D0338153

All the World's a Fair

ROBERT W. RYDELL

All the World's a Fair

Visions of Empire at
American International
Expositions, 1876–1916

The University of Chicago Press

Chicago and London

The University of Chicago Press, Chicago 60637
The University of Chicago Press, Ltd., London

© 1984 by The University of Chicago
All rights reserved. Published 1984
Paperback edition 1987
Printed in the United States of America

08 07 06 05 04 03 02   6 7 8 9

Library of Congress Cataloging in Publication Data

Rydell, Robert W.
  All the world's a fair.

  Bibliography: p.
  Includes index.
  1. Exhibitions—History. I. Title.
T395.5.U6R93   1984   909.81′074′013   84-2674

ISBN 0-226-73240-1 (paper)

♾ The paper used in this publication meets the minimum
requirements of the American National Standard for
Information Sciences—Permanence of Paper for Printed
Library Materials, ANSI Z39.48-1992.

To Kiki and to the memory of my parents

Contents

Acknowledgments   viii

Introduction   1

1. **The Centennial Exhibition, Philadelphia, 1876**
   The Exposition as a "Moral Influence"   9

2. **The Chicago World's Columbian Exposition of 1893**
   "And Was Jerusalem Builded Here?"   38

3. **The New Orleans, Atlanta, and Nashville Expositions**
   New Markets, "New Negroes," and a New South   72

4. **The Trans-Mississippi and International Exposition, Omaha, 1898:** "Concomitant to Empire"   105

5. **The Pan-American Exposition, Buffalo**
   "Pax 1901"   126

6. **The Louisiana Purchase Exposition, Saint Louis, 1904**
   "The Coronation of Civilization"   154

7. **The Expositions in Portland and Seattle**
   "To Celebrate the Past and to Exploit the Future"   184

8. **The Expositions in San Francisco and San Diego**
   Toward the World of Tomorrow   208

Conclusion   234

Notes   239

Bibliography   293

Index   317

Acknowledgments

The intellectual debts I have accumulated in completing this book can never be adequately repaid. They begin with public school teachers up and down the state of California who taught me the value of studying history. My interest in American culture generally, and world's fairs specifically, developed while I was an undergraduate at Berkeley. Michael P. Rogin and Kenneth M. Stampp sparked my interest in American culture, and John Lottier and Mark Wilson called to my attention the importance of international expositions.

That my curiosity about world's fairs and American culture ever developed into a book is due in large measure to Alexander P. Saxton and members of his UCLA graduate seminar on race, culture, and ideology. From the beginning, I have relied on Alex for guidance, inspiration, and friendship. At one critical juncture, he shared with me his appreciation of cacti blooming in the desert mountains, and I will never forget.

Other members of the UCLA faculty were generous with their advice, and the end product has benefited immensely. Thomas S. Hines served as my committee co-chair and led me to think hard about the relation between architecture and social change. Daniel Walker Howe offered valuable insight into the meaning the fairs held for Victorian America. Richard Lehan and Gary Nash also helped clarify my thoughts with their thorough readings of the manuscript, and Fawn Brodie and Blake Nevius offered constant encouragement that hastened its completion.

While this project was developing, many people took time to offer valuable suggestions for improvement. Merle Curti read an early draft of my research proposal and encouraged me to pursue my work. Neil Harris and Helen Lefkowitz Horowitz read the entire manuscript, and the book is much better as a result. I am particularly grateful to David Hollinger for his critical insights and for his helping hand along the way. Robert Abzug, Edward Barry, George B. Cotkin, George A. Frickman, James Henretta, Norris Hundley, Josiah Ober, Edwin J. Perkins, G. Terry Sharrer, Billy Smith, Robert Twombly, and Herman

Viola also tendered advice that saved me from many pitfalls. I am equally indebted to the following individuals for reading and improving drafts of my chapters: Pete Daniel, Deborah A. Forczek, David A. Johnson, Lesley Kawaguchi, Harry Liebersohn, Jonathan McLeod, Janet T. Marquardt, Adrienne Mayor, Judy Powers, Marianne Roos, and Patricia A. Roos. In the course of completing this study, much of the burden fell on Jonathan and Nantawan McLeod. I shall always treasure their friendship.

My colleagues in the Department of History and Philosophy at Montana State University and members of the Society of American Historians, especially Kenneth Jackson, have my lasting gratitude for their support.

To librarians and library staff at the following institutions I owe a special debt: the Atlanta Historical Society; the Bancroft Library; the Beinecke and Sterling libraries at Yale; the Buffalo and Erie County Historical Society; the Department of Special Collections at California State University, Fresno; the Chicago Historical Society; the City Archives of Philadelphia; the Honnold Library at Claremont Colleges; the Denver Public Library; the Perkins Library at Duke University; the Georgia State Archives; the Historical Society of Pennsylvania; the Library of Congress, Manuscripts Division; the Missouri Historical Society; the National Anthropology Archives; the National Archives; the National Museum of American History Library; the New York Public Library; the Oregon Historical Society; the Portland Public Library; the San Diego Historical Society; the Smithsonian Institution Archives; the Southwest Museum; the Tennessee State Library and Archives; the Department of Special Collections at UCLA; the Western History Collection at the University of Colorado; the University of Oregon; and the University of Washington. Without their cooperation, I could not have written this book. Members of the interlibrary loan and reference departments at UCLA deserve special mention for their support. Edith Fuller, Janet Ziegler, Norma Pasillas, Jo Crawford, and Carolee Shoemaker did a first-rate job in tracking down my endless requests, and their unfailing cheerfulness made the research a pleasure. At the Smithsonian Institution, Scott Berger, William Cox, William Deiss, James Glenn, William Massa, Rhoda Ratner, and Rich Szary helped me to mine the rich resources of the archives with their knowledge and skill. Ron Mahoney, head of the Department of Special Collections at California State University, Fresno, has turned the exposition collection into one of the finest in the country. Ward Childs, James Hoobler, and Renée Jaussaud—respectively at the City Archives of Philadelphia, the Tennessee State Library and Archives, and the National Archives—also have my gratitude for their assistance.

Grateful acknowledgment is also made to the editors of *American Quarterly*, *Journal of American Culture*, and *Pacific Historical Review* for permission to reprint revisions of articles that first appeared in those journals.

Completion of the book was aided by grants from Montana State University, the Institute of American Cultures at UCLA, and the Smithsonian Institution.

I deeply appreciate their support for this project.

Brett Gary, Nanci Brug, and Dianne Ostermiller typed the manuscript and endured my requests for last-minute changes.

Finally, who could be more fortunate? My mother and father encouraged my love for history and urged me to become a teacher. They also encouraged me to pursue a dream that my wife, Kiki Leigh Rydell, has helped me fulfill.

Introduction

And when these days were expired, the king made a feast unto all the people that were present in Shushan the palace, both unto great and small, seven days, in the court of the garden of the king's palace; where were white, green, and blue hangings, fastened with cords of fine linen and purple to silver rings and pillars of marble: the beds were of gold and silver, upon a pavement of red, and blue, and white, and black marble. And they gave them drink in vessels of gold, (the vessels being diverse one from another,) and royal wine in abundance, according to the state of the king. And the drinking was according to the law; none did compel: for so the king had appointed to all the officers of his house, that they should do according to every man's pleasure. Also Vashti the queen made a feast for the women in the royal house which belonged to king Ahasuerus.

Esther 1:5–9

BETWEEN 1876 AND 1916, nearly one hundred million people visited the international expositions held at Philadelphia, New Orleans, Chicago, Atlanta, Nashville, Omaha, Buffalo, Saint Louis, Portland, Seattle, San Francisco, and San Diego.[1] The promoters of these extravaganzas attempted to boost the economic development of the cities and regions in which they were held as well as to advance the material growth of the country at large. Fairs provided manufacturing and commercial interests with opportunities to promote the mass consumption of their products. They showed off the nation's economic strength and artistic resources, highlighting new architectural forms and offering models for urban planning. They presented new mediums of entertainment and opportunities for vicarious travel in other lands. Diversity characterized the expositions, and this heterogeneity was part of their attraction. Diversity, however, was inseparable from the larger constellation of ideas about race, nationality, and progress that molded the fairs into ideologically coherent "symbolic universes" confirming and extending the authority of the country's corporate, political, and scientific leadership.[2]

Sociologists Peter L. Berger and Thomas Luckmann have described a "symbolic universe" as a structure of legitimation that provides meaning for social experience, placing "all collective events in a cohesive unity that includes past, present, and future. With regard to the future, it establishes a common frame of reference for the projection of individual actions." The net result, according to Berger and Luckmann, is that "the symbolic universe links men with their successors in a meaningful totality, serving to transcend the finitude of individual existence and bestowing meaning upon the individual's death. All the members of society can now conceive of themselves as belonging to a meaningful universe, which was there before they were born and will be there after they die."[3] This cohesive explanatory blueprint of social experience is what the sponsors of the fairs offered to millions of fairgoers in the wake of the industrial depressions and outbursts of class warfare that occurred between the end of Reconstruction and United States entry into World War I.

If one function of the expositions was to make the social world comprehensible, the directors of the fairs attempted to organize the direction of society from a particular class perspective. These events were triumphs of hegemony as well as symbolic edifices. By hegemony, I mean the exercise of economic and political power in cultural terms by the established leaders of American society and "the 'spontaneous' consent given by the great masses of the population to the general direction imposed on social life by the dominant fundamental group; this consent is 'historically' caused by the prestige (and consequent confidence) which the dominant group enjoys because of its position and function in the world of production."[4] Hegemony, moreover, is the normal means of state control in a pluralistic society; force is used when power exercised in cultural terms is no longer capable of maintaining the order on which the state is founded.

2

World's fairs performed a hegemonic function precisely because they propagated the ideas and values of the country's political, financial, corporate, and intellectual leaders and offered these ideas as the proper interpretation of social and political reality. While expositions were arenas for asserting the moral authority of the United States government as opposed to its coercive power, numerous military exhibits suggested that force was available to maintain order whenever and wherever necessary. Congressional acts providing for the establishment of exhibits by the federal government generally mandated that such displays "illustrate the function and administrative faculty of the Government in time of peace and its resources as a war power, tending to demonstrate the nature of our institutions and their adaptation to the wants of the people."[5] Fairs therefore were to serve as reminders of the belief that in America the people were sovereign.

In the early years of the twentieth century, a visitor to several of the expositions spoke directly to the significance of the fairs. Henry Adams, a historian sensitive to the social transformations taking place in America, "professed the religion of World's Fairs, without which he held education to be a blind impossibility." His equation of religion and expositions was layered with irony and insight. He expressed concern over the growing impersonality that permeated the United States, as symbolized by the dynamos he saw at the Chicago World's Columbian Exposition of 1893. Far more satisfying to his humanistic sensibilities were the great cathedrals of the Middle Ages. One imposing structure he particularly admired was in Coutances, France. There, Adams remarked, "the people of Normandy had built, towards the year 1250, an Exposition which architects still admired and tourists visited, for it was thought singularly expressive of force as well as of grace in the Virgin."[6]

The elegantly arched connection Adams drew between the medieval cathedral and more recent expositions had a basis in etymology as well as historical fact. The term "fair" derives from the Latin *feria*, "holy day." More explicitly, the German *Messe* connotes both "mass" and "fair."[7] America's world's fairs resembled religious celebrations in their emphasis on symbols and ritualistic behavior. They provided visitors with a galaxy of symbols that cohered as "symbolic universes." These constellations, in turn, ritualistically affirmed fairgoers' faith in American institutions and social organization, evoked a community of shared experience, and formulated responses to questions about the ultimate destiny of mankind in general and of Americans in particular.

The sheer number of fairgoers testified that the expositions struck a responsive chord in the lives of many Americans. While the fairs obviously failed to provide a vision that all who experienced them shared equally, they did deeply influence the content of many individual and collective beliefs and values. The social prestige and authority of the financial and political leaders who sponsored the fairs played an important part in this complex process. Perhaps another factor was a psychological dynamic that literary critic Norman

Holland has explored with respect to an individual reader's reaction to a masterpiece of literature. In Holland's "reader-response" schema, the reader experiences more than the objective external creation of the artist. A given text does not necessarily produce a fixed reaction but presents "a structure which the reader creates for himself" according to "his own characteristic transformations of his identity theme. He no longer feels any distinction between 'in here' and 'out there,' between him and it. Indeed, there is none, and he becomes 'absorbed.' "[8] In the course of "doing the fair," or "taking it in," many visitors made the exposition a part of their lives.

This was no accident. Between 1876 and 1916, Americans were engaged, as one historian has written, in "a search for order." Increasing industrialization and cyclical industrial depressions, beginning in 1873, resulted in frequent outbursts of open class warfare. The urgency expressed in social reform movements and in the flood of utopian writings at the century's end reflected the country's unsettled condition. Adding to the worries of the times was the discovery of unfathomable multiplicity in the universe. All these concerns gave troubled American Victorians an intense drive to organize experience. And herein lay part of the appeal of the expositions. To alleviate the intense and widespread anxiety that pervaded the United States, the directors of the expositions offered millions of fairgoers an opportunity to reaffirm their collective national identity in an updated synthesis of progress and white supremacy that suffused the blueprints of future perfection offered by the fairs.[9]

President William McKinley, before his assassination at the Pan-American Exposition at Buffalo in 1901, made explicit the connection between the fairs and progress: "Expositions are the timekeepers of progress. They record the world's advancement. They stimulate the energy, enterprise, and intellect of the people and quicken human genius. They go into the home. They broaden and brighten the daily life of the people. They open mighty storehouses of information to the student. Every exposition, great or small, has helped this onward step."[10] McKinley presented his explanation of progress as a forward movement through time in the context of a necessity for expanding American markets, finding new supplies of natural resources, and imposing American civilization overseas. For McKinley, as for the directors of the fairs, progress was synonymous with America's material growth and economic expansion, which in turn was predicated on the subordination of nonwhite people.

Progress, however, is not necessarily inherent in change or development or growth. Progress is a positive value linked to change. At a time when the American economy was becoming increasingly consolidated and when the wealth generated by the country's economic expansion was concentrated in fewer and fewer hands, the exposition builders promised that continued growth would result in eventual utopia. Therein lay the mythopoeic grandeur of the fairs: an ideology of economic development, labeled "progress," was translated into a utopian statement about the future. An ideology, an idea complex

tied to socioeconomic cleavages in a particular historical era, was presented
as the transcendent answer to the problems besetting America.

Powerful and subtle, flawed and pliable, the road map to future perfection
offered by the exposition directors also involved a comparative dimension.
World's fairs, often christened "world's universities,"[11] put the nations and
people of the world on display for comparative purposes. Americans had often
measured their achievements against those of different nations. But at the
fairs, the idea of technological and national progress became laced with scientific racism.

Racism signifies a system of beliefs that holds that one group of people is
superior to another in moral, cultural, and intellectual qualities—qualities
that are alleged to pass from one generation to another through heredity.[12]
That American culture at the turn of the century was imbued with racist ideas
and that these prevailing assumptions were given added support with the popularization of evolutionary theories about race and culture has been abun-
dantly demonstrated by recent historians. Exactly how scientific ideas about
evolution, race, and culture were disseminated from academic circles to the
level of popular consumption, however, is less well understood and has led a
handful of historians to question the legitimating function of Darwinian
ideas.[13] World's fairs provide a partial but crucial explanation for the interpenetration and popularization of evolutionary ideas about race and progress.

In one sense the juncture of racism and progress as revealed at the fairs
echoed the not-too-distant past. Several antebellum ethnologists had effected
a similar equation in an attempt to construct an intellectual framework for
justifying slavery. Their efforts had been seriously undercut by the challenge
they posed to deeply felt Christian attitudes about the essential worth of all
human beings in the eyes of God. But by the final quarter of the nineteenth
century, the epistemological frame of reference was shifting from religion to
science.[14] Scientific explanations about natural and social phenomena became
increasingly authoritative, and the exposition planners enhanced and drew
upon the prestige of science to make the presentation of America's progress
more convincing.

The scientific approach, with its emphasis on classification, stressed the
diversity of racial "types" and an evolutionary hierarchy that tended to blur
class distinctions among whites while it invited them to appraise the relative
capabilities of different groups of nonwhites for emulating the American model
of progress. But this more complex hierarchical perception of races also suggested that there were gradations among European populations as well as
among Asians, Africans, Afro-Americans, Native Americans, American Hispanics, and other nonwhite people of the world. By 1916, eugenicists had
joined anthropologists in applying hierarchical ideas about race and culture to
selected white populations, thereby laying the intellectual foundation for mass
support of immigration restriction.[15]

World's fairs, held at different times in different regions of the country, did not stand in isolation as creators of popular racial images. Exposition promoters drew upon and reshaped such sources of entertainment as the zoological garden, the minstrel show, the circus, the museum of curiosities, the dime novel, and the Wild West show. World's fairs existed as part of a broader universe of white supremacist entertainments; what distinguished them were their scientific, artistic, and political underpinnings. Whether or not they were the most important source for shaping racial beliefs, they certainly were among the most authoritative. International expositions, where science, religion, the arts, and architecture reinforced each other, offered Americans a powerful and highly visible, modern, evolutionary justification for long-standing racial and cultural prejudices. The consequences were profound. For, as vehicles that endowed popular racial attitudes with apparent scientific credibility, the fairs helped to build public support for the acceptance of specific foreign and domestic policies.[16]

The most frequent contributions to the scientific exhibits at the fairs came from the Smithsonian Institution. Given that the Smithsonian had been founded "for the increase and diffusion of knowledge among men," its scientists took a measure of delight in participating in events that enabled them to reach a wide audience with the latest findings of scientific research. But the directors and scientists of the Smithsonian viewed the expositions as nuisances as well as godsends, for the problems involved in setting up exhibits were enormous. One assistant secretary of the Smithsonian, Richard Rathbun, compiled a compendium of evils that befell the institution as a result of congressional decisions to fund exposition displays by the federal government. Valuable staff time went into organizing collections for expositions, and exhibit halls in the United States National Museum (USNM) were "emptied to a greater or less extent" because of them. Frequently, exhibits sent to the fairs required repair before they could be reinstalled. But, Rathbun recognized, "a government participation in expositions in which the Museum, the one establishment designed for exhibition, was not represented would appear almost farcical." Bearing this point in mind, he reported that "an effort has generally been made to present an exhibit which, in greater or less part, is germane to the specified objects of the exposition."[17]

Walter Hough, an assistant curator in the Division of Anthropology at the USNM, found the fairs more alluring than did Rathbun. The fairs, he declared, offered two important benefits. First, they presented "the opportunity to make an impressive education display, following out an appropriate idea." Second, they added significantly to museum collections. Admitting that the fairs interfered with the routine operation of the USNM, Hough nevertheless considered them of "immense significance."[18]

Ultimately, every Smithsonian official connected with the fairs had reservations about them. Yet few of them would have disagreed with the view expressed by G. Browne Goode, Rathbun's predecessor as assistant secretary of the Smithsonian and one of the pioneers of museum development in the United States. "All of this," Goode wrote concerning the manifold inconveniences caused by the fairs, "is accepted without complaint, because, though the Museum undoubtedly loses much more than it gains on such occasions, the opportunity for popular education is too important to be neglected."[19]

The possibility for educating the public through the medium of the fairs motivated not only the scientists at the Smithsonian, but federal officials generally. The didactic mission entailed several assumptions that Wilbur O. Atwater of the Agriculture Department best articulated in a statement occasioned by the World's Columbian Exposition. Atwater stated his conviction that the American public demanded scientific knowledge and that scientists could oblige them better than ever before: "Let the exposition be a display, not merely of material products, but of the teachings of science and experience as regards their value, importance and use." For Atwater, the role of science at the fair bore a direct relation to national destiny: "The exposition should not be merely a show, a fair or a colossal shop, but also and pre-eminently an exposition of the principles which underlie our national and individual welfare, of our material, intellectual and moral status; of the elements of our weakness and our strength, of the progress we have made, the plane on which we live and the ways in which we shall rise higher." Expositions must "teach not only to our people, but to the world, what a young republic, with all the crudeness of youth, but heir to the experience of the ages, has done in its brief past, is doing in the present, and hopes to do in the greater future for its people and for mankind."[20] Science and salvation seemed to march hand in hand. One purpose of this book is to explore how Smithsonian scientists, especially ethnologists and anthropologists at the USNM and Bureau of American Ethnology (BAE) shaped this faith at the fairs.

The Smithsonian Institution played a central role in shaping ethnological features of the fairs, but the directors of the World's Columbian Exposition and several subsequent fairs brought in anthropologists and materials from other museums and universities to supplement exhibits established by government scientists. Several of the fairs provided separate buildings for anthropological materials. Following the example of colonial villages established at the 1889 Paris Exhibition, living ethnological displays of Native Americans and other nonwhite people were introduced en masse at the Chicago fair and appeared at subsequent expositions as well. Significantly, such "villages" were honky-tonk concessions often located in the amusement sections of the fairs alongside wild animal exhibits, joyrides, and other entertainment features. Although these villages degraded and exploited the people on display, anthropologists generally testified to the ethnological value of the exhibits. The result was that scientific and pseudoscientific anthropology became instrumental in buttressing the legitimacy of the utopian artifacts created by the directors of the fairs. The fairs certainly popularized anthropological findings, and the science of man that reached the fair-going public had a distinct hierarchical message and served a hegemonic function.

The web of world's fairs that stretched across the widening economic fault lines of American society between 1876 and 1916 reflected the efforts by America's intellectual, political, and business leaders to establish a consensus about their priorities and their vision of progress as racial dominance and economic growth. How each fair contributed to this ideological process is the burden of my analysis. I concentrate on American fairs because they remain largely unstudied and because their influence was pervasive in American culture at the turn of the century. Yet they were part of what became, after the success of London's Crystal Palace Exhibition of 1851, a worldwide movement. Fairs were held around the world, in cities ranging from Saint Petersburg and Brussels to Rio de Janeiro and Hanoi. These fairs were linked to the massive industrial developments in the Western world and to imperialist expansion into Asia, Africa, and Latin America. America's expositions, while part of the American grain, were unique only in that they helped shape the increasing efforts by the United States to manage the world from its own rapidly expanding imperial perspective.[21]

1

The Centennial Exhibition, Philadelphia, 1876: The Exposition as a "Moral Influence"

Come back across the bridge of time
And swear an oath that holds you fast,
To make the future as sublime
As is the memory of the past!

Fourth of July Memorial, 1876

He was a young man, evidently just fresh from some interior village. He was naturally no fool, but it could be plainly seen that he knew next to nothing of men or of the world, and that his visit to the world's fair was the crowning event in his quiet life.

New York Times, 1876

The teachings survive the demolition of the buildings.

William P. Blake, 1872[1]

ON THE OVERCAST MORNING of 10 May 1876, the Centennial Exhibition in Philadelphia officially opened to the public. The 186,672 visitors to the fairgrounds that first day began a stream of almost ten million people who saw the exhibition. Before its conclusion in mid-November, nearly one-fifth of the population of the United States passed through the turnstiles, making the attendance at this international exposition larger than at any held previously in any country.[2]

After early apathy, ambivalence, and even outright hostility to the enterprise, a sense of growing anticipation began building in the City of Brotherly Love in early 1876 and spread throughout the country. It had become, in the words of one newspaper, a "swelling act." Foreign and domestic newspaper correspondents found ample copy as exhibit halls filled with displays ranging from exquisite, exotic silks to practical tools and to "Old Abe," the Wisconsin war eagle that had been in thirty-six Civil War battles.[3]

Life in Philadelphia was a story. With the price of lodging in the lead, the cost of living soared. "Prices have gone up fifty per cent, with indications that the maximum of extortion has not been reached by any means," declared the *New York Times*. One firm went so far as to purchase Oak Cemetery, remove the tombstones, and erect a campground to handle the expected overflow crowds from boardinghouses. "Philadelphia," *Harper's Bazaar* had quipped in March, "appears for the nonce to have thrown off her sombre Quaker apparel, and to have ushered in the Centennial with much the air of a venerable old lady endeavoring to execute some difficult steps in the can-can." This description, while good-natured, was both revealing and misleading. The international exposition, like the cancan, was a novelty of comparatively recent origin, the first international exposition having taken place in London in 1851. Yet the men and women who organized the Centennial Exhibition were not wholly inexperienced with the medium of fairs. Several of the directors had participated in the Sanitary Fairs held in Philadelphia during the Civil War. And the war itself had taught many army officers, who later became exposition officials, lessons in efficient management and organization. Furthermore, Alfred T. Goshorn, director-general of the Centennial Commission, far from being a newcomer to fairs, had been in charge of industrial exhibitions in Cincinnati since the conclusion of the war. And, if *Harper's* metaphor of the cancan was not entirely apt, neither was its stereotypical conception of Philadelphia's earlier dourness. Philadelphia's Quaker roots had nothing to do with the gloom that had settled over the city and the whole country. The unhealed social and political wounds left by the war would have been difficult to cope with in the best of circumstances, but these problems had been compounded manyfold by the industrial depression of 1873. By 1876 the Gilded Age had already earned its name. But if Philadelphians could find an almost comic relief from the unsettled condition of the country in the spectacle of a world's fair, perhaps other Americans, as *Harper's* recommended, could do

likewise. Minimally, the exposition promised a diversion from endless accounts of political corruption in Washington, collapse of financial and mercantile establishments, and stories of working-class discontent with the industrial
system.[4]

From such gloomy vistas, the Centennial Exhibition provided a welcome
change. Yet, rather than merely offering an escape from the economic and
political uncertainties of the Reconstruction years, the fair was a calculated
response to these conditions. Its organizers sought to challenge doubts and
restore confidence in the vitality of America's system of government as well as
in the social and economic structure of the country. From the moment the
gates swung open at nine o'clock on the morning of 10 May, the fair operated
as "a school for the nation," a working model of an "American Mecca."[5]

Despite the rain, which the day before had drenched the city and turned
portions of the fairgrounds into a quagmire of mud and rotting straw, crowds
began arriving several hours before the ceremonies were scheduled to get under way. The fair, occupying a portion of Fairmount Park's three thousand
acres, was situated on a plateau intersected by wooded dells and meandering
streams. From the high points of the elevation visitors could gaze upon the
Schuylkill River, the exhibition buildings, and the central city.[6]

The major buildings themselves were colossal edifices. Along the southern
edge of the grounds was the Main Building, 1,880 feet long by 464 feet wide.
The wood, iron, and glass structure was the largest in the world. West of the
Main Building, and next largest, was Machinery Hall. On the northern portion
of the fairgrounds was another gigantic structure, Agricultural Hall. Devoted
to displays of agricultural machinery, its modified Gothic outlines covered
more than ten acres. On a line between Agricultural Hall and the Main Building was Horticultural Hall, the most ornamental of the exposition buildings.
The interior contained specimens of exotic plants, model greenhouses, garden-
ing tools, and elegant containers. Twenty feet above the floor a gallery encircling the building afforded a view "as entrancing as a poet's dream." Taken
in its totality, the interior scene added up to "an Arabian Nights' sort of
gorgeousness." Between Horticultural Hall and the Main Building was Memorial Hall, "the most imposing and substantial of all the Exhibition structures," which housed paintings and sculpture from around the world, including "Iolanthe," an extraordinary "alto-relievo . . . in butter," sculpted by an
Arkansas woman.[7]

In addition to the five main exhibition buildings, there were seventeen state
buildings, nine foreign government buildings, many restaurants, six cigar pa-
vilions, popcorn stands, beer gardens, the Singer Sewing Machine Building,
the Photograph Gallery, the Turkish Coffee Building, the Shoe and Leather
Building, the Bible Pavilion, the Centennial National Bank, the New England
Log House, a Nevada Quartz Mill, a Woman's School House, and, signifi-

cantly, the Woman's Pavilion. The exhibition directors had even granted permission for a Burial Casket Building—much to the embarrassment of Americans concerned with proving the cultural worth of their country to European visitors.[8]

The throngs rushing through the 106 entrances, each adorned with "American trophies, shields, flags, eagles, etc.," could well anticipate all of this and a great deal more with the help of newspaper coverage and guidebooks to the exposition. But seeing was believing. Statues and fountains added to the splendor. West of Machinery Hall was the immense, but incomplete, Centennial Fountain, designed by Herman Kirn and funded by the Catholic Total Abstinence Union of America. The central figure was an enormous statue of Moses atop a granite mass in the midst of a circular basin forty feet in diameter. Around the basin, drinking fountains were set at the bases of nine-foot marble statues representing prominent American Catholics. Other monumental figures abounded. B'nai B'rith erected a statue of Religious Liberty, twenty feet tall, that had as its centerpiece a female warrior with the American shield for a breastplate, typifying "the genius of liberty." Near the base of the figure was an eagle clutching a snake in its talons, representing the end of slavery. Completing the allegory were inscriptions from the Constitution. Other heroic statues dotted the exhibition grounds. In addition to representations of Columbus and Elias Howe, there was the American Soldier's Monument, weighing thirty tons, and the John Witherspoon Memorial erected by American Presbyterians. French sculptor Frédéric Bartholdi sent over the Torch of Liberty from the as yet unfinished Statue of Liberty. And, as a monument to the Victorian age of which the Centennial Exhibition was a part, there was also a statue of Thomas Carlyle. This setting, at once pastoral and heroic, appealed to many fairgoers. "Dear Mother," wrote a young woman after seeing the grounds, "Oh! Oh!! O-o-o-o-o-o-o-o-o!!!!!!"[9]

Unlike many subsequent fairs, the landscaping was largely completed and almost all the buildings and exhibits were ready by opening day. The crowds rapidly filled every available space across from the platforms erected for the ceremonies between the Art Building and the Main Building. Some climbed statues, and others found their way to rooftops. "A hundred thousand people in a crowd and not one peasant," commented a journalist. A local correspondent found in the crowd a hierarchy "suggestive of a modernized Babel without its guilt and folly, in the confusion of the various forms of human language to be heard, from our own familiar and vigorous Anglo-Saxon to the guttural of our barbaric Aboriginese, or the sing-sing jargon of the 'heathen Chinese.' "

Fig. 1. *(opposite)* Centennial vision of American progress. Cover, *Frank Leslie's Illustrated Monthly*, 1, no. 3 (1876), courtesy of Department of Special Collections, Library, California State University, Fresno.

Fig. 2. Main Building, Centennial Exhibition. Lithograph courtesy of
Smithsonian Institution Archives, Record Unit 95, Photograph Collection.

Newspapers tried to foster the impression that people from foreign countries
were "treated with the utmost respect and courtesy" and that the crowd, above
all, was orderly even in the absense of direct military supervision. Generally
overlooked were expressions of racial hostility that followed the decorous
opening proceedings. Turks, Egyptians, Spaniards, Japanese, and the
Chinese, a contemporary noted, "were followed by large crowds of idle boys
and men, who hooted and shouted at them as if they had been animals of a
strange species instead of visitors who were entitled to only the most courteous
attention." This outburst of racial hostility did not detract entirely from the
general orderliness of the crowd during the ceremonies and the exposition as
a whole. Rather, it revealed that white Americans brought their accumulated
racial attitudes with them to the fair and that fairgoers found nothing in the
opening ceremonies to negate their racial assumptions.[10]

In describing the opening ceremony, Reverend D. Otis Kellogg explained
the orderly nature of the crowds as being a direct result of the impression
created by "the majesty of the exposition itself." "The imposing edifices were
there to speak," he observed, "and emphatically do they do their work. With
an effect like some of the European Cathedrals, the Main Building exceeds
any of them in extent many times over. . . . Then there were the eminent
men of the land coming as representatives of the power of the country to
acknowledge the grandeur of Industry." It was precisely the religious aura
about the opening that led the Philadelphia *Press* to declare: "Let us, therefore, to-day bare our heads and take off our sandals, for we tread on holy
ground." This effort to shape American culture, however, would have been
incomplete without the explicitly didactic lessons provided by the speakers
themselves.[11]

Introduced with music composed by Richard Wagner and conducted by
Theodore Thomas, the ceremonies emphasized national unity and America's

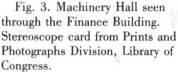

Fig. 3. Machinery Hall seen through the Finance Building. Stereoscope card from Prints and Photographs Division, Library of Congress.

destiny as God's chosen nation. Hope for the future provided the text for the speech delivered by Joseph R. Hawley, president of the Centennial Commission. He expressed his "fervent hope" that "all parties and classes" would come to the exhibition "to study the evidence of our resources, to measure the progress of a hundred years, and to examine to our profit the wonderful products of other lands." President Grant concluded the speechmaking by urging the audience to make "a careful examination of what is about to be exhibited to you," bearing in mind that America's greatest achievements still lay in the future.[12]

When the orchestra and chorus played the "Hallelujah Chorus" at the conclusion of Grant's remarks, one phase of the inaugural proceedings was complete. The climax, however, had yet to occur. President Grant, Emperor Dom Pedro of Brazil, and Director-General Goshorn took their places at the head of a procession of four thousand invited dignitaries. After reviewing the foreign and domestic displays in the Main Building, they arrived at the exposition's centerpiece, the Corliss engine, in Machinery Hall. George Corliss, commissioner from Rhode Island and designer of the machine, gave operating instructions to the two heads of state. Then both men turned wheels and started the generator that provided the power for the exhibits in Machinery Hall.[13]

The Corliss engine was the most impressive display on the exhibition grounds. With its steam boiler tucked out of sight and earshot in an adjacent power supply building, the engine, despite its size, ran with an awesome, silent power—"an athlete of steel and iron." When Walt Whitman visited Machinery Hall several weeks later, "he ordered his chair to be stopped before the great, great engine . . . and there he sat looking at this colossal and

Fig. 4. Corliss engine: "An athlete of steel and iron."
From Prints and Photographs Division, Library of
Congress.

mighty piece of machinery for half an hour in silence . . . contemplating the
ponderous motions of the greatest machinery man has built." His less renowned companion, California poet Joaquin Miller, summed up the reaction
of many not only to the Corliss engine, but to the fair as a whole: "How the
American's heart thrills with pride and love of his land as he contemplates
the vast exhibition of art and prowess here." "Great as it seems today," Miller
forecast, "it is but the acorn from which shall grow the wide-spreading oak of
a century's growth."[14]

Any number of exhibits—the Westinghouse air brake, various refrigeration
processes, the telephone, Vienna bread, Fleischmann's yeast—could be sin-
gled out as ample proof of Miller's prediction that the fair would have a lasting
impact on American life. Just as profound as any single exhibit or group of
displays, however, were the values and ideas that channeled the exhibits into
a coherent picture. As the opening-day speeches made clear, the exposition

was intended to teach a lesson about progress. The lesson was far from benign, for the artifacts and people embodied in the "world's epitome" at the
fair were presented in hierarchical fashion and in the context of America's
material growth and development. This design well suited the small group of
affluent citizens who organized the Centennial into a dynamic vision of past,
present, and future.[15]

   Several persons originated the idea of celebrating America's centennial with
an international exhibition. The most influential was probably John L. Campbell, a professor at Wabash College in Indiana, who proposed a commemorative fair in an 1864 address delivered at the Smithsonian Institution. In the
heat of the war the response to his proposal was lukewarm. Selective prodding
of congressmen and public officials in Philadelphia by Campbell, John Bige-
low, Charles B. Norton, and M. Richards Mucklé, however, finally led the
Select Council of Philadelphia, on 20 January 1870, to endorse unanimously
the plan for an international exhibition. The council was next joined by the
Franklin Institute and the state legislature, which presented memorials to
Congress urging federal sanction for the event. Daniel J. Morrell, representative from Pennsylvania, chairman of the House Committee on Manufactures,
and "one of the most eminent and successful [iron] manufacturers of Pennsylvania," guided the bill through Congress. In its final form the bill empowered
the president to appoint commissioners from the states and territories upon
the recommendation of the governors. At its first meeting in March 1872,
Joseph R. Hawley was elected president of the United States Centennial Commission and Campbell, by this time a commissioner from Indiana, was elected
secretary. Hawley, formerly a Civil War major general, had served as governor
and congressman from Connecticut and become a successful Hartford newspaper publisher. His administrative skill was widely recognized, but the Centennial promised to be an immense project. So, soon after the first meeting of
the commission, Alfred T. Goshorn was elected director-general. Goshorn, a
Cincinnati white-lead manufacturer, city councilman, and member of the local
Board of Trade, had made the annual Cincinnati industrial exposition the
largest American fair before the Centennial. His first assignment as director-
general was to visit the 1873 Vienna international exhibition to gain insights
applicable to the Philadelphia celebration.[16]
   To raise funds for the Centennial, Congress created a separate commission,
the Centennial Board of Finance, chaired by John Welsh and authorized it to
raise $10 million by selling stock subscriptions to the public. Welsh, a prom-
inent Philadelphia businessman, organized the financing of the exhibition. He
personally persuaded one hundred "of the most prominent and wealthy of the
citizens of Philadelphia to affix their names as sureties to the bond of
$500,000, required for the faithful disbursement of the congressional appro-
priation of $1,500,000." Yet the Centennial was more than a local or state

venture. The depression of 1873 made it imperative for organizers to seek nationwide support for the fair, and both commissions solicited the aid of prominent people throughout the country. A letter to George Clarkson, an influential citizen of Rochester, New York, testified to the thoroughness with which this solicitation was carried out. In 1875 the Board of Finance informed Clarkson that the general agent of the brokerage firm, Peasler and Company, would contact him "to canvass the city for the sale of Centennial Stock and medals and above all will he need your influence among your neighbors." "Our experience," the letter continued, "so far shows that a local committee of citizens using their personal influence is the most effective means of raising the quota of a city, town, or county." Especially valuable in the task would be tax lists, which would suggest "what would be a proper sum for the citizens of their district to contribute."[17]

From beginning to end, the exposition illustrated the consolidation and unequal distribution of wealth and power in the United States. The list of voters casting ballots for the Board of Finance underscored this fact. Out of 22,776 total votes, the Philadelphia and Pennsylvania Railroad had 11,400, the Lehigh Valley Railroad 2,400, the A.P. Railroad 1,420, Thomas W. Price 1,000, John B. Ellison and Sons 900, and Lippincott Publishing Company 500. Many individuals and firms of lesser means subscribed to exposition stock, but they had little voice in the management of exposition affairs. A notice "To Our Employees," posted in several Philadelphia firms, urged workers to subscribe to stock, promising that "no class will receive a more speedy return than the Artisan, Mechanic, and Workingman, by whom the necessary labor must be performed." The number of working people who responded is unknown. It is clear, however, that a small number of wealthy individuals, railroads, and large mercantile establishments held controlling interest.[18]

The motives of those who took large subscriptions of exhibition stock went beyond the anticipation of immediate profit. William P. Blake, who played a central, though little publicized role in the fair, cautioned Goshorn in late 1872 that the attendance might be less than at the 1867 Paris Exposition. Consequently, he advised against promising a full return with profit on investments. He counseled a different strategy: "We must fall back upon patriotism and such other incentives as we may be able to present in the shape of Honors or Recognitions distinguishing the subscribers in some way." Although Blake's advice was not always heeded, the call to patriotism resonated strongly throughout the exposition years.[19]

Patriotism was explicitly linked to the need for continued economic growth as well as political and social stability. Goshorn, outlining the scope of the fair, stressed the opportunity the exhibition presented for comparing the "resources and present state of industrial and social development" of different countries. This "true picture," he explained, not only would foster "the well being and happiness of the human race, but . . . will have a direct and special influence in promoting the already large trade existing with the United States, establish profitable connections, and open new and extended markets for many European industries hitherto comparatively unknown in the United States." For large investors, it was suggested that immediate profit on stock subscriptions could be outweighed by the lure of long-term economic gain resulting from the exposition. This anticipated result, however, was contingent upon the persistence of faith in the existing social and political order. The authors of an address to the "People of New York by Prominent and Influential Citizens" argued on behalf of the plans for the Centennial celebration that an exhibition would produce "a stronger confidence at home and abroad in the peaceful endurance of our free institutions."[20]

How this stability could be promoted by an international fair was the subject of an address at the organizational meeting of the Centennial Commission. William Bigler, former governor and senator from Pennsylvania, asked to be "indulged in the expression of the belief that the proposed gathering of the people together from all sections commingling and coming together, with their hearts naturally open to the best impressions, cannot fail to have the happiest influence upon the relations existing between the States and the people." Visitors to the fair would have occasion to learn of the "crowning glory" of America, namely: "That the mass of the people whilst engaged in their daily and necessary pursuits, enjoy a larger measure of personal comforts and dignity than those of any other nation." The exposition would address the social and economic problems of the 1870s by equating material gain and human dignity. This linkage would be endowed with a positive value—progress. And progress, as the *Georgia Telegraph and Messenger* suggested, was related to "the glorious principle of self-government, and the rights of man, abstract and undeniable postulates, whose triumph it is now proposed to celebrate in the Centennial of 1876." In a general letter to clergy, Bishop William Bacon Stevens, of the Episcopal Diocese of Pennsylvania, expressed his wish that "people from all parts of our recently divided country will meet around the old family hearthstone of Independence Hall and pledge anew heart and hand in a social and political brotherhood never to be broken." These various celebrations of the exposition converged on the belief that material growth and universal brotherhood marched hand in hand along the pathway to a better future for mankind. From the beginning, however, the route was laid out in terms of long-standing racial assumptions common to most white Americans. The exposition reflected and solidified the deep-seated belief in a hierarchy of "progressive" and "regressive" nations and peoples.[21]

The idea for an international exhibition to commemorate the centennial of the Revolution originated in a lecture delivered by a scientist at the Smithsonian Institution and was brought to fruition by the efforts of businessmen and politicians interested in promoting the stability and further economic growth of the country. In the course of planning the exposition, the role of scientists, especially those of the Smithsonian, expanded until, at crucial junctures, the histories of the Centennial and American science became interwoven.

When the exposition directors needed assistance in developing a way to organize the thousands of exhibits, they turned to the commissioner from Connecticut, William Phipps Blake. Blake, a lineal descendant of one of the earliest settlers of the Massachusetts Bay Colony, had established a solid reputation as a geologist and mining engineer. He also possessed impressive credentials as an exhibition specialist, having organized the Mineralogy Department at the New York Crystal Palace Exhibition of 1853 and served as a member of the United States delegation to the 1867 Paris Exposition. This experience, coupled with world travel as a mining engineer, led to his selection to organize and classify the exhibits for the Centennial.[22]

The problem of devising a satisfactory systematic arrangement of exhibits had bewildered the planners of expositions since 1851. Yet, as the *Report on the Classification* made clear, it was a critical issue. The *Report*, delivered to the United States Commission in 1874, recognized that classification brought order out of chaos but emphasized that "a classification goes further than this: it serves to indicate generally and specifically the nature of the exhibition; it is the organic basis or expression of the whole; it is the foundation of organization and effort. It may be called the framework or skeleton from which exhibitions take their shape and character." Organization, as the *Report* made clear, must be determined by the purposes of an exposition. In the case of the Centennial, Blake's task was made easier because the authorizing act of Congress clearly stated the intent of the fair. The "one hundredth anniversary of American Independence" was to be commemorated "by holding an International Exhibition of Arts, Manufactures, and Products of the Soil and Mine . . . , the natural resources of the country and their development, and of its progress in those arts which benefit mankind, in comparison with those of older nations." As the *New York Times* explained Blake's plan: "It is designed to carry the spectator through the successive steps of human progress."[23]

Exhibitors were notified that the exhibition would contain ten departments:

1. Raw materials—mineral, vegetable, and animal
2. Materials and manufactures used for food, or in the arts, the result of extractive or combining processes
3. Textile and felted fabrics—apparel, costumes, and ornaments for the person
4. Furniture and manufactures of general use in construction and in dwellings
5. Tools, implements, machines, and processes
6. Motors and transportation
7. Apparatus and methods for the increase and diffusion of knowledge

8. Engineering, public works, architecture, and so forth
9. Plastic and graphic arts
10. Objects illustrating efforts for the improvement of the physical, intellectual, and moral condition of man.

As the Centennial Commission explained, raw materials came first as the necessary "foundation" for progress. Each of the succeeding steps represented "as nearly as possible in the order of their development, the results of the use of these materials, placing at the end the higher achievements of intellect and imagination." Blake's scheme was an ingenious conception for illustrating what progress was and how and where it occurred. The feasibility of the system for ordering experience received its highest, if unacknowledged, tribute from Melvil Dewey, who apparently used Blake's system as the basis for his own decimal arrangement of books in public libraries.[24]

In the short run, however, Blake's scheme ran into difficulty. Initially, he and the other commissioners had assumed that the Centennial Exhibition would follow the precedent established by earlier international exhibitions of having one grand building to house all the major exhibits. By 1873, however, because of delays in raising funds and the overwhelming number of exhibits, it became plain that additional structures would be needed. Even the Main Building itself underwent changes as additional space requirements had to be met. The decision to have several large structures instead of one called for changes in the classification system. The new arrangement, by necessity, was determined in part by the intended functions of the buildings. The result was a certain degree of disarray, not altogether displeasing to observers and certainly not devoid of symbolic portent for the future of American expansionism. For instance, the locomotive built for Dom Pedro by the Baldwin Locomotive Company was next to displays illustrating the process of making finished material out of raw wool. Together these exhibits suggested possibilities for the economic development of Latin America that promoters of succeeding fairs would attempt to clarify.[25]

Blake's reaction to the necessity for reworking his original classification is not recorded, but within the constraints imposed by the addition of new buildings the new arrangement—worked out by Campbell and his assistant Dorsey Gardner—was effected "with as little departure as possible from its original form." The idea of progress was still the central theme, and one of the assumptions implicit in the earlier classification was worked out in explicit fashion for the exhibits in the Main Building.[26]

Displays from around the world were organized in the Main Building according to race. It was an "installation by races," Gardner recorded. The United States, England, France, and Germany were given the most prominent display areas. "France and Colonies, representing the Latin races, were given space adjacent to the northeast central tower. England and Colonies, representing the Anglo-Saxon races, were given space adjacent to the northwest central tower. The German Empire, and Austria and Hungary, representing the Teutonic races, were granted space adjacent to the southwest tower." In a show of modesty, the United States took the "least desirable" location, though America was still presented as the geographic hub of the world—Mexico's and Brazil's displays were placed across from the United States exhibit, while displays from China and Japan were in the west wing, "being geographically west of America." The plan, according to Gardner, was "to place all the exhibiting nations of Latin extraction in the northeast quarter, adjacent to France, and of Teutonic extraction in the southwest quarter, with Germany, etc., etc."[27]

The idea of progress made manifest at the Centennial International Exhibition of 1876, in short, was presented along racial lines in an organizational system devised by several eminent scientists. This classification scheme joined politicians, business leaders, and scientists in the development and presentation of an ideology of progress that linked ideas about race to nationalism and industrial growth. The knot tightened as a result of direct involvement by the Smithsonian Institution, especially in the area of ethnology.

In January 1874 President Grant, by executive order, created a government board to set up a United States government display at the Centennial that "would illustrate the functions and administrative faculties of the Government in time of peace and its resources as a war power, and thereby serve to demonstrate the nature of our institutions and their adaptation to the wants of the people." Two years later, as the Government Building neared completion, the *New York Times* wrote of the display:

A veritable *multum in parvo*, it will convince the world, or rather that part of it that has eyes to see and intelligence to comprehend, that the future of America is based upon a rock and will endure. . . . Here in this comparatively small building will be shown the grandeur and extent of those resources, which in spite of taxation and depression will sooner or later lift the nation from its slough of despond, and place it at the head of the phalanx of progress.

When seen in this light, the Smithsonian's 20,600 square feet of display space, an exhibit area equaled only by that given to the Interior Department, took on an explicit ideological role in the centennial celebration of American progress.[28]

Spencer F. Baird, renowned naturalist and assistant secretary of the Smithsonian, was selected by Smithsonian secretary Joseph Henry to serve on the government board composed of executive department heads. As far as Henry and Baird were concerned, the Centennial came at a pivotal moment, for both men were edging the institution away from its earlier research orientation and

giving increasing emphasis to the Smithsonian as a museum that would educate and uplift the public. Baird had devoted over twenty years of his life to
its development as a paramount scientific organization. He plunged into the
task of organizing exhibits for the fair, recognizing in the Centennial an opportunity to illustrate the importance of the Smithsonian's activities to the
American people and to Congress. Baird also saw in the fair a chance to
gather additional materials and to formulate an argument that could persuade
Congress to provide the Smithsonian with a new building to be used as a
national museum.[29]

In his 1875 *Report to the Secretary,* Baird outlined plans for a display that
would encompass the activities of both the Smithsonian and the United States
National Museum. Exhibits would include fisheries and animal and mineral
"resources," as well as several display cases devoted to Smithsonian publications about the institution and its research undertakings. Additionally, Baird
advocated a "special effort" for an "exhaustive and complete" display to "illustrate the past and present condition of the native tribes of the United
States, or its anthropology." Initially, the Indian Bureau of the Interior Department contemplated an Indian exhibit of its own, but to expedite the collection and arrangement of material the bureau agreed to give the Smithsonian
control of the Indian exhibit.[30]

Collecting material for the exposition was no small matter. Baird organized
several ethnological expeditions to the Pacific Northwest, the West Coast, and
the upper Rocky Mountain states. James G. Swan, John Wesley Powell, and
Stephen Powers were placed in charge of the respective expeditions, and each
contributed a number of artifacts to the exposition. Baird also relied on federal
Indian agents on the reservations to round out the ethnological collection. To
aid these agents in determining what to collect, the Indian Bureau assigned
Otis T. Mason, a professor at Columbian (later Geoge Washington) University,
to devise a systematic set of "ethnological directions." Mason incorporated
into his instructions a plan of ethnological classification developed by Gustav
Klemm for the Leipzig Museum of Ethnology. Mason had translated Klemm's
work in 1873, and it subsequently became the basis for the arrangement of
exhibits in the National Museum. Klemm's theory, *Kulturgeschichte,* was reflected in Mason's appeal for materials to illustrate "the history of culture
among the aborigines of America, including the tribes now in existence, and
those which are nearly or quite extinct." Mason instructed the agents, many
of whom cared little about Indians and even less about ethnology, to gather
artifacts that would "present savage life and condition in all grades and
places," not omitting objects "because they are either rude or homely." He
demanded clear descriptions of the items collected, accurate models of artifacts, and care in exploring Indian mounds and caves. "The fact that the
monuments of the past and the savage tribes of men are rapidly disappearing
from our continent," he explained, "and that, ere another century will renew

an incentive so great and universal as this Exposition, they will have disappeared forever, should be all the stimulus required to give to the enterprise
the conscientious labor which it demands." Mason was genuinely impressed
by Indian life, but his emphasis on the "history of culture" betrayed a famil-
iarity with another aspect of Klemm's work. Klemm's *Allgemeine Cultur-Ges-
chichte der Menscheit* a ten-volume study of the history of culture, organized
mankind into "active" and "passive" races. In Mason's scheme, American
Indians were relegated to a passive role and were assumed to be en route to
extinction. Baird modified this view only slightly when he expressed his belief
that within the next century Indians "will have entirely ceased to present any
distinctive characters, and will be merged in the general population." Baird's
faith in assimilation—again echoing Klemm—reflected an all-or-nothing view
of the future of America's Indian population. Distinctiveness would be incompatible with assimilation. Ironically, while Baird, taken on his own terms,
appeared to believe that American Indians could be incorporated into the
larger American society, the exhibit itself attempted "to reconstruct the past
history of the different races of man" and to offer visitors "an opportunity of
studying these tribes of Indians which have come least under the influence of
civilization."[31]

While Baird worked out the plans in Washington, he left the organization
of the exhibit under the supervision of Charles Rau. Described by one historian as "a lonely, ascetic German immigrant," Rau had earned his livelihood
as a schoolteacher in the Midwest and in New York City. In the 1860s he had
collaborated with the Smithsonian in the study of archaeology. By the time he
received a year-long appointment in 1875 to organize the ethnological collection of the Smithsonian, he had become "one of the most eminent of American
ethnologists." Rau's ideas about ethnology, not surprisingly, resembled
Baird's and merged into the central themes of the Centennial. In a lecture
entitled "The Happy Age," delivered before the New York Liberal Club, Rau
argued: "the extreme lowness of our remote ancestors cannot be a source of
humiliation; on the contrary, we should glory in our having advanced so far
above them, and recognize the great truth that *progress* is the law that governs
the development of mankind." He concluded his address with a promise:
"Those who come after us will see better times." Rau's observations about
progress were seemingly confirmed at the exhibition when his assistant, Frank
Hamilton Cushing, spied a quartz nugget protruding from the ground across
from Agricultural Hall. Closer examination revealed the stone to be part of an
Indian club. A newspaper correspondent observing the scene noted that this
"reminding of another age and another people, provides the strongest imagin-
able contrast to the mechanical progress of the present."[32]

The central conception underlying the Indian exhibit at the Centennial, in
short, was that Native American cultures and people belonged to the intermin-

able wasteland of humanity's dark and stormy beginnings. The Indians' worth as human beings was determined by their usefulness as counterpoint to the unfolding progress of the ages.

This idea became manifest in the exhibit of Indian artifacts in the Smithsonian section of the Government Building, which took up nearly one-third of the space. Display cases were filled with examples of pottery, weapons, and tools. Between the cases stood tepees and other models of Indian homes. Photographs of Indians hung on the walls, and Swan's major acquisition, a sixty-five foot Haida canoe, occupied a central position. Life-size papier-mâché and wax figures were placed along the aisles to illustrate Indian costumes. The display itself struck many visitors as chaotic, though Rau and Cushing apparently tried to arrange the artifacts genetically, following Mason's dictum that similar objects be placed in evolutionary sequence, regardless of origin.[33]

As an exercise in organization the display may have been a hodgepodge bordering on failure. But as an attempt to create an impression of Indians as an antithesis to the forces of progress, it was successful. Few observers dem-

Fig. 5. Smithsonian Institution exhibit, United States Government Building. Courtesy of Smithsonian Institution Archives, Record Unit 95, Photograph Collection.

onstrated empathy for the Indians. James L. Dale offered a typical response to the exhibit in his popular novel, *What Ben Beverly Saw at the Great Exposition:*

> There are also wax figures of celebrated Indian braves, with names indicating their bloodthirsty disposition, and terrible fighting qualities. . . . Novelists with unsubdued fancies, may sit in their cozy back parlors, and write pretty little stories of the noble red man, bounding over his native wilds in all the untrammelled freedom of his irrepressible nature . . . ; but let one of these red gentlemen, with his small, cruel, black eyes, his coarse, unkempt locks, and the chains [*sic*] of his wide cheekbones, and large animal mouth, heightened by a skillful application of red and yellow ochres; I say, should this attractive creature meet our charming story writer on those same native wilds, I fancy the next novel, if by some miraculous interposition of Providence it should be permitted at all, would indicate a very sudden change of base on the Indian question.

Influential editor William Dean Howells concurred in the pages of the *Atlantic Monthly:* "The red man, as he appears in effigy and in photograph in this collection, is a hideous demon, whose malign traits can hardly inspire any emotion softer than abhorrence." Howells, moreover, defended Indian agents against charges of incompetence: "we do not sufficiently account for the demoralizing influence of merely beholding those false and pitiless savage faces; moldy flour and corrupt beef must seem altogether too good for them." For Howells, the solution to the Indian problem was simple and obvious: "extinction."[34]

In addition to the collection of artifacts in the Smithsonian display, the exposition offered visitors an opportunity to apply the lessons learned from the scientific exhibits to living representatives of various Indian tribes. Until their efforts were thwarted by the failure of an anticipated congressional appropriation, both the Smithsonian and the Bureau of Indian Affairs contemplated a living display of Indians under their joint supervision as a key attraction at the fair. The lack of congressional sanction rendered impossible an official display of Indians by the government. At one point the Indian Office even appeared reluctant to allow any Native Americans to journey to Philadelphia because of fears that any gathering of Indians would become a "sideshow." However, popular interest in Indians and the desire of the government "to impress the Indians themselves, through their representatives on the occasion in question with the powers and resources of the United States and of civilization generally" overcame the initial hesitancy about Indian participation in the Centennial. Various Indian agents, often on behalf of Indians, requested permission to allow delegations of Indians to attend the fair.[35]

Several Missouri chiefs dictated a simple request: "We have many friends in Philadelphia that we wish to shake hands with." En route, they hoped to be able to meet with the president, since he had not responded to their letters.

John Q. Smith, Indian commissioner, responded favorably—albeit in bureau-
cratic doublespeak—to a number of these appeals from Indian agents: "Cannot authorize absence of any Indians from their reservation. If you are satisfied, and will be responsible that Menomenees will go as visitors only in
charge of competent and proper persons, will not discredit themselves or the
Indian service, and will return without expense to government, I will not object." A small Indian encampment apparently was situated at the base of
George's Hill on the fairgrounds and placed under the supervision of the famous Texas scout and Indian fighter George Anderson. The Indians, described
by one newspaper as "the *crème de la crème*" of Indian society, were presented
and generally viewed as leftovers from a bygone age.[36]

The image of Indians as unassimilable savages took on an immediate political importance when the northern Great Plains exploded in warfare. The exposition, of course, was not directly responsible for the series of events culminating in George Armstrong Custer's debacle in June 1876. But the images
of the Indians fostered by the Smithsonian and Indian Office at the exhibition
left little room for doubt about the identity of heroes and villains in the American West.

The rationale behind the need for negative perceptions of Indians was underscored in the certificate the Smithsonian received: "For a very superior
scientifically and practically arranged display of the vast natural resources of
the United States . . . and the collections of Ethnological objects of the greatest interest for this branch of science." The displays of natural resources and
ethnological exhibits were intimately related. Both Indians and raw materials
could legitimately be exploited in the interest of American expansion. The
Smithsonian Institution's exhibit, in short, provided the cement for integrating
ideas about progress and race into a coherent ideological whole. The Smithsonian's exhibits, moreover, were at least as important in laying the groundwork for favorable reception of evolutionary ideas about race in the United
States as was the centennial visit to America of Thomas H. Huxley, popular-
izer of Charles Darwin's theory of evolution.[37]

The attention paid to Native American exhibits contrasted sharply with the
neglect accorded blacks at the exposition. Initially, many blacks expected to
play a large part in the Centennial and looked upon the fair as an opportunity
to demonstrate their contributions to America's historical development. They
were sorely disappointed by the actions of the exposition directors. The *Death
of Cleopatra*, by Edmonia Lewis, and *Under the Oaks*, by Edward M. Bannister, were the only representations of the work of black artists. And the only
exhibit directly related to American blacks was a statue, *The Freed Slave*.
Blacks, moreover, were discriminated against during the construction of the
fair. Philip Foner notes the complete absence of black workers in construction
crews despite the 70 percent unemployment rate among blacks in Philadelphia. Once the fair opened, the only employment available for blacks was as

entertainers or as waiters, hotel clerks, messengers, and janitors. Even the most influential black in American society, Frederick Douglass, suffered humiliation at the fair. For opening day he had been invited to sit on the platform with other dignitaries, but police officers refused him admittance to the stand. Had it not been for the personal intervention of New York's Senator Roscoe Conkling, he would have been compelled to watch the proceedings from afar. As it was, Douglass, a magnificent orator, was not permitted to address the crowd.[38]

In the early years of preparation, white women sponsors of the exposition had asked black women to help raise funds by selling stock subscriptions. At the first organizational meeting, black women discovered that "we were to be *classed*." "It was then, and not till then," according to Miss R. Cole, "that I had any idea that our work was to be confined exclusively among our own color, and that we were to have no voice nor to form any part of the local committee in the wards." The Afro-Americans' protest about being manipulated resulted in the white women's passing a resolution expressing their regret that the executive committee had appointed a committee of black women in the first place. They granted Miss Cole and her committee "an honorable discharge." The unfavorable publicity generated by this controversy ultimately resulted in the executive committee's issuing an apology to the black subcommittee and a promise that fund-raising activities would take place without racial discrimination. Yet, having raised funds for the exposition, black women received neither mention nor exhibit space in the Woman's Building.[39]

Another dispute ensued over an offer by the exposition commissioners to allow blacks to place a statue on the grounds memorializing one of their heroes. The offer was refused, in part because some black community leaders felt such a monument would create an impression of separateness. There was also indecision about who the statue should represent. But the most important reason for refusal was the unwillingness of blacks approached by the Centennial Commission to obey its guideline that all monuments come down thirty days after the close of the fair. Regardless of whom the statue represented, blacks felt it imperative that the monument be as enduring as their contributions to the republic.[40]

Instead of monuments and exhibits of their own, American blacks were represented at the fair in a concession variously called "The South," or the "Southern Restaurant." The commissioners "cheerfully" granted this concession to Edward Mercer, a white businessman from Atlanta. A guidebook informed visitors that there would be "a band of old-time plantation 'darkies' who will sing their quaint melodies and strum the banjo before visitors of every clime." The possibilities for excitement were unbounded: "Imagine the phlegmatic German exhibitor with his 'frau und kinder' gazing with astonishment at the pure and unadulterated 'Essence of Ole Virginny' expounded by a hand from the cotton field, or a solemn-visaged Turk receiving with ill-

concealed horror, a dusky son of Tophet 'rattling of the bones.' " The guidebook ended its description with the promise: "To a student of human nature
it will be one of the most interesting sights in the Exhibition." Blacks, in
other words, were seen as examples of certain aspects of human nature, particularly of the child in man, and not as full human beings in their own right.
Another impression created by the concession was that newly freed blacks in
the South were happy, carefree, and in good hands. The harsh realities of
sharecropping, lynching, and political exclusion were ignored. Joaquin Miller,
in his epic "Song of the Centennial," summed up the place assigned to American blacks at the Centennial Exhibition and in American society: "A new and
black brother, half troubador, / A stray piece of midnight comes grinning on
deck." William Dean Howells described the bronze *Freed Slave* in equally
revealing terms: "a most offensively Frenchy negro, who has broken his chain,
and spreading both his arms and legs abroad is rioting in a declamation of
something (I should say) from Victor Hugo; one longs to clap him back into
hopeless bondage." Feared as insurrectionists and barely tolerated as minstrels, blacks were relegated to the shadows of the vision of progress projected
at the fair.[41]

   If the Centennial projected a distorted image of Native Americans and
blacks, the racial classification of exhibits suggested an equally skewed
impression of other nonwhite peoples from around the world. As in the instance of the Indian, a negative impression of a selected group of people could
be manipulated in the interests of economic expansion. Philadelphia newspapers, throughout the months of the fair, made repeated reference to the exhaustion of the home market for American manufactured goods and the absolute necessity for foreign markets "to prevent continued depression." The field
most often mentioned in this context was Asia. One newspaper found this "to
be an almost unlimited field for the disposal of many articles of American
manufacture, where up to this very moment, such goods are almost unknown."
Another press report noted the volume of trade generated by Asian countries
and pointed out that with increased efficiency in the native labor force productivity could skyrocket. The *Philadelphia Inquirer* was enthusiastic: "American enterprise is wanted in that region, and our people need only to be shown
the value of the field to go to work there." The prospective value of the Asian
market, however, was bound up with the perceived qualities and capabilities
of Asian peoples.[42]
   For the most part Asians were puzzling to Americans. Their architecture,
music, art, and religion seemed curious and strange. The reaction to displays
from China and Japan, however, was by no means uniform. Japan excited
more favorable comment than its neighbor, but the Japanese were only comparatively well received. The elegance of the Japanese display was particularly remarkable, according to most observers, because the Centennial marked

only the second time the Japanese government had participated in an international exhibition—the first being the Vienna fair of 1873. "The quaint little people," one visitor commented, "with their shambling gait, their eyes set awry in their head, and their grave and gentle ways, how can it be in them . . . to make such wonderful things?" This was truly a disquieting question in view of the magnificent displays of Japanese bronze and porcelain vases, basketry, screens, and two entire buildings crafted by Japanese workmen. The beauty of the exhibits, coupled with the industriousness of the Japanese workers, seemed incompatible with the prevailing stereotypes of nonwhite people. Nevertheless, these preexisting racial attitudes formed the starting point for the response to Japanese creativity. One reaction of white Americans was to assume sponsorship. As a Philadelphia newspaper reminded exposition-goers, it was America's Commodore Perry who had "discovered" the Japanese in 1854. Another account of the exhibits noted that the Japanese had developed an acute sense of "moral obligations." This moral sense was seemingly amplified by the Japanese emphasis on order—a quality greatly admired by Victorian Americans. Furthermore, the attention the Japanese *Catalogue of Exhibits* gave to gardens suggested that the Japanese were a pastoral people. The highest praise came from the *Inquirer:* "Japan renders her verdict in favor of American machinery. The Japanese have already adopted the American costume in dress, and the progressive spirit pervading the Old World is inclining her people to adopt American ideas and American machinery." Japan, it seemed, was ready to incorporate the American machine into its garden. Even before the exhibition opened formally, a reporter had observed, after visiting the Main Building: "Japan is bound to be more and more progressive, and China must be more and more conservative."[43]

The reaction to the Chinese exhibit, established by Chinese customs officials, was extremely ambivalent. "Cut off from the rest of the world by its great wall, and isolated behind her old feeling of distrust and apathy towards the peoples of Europe," reported the *Public Record*, "the old empire of China has received but little benefit from western civilization and advancement, and as a consequence, makes a display at the exposition which is curious, rich, and rare." Like the Japanese, the Chinese were viewed as peculiar, yet they were seen as very different from the Japanese. Even the beauty of their display could not dispel the American belief that they posed a threat. Easterners were aware of the mounting anti-Chinese agitation in California, and similar fears were taken up in accounts of Chinese displays at the fair. After favorable reference to silks, jade, and ivory carvings, a contemporary exposition historian stated: "A Chinaman would rather swallow a decoction of opium and tobacco than one of the green tea prepared by himself." A visitor recorded his recollection of "the long-tailed coolies working there for some time past, amid boxes and bales all redolent with the peculiar odor which belongs to China." In discussing the "Chinese problem," the *Inquirer* asked: "Where comes the benefit of hiring men for a pittance when their very presence spreads a moral and physical leprosy, contaminating everything it touches, and corrupting the very air with the poison of a loathsome disease?" The crux of the issue was simply stated: "The Chinese will not assimilate with our population. . . . From a plaything and curiosity John has become a vexing problem."[44]

The negative perception of the Chinese was ironic given the tremendous profit Philadelphia financiers reaped from the China trade—profits that were invested in Philadelphia's shipping industry. But China had never been viewed or treated as an equal partner in trade relations with the United States. Indeed, negative stereotypes of the Chinese made the China market all the more accessible to American commercial ventures. For if the Chinese were inferior, they could not be expected to make decisions concerning the use of their resources that would affect the course of world progress. The same logic easily applied to other Asian countries as well: "A moderate calculation of the trade done by these people places it as five hundred millions of dollars annually. This result is attained for the most part by active enterprise, in a very inefficient manner, and without much industry or energy. But for that reason it is more valuable, as showing what might be done by the active labors of the American people."[45]

Not all fairgoers, however, drew a sharp distinction between the Chinese and the Japanese, stressing instead the difference between Orient and Occident. Birdsley Grant Northrup, Congregational minister and educator, found that the exhibits in the Main Building revealed "a radical difference of type between the Occidental and Oriental Mind." Christian nations were "largely inventive," whereas Asian nations were "essentially and laboriously *imitative*." These complementary characteristics, Northrup suggested, would lead to closer trade relations with China and Japan. Both countries, he noted, "may contribute immensely to our prosperity." The perpetrators of the racial violence that erupted on opening day also lumped Asians together. While one Chinese official was practically stripped of his robes and another was threatened with having his queue cut off, several Japanese were assaulted. Racial violence, seemingly contradictory to the messages delivered by opening-day speakers, in reality confirmed the lessons of *herrenvolk* democracy so deeply embedded in the ideology of progress presented at the fair.[46]

Ideas about racial hierarchy were further amplified by the displays from Africa. African cultures were generally ignored by the colonial powers that controlled the African exhibits. The colonizers emphasized the natural resources of the African continent. The display by the Orange Free State, "a plucky little faraway African state," received the most favorable and sympathetic notice. Many Americans had no idea that the Orange Free State was in South Africa until coming to the exhibition. After viewing the exhibits of diamonds, wool, coal, cream of tartar, and corn, few fairgoers would have disagreed with the forecast that this region would have "a career of prosperity equaled only by that of California after the discovery of gold." Even more impressive than the exhibit proper was the history it represented, for the display had been set up by "enterprising Dutchmen" in the process of "civilizing a barbarous land." The empathy of many white Americans for the white Afrikaner was reflected in the feeling of one observer that future historians would have to record "the great trecken or emigration of thousands of Dutch colonists from the Cape of Good Hope; of their struggles with warlike blacks, who harassed their settlements just as the Indians did those of our forefathers." Attitudes toward black Africans received ample illustration in a cartoon in a popular history of the fair showing the "Boo Choo" African delegation marching in a parade. Equally revealing was the description by Charles B. Norton of L'Africaine, a statue by the Italian sculptor Emanuele Caroni: "Africa—stagnant, blind, and neglected among the countries of the earth! Whose vast desert is but the outward symbol of the desolation beyond. The desolation where nature is luxuriant, perhaps, but where man is alike uncultured and unconscious; sunk, alas! in that most melancholy degradation which knows no better sphere." The statue seemed to Norton a perfect description of the African as a "partially awakened soul striving to grasp its real position, that it may the better grope—though blindly and feebly—toward a more friendly and beneficent future!"[47]

"Comparison," Joseph Hawley stressed in 1879, "is vital to the success of any exposition. . . . You can never discover your success or your failure without comparison. You cannot gauge your status without comparison with other nations." "Comparison," he underlined, "is essential to show the effects on the industries and the arts of climate, of race, of geographical position, of raw materials, of social and political institutions." Hawley believed that studying different peoples and exhibits held value for all fairgoers, regardless of class. But the volatile economic situation of the country led the directors to place particular importance on attracting the working classes to the exhibits illustrating comparative racial and material progress.[48]

The N. and G. Taylor Company of Philadelphia urged its employees to subscribe twenty-five cents a week to exposition stock out of their wages, with the admonition that the exposition would give them an opportunity "to prove their superiority." The fair, the circular claimed, "will, in effect, be a test of two systems, one the poorly paid, poorly fed and uneducated cheap labor of the old world, against the intelligent, contented, protected labor of the new." The advantages that workers "have gained in their larger freedom they enjoy here, over that which is the lot of their fellows in other lands, is to be measured." Once the exposition opened, newspapers urged local workers to visit the Centennial, reminding them that the only cost was for their carfare and entrance fees for themselves and their families. At one point the House of Representatives formulated plans, never implemented, to provide funds for one skilled mechanic from every congressional district to visit the fair.[49]

When a Philadelphia newspaper discovered that the Artisans' Institute for Promoting General and Technical Knowledge in London was sending a delegation to the fair, it appealed to American manufacturers to send their workers to the exposition. "Here is the rare opportunity for study and comparison," the *Inquirer* proposed, "and it will be suicidal for us to neglect making the Centennial an engine to stir our workmen into a greater interest in this matter of technology." Workers would discover new "practical ideas." Furthermore, the newspaper later added, the laborer would "discover that not merely his life, but his elevation in wealth and comfort depend upon his acceptance of what invention has achieved, and his efforts to appropriate its benefits, and, perchance, to earn fortune by improving upon what he sees." Most important, workers would "learn to value the irresistible competition" confronting them in the workplace. One exhibit that conveyed these lessons was a working model of a screw-making apparatus in Machinery Hall that produced 80,000 screws daily. The beauty of the machine, visitors were informed, was that one operator, in this case a woman, could attend ten machines at once.[50]

Several manufacturers heeded the advice of the press and gave their employees an opportunity to see the fair. Owners of the Yale Lock Company sent 120 employees to the fair, and Baltimore cotton mill owners sent 4,000 women workers. The largest excursions were organized by the railroads and coal-mining companies. At least a half-dozen excursions of miners numbering in the thousands were brought to the Centennial. The impelling motives behind these ventures were the turmoil in the mining regions involving the Molly Maguires and the opportunity the Centennial offered to reorient the values of the miners. A typical excursion was arranged by the Philadelphia and Reading Coal and Iron Company. Miners and their wives and children, 1,100 strong, received an all-expense-paid trip to the fair, and a dinner of vegetables, meat, and ice cream was provided by the company. A vice-president and other company officials "were unremitting in their efforts to make their grateful guests as comfortable and happy as possible." The company officials expressed satisfaction with the result: "Not only the faces but the words of the honest folk attested how successful the endeavor was." The importance manufacturers attached to working people's visiting the fair was further reflected in the efforts to keep the fair open on Sundays and past 6 P.M. on working days. Although both of these efforts failed in the face of opposition from the clergy and because of insufficient illumination afforded by the gas lamps, the directors of the exposition did set aside a "poor man's day" with reduced admission rates.[51]

That the Centennial Exhibition was in certain respects a counterculture—more precisely, an effort to counter a tenderloin culture—was testified to by the rough-and-tumble "Centennial City" that appeared along Elm Avenue, just across from the Main Building. Stretching for almost a mile were "restaurants, small hotels, beer-gardens, ice-cream saloons, and small shows that have sprung up as if by magic." In sharp contrast to the stately exposition buildings, the structures of the adjacent shantytown were "flimsy," constructed of wood, with pieces of canvas frequently serving as roofing. The buildings were decorated in festive colors, and the proprietors hired bands to entertain their guests. In addition to restaurants, bars, and hotels, there were dioramas, working models of oil wells, "pea-nut stands, pie-stalls, the applemen and women, Bologna sausage-vendors, dealers in cakes and lemonade, and the inevitable balloon-man." One of the more popular attractions was a "museum" that put on display "the wild men of Borneo, and the wild children of Australia, the fat woman . . . heavy enough to entitle her to a place in Machinery Hall, and a collection of 'Feejees,' who were vouched for by the exhibitors as 'pure and unadulterated man-eaters.' "[52]

Reminiscent of the popular street shows and museums of Europe and America, the chaotic Centennial City offered a vivid contrast to the carefully orchestrated entertainment at the exposition. The directors of the fair were concerned about what went into the "mental valise" of the visitor who wandered into the Centennial City.[53]

From the perspective of the exposition directors and city officials, elements associated with vice seemed to be the lifeblood of the Centennial City. A police report noted that the area around the railroad station, directly across from the Main Building, was the congregating point "for many tramps, peddlers, and boot-blacks" who frequently were found sleeping in fields, "in outhouses, in empty cars of the Pennsylvania Railroad Company, and, in one instance, in a cave." The contrast between the wealth contained in the exposition grounds and the poverty around them was compelling, but such a poignant reminder of the industrial depression was hard for the exposition and city officials to brook. Many of the inhabitants of the area adjacent to the exposition were soon labeled "pests and nuisances." An incident in late June was particularly vexing. Two women, Isabella Parker and Maggie Peterson (also known as Maggie Pooler and Irish Maggie), met James M. Canfield, an exhibitor at the Centennial. In the evening they visited several saloons. The following day Canfield was discovered "in an insensible condition" in an apartment above the Fish House Saloon. Canfield's death prompted a police investigation of the entire area. Meanwhile, a serious fire in an oyster house, which spread over four acres of adjoining structures, provided the mayor with a reason to evict all residents from illegally built structures on Elm Street. By the end of September an additional twenty-seven buildings in the Centennial City had been demolished by Philadelphia authorities.[54]

Elm Street typified certain aspects of tenderloin culture that involved values different from those etched by the exposition promoters. Seventeen years would pass before exposition designers found a way to incorporate popular amusements into the ideological framework of the fair. In 1876, the popular entertainments along Elm Street posed a threat precisely because they were not explicitly incorporated into this ideological construct. The popular museum seemed to be simply a freak show, and the various bars and saloons typified a social reality different from that projected by the fountains that temperance societies erected on the exposition grounds. The Centennial City, in short, seemed diametrically opposed to the exposition sponsors' efforts to render all visitors, especially workers, expectant capitalists with a shared faith in American progress. Consequently, shantytown had to be destroyed.

The Centennial Exhibition closed with a flourish. Dignitaries circulated ceaselessly. Wagner's Inaugural March received another hearing, Beethoven's Sixth Symphony and the Hallelujah Chorus were performed, and speechmaking once again characterized the occasion. There was, however, one difference from opening day: it rained so hard that the ceremonies had to be moved indoors.[55]

" 'As a woman who is in travail hath sorrow,' but afterwards 'she remembereth no more her anguish for the joy that a man is born into the world,' " so with the Centennial, at least as Congressman Morrell summed up the history of the enterprise. He reminded his listeners that early opposition to the fair had given way to support for an event that demonstrated that America had grown up, arrived at full "manhood," and could take its place alongside the older nations of Europe. The pulse of the fair, Morrell mentioned, was the Corliss engine: "Silent and irresistible, it affects the imagination as realizing the fabled powers of genii and afrit in Arabian tales, and like them it is subject to subtle control." The exposition signified the permanence of the machine in American life. Who would control the forces of machinofacture? What form would the control take? These were questions that the sponsors of the exposition had endeavored to resolve.[56]

One particularly instructive exhibit along these lines was a nine-foot-tall working model of George Washington's tomb, which demonstrated that history itself could be automated and manipulated in apparent support of the world view offered by the directors of the exposition. At regular intervals Washington rose from the dead, as it were, and the toy soldiers keeping guard saluted. In this display the glories of the republic's past were used to bestow a benediction on America's present condition and to anticipate future development.[57]

Six years after the Centennial closed, John Welsh summed up the effects of the exhibition in a *Memorial* to Congress. He lauded the educational accomplishments of the fair, commented favorably on the increased domestic and foreign markets that resulted from it, and noted that the exposition had promoted immigration to the United States. In the last analysis, however, Welsh argued that "the material result was in reality greatly short of the moral influence which the United States gained by the Exhibition." Affixing a moral quality to the exposition had several implications. First, if the exposition was a moral compass, present and future social, political, and economic choices could be judged as right or wrong, good or bad, by using the exposition as a fixed coordinate. As Morrell exclaimed during the closing ceremony: "the full measure of our manhood will go down to [future generations] untouched by the gnawing tooth of Time." Second, if the exposition proved America's material and moral standing in the eyes of the civilized world, there could be little doubt that the United States should assume the role of moral arbiter of world affairs. Finally, if the fair exerted a moral influence, it seemed to follow that this ethical force resulted from the leadership exerted by the sponsors of the fair.[58]

Immediately upon the exposition's conclusion, the Board of Finance distributed to bankers, steamship companies, railroads, insurance firms, and Philadelphia's leading merchants a circular requesting written tributes to Welsh and asking that contributions of fifty or one hundred dollars be given to him in recognition of his services. Donations totaled fifty thousand dollars, which Welsh turned over to the University of Pennsylvania to endow a chair in history and literature. One contributor found this testament particularly appropriate: "and as it was in the beneficent cause of education that this splendid success was [won], its record cannot take a better form than the educational endowment Mr. Welsh modestly proposes. May the endowment be as enduring as the glorious memory of the Centennial and of the services of its Chairman of Finance." John Wanamaker, Philadelphia's leading merchant and founder of the department store bearing his name, was even more enthusiastic: "The bright path through the Centennial Alps was flooded with sunshine by the beautiful spirit of the undaunted leader." An early historian of the fair allowed other commissioners to bask in the reflected glow of Welsh's glory: "John Welsh and his coadjutors have held the magician's wand that conjured up Aladdin's Palace in Fairmount Park."[59]

As recently as the Bicentennial celebration in 1976, Americans were reminded of the work of Welsh and the other directors of the Centennial: "They did well." The Bicentennial was also a time for the Smithsonian to recall the tremendous benefits it had reaped from the Philadelphia celebration of a hundred years earlier. In the Arts and Industries Building, constructed in 1880 to house the millions of dollars worth of artifacts donated to the government as a result of the fair, the Smithsonian recreated the Centennial Exhibition on a small scale. The 1976 exhibit was appropriately commemorative, for the Centennial Exhibition had marked a second birth for the Smithsonian Institution, and each subsequent fair contributed to its growth and popularity.[60]

The most important result of the Centennial was simply its success. The Board of Finance was left with a two million dollar surplus before repaying the government loan. This was an unexpected bonus and a further incentive to other would-be "custodians of culture" to organize world's fairs. The overarching lesson of the fair was passed on by Francis A. Walker, chief of the Bureau of Awards and future president of the Massachusetts Institute of Technology, when he compared the guiding principle of a world's fair to that of an ecumenical council: "A council of the church does not derive its authority merely from the presence of so many dignitaries of such an aggregate weight of holiness, learning, and experience. A larger array of men of greater talents and virtues might possess no authority at all to enunciate doctrine. The council speaks with effect because, in the theory of its constitution, the church—the whole body, not only of actual but of potential believers—throughout the inhabited world is there present. Its universality is of the essence of its authority."[61] For the next forty years, America's upper classes, confronted by growing class unrest, would redouble the efforts begun at Philadelphia to speak with the voice of authority, "enunciate doctrine," and affirm their cultural hegemony through the medium of international expositions.

2

The Chicago World's Columbian Exposition of 1893: "And Was Jerusalem Builded Here?"

The long lines of white buildings were ablaze with countless lights; the music from the bands scattered over the grounds floated softly out upon the water; all else was silent and dark. In that lovely hour, soft and gentle as was ever a summer night, the toil and trouble of men, the fear that was gripping men's hearts in the markets, fell away from men and in its place came Faith. The people who could dream this vision and make it real, those people . . . would press on to greater victories than this triumph of beauty—victories greater than the world had yet witnessed.

Robert Herrick, *Memoirs of an American Citizen*, 1905[1]

THE DIRECTORS OF THE CENTENNIAL EXHIBITION began the task of providing industrialized America with a cultural synthesis through the medium of the international exposition. This effort by America's leaders to define social reality reached a new level of sophistication with the Chicago World's Columbian Exposition of 1893.[2]

In the midst of the Mauve Decade, five years after the outbreak of class violence at Haymarket Square in Chicago, a neoclassical wonderland, an imposing White City suddenly appeared on the desolate marshlands of the Lake Michigan shore, seven miles south of the downtown Loop. To a country on the brink of yet another financial panic, the fair seemed "a little ideal world, a realization of Utopia . . . [foreshadowing] some far away time when the earth should be as pure, as beautiful, and as joyous as the White City itself." For Meg and Robin Macleod, two orphans with "elflocks and pink cheeks" in a Frances Hodgson Burnett novel, the fair took on similar importance. "I've been reading the *Pilgrim's Progress*," Meg said to her brother, "and I do *wish*—I do so wish there *was* a City Beautiful." The two waifs, upon hearing about the ivory palaces, amethystine lakes, and enormous crowds, adopted the role of Christian and made a pilgrimage to the City Beautiful reincarnate in Jackson Park.[3]

They were not alone. In February 1892 Harlow N. Higinbotham, a partner in Marshall Field's mercantile empire and chairman of the exposition's committee on ways and means, appeared before the House Appropriations Com-

Fig. 6. Court of Honor. Courtesy of Smithsonian Institution Archives, Record Unit 95, Photograph Collection.

mittee. He estimated that twenty million people would visit the fair once and that nearly half of them would make a second visit. His estimate proved to be only slightly inflated. Admissions totaled 27,529,400 adults and children. Pilgrims all, many visitors, like the twins, were lifted into ecstasy at the spectacle. "Everything is buzz and clatter and confusion, an unending, everlasting labyrinth of grandeur," wrote Horace G. Benson, a Denver attorney. "I am dazzled, captivated and bewildered, and return to my room, tired in mind, eyes, ears and body, so much to think about, so much to entice you on from place to place, until your knees clatter and you fall into a chair completely exhausted." "However," he concluded, "it is very pleasant to lay here and think of it all." Other visitors, like the fictitious Uncle Jeremiah, a midwestern farmer, found reassurance and justification: "I used to be afraid that the government was all a goin' to pieces and that my fighting for Uncle Sam at Gettysburg was of no use, but I ain't any more afraid of the world bustin' up. People that made the machinery that I've seen and all that have too much sense."[4]

William Dean Howells, at the peak of his career, again journeyed to a world's fair and like many of his middle-class contemporaries looked upon the White City as a manifestation of what was good in American life and as an ennobling vision Americans should strive to effectuate. In *Letters of an Altrurian Traveller*, originally serialized for the *Cosmopolitan*, Howells, through the character of Homos, sought to direct Americans toward building a commonwealth based on the New Testament. To the dismayed Homos, Chicago, the burgeoning metropolis of the West, with its corruption and filth, seemed a "Newer York, an ultimated Manhattan, the realized ideal of largeness, loudness, and fastness, which New York has persuaded the American is metropolitan." After seeing the fair, however, Homos found cause for optimism that in the future of America urban problems "shall seem as impossible as they would seem to any Altrurian now." The "Fair City," Howells proclaimed, "is a bit of Altruria: it is as if the Capitol of one of our Regions has set sail and landed on the shores of the vast inland sea where the Fair City lifts its domes and columns."[5]

In actuality, the utopian vision projected by the exposition directors had a dual foundation: the monumental White City and the Midway Plaisance. The Midway, the honky-tonk sector of the fair, was officially classified under the auspices of the exposition's Department of Ethnology. Hailed as a "great object lesson" in anthropology by leading anthropologists, the Midway provided visitors with ethnological, scientific sanction for the American view of the nonwhite world as barbaric and childlike and gave a scientific basis to the racial blueprint for building a utopia. The Chicago world's fair, generally recognized for its contributions to urban planning, beaux-arts architecture, and institutions of the arts and sciences, just as importantly introduced millions of fairgoers to evolutionary ideas about race—ideas that were presented in a

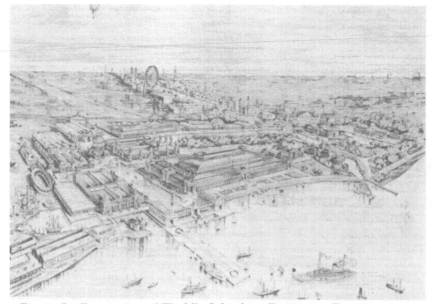

Fig. 7. Bird's-eye view of World's Columbian Exposition. Engraving from Prints and Photographs Division, Library of Congress.

utopian context and often conveyed by exhibits that were ostensibly amusing. On the Midway at the World's Columbian Exposition, evolution, ethnology, and popular amusements interlocked as active agents and bulwarks of hegemonic assertion of ruling-class authority. In addition to its ethnological underpinnings, the cultural force of the fair was further augmented by a series of international congresses. Organized by the exposition directors, these public conferences brought together the world's leading authorities to discuss religion, labor, women, and other important concerns of the day. George Alfred Townsend, columnist for the *Chicago Tribune*, described the heart of the fair when he wrote: "The motives and facts around this exposition are the confessions of faith of a new dispensation." This new dispensation gave to the creed of American progress a new tenet: evolution.[6]

One of the sidelights of the persisting tensions and uncertainties about industrialization that characterized American life in the 1880s and early 1890s was the tug-of-war between urban elites over the site for the international exposition that would commemorate the four hundredth anniversary of the landfall of Columbus. Minneapolis, Washington, DC., and Saint Louis had their staunch supporters, but the leading contenders were the businessmen and financiers of New York and Chicago. There was something ridiculous about either New York, with its obvious Dutch and English beginnings, or Chicago, situated a thousand miles from the Atlantic seaboard, proposing to commemorate Columbus's landing in the West Indies, but the urgency of the country's social and economic situation as well as the prospects for profit rendered such objections trivial. Leading businessmen in both cities undoubtedly were familiar with the United States Centennial Commission's final report, which estimated that each visitor to the Centennial had contributed $4.50 to Philadelphia's economy. Many businesses in the city chosen for the next fair clearly stood to reap enormous benefits. Proponents of the Columbian celebration, however, included not only businessmen, but the financial titans of the respective cities. In New York, Chauncey Depew (president of the New York Central Railroad) was in the forefront of the exposition effort. William Waldorf Astor, J. P. Morgan, Cornelius Vanderbilt, Grover Cleveland, William Rockefeller, Jay Gould, Elihu Root, and August Belmont contributed time, money, and their not inconsiderable political influence to gain state and federal support for the fair. Their counterparts in Chicago's financial world fought equally hard. Philip Armour, Charles B. Holmes, Charles T. Yerkes, Gustavus Swift, Cyrus McCormick, George Pullman, and Marshall Field spearheaded the drive to bring the fair to Chicago. [7]

Although New York financial interests eventually pledged fifteen million dollars on behalf of the exposition, a political schism in Republican ranks, complicated by conflicts with Tammany Hall, eroded the efforts of New York's backers. While their plans hovered uncertainly in the state legislature, the Chicago boosters organized an effective corporation and began lobbying in Congress five weeks before the New York delegation arrived. Even before President Harrison formally approved the congressional act that sanctioned a commemorative exposition, nearly thirty thousand subscriptions to $5,407,350 of exposition stock had been gathered. The number of subscriptions was as impressive as the distribution was consolidated: 948 people purchased 70 percent of the stock, and of those individuals sixteen controlled 18 percent of the stock. The consolidation of control was confirmed when, before the election of the first board of directors, a decision was made to count each share as one vote rather than give one vote to each stockholder. At the first meeting Lyman Gage, president of the First National Bank, was elected first president of the board of directors and became part of the congressional lobbying effort. His acumen proved decisive, for at the last minute the congressional committee balked at the Chicago offer and seemed ready to award the exposition prize to New York. The committee gave Gage twenty-four hours to raise an additional $5 million as a guarantee. He immediately approached the exposition's financial backers in Chicago to obtain the necessary pledges. As he later recalled, "we received a fully supporting telegram signed by thirty or more citizens whose aggregate wealth was known to be more than a hundred millions of dollars." In the succeeding months, as the country's financial condition worsened and the size of the exposition increased, additional funding became necessary. More stock was issued, and the federal government appropriated $2.5

million in the form of souvenir half-dollars—which the exposition directors sold for one dollar apiece, thereby doubling in effect the amount of the appropriation. In April 1893, a month before the opening of the fair, the exposition's finance committee voted $5 million of bonds at 6 percent interest. Chicago banks purchased $2.3 million, and "leading capitalists" throughout the country absorbed $1.5 million.[8]

If these investors sought a return on their capital outlay, they also had broader cultural goals. Two years before the fair opened, Gage rhapsodized on what a visitor could expect to see from the "dizzy height" of the Proctor Tower, an abortive plan to imitate the Eiffel Tower erected in Paris for the 1889 exposition. The fairgoer, Gage promised, "will see beautiful buildings radiate with color and flashing the sunlight from their gilded pinnacles and domes." "And beyond all," Gage suggested, visitors "will behold the boundless waters of Lake Michigan, linking the beautiful with the sublime, the present with the past, the finite with the infinite."[9]

As was the case in 1876, the Smithsonian Institution again contributed materially and conceptually to the organic whole of the exposition. Following the Centennial, the Smithsonian participated in many local, national, and international fairs. Exhibits traveled to the International Fisheries Exhibitions in Berlin and London (1880 and 1883), to Boston's Foreign Exhibition (1883), and to the Chicago Railway Exhibition (1883). Over the next two years exhibits went to the International Electrical Exhibition in Philadelphia (1884), the Southern Exposition in Louisville (1884), Cincinnati's Industrial Exposition (1884), and the World's Industrial and Cotton Exposition at New Orleans (1885). Between 1887 and 1893 the Smithsonian also provided displays for the Minneapolis Industrial Exposition (1887), the Centennial Exposition of the Ohio Valley (1888), the Marietta, Ohio, Exposition, the Paris International Exposition (1889), the Patent Centennial (1891), and the Columbian Historical Exposition in Madrid (1892). By 1893 the Smithsonian had earned a well-deserved reputation "as the one bureau of Government whose special function is that of exhibition."[10]

With its experience in exposition matters, the Smithsonian was the place the directors of the Chicago fair naturally turned for assistance in classifying exhibits. The institution assigned the task to its assistant secretary, G. Brown Goode.

Goode, highly regarded as an ichthyologist and museum administrator, had studied under Louis Agassiz at Harvard. He was also knowledgable in physics, astronomy, and comparative philology, versed in anthropology and American history, and an authority on genealogy. Samuel Pierpont Langley, Baird's successor as secretary of the Smithsonian, explained how this latter interest related to science: "Doctor Goode was a strong believer in heredity, and he was profoundly impressed with the idea that man's capabilities and tendencies were to be explained by the characteristics of the men and women whose blood flowed through their veins." Goode, however, devoted himself primarily to museum work, which he considered intimately related to expositions. International fairs and museums, Goode felt, both possessed great educational value as well as vast potential for creating the good citizenship necessary for advancing civilization.[11]

Goode's exposition experience had started at age twenty-five when Baird appointed him to arrange the Smithsonian's exhibit of animal resources of the United States at the Philadelphia Centennial. He subsequently served as a federal commissioner to the Fisheries Exhibitions in London and Berlin and represented the Smithsonian at every major United States exposition between 1884 and 1895. At the Madrid exposition, just before the Chicago world's fair, Goode briefly held the post as commissioner-general. His exposition experience in the 1880s and his organizational efforts within the National Museum formed the backdrop for his seminal address "The Museums of the Future," delivered at the Brooklyn Institute in early 1889.[12]

"There is an Oriental saying," Goode told his audience, "that the distance between ear and eye is small, but the difference between hearing and seeing is very great." He was referring to the growing importance of visual arts in the late nineteenth century, perhaps best typified by the separate building that had been provided for photographic exhibits at the Centennial. The increasing prominence of the visual arts, according to Goode, marked a fundamental cognitive shift. He put it bluntly: "To see is to know." In this context, he urged that the museum ought to become a major influence, "for it is the most powerful and useful auxiliary of all systems of teaching by means of object

Fig. 8. G. Brown Goode (1851–96). Courtesy of Smithsonian Institution Archives, Record Unit 7177, George P. Merrill Collection.

lessons." The problem was that museums were too few and generally were antiquated in their display techniques. "This can not long continue," he warned. "The museum of the past must be set aside, reconstructed, transformed from a cemetery of bric-à-brac into a nursery of living thoughts. The museum of the future must stand side by side with the library and the laboratory, as part of the teaching equipment of the college and university, and in the great cities cooperate with the public library as one of the principal agencies for the enlightenment of the people." Above all, Goode stressed, future muscums "in this democratic land should be adapted to the needs of the mechanic, the factory operator, the day laborer, the salesman, and the clerk, as much as to those of the professional man and the man of leisure." They should give adults the opportunity to continue the learning process begun in the schools. "[T]he people's museum should be much more than a house full of specimens in glass cases. It should be a house full of ideas, arranged with the strictest attention to system."[13]

The exposition directors gave Goode the opportunity to arrange their "house full of ideas." In his "First Draft of a System of Classification for the World's Columbian Exposition," he reiterated the central theme of his Brooklyn Institute lecture. *"The exhibition of the future will be an exhibition of ideas rather than of objects, and nothing will be deemed worthy of admission to its halls which has not some living, inspiring thought behind it, and which is not capable of teaching some valuable lesson."* The guiding thought he had in mind for the World's Columbian Exposition was progress. The fair, he wrote, would illustrate "the steps of progress of civilization and its arts in successive centuries, and in all lands up to the present time." It would become, "in fact, an *illustrated encyclopedia of civilization."*[14]

Once he had completed the classification for the fair, Goode returned to Washington to supervise the Smithsonian's plans for an exhibition of scientific progress at Chicago. Goode's ideas about the specific role of science at the exposition can be inferred from his 1894 address "America's Relation to the Advance of Science." "Is it not possible," he asked his audience at the Philosophical Society of Washington, "that [science in America] may hereafter become the chief of the conservative forces in civilization rather than, as in the past, be exerted mainly in the direction of change and reform?" After informing the audience that "the Renascence of today is leading men to think not only with personal freedom, but accurately and rightly," Goode concluded with a quotation from Whitman's *Leaves of Grass:*

> Brain of the New World, what a task is thine,
> To formulate the Modern—out of the peerless grandeur
> of the Modern,
> Out of thyself . . .
> Thou mental orb, thou new, indeed new, spiritual world,
> The Present holds thee not—for such vast growth as thine,

> For such unparalleled flight as thine, such brood as
> thine,
> The Future only holds thee and can hold thee.

Goode's definition of science as the guarantor of civilization into the future
also pinpointed the function of science at the Chicago exposition—an exposition that in its very essence was an effort to educate and "to formulate the
Modern."[15]

At the public dedication, held 12 October 1892, Potter Palmer, Gage's
successor as president of the World's Columbian Commission and owner of
Chicago's most fashionable hotel, expressed the enthusiasm he and the other
directors felt for the educational value of the exposition: "May we not hope
that lessons here learned, transmitted to the future, will be potent forces long
after the multitudes which will throng these aisles shall have measured their
span and faded away?" Francis J. Bellamy, an editor of *Youth's Companion*,
substantially aided the realization of these hopes when he devised a plan
whereby schoolchildren across the country could feel themselves a part of the
exposition's quadricentennial liturgy. He urged that the dedication day of the
fair be set aside as a national holiday and that children congregate in their
schools and churches to celebrate Columbus's achievement and the fair designed to commemorate it. To make the event truly national in character,
Bellamy drafted the Pledge of Allegiance to the flag of the United States. The
Federal Bureau of Education circulated copies to teachers throughout the
country. Presidential candidates Harrison and Cleveland endorsed the operation, as did the exposition directors. At the ceremonies themselves schoolgirls
dressed in red, white, and blue formed a living flag. The result was that while
well over one hundred thousand people witnessed the dedication of the fair,
millions of children around the country pledged "allegiance to my flag and the
Republic for which it stands, one Nation indivisible with Liberty and Justice
for all." And as Annie Randall White, author of a children's history of Columbus and the fair, reminded her young readers, the fair "involved more than an
exhibit of wonderful productions. It means a new era in the onward march of
civilization."[16]

The fair, which opened seven months after the dedication proceedings,
served as an exercise in educating the nation on the concept of progress as a
willed national activity toward a determined, utopian goal. The interplay of
progress and human will was constantly repeated in the contemporary literature on the fair. But will was not enough. The pathway to the future could be
constructed only out of fibers of human will rightly informed. "Education," as
Henry Adams ruefully observed, "ran riot" at the World's Columbian Exposition of 1893.[17]

Because the central message of the fair emphasized American progress

Fig. 9. President Grover Cleveland at the opening-day ceremonies.
Photograph by C. D. Arnold, courtesy of Chicago Historical Society.

through time and space since 1492, it was appropriate that Frederick Jackson
Turner chose the American Historical Association's meeting, held in conjunction with the exposition that summer, for the presentation of his frontier thesis.
He informed his colleagues that the individual "would be a rash prophet who
should assert that the expansive character of American life has now entirely
ceased." Turner's admonition found support in an exposition that strongly suggested that America's past achievements were indicative of the future direction
of society. Pilgrims to the various shrines in the White City caught glimpses
of such sacred articles as a lock of Thomas Jefferson's red hair and Miles
Standish's pipe. Relics abounded that traced the road already traveled; yet
Americans were asking where the country was headed.[18]

That such fundamental questions were thought relevant to the Columbian
Exposition was indicated by the title of a sonnet in the Chicago *Daily Inter
Ocean:* "The Perfection of Society in Columbia's Future." To arrive at this
perfected state, visitors were told they first needed to absorb the spirit of the
fair. Mariana G. van Rensselaer, art critic for *Century Magazine,* urged her
readers to go to the fair "wholly conscienceless—not like a painstaking drafts-
man, but like a human kodak, caring only for as many pleasing impressions
as possible, not for analyzing their worth." Thus, lying back in Venetian gon-
dolas or electric motor launches, drifting idly about ethereal fountains, they
could imbibe what Potter Palmer termed "a vision snatched from dreams

whose lines have been brought out and well-defined by the iodine of art." How was the vision to be actualized? Youthful Meg Macleod explained to her brother that although the idea of the fair had originated with a great magician who was the ruler of all the genii in the world, the fair was designed to make people "know what *they* are like themselves, because the wonders will be made by hands and feet and brains just like their own. And so they will understand how strong they are—if they only knew it— and it will give them courage and fill them with thoughts." Courageous human will, inspired by the vision of America's future triumph, could begin the task of restructuring America.[19]

In the light of such visions it was also essential to ask who would be the builders of the "New Jerusalem" and, more important, to determine who would be included in:

> The city so holy and clean,
> No sorrow can breathe in the air;
> No gloom of affliction or sin,
> No shadow of evil is there.

As explained in a Fourth of July oration published in the Chicago *Tribune*, the "far-off divine event" would be accomplished "by the average citizen— that plain, sturdy, self-reliant, ambitious man, who is known as the typical American." The *Cosmopolitan* assured its readers that the fair was for "the Average People . . . not for the few at the top or for the helpless lot in the gutter, but for the Average." Rightly instructed by Daniel Burnham's neo-classical exposition forms, average Americans were told they could at long last fulfill their destiny as "the solvent the alchemists of politics groped for." Their task, however, was enormous, for the exposition made clear that not only the national, but also the international, body politic needed much racial purification before the dream of perfection could be realized. The White City was a utopian construct built upon racist assumptions. Yet this did not mean that all nonwhites were perceived uniformly.[20]

When invitations were sent to foreign governments, Japan was among the first to respond, and it eventually invested more than $630,000, one of the largest sums spent by any foreign country, in setting up its exhibits. Japan, moreover, was given what many considered the choicest location on the fair-grounds, the Wooded Isle, for its official building. Whereas American workers built the other foreign structures, Japanese workers were sent from Japan to build the Ho-o-den Palace. The building was designed by a Japanese archi-tect, the interior decorated by members of the Tokyo Art Academy. Gozo Tateno, Japanese minister to Washington, explained that his country was en-thusiastic about participating in the exposition because of Japan's interest in furthering commercial ties with America as well as proving "that Japan is a country worthy of full fellowship in the family of nations." American officials welcomed the Japanese, apparently with few reservations.[21]

The situation with respect to China provided a contrast. Earlier ambivalence about the Chinese in 1876 had given way to hostility. Because of the Geary Law, which renewed the restrictions placed on Chinese immigration by the Exclusion Act of 1882, China declined to send a commissioner to Chicago. More important, China refused to set up an official exhibit at the fair. But since it seemed essential that China be represented in some capacity in an exposition supposedly international in character, the Chinese exhibit was leased to "patriotic and commercially interested Chinese" in America and was placed on the Midway Plaisance, with its theater set next to the Captive Bal-

Fig. 10. Japanese Buildings with members of Japanese delegation. Courtesy of Chicago Historical Society.

loon concession and its teahouse adjoining the Ice Railway. Sandwiched between entertainment facilities, both Chinese displays became a source of amusement, not respect.[22]

The disparities in the reception and treatment of China and Japan were reminiscent of the situation at the Centennial; but at Chicago, American attitudes more explicitly revolved around the cultural and racial capacities attributed to the two nations to attain and carry forward the banner of Anglo-Saxon civilization. Although the Japanese seemed to be more highly regarded than the Chinese, on closer examination the esteem shown them was not without qualification.

In the opinion of most observers, Japan had the potential for reconciling its preindustrial culture with the example of American industrial growth. "The astonishing progress of Japan in arts and civilization," reported the *Inter Ocean*, "is one of the wonders of the age." Not only was Japan rapidly progressing, it was doing so without moral decadence. *The Popular Science Monthly* attested to the purity and decency of Japanese life: "Filial piety, connubial affection, parental tenderness, fraternal fondness . . . and above all this is that ardent spirit of patriotism and love for home that so preserves the unity of the Japanese people." Nowhere was the morality of the Japanese and the belief that they could even influence American culture given more pointed expression than in an anecdote related by Charles Stevens, author of the popular novel *Uncle Jeremiah and Family Go to the Fair*. Uncle Jeremiah, perpetually awestruck at the sights and sounds in the Manufacturer's Building, saw two elderly ladies sit down in the Japanese section to admire a display of pottery and managed to overhear their conversation. "I don't see the use of sending missionaries to Japan," said the first. Nodding her head in agreement, the other replied: "I don't believe they are so very bad after all. I can't believe that anyone who could make such lovely things could be a very wicked heathen. I should think the Japanese would almost feel like sending missionaries over here." At first glance, the American posture toward the Japanese conveyed the same goodwill as this conversation. Yet, notwithstanding the pronouncement of one souvenir publication that "because of their intelligence and ingenuity not a race prejudice exists against them," the Japanese were central to the racial economics of the fair.[23]

Japan, because of its moral and industrial progress, was portrayed as on the verge of leaping "at one bound to those things for which the Caucasians battled during succeeding centuries." "If the modern civilization of Japan stands," a newspaper predicted, "the cradle of humanity will become worthy of its children, the races of civilized men." An early historian of the fair offered another version of the same theme: "Japan, the Great Britain of Asia, . . . with every day is making some new stride toward the Western spirit of enterprise and civilization." Japan, in short, was expected to have an uplifting—that is, Americanizing—influence on an otherwise backward Asian continent.[24]

The subordinate status accorded the Japanese in hastening the realization of the vision of the White City was clear in the same souvenir folio that denied the existence of any race prejudice against the Japanese. "Everybody wanted to know, and knowing, liked the Japs. They were so quiet, and so good-natured," asserted the author. As long as Japan remained a "Children's Paradise," and the Japanese, as "Yankees of the East," showed deference to the desires of the United States, there was every reason to believe that the Japanese people could be accommodated after a fashion in the future utopia. But once the Japanese began striking out on their own, once they began to loom large as an actual Great Britain of Asia over the next decade, they could no longer be seen in the same perspective, much less be permitted to send "missionaries" to this country.[25]

In 1893 Americans' positive attitude toward the Japanese was also demeaning and patronizing. The nuance at the Columbian Exposition became explicit at the San Francisco Midwinter Exposition of 1893–94—brainchild of M. H. De Young and largely imitative of the Chicago fair—where Japanese were portrayed as "cousins" of the Chinese and visitors to the Japanese Village were invited to view "part and parcel of the home life of the little brown men." The possibility that the Japanese might become full citizens of the City Beautiful of the future was increasingly problematic.[26]

If, however, the Japanese were given at least a semblance of respect in 1893, the Chinese were seen as replicas of the old stereotype of the shrewd, cunning, and threatening "John Chinaman." The *Chicago Tribune*, in an article titled "Freaks of Chinese Fancy at the Fair," reported that, despite their inability to speak English fluently, the Chinese never made a mistake against themselves in giving change. On the apparent slowness of the Chinese fortuneteller, the *Tribune* commented: "'hustle' is something to which Professor Hin has hereditary objection." References to "almond-eyed" and "saffron-colored mongolians" abounded. Hubert Howe Bancroft, who in the 1880s had written that "as a progressive people we reveal a race prejudice intolerable to civilization," looked disdainfully upon the Chinese theater for the "oddity of the performance and for the nature of its themes." Comparing theatrical themes to those of Chinese literature and denigrating both, Bancroft found "the pervading tone is morbid and ultra pessimistic, virtue in woman and honor in man being conceded only to a few." China, he continued, "is a country where the seat of honor is the stomach; where the roses have no fragrance and women no petticoats; where the laborer has no sabbath and the magistrate no sense of integrity."[27]

Charles Stevens, author of *Uncle Jeremiah*, expressed pleasure that a few "decent-looking Chinamen" who did not "look like rats and whose fluent English proclaims their long stay in 'Flisco' were serving tea at the entrance to the theater," but he also stated his suspicion that the joss house contained the opium bunks of the Chinese actors. *Harper's Weekly*, in an article on the Fourth of July parade staged by the villagers of the Midway Plaisance, wrote of the Chinese: "[They] are a meek people, but seem anxious to apologize and make atonement for their humility by the extraordinarily aggressive dragons and devils which they contrived. The dragon did much to raise the standing of the Midway Chinese among other more savage and not half so ingenious races." Viewed as a race, the timid but cunning, immoral, and uncivilized Chinese were considered to be closer to the lower orders of mankind than to visions of future possibilities and perfections.[28]

If, to white Americans, the fair was a reaffirmation of the nation's unity, self-confidence, and triumphant progress, despite a devastating Civil War and mounting social-industrial turmoil, its impact on American blacks was quite different. A black newspaper in Cleveland described it as "the great American white elephant." Earlier anticipations by blacks that the fair might serve as a forum for displaying their achievements since emancipation quickly disappeared as it became apparent that no black representative would be appointed to positions of authority on any of the various commissions governing the fair. When the Board of Lady Managers refused to appoint a black woman to its committee, the *New York Age* reported bitterly: "We object. We carry our objection so far that if the matter was left to our determination we would advise the race to have nothing whatever to do with the Columbian Exposition or the management of it. . . . The glory and the profit of the whole thing, is in the hands of white 'gentlemen' and 'ladies' and in all charity they should be allowed to share all the glory or failure of the undertaking." As a result of such protests, a Saint Louis school principal, Hale G. Parker, who considered himself "above" other blacks by virtue of his professional status, was finally appointed to the National Commission, but he served only as an alternate.[29]

Controversy divided the black community. Frederick Douglass and Ida Wells, longtime advocates of black political and economic rights, wanted to publish a pamphlet in foreign languages informing the rest of the world of the travails of black Americans in both North and South. Many editors of black newspapers, however, argued that such an action would increase white hostility and disgrace blacks before foreign visitors. Lack of funds eventually compelled Wells and Douglass to publish only an English edition of their pamphlet, with prefaces in French and German that referred to the exposition as a "whited sepulcher." Discussion also developed over the idea of an Afro-American exhibit, which proponents argued would encourage black participation in the fair. Blacks laid plans to rely on the Southern Exposition in Raleigh, North Carolina, in 1891 as a gathering point for black exhibits to be sent to the world's fair two years later. But the idea of a separate exhibit aroused opposition as de facto surrender to segregation. The issue in many respects became moot when the directors ruled against racially separate exhibits. Instead, they encouraged blacks to participate in existing state displays but tempered their encouragement by the requirement that black exhibits be submitted to and approved by all-white committees in the various states. Few black exhibits made their way through the screening apparatus.[30]

A further source of contention was the exposition management's decision to grant demands some blacks made for a special day of their own—"Jubilee" or "Colored People's Day" as it was variously called. Since there had been other days set aside for specific ethnic groups, Douglass favored the proposal. Ida Wells, conversely, saw the gesture as condescending and urged blacks to avoid the fair. The black community again divided. The *Indianapolis Freeman*, the nation's most widely circulated black newspaper, argued that the day, "if carried out . . . will only serve to attract invidious and patronizing attention to the race, unattended with practical recompense or reward." As Jubilee Day, 25 August, drew nearer, the *Freeman* became increasingly sarcastic: "The Board of Directors have furnished the day, some members of the race have pledged to furnish the 'niggers,' (in our presence Negroes), and if some thoughtful and philanthropic white man is willing to furnish watermelons, why should he be gibbeted?" A revealing cartoon in *Puck* (fig. 11) suggests why all but one thousand blacks stayed away from the fair on the day set aside for them. Frederick Douglass, however, availed himself of the opportunity to address those white Americans who branded the black "a moral monster." Douglass, United States minister to Haiti, had been appointed by the Haitian government as its delegate and delivered his message from the Haitian Building: "Men talk of the Negro Problem. There is no Negro Problem. The problem is whether the American people have honesty enough, loyalty enough, honor enough, patriotism enough to live up to their own Constitution." "We have come out of Dahomey into this, " he declared. "Measure the Negro," he urged. "But not by the standard of the splendid civilization of the Caucasian. Bend down and measure him—from the depths out of which he has risen."[31]

Whites were only too happy to measure blacks. Shortly after the close of the fair, a souvenir book of photographs appeared. The caption to one of the illustrations read: "Perhaps one of the most striking lessons which the Columbian Exposition taught was the fact that African slavery in America had not, after all, been an unmixed evil, for of a truth, the advanced social conditions of American Africans over that of their barbarous countrymen is most encouraging and wonderful."[32]

Black visitors apparently experienced little overt discrimination in public facilities at the fair, since only one instance was reported. The case involved a black woman who was refused admission to the entertainment program in the Kentucky Pavilion. Racism, however, existed in other forms. Popular attitudes embracing the spectrum of racist notions were articulated in a series of cartoons that appeared in *Harper's Weekly*, depicting the adventures of a black family at the fair. The first of the series ridiculed blacks' aspirations to advance in American society as well as their intellectual ability to comprehend the lessons of the fair. Mr. Johnson, wide-eyed and viscid-lipped, ex-

DARKIES' DAY AT THE FAIR.

(A Tale of Poetic Retribution.)

claimed to his wife as they first caught sight of the buildings from the Peristyle entrance: "Great Lan' Gloriah! I'd a given dat spotted mule ob mine for de contrac' of whitewashing dis yer place." Another cartoon found Johnson in agitated dialogue with a South Sea Islander: "Does you speak Inglish?" With the crowd chortling in the background, the Samoan responded: "Yes, does you?" Another caricature followed in which Johnson paused at the Dahomeyan Village to shake hands with one of the villagers. His wife, menacing him with her parasol, shouted: "Ezwell Johnson, stop shakin' hands wid dat heathen! You want de hull fair ter t'ink you's found a poo' relation!" The most suggestive illustration, however, placed the Johnson family in the Kentucky exhibit. There Johnson met his former master, who asked him what he was doing at the fair. Johnson, with a trace of deference, answered, "Well, sah, I's lak a noble shoe dat's been blacked—'bout time I's gettin' some polish!"[33]

The fair did not merely reflect American racial attitudes, it grounded them on ethnological bedrock. So pervasive was the opportunity to study anthropology at the World's Columbian Exposition that Otis T. Mason, curator of the Smithsonian's Bureau of American Ethnology since 1884, exclaimed: "Indeed, it would not be too much to say that the World's Columbian Exposition was one vast anthropological revelation. Not all mankind were there, but either in persons or pictures their representatives were." Anthropological exhibits— including "representatives of living races in native garb and activities," photographs and drawings, books, and "objects connected with every phase of human life"—seemed to be everywhere. The exposition directors hired Frederic Ward Putnam, head of Harvard's Peabody Museum of American Archaeology and Ethnology, to take charge of the exposition's Department M, which included the anthropological exhibits. The National Museum and the Bureau of American Ethnology of the Smithsonian contributed a separate and sizable ethnological display. Foreign governments and concessionaires also contributed ethnological materials. According to William H. Dall, a naturalist and scientific correspondent for the *Nation*, America's leading and soon-to-be leading anthropologists, including Franz Boas, Alice Fletcher, George A. Dorsey, John Wesley Powell, Elizabeth Coxe Stevenson, and James Mooney, "brought together . . . an anthropological collection hitherto unequalled and hereafter not likely to be surpassed."[34]

The immediate starting point for the ethnological ventures at the Chicago fair was the tenth Congrès Internationale d'Anthropologie et d'Archéologie Préhistoriques held in conjunction with the Paris Exposition of 1889. The two members of the United States delegation to this meeting of the world's foremost anthropologists were from the Smithsonian—Otis Mason and Thomas

---

Fig. 11. *(opposite)* "Darkies' Day at the fair." Cartoon from *World's Fair Puck*, from Prints and Photographs Division, Library of Congress.

Wilson, Rau's successor as curator of prehistoric anthropology in the USNM. Delegates listened to presentations of scholarly papers and, under the guidance of renowned French anthropologists, toured the exposition and the museums of Paris. Mason was particularly impressed by the Paris fair: "to the eye of the anthropologist the whole Exposition seemed to have been arranged for his special pleasure and profit by his colleagues there."[35]

Much of Mason's enthusiasm centered on the colonial city, where 182 Asians and Africans had been installed in simulated native villages, presumably to quell French anxieties over the government's policies of empire. In late summer the congress met on the esplanade for a special all-day tour of exhibits with anthropological content. M. G. Dumotier, minister of education in the Tonkin Bureau, delivered the welcoming address. Dumotier and E. T. Hamy, curator of the Paris Musée d'Ethnographie, conducted the visitors on a guided tour through the colonial city. When they arrived at the Okanda and Adouma villages, the lieutenant governor of Gabon introduced the inhabitants of the villages as examples of two different races, "en insistant sur les différences de leurs caractères extérieurs, taille, indices céphaliques, etc." Mason, impressed by the colonial city, was especially pleased by the History of Human Habitations display fronting the Eiffel Tower, which demonstrated the evolution of human dwellings from prehistoric to present times. "[A] most interesting series of structures illustrative of human habitations in all grades of culture," Mason declared. To his way of thinking the Paris exposition had triumphed precisely because it had demonstrated "this living connection between men and things."[36]

Mason would try to surpass the achievements of the Paris exposition at the World's Columbian celebration. His account of the Paris exhibits laid the basis for the plans Langley and Goode first proposed to the United States Congress in 1890 for the Smithsonian's ethnological display at Chicago. Its purpose would be "to show the physical and other characteristics of the principal races of men and the very early stages of the history of civilization as shown by the evolution of certain selected primitive arts and industries." The Paris exposition, they noted, had accomplished this task in "a popular and effective" manner. These plans, moreover, were wholly compatible with Goode's intent to classify exhibits at the fair so as to illustrate the progress of civilization.[37]

The exposition management, always concerned about the escalating costs of the project, was well aware that the ethnological villages at Paris had been one of the main attractions for over thirty million visitors. Thomas W. Palmer, president of the National Commission, was particularly interested in an ethnological display and advocated placing living villages on the narrow strip of land known as the Midway Plaisance.[38]

The efforts of Goode and Palmer to mount an ethnological display at least on par with that at Paris were further supported by Putnam. Putnam, like

Goode a former student of Agassiz, had developed while at Harvard an expertise in museum work for which he became nationally famous. An "institutional
entrepreneur in an age of organizing genius," he regarded the Chicago fair as
a tremendous opportunity to introduce the science of anthropology to
the American public and to build a collection that would lead to the establishment of a great ethnological museum in Chicago. He explained his ideas for
the fair in a letter to the *Tribune* in May 1890. So impressive were his plans
for a detailed exhibit of "the stages of the development of man on the American continent" that in early 1891 the directors appointed him chief of the
Department of Ethnology and Archaeology.[39]

In the course of planning their exhibits, the scientists in the Smithsonian
and Department M sought to avoid duplication. Putnam and his assistants
concentrated on a living ethnological display of American Indians and on collecting and organizing ethnological artifacts from around the world. The vast
amount of material they acquired led the directors of the fair, after repeated
prodding by Putnam, to establish a separate Anthropology Building on the
fairgrounds. This building, one of Putnam's major achievements in trying to
popularize anthropology and to prove the worth of building a permanent ethnological museum, contained archaeological exhibits, laboratories, a library,
and a large collection on religion and folklore. Visitors to this building could
be examined and measured by physical anthropologists under the direction of
Putnam's assistants, Franz Boas and Joseph Jastrow. For fairgoers who har-
bored doubts about the ideal types they were to conform to, statues of a male
and female student from Harvard and Radcliffe stood nearby. The overriding
aim of the department was stated by an ethnologist and one of Putnam's assistants, Harlan Ingersoll Smith: "From the first to the last," he declared, "the
exhibits of this department will be arranged and grouped to teach a lesson; to
show the advancement of evolution of man."[40]

The Smithsonian's display in the Government Building was smaller than
Putnam's but equally significant. Thomas Wilson arranged an exhibit of prehistoric people between the stone ages, while William Henry Holmes organized an exhibit based on his own archaeological research. The most important ethnological display by the Smithsonian was planned by Mason, who,
after consulting with Putnam, agreed to avoid duplicating Putnam's efforts and
to organize an Indian exhibit that would reflect life in America at the time
Columbus landed. In the wake of the exposition directors' decision to set up
an ethnological department, Mason determined to create a display that would
demonstrate the value of John Wesley Powell's recently completed linguistic
map of Native American speech patterns. "The Chicago Exposition," Mason
wrote in his annual report for 1892, "furnishes an excellent opportunity for
testing the question—how far language co-ordinated itself with industries and
activities as a mark of kinship and race, and how far climate and the resources
of the earth control the arts and industries of mankind in the sphere of lan-

guage and race." Often described as a striking departure from Baird and Rau's arrangement of the ethnological display at the Centennial, Mason's exhibit was a variation on the theme of racial progress. Life-size statues of Indian adults and children of a given language grouping were dressed in characteristic clothing and shown working at typical tasks in their natural environments. The emphasis on culture areas, occupational groups, and environment would have a significant impact on twentieth-century anthropology. Yet, if the exhibit technique was a milepost in the development of the science of anthropology, the concept of culture areas fit snugly with a view of Native Americans as "lower races in costume," living an outmoded life. The Smithsonian display at the World's Columbian Exposition presented Indians as culturally distinct from one another and racially inferior to other "types" of humanity, especially when viewed against the backdrop of the White City.[41]

At a meeting of the International Congress of Anthropology, which met from 28 August to 2 September at Chicago's Art Institute and on the exposition grounds, Mason described the Smithsonian exhibit for his colleagues. In the course of his presentation he suggested that the idea of culture areas might resolve the ongoing dispute between Daniel G. Brinton, America's foremost ethnologist, and Putnam whether Indians in North America constituted one race or two. Mason argued that Indians had not been in North America long enough "to breed races with differential and hereditable characteristics." Rather than viewing Indians as plural races, Mason counseled anthropologists to study Indians from the standpoint of different cultural regions in which they lived. That different cultural areas existed, however, was not at all incompatible with understanding Indian life in racial terms. "Among the civilized com-

Fig. 12. Otis T. Mason (1838–1908). Courtesy of Smithsonian Institution Archives, Record Unit 7177, George P. Merrill Collection.

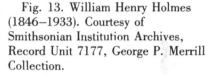

Fig. 13. William Henry Holmes
(1846–1933). Courtesy of
Smithsonian Institution Archives,
Record Unit 7177, George P. Merrill
Collection.

munities," Mason noted, "there has grown up a reverence for the government, called patriotism, and from this, combined with the love of one's native land, comes a strong motive in holding the people of a nation together." "Not so in savagery," he added. "Among the American tribes of Indians, indeed, the strongest civilized bond is that of kinship, which, after all, is a racial characteristic."[42]

That the concept of culture areas was compatible with a belief in cultural/racial grades became further apparent in Mason's plans to round out the Smithsonian's ethnological collection with a presentation of American and Afro-American types. To understand what America "has done and undone" to blacks, Mason urged that a display of the industries of western African and Afro-Americans be established at the fair so visitors could compare their respective levels of culture. Anthropologists, Mason felt, should be encouraged to make forays into Africa to gather artifacts because, as was the case with the Indians, it was only a matter of time until their "rude arts" would be supplanted by those of Western nations. The exhibit would have immense scholarly importance and enable ethnologists "to comprehend many things observable in the present condition of the United States and to trace them to their true source."[43]

Funding for this plan was not forthcoming, but the ethnological display in the Woman's Building gave Mason the opportunity to locate for visitors the "source" of contemporary Afro-American difficulties in adjusting to the demands of white society. To illustrate women's role in peacemaking through the ages, Mason synoptically arranged twelve groups of objects in such a way that "in each group a certain art is traced in its manifestation among the three modern types of savagery, namely: the American, the Negroid and the Malayo-

Polynesian." Within this framework, the political and economic situation of American blacks would easily be explained as an outgrowth of their "savage" heritage. He allowed that blacks, Indians, and Malaysians might have distinct cultures, but his presentation of different peoples and cultures formed a crucial link in the chain of human progress along racial lines that the fair presented.[44]

Shortly after the fair concluded, Mason mentioned that he had been deeply affected by a bas-relief of a "forlorn savage woman depicted on the doorway of the Transportation Building at one end of a series of weary burden bearers," who "was in strange contrast with the spirituelle painting of angels on the walls above her head." The contrast became even more dramatic on the Midway Plaisance, where the "savages" frozen in art and in the Smithsonian's lay figures seemed to come alive.[45]

The Midway Plaisance was a strip of land a mile long and nearly six hundred feet wide, formerly a wooded drive connecting Jackson Park with Washington Park. By opening day of the fair, its serenity had been transformed into what the *Tribune* labeled the "Royal Road of Gaiety." On either side of the street the visitor could find restaurants, entertainment facilities, ethnic villages, and above all enormous crowds. Historian Hubert Howe Bancroft described it as follows:

> Entering the avenue a little to the west of the Woman's Building [the visitor] would pass between the walls of mediaeval villages, between mosques and pagodas, past the dwellings of colonial days, past the cabins of South Seas islanders, of Javanese, Egyptians, Bedouins, Indians, among them huts of bark and straw that tell of yet ruder environment. They would be met on their way by German and Hungarian bands, by the discord of . . . camel drivers and donkey-boys, dancing girls from Cairo and Algiers, from Samoa and Brazil, with men and women of all nationalities, some lounging in oriental indifference, some shrieking in unison or striving to outshriek each other, in the hope of transferring his superfluous change from the pocket of the unwary pilgrim. Then, as taste and length of purse determined, for fees were demanded from those who would penetrate the hidden mysteries of the plaisance, they might enter the Congress of Beauty with its plump and piquant damsels, might pass an hour in one of the theatres or villages, or partake of harmless beverages served by native waiters. Finally they would betake themselves to the Ferris Wheel, on which they were conveyed with smooth, gliding motion to a height of 260 feet, affording a transient and kaleidoscopic view of the park and all it contains.

Rao Telang, a visitor from India, outlined the scene in the center of the Midway: "the mania for buying tickets, the anxiety to get there first to secure the best seat, the excitement of the orator assisted by the salesman . . ., the distant roar of the lions from the show of wild beasts . . . make the place unbearable for a quiet sort of person." The *New York Times* put the matter succinctly: "The late P. T. Barnum should have lived to see this day."[46]

Several visitors to the fair denied the ethnological value of the Midway, believing it was "a sideshow pure and simple." To others it appeared the Midway had strayed far from its ethnological origins. An early history of the fair suggested that the Midway exhibits were grouped under Department M solely for classification and were not directly connected with it. Putnam, however, made the most of the situation and attested to the anthropological value of the Javanese, Samoan, and Dahomeyan villages and others. Significantly,

Fig. 14. Ferris wheel. From Prints and Photographs Division, Library of Congress.

the Rand-McNally guidebook to the fair suggested that people visit the Midway and view the exhibits—none of which were national displays, though several had government approval from the countries represented—only after having seen the edifices of modern civilization in the White City. There was a lesson to be learned from the apparent contrast.[47]

The Midway's didactic function was related to its history. From the time Thomas Palmer first proposed confining villages of people within its bounds, there existed strong sentiment that no cheap entertainment be permitted to clutter the magnificence of the White City. That as late as spring 1892 no firm plans had been made for the exhibits to be located on the Midway suggests the ambivalence felt by many exposition backers, harking back to the precedent of the Philadelphia Centennial, about making popular entertainments part of the spectacle. But once again the example of the Paris fair loomed large. Concessionaires had contributed over $700,000 to the coffers of the 1889 exposition. Furthermore, the decision by the Committee on Ways and Means that most of the attractions proposed for the Midway had certain "ethnological and historical significance" and therefore should be located in the Department of Ethnology and Archaeology gave the Midway an aura of scientific respectability. As it became apparent that instruction and entertainment could complement one another, the fairgoer became more than welcome to ride the Ferris wheel or to sip a glass of Dr. Welch's grape juice while waiting in line to see Fatima perform her titillating hootchy-kootchy dance.[48]

The installation of Midway exhibits was put in the hands of a twenty-one-year-old San Franciscan, Sol Bloom, who would later build a name for himself in real estate and national politics as well as help draft the United Nations charter. Bloom had visited the 1889 exposition and recorded that "of all the exhibits at the fair I had found those of the French colonies most fascinating." He had discovered as he walked among the exhibits that "a kind of natural selection (though not precisely the theory enunciated by Darwin) was governing my movements." He noted "that the spiritual intensity of the performance presented by a troupe of Bedouin acrobats exceeded the emotional power of a pre-Renaissance tapestry" and that "a tall, skinny chap from Arabia with a talent for swallowing swords expressed a culture which to me was on a higher plane than one demonstrated by a group of earnest Swiss peasants who passed their days making cheese and milk chocolate." Before leaving Paris, Bloom signed a contract to bring the Algerian Village to the United States for a tour. Arrival of the Algerians was delayed until shortly before the Chicago fair opened, but Bloom busied himself superintending the installation of other Midway exhibits from his position in Burnham's Division of Works. He was astonished to find that the Midway was part of Frederic Putnam's domain. While Bloom had no quarrel with Putnam's scientific capabilities, he felt, as he later recalled, that placing him in charge of the Midway was tantamount to making Albert Einstein manager of Barnum and Bailey's Circus. Although

Bloom and Putnam worked separately, the net result of their efforts was an alliance between entertainment and anthropology replicated in subsequent fairs.[49]

Putnam's major contribution to the ethnological display was organizing living representatives of various Indian tribes into an exhibit. To persuade Indians to participate, he relied primarily on Indian agents and on a young Apache, Antonio, who had been captured and "civilized." When various displays of Indian life and handicrafts were being considered, Putnam wrote that he intended "the presentation of native life [to] be in every way satisfactory and creditable to the native peoples, and no exhibition of a degrading or derogatory character will be permitted." Putnam believed that "this gathering of different natives of this continent at such a time and place can but be beneficial, as it will afford them a grand opportunity to see and understand the relations of different nations and the material advantages which civilization brings to mankind." A fundamental flaw in Putnam's scheme was that several of the exhibits of Dakota Sioux, Navajos, Apaches, and various northwestern tribes were on or near the Midway Plaisance, which immediately degraded them as had happened with the Chinese exhibits.[50]

Emma Sickles, one of Putnam's staff members, raised the only objection to the treatment of Indians that was heard throughout the duration of the exposition, and she was summarily dismissed from her position. In a letter of protest to the *New York Times,* she charged that every effort had been made to use the Indian exhibits to mislead the American people. The display, she wrote, "has been used to work up sentiment against the Indian by showing that he is either savage or can be educated only by Government agencies. . . . Every means was used to keep the self-civilized Indians out of the Fair." Putman dismissed the charges against the Department of Ethnology as "simply a tissue of misrepresentations and false statements." Yet if the Sickles indictment needed qualification, so did Putnam's claim to be "a true friend to [the Indian] race."[51]

The Native Americans who participated in the exhibits did not benefit from the exposition. Rather, they were the victims of a torrent of abuse and ridicule. With Wounded Knee only three years removed, the Indians were regarded as apocalyptic threats to the values embodied in the White City who had to be tamed—an idea already captured and put into effect in Wild Bill's Congress of Rough Riders, which was performing on Sixty-third Street, several blocks from the fair.[52]

To illustrate the inevitable triumph of white civilization over the Indian nations, the exposition management had invited several Sioux chiefs to the opening ceremonies and permitted them to view the proceedings from the highest point of the Administration Building. The Indians appeared at the climax of the ceremony, just as the chorus began singing "My Country 'Tis of Thee." As one newspaper correspondent later reported the effect of the scene:

"Nothing in the day's occurrences appealed to sympathetic patriotism so much
as this fallen majesty slowly filing out of sight as the flags of all nations swept
satin kisses through the air, waving congratulations to cultured achievement
and submissive admiration to a new world."[53]

The significance of the Midway as a bulwark of the utopian dream projected
by the White City cannot be underestimated. "The Midway Plaisance," explained correspondent Amy Leslie, "seems to be a magnet of deepest and most
lasting significance." Its greatest importance lay simply in the vivid illustrations of evolutionary principles provided by ethnological villages.[54]

Since Putnam was a student and colleague of Agassiz, one might suspect
that he was somewhat unreceptive to the evolutionary ideas of Darwin. But as
early as 1880, *Popular Science Monthly* pointed out that Agassiz was becoming increasingly isolated in academic circles: "Of all the younger brood of
working naturalists who Agassiz educated, every one—Morse, Shaler, Verrill,
Niles, Hyatt, Schudder, Putnam, even his own son—has accepted evolution."
While Putnam was "more interested in institutional development than in evolutionary theory," he nevertheless did intend the exhibits in his department to
portray the stages of development of man from prehistoric times to the present.
As with his chief assistant at the fair, Franz Boas, who had not yet moved
into the camp of cultural relativism, Putnam's thoughts were in flux concerning the wisdom of conventional racial attitudes. Putnam clearly hoped American civilization could accommodate different races. Yet he was so eager to
popularize anthropology that he acquiesced in the amalgamation of honky-tonk
concessions and living ethnological displays on the Midway Plaisance. The
results were devastating not only for Africans, Native Americans, and
Chinese, but also for other nonwhite people of the world. For Putnam, it was
sufficient to believe that "there was much of instruction as well as of joy on
the Merry Midway."[55]

Nathaniel Hawthorne's son Julian revealed the educational thrust of the
Midway: "Roughly speaking, you have before you the civilized, the half civilized, and the savage worlds to choose from—or rather to take one after the
other." Department M, he decided, could better be titled "The World as Plaything." On the Midway, presented as being under the control of the well-
meaning professor from Harvard, the world became a bauble with which
Americans might amuse themselves and a standard against which they might
measure their achievements. Alternating between specimens and toys in the
eyes of observers, the nonwhite people living in villages along the Midway not
only were seen through the lens of America's material and presumed racial
progress leading to future utopia, but were neatly categorized into the niches
of a racial hierarchy.[56]

A strong possibility exists that such racial compartmentalization reflected
the intended organization of the Midway Plaisance. Denton J. Snider, a con-

Fig. 15. Frederic Ward Putnam
(1839–1915). Photograph by D. I.
Bushnell, Jr., courtesy of National
Anthropology Archives.

temporary literary critic, suggested that the Midway consisted of a "sliding scale of humanity." Nearest to the White City were the Teutonic and Celtic races as represented by the two German and two Irish villages. The center of the Midway contained the Mohammedan world, West Asia, and East Asia. Then, "we descend to the savage races, the African of Dahomey and the North American Indian, each of which has its place" at the opposite end of the Plaisance. For Snider, there was only one way to understand this "living museum of humanity." "Undoubtedly," he declared, "the best way of looking at these races is to behold them in the ascending scale, in the progressive movement; thus we can march forward with them starting with the lowest specimens of humanity, and reaching continually upward to the highest stage." "In that way," he suggested, "we move in harmony with the thought of evolution, and not with that of the lapse or fall." The *Chicago Tribune* also hinted that the Midway was organized along evolutionary lines. In retrospect, the *Tribune* recalled that the "reconvening of Babel" on the Midway Plaisance afforded the American people an unequaled opportunity to compare themselves scientifically with others: "What an opportunity was here afforded to the scientific mind to descend the spiral of evolution," the newspaper affirmed, "tracing humanity in its highest phases down almost to its animalistic origins."[57]

Among white visitors there seems to have been nearly unanimous consent about which people belonged at the respective extremes of the racial spectrum. With the Anglo-Saxons at one end, "the negro types at the fair," according to one publication, "represented very fairly the barbarous or half-civilized state of a people who are a numerous and rapidly increasing class of American citizens." White observers generally agreed that, of the blacks, the Dahomeyans were the most savage and threatening. "Sixty-nine of them are here in all their barbaric ugliness," a correspondent wrote for *Frank Leslie's Popular Monthly,* "blacker than buried midnight and as degraded as the animals which prowl the jungles of their dark land. . . . In these wild people we easily detect many characteristics of the American negro." A woman from Boston expressed regret at having seen the Africans when she considered "the gulf between them and Emerson." By contrast to the Dahomeyans, with their war dances and rumored cannibalism, the American Indian became, according to a souvenir publication, "a thing of beauty and joy forever."[58]

Climbing the rungs of the evolutionary ladder, a Midway tourist moved from the "savagery" of the Dahomeyans to the delightful and engaging Javanese— the "Brownies." "About the shade of a well-done sweet potato," the *Popular Monthly* reported, "the Javanese holds the position closest to the American heart of all the semi-civilized races." Javanese men were described as industrious workers, the women as untiring in their domestic duties. Described as cute and frisky, mild and inoffensive, but childlike above all else, the Javanese seemingly could be accommodated in America's commercial empire as long as they remained in their evolutionary niche.[59]

Like the Javanese, the Samoans, popularized in the writings of Robert Louis Stevenson, were well received. Yet an incident reported in the *Inter Ocean*

Fig. 16. Dahomey Village on the Midway Plaisance. From Department of Special Collections, Library, California State University, Fresno.

revealed the limits within which such hospitality was contained. The prospect of coming to the United States, according to the *Inter Ocean,* had sparked in the Samoans an ambition to reform. Upon arriving in Chicago, much to their manager's horror, they had given one another haircuts and begun dressing in American garb. The manager had put a halt to the "civilizing process," and the *Inter Ocean* reported that "the Samoans [were] making a heroic and laudable effort to resume their natural state of barbarism." In an exhibit portraying the tiers of mankind, every race had its own permanent racial position.[60]

The Midway Plaisance, a place where Americans regardless of class could "study ethnography practically," linked equality to race. In blurring class lines and providing a quasi-scientific basis for the American image of the nonwhite world as barbaric and childlike, the Midway fed directly into the utopian vision of the White City. For Miss Berry, a character in a contemporary novel titled *Sweet Clover,* the relation between the two sides of the fair was crystal clear:

> That Midway is just a representation of matter, and this great White
> City is an emblem of mind. In the Midway it's some dirty and all
> barbaric. It deafens you with noise; the worst folks in there are
> avaricious and bad; and the best are just children in their ignorance,
> and when you're feelin' bewildered with the smells and sounds and
> sights, always changin' like one o' these kaleidoscopes, and when you
> come out o' that mile-long babel where you've been elbowed and
> cheated, you pass under a bridge—and all of a sudden you are in a
> great, beautiful silence. The angels on the Woman's Buildin' smile
> down and bless you, and you know that in what seemed like one step,
> you've passed out o' darkness and into light.

The Midway made the dream of the future seem all the brighter and the present civilization all the more progressive.[61]

With the forces of mind and light counterposed to ignorance, dirt, smells, and matter, the White City and the Midway were truly symbolic, but not antithetical, constructs. Rather, the vision of the future and the depiction of the nonwhite world as savage were two sides of the same coin—a coin minted in the tradition of American racism, in which the forbidden desires of whites were projected onto dark-skinned peoples, who consequently had to be degraded so white purity could be maintained.[62] The Midway, with its half-naked "savages" and hootchy-kootchy dancers, provided white Americans with a grand opportunity for a subliminal journey into the recesses of their own repressed desires. Like Miss Berry, however, Americans were expected to leave what was filthy behind them and accept what was pure of mind and vision. Miss Berry's escort, Aunt Love, remarked: "It's come to me, Mr. Gorham, that perhaps dyin' is goin' to be somethin' like crossin' the dividin' line that separates the Midway from the White City." On the downhill side of the dividing line were designated displays of various racial types that the *Chicago*

Tribune had described as a "Sort of Universal Stew / A Pot Pie of the Earth."
On the other side rose the antiseptic structures of the White City.[63]

The evolutionary steps in human progress presented by the spectrum of
human "types" along the Midway leading up to the White City were further
explained in September by the Congress on Evolution, a part of the World's
Parliament of Religion. This conference was one of several sponsored by the
World's Congress Auxiliary, which had been organized by Charles C. Bonney,
Thomas B. Bryan, Lyman Gage, and Benjamin Butterworth. These men had
been concerned that the overwhelming number of exhibits at the fair might
obscure the fair's larger lessons about progress. To prevent fairgoers from
losing sight of the whole, the World's Congress Auxiliary was formed as the
"Intellectual and Moral Exposition of the Progress of Mankind" that would
bring "all the departments of human progress into harmonious relations with
each other." The Congress on Evolution, specifically intended to reconcile the
teachings of evolution with Christianity, also attempted, as Herbert Spencer
noted, "to advance ethics and politics by diffusing evolutionary ideas." Spencer provided the starting point for this congress with a short paper in which
he asserted that the "highest social type and production of the greatest general
happiness" would result only when a balance was struck between egoism and
altruism. Other contributors to the conference included John Fiske, T. H.
Huxley, and a number of lesser-known scientists and religious leaders. One
of these, James A. Skilton, called Spencer the "Columbus of the new epoch,"
because he had "discovered the unity of the universe and taught us how to
make that discovery plain to others." It was left to the Reverend James T.
Bixby to express the central lesson of the congress: "Evolution from lower to
the higher, from the carnal to the spiritual, is not merely the path of man's
past pilgrimage, but the destiny to which the future calls him, for it is the
path that brings his spirit into closest resemblance and most intimate union
with the divine essence itself." The congress, in short, synthesized and validated the theory of racial and material progress along evolutionary lines that
the exposition itself presented in visible form. "Chicago," Henry Adams confirmed in retrospect, "was the first expression of American thought as a unity;
one must start there."[64]

The fair lasted only six months. But through the City Beautiful Movement,
popular novels, pulp fiction, souvenir albums, theatrical performances, and
even a scale model of the White City built by George Ferris, which traveled
to subsequent fairs, the World's Columbian Exposition left a lasting imprint
on the American cultural landscape. Louis Sullivan, contemptuous though he
was of the artistic quality of the White City, nonetheless testified to its importance: "The damage wrought by the World's Fair will last for half a century
from its date, if not longer. It has penetrated deep into the constitution of the
American mind, effecting there lesions significant of dementia." Thirty years

later George F. Babbitt, Sinclair Lewis's prototypical businessman and urban
booster, nervously awaited the arrival of his paramour while thumbing through
a photograph book of the world's fair. "Fifty times," Lewis wrote, Babbitt
"looked at the picture of the Court of Honor." The irony was not lost on the
millions who had either been to the fair or read about it in the multitude of
literary accounts. A decade after the close of the fair, Joe Mitchell Chapple,
editor of *National Magazine*, made a nostalgic return to Jackson Park and
reported that "a permanent uplifting of the people" had resulted from the fair
and that this moral elevation of the people had been perpetuated in the beauty
of the park itself and in the Field Columbian Museum.[65]

The museum, a modified version of Putnam's original idea for a grand ethnological institution, was established by Marshall Field and other cultural
barons of Chicago who had been responsible for the fair to institutionalize
selected exhibits from the exposition and continue its didactic mission. Under
the direction of Frederick J. V. Skiff, a Colorado mining investor and Denver
newspaper editor, who had been chief of the Department of Mines at the fair,
the Field Museum became "in the widest sense an educational institution."
Its early collections included industrial and commercial displays from the fair,
but after these were returned to their donors the emphasis shifted to natural
history. From the beginning the museum had a department of anthropology
established by Putnam and Boas, who were followed in succession by William
Henry Holmes and George Dorsey. Under the latter's guidance, anthropological exhibits illustrated "the stages of culture and the physical characteristics"
of Native Americans. The museum, moreover, became a repository of exposition ideas. In succeeding years, Skiff became active in promoting and classifying exhibits for subsequent fairs. By 1915 he was considered the world's
foremost authority on expositions. Skiff's tie both to a major museum and to
world's fairs would provide continuity to the attempts by other political and
industrial leaders in other sections of the country to present Americans with
visions of progress and cultural unity.[66]

In 1909 the benefits exposition promoters had realized from providing
Americans with a utopian social vision at the Chicago fair were reviewed by
exposition president Higinbotham for members of the Chicago Association of
Commerce. Exemplifying the "benign influence of our exposition," Higinbotham told his audience, was its effect on potential troublemakers. "[I]f people came there to commit depredations," he stated, "they were disarmed when
they witnessed the matchless beauty of the situation." Plunder was averted
because the people believed they were responsible for the fair. "The exposition," he argued, "was really the flower or culmination of the civic pride of
the citizens of this great city. There was no aristocracy in its creation or
management; it was of and for the people, and the joy and profit was theirs."[67]

The exposition, "an epitome of progress" in Higinbotham's eyes, was not
produced by the people, but to the extent that Americans felt that the fair was

actually theirs, the cultural authority of the exposition directors was validated, as were the imperial directions in which they were pushing American society. Secure in the belief that his values were widely shared throughout the country, Higinbotham apologized to his listeners for the military hardware displayed at the fair, telling them he had since acquired "a higher and grander appreciation of the implements of peace and an intense dislike, amounting to a hatred, of war and all its trappings." In this context he stressed that, just as the Chicago fair had exerted a calming influence on the volatile social situation in America in 1893, so future expositions would contribute to world peace by minimizing the friction arising from the expansion of American capitalism. His remarks were appropriate to the occasion, for the businessmen who heard his address were considering ways to aid the Tokyo exposition of 1917. The medium of the fair clearly held grand potential for rendering America's civil religion of progress an international faith.[68]

Fig. 17. "Grand finale of . . . 'Uncle Sam's show.' " Cartoon from Prints and Photographs Division, Library of Congress.

"Man's temples typify his concepts," concluded journalist Frederick F. Cook shortly after the fair closed. "I cherish the thought that America stands on the threshold of a great awakening. The impulse which this Phantom City will give to American culture cannot be overestimated. The fact that such a wonder could rise in our midst is proof that the spirit is with us." Possessed of this spirit, millions of Americans would understand the ensuing decades of social struggle and imperial adventure as an integral part of the evolutionary process that accompanied progress. Their understanding would be furthered by a series of smaller international fairs in the South and in the Midwest that followed the Chicago fair. Although the World's Columbian Exposition became the standard with which every subsequent fair would be compared, these later fairs were not carbon copies. The directors of each attempted to improve on one or more aspects of the Chicago venture in order to clarify and hasten the national and international realization of utopia.[69]

3

The New Orleans, Atlanta, and Nashville Expositions: New Markets, "New Negroes," and a New South

The wisest among my race understand that the agitation of questions of social equality is the extremest folly, and that progress in the enjoyment of all privileges that will come to us must be the result of severe and constant struggle rather than of artificial forcing. No race that has anything to contribute to the markets of the world is long, in any degree, ostracized.

Booker T. Washington, 1895[1]

BETWEEN 1885 AND 1907, international expositions spanned the South: the New Orleans World's Industrial and Cotton Exposition (1885); the Atlanta Cotton States and International Exposition (1895); the Tennessee Centennial Exposition (1897); the South Carolina Interstate and West Indian Exposition (1901–2); and the Jamestown Tercentenary Exposition (1907). Each fair presented an image of a New South imbued with the spirit of progress and patriotism. Embodying the purposes and thematic content of the southern fairs were the expositions held at New Orleans, Atlanta, and Nashville.[2]

Signs of sectional accord abounded at these fairs. Confederate and Union veterans held reunions with great fanfare. At the Tennessee Centennial the veterans enacted sham battles, and fairgoers could see reconstructed on the exposition grounds the boyhood cabins of Abraham Lincoln and Jefferson Davis. Julia Ward Howe, author of "Battle Hymn of the Republic," directed the Woman's Department at the New Orleans fair. Presidents Grover Cleveland and William McKinley visited the Atlanta and Nashville expositions and received enthusiastic receptions. Although exposition directors in New Orleans were unable to boast of a presidential visit, a large portrait of Chester A. Arthur was hoisted behind the speakers' stand during the opening ceremonies. One of the most noteworthy national heirlooms, the Liberty Bell, traveled from Philadelphia to the New Orleans and Atlanta fairs. Atlanta's response to its arrival was characteristic. So important was the occasion that a public holiday was proclaimed. The day before its arrival, teachers, on orders from the Board of Education, told their students the history of the bell. Children, moreover, received discounts on transportation to the fair to see the exhibit. When it arrived at the railroad depot, pandemonium broke loose as the crowd spilled over the guardrails and rushed to the railroad car bearing the bell. According to the *Constitution:* "Several children, held up by their parents, kissed the revered old bell and happily patted its great brazen sides, hardly knowing what they were doing or why, but feeling, as all present did, that electric thrill of self-satisfaction and national pride."[3]

Supercharged with symbols of patriotism designed to promote sectional reconciliation, these fairs also represented attempts to catapult the poverty-ridden South into the forefront of national and international economic growth and were meant to demonstrate to the rest of the country that the leaders of the New South were capable of guiding their own section and the nation at large toward further progress. Like the directors of the Philadelphia and Chicago expositions, promoters of the southern fairs attempted to establish a consensus about progress. But these fairs were not simply exercises in mimicry. They projected a vision of national and international progress shaped by the peculiar social and economic circumstances of the South.

Each exposition conveyed the message that the prosperity of the country as a whole was contingent upon economic development of the South, especially of its natural resources, and subsequent export through southern ports of both

Fig. 18. Liberty Bell at Atlanta. Courtesy of Smithsonian Institution
Archives, Record Unit 95, Photograph Collection.

raw and finished materials to Latin America and Asia. The fairs further suggested that the South, in addition to holding the key to national economic
recovery, also possessed the solution to the "Negro question." What especially
distinguished southern fairs from their northern counterparts was the important
role assigned to Afro-Americans in the larger picture of developing domestic
and foreign markets. Where the directors of the Philadelphia and Chicago
expositions had been ambivalent toward black exhibits, if not adamantly opposed, the directors of the southern fairs established Negro departments to
illustrate the compatability of blacks and whites in the South.

These efforts to create an impression of racial harmony culminated when
the directors of the Atlanta Cotton States and International Exposition invited
Booker T. Washington to deliver one of the opening addresses. Washington's
speech, later dubbed the "Atlanta Compromise," attracted immediate and
widespread national attention as a solution to racial tensions that apparently
satisfied both blacks and whites. The setting of Washington's speech, however, was just as important as its content. His address was part of an international fair concerned with finding new markets to sustain growth. Indeed,
the impression of racial harmony that the directors of the Atlanta exposition
and every other world's fair in the South attempted to convey was predicated
upon expanding America's industrial and agricultural productivity through the
discovery of new markets and new supplies of natural resources. Growth along
these lines required a large industrial and agricultural labor force. This was
precisely the guarantee Washington offered. He depicted blacks as best suited

Fig. 19. Overview of the Cotton States and International Exposition. From Division of Prints and Photographs, Library of Congress.

to industrial and agricultural labor and urged them to remain socially separate from whites. Washington's speech was a key element in a fair that represented an attempt to fix class relations in the South within the confines of a racial pyramid.

The racial distinctions drawn at the southern fairs, however, suggested increasing differentiation among whites as well as blacks. These possibilities were brought into sharp focus on South Carolina Day at the Atlanta exposition, when Senator Ben Tillman earned the nickname "Pitchfork." Where the exposition directors spoke of harmony between North and South, Tillman pointed to the financial depletion of the South by northern financial policies and condemned those who said " 'me too,' every time the *New York World* and Grover Cleveland grunt[ed]." He not only threatened to prod Cleveland with a pitchfork to persuade him to change his tariff policy, but sounded an ominous warning: "with the negro problem in the South, with the immigration problem in the North; with the great burden of ignorant and debased foreigners who are up there living in the very dregs of degradation and ignorance and anarchism and communism and all the otherisms that go to pull down; that the time will come when the Southern farmers will be the saving salt that will keep this Republic from toppling over and becoming a military despotism." Tillman's speech, while inflammatory and acutely embarrassing to the directors, was not wholly out of keeping with the intent of the exposition. At a time when closer trade relations with Latin America meant greater contact with Hispanics and when immigrants from southeastern Europe were arriving in increasing num-

bers at northern ports, the exposition made clear that the only immigrants who
would be welcomed in the South were those racially compatible with the "old
Anglo-Saxon stock" already there. Endorsed by national statesmen, educators,
scientists, and businessmen, the southern fairs forged a link between race and
progress that prepared the way for national acceptance of *Plessy v. Ferguson*
and for the increasing agitation for immigration restriction.[4]

Indicative of the national response to the southern fairs was California poet
Joaquin Miller's generous tribute to the New Orleans exposition:

> The banners! The bells! The red banners!
> The rainbows of banners! The chimes!
> The music of stars! The sweet manners
> of Peace in old pastoral times!
>
> The coming of nations! Kings bringing
> Rich gifts to republics! The trees
> Of Paradise and birds singing
> By the side of De Soto's swift seas!

The melodious tones of bells and birds, however, were not the only sounds
heard at the southern expositions. While the fair was under construction, the
Atlanta exposition grounds resonated with the clang of chain-gang hammers.[5]

The international expositions in the South originated from three sources:
embarrassment felt by New South ideologues over the poor showing of southern resources at the Philadelphia and Chicago fairs; successful local industrial
and cotton expositions sponsored by these same interests in Atlanta and in
Waco, Texas; and, most important, the nationwide search for new markets to
alleviate the industrial downturns of the national economy and concurrent social protests.[6] At the opening of the New Orleans celebration, the Reverend
T. Dewitt Talmadge prayed for God's assistance in putting the country on the
right track through the World's Industrial and Cotton Exposition: "Gracious
God! We pray Thee, by means of this Exposition, solve for us the agonizing
question of supply and demand." A circular announcing the forthcoming Atlanta Cotton States and International Exposition explained why another fair
was needed so soon after the Chicago colossus: "The answer is in the peculiar
economic conditions now prevalent. The condition of the industrial world is
expressed in one word—overproduction." Surplus production, the circular
stressed, meant the "absolute necessity for an expansion of trade beyond the
limits of the home market." Another international fair, the circular stated,
would be the best means to effect this end. Herman Justi, head of the Department of Publicity and Promotion as well as official historian of the Nashville exposition, located the reasons for the Tennessee Centennial in the depressed economic circumstances of the early 1890s. "There was an all-
pervading despondency in the community," he wrote. "Labor was idle, capital

in hiding. The gaunt spectre of want, always more terrible in anticipation than in reality, seemed to perch itself above the rich man's mansion, no less than over the door of the day-laborer. To men of weak nerves, limited resources, or restricted vision, all this was dreadful; but to men inbred with the spirit of progress and patriotism this trial was only an incentive to noble endeavor."[7]

Several men rose to meet the threatening realities of southern poverty and nationwide class conflict. The names of E. A. Burke, Charles A. Collier, Samuel Inman, Isaac W. Avery, William A. Hemphill, John W. Thomas, Joseph B. Killebrew, and Eugene Castner Lewis have been overshadowed by another New South advocate, Henry Grady. But these men were no less apostles of the New South movement than Grady and contributed as much to its spirit and popularization. They too shared in the New South dream—a dream Grady described before his death in 1889 as "a perfect democracy, the oligarchs leading in the popular movement: a social system compact and closely knitted, less splendid on the surface, but stronger at the core; a hundred farms for every plantation, fifty homes for every palace; and a diversified industry that meets the complex needs of this complex age."[8]

One of the early advocates of the New South, E. A. Burke, director-general of the New Orleans exposition, was a southern patriot. In 1874, as a local railroad official, he singlehandedly delayed the train bearing federal troops to the Battle of New Orleans, thereby assuring the triumph of the Redeemers. On the wings of that triumph, he was elected state treasurer in 1887. He subsequently purchased two major newspapers in New Orleans, giving him

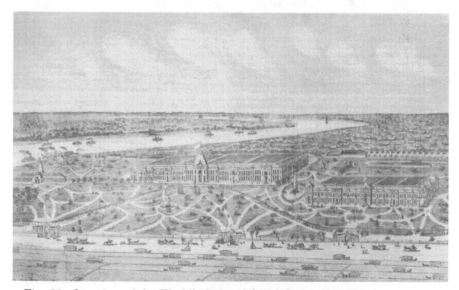

Fig. 20. Overview of the World's Industrial and Cotton Exposition. Lithograph courtesy of Historic New Orleans Collection.

unsurpassed power in Louisiana. The high point of his career came when the National Cotton Planters Association, headed by Edmund Richardson, one of the world's largest cotton planters, selected him to superintend the World's Industrial and Cotton Exposition. One admirer described Burke as a "man of iron," but this latter-day Andrew Jackson later embezzled nearly two million dollars of state funds and fled to Europe.[9]

The sponsors of the Atlanta exposition exercised nearly as much power as Burke. They too had at their disposal a major newspaper—the Atlanta *Constitution*, which Grady had purchased with the aid of a loan from Chicago industrialist Cyrus P. McCormick. Not surprisingly, the idea for holding a world's fair in Atlanta originated with William A. Hemphill, one of Grady's former associates and business manager of the *Constitution*. For Hemphill, as for most other backers of the Atlanta fair, the newspaper was one of many interests. In addition to presiding over the Board of Education and the Young Men's Library Association, Hemphill controlled two banks, the Atlanta Street Car Line, and a real estate development firm. Samuel M. Inman, who chaired the exposition's finance committee, not only was a trustee of Grady Hospital, but served on the boards of directors of several banks, operated an insurance company, and headed a firm that did "the largest cotton business in the world, and [controlled] more markets than would sound credible." To extend cotton markets even further and open new outlets for other commodities, promoters of the Atlanta fair appointed Isaac W. Avery as the exposition's commissioner to South America. Avery, an Atlanta lawyer, historian, and editorial writer for the *Constitution*, had for the past decade advocated the "movement to build up the trade of the United States with foreign countries through southern ports." Overseeing the entire exposition operation was its president, Charles A. Collier, cotton mill operator and banker.[10]

The control these men exercised over the Atlanta exposition was immense, as John W. Thomas, president of the Tennessee Centennial Exposition, would discover. When Thomas requested information from the Atlanta exposition directors concerning the financial structure of their 1895 fair, the backers responded that, of the $300,000 in bonds first issued by the exposition corporation, the directors, railroad companies, and brewing companies had purchased $250,000, with concessionaires absorbing the remaining $50,000. When it became necessary to issue first-mortgage bonds in the amount of $100,000, Inman had personally purchased $50,000 worth, and the other directors the remainder. "This," Thomas discovered, "is the true inwardness of the great Exposition."[11]

The pattern repeated itself at Nashville, where "the foremost and firmest allies of the expositions were the railroads." George Pullman made several cash contributions to the fair, and for the railroad exhibit he sent four passenger cars originally built for display at the World's Columbian Exposition and all named in honor of Columbus. On several occasions Thomas, president of the Nashville, Chattanooga and St. Louis Railway, personally guaranteed bank loans to the exposition company he directed. Two of his railroad associates, moreover, played crucial roles in organizing the fair. Major Eugene Castner Lewis, chairman of the board of the NC&SL, was selected director-general of the exposition and originated the idea for its most lasting monument—the Parthenon. J. B. Killebrew, the industrial and immigration agent for the same railroad, took charge of the railroad exhibits and did much publicity work for the fair throughout the South. The *Nashville Banner* justified this preponderance of railroad influence in the Tennessee Centennial on the grounds that the directors had vast experience in resolving the "plain, sensible question—How shall we make two blades of grass to grow where only one grew before?" Railroads, the newspaper continued, more than any other agency, pointed the way to "interlocking our interests more and more with those of other nations, in the van of civilization."[12]

Regional, national, and international economic expansion were bywords of the various fairs. To further this process, backers of the southern fairs urged northern capitalists to invest in the development of southern resources. One Atlanta wag offered his encouragement: "Thirty years ago the Yankees came down here and captured the town, and now they have come down and captured it again, and we like the second capture better than the first." The *New York Times* stripped the issue of humor: "It is the prime object of the Cotton States and International Exposition to make an effective presentation . . . that their region needs only adequate development of its abundant resources to make it a leading manufacturing center, an agricultural center of unsurpassed productiveness, and part of the country of almost general prosperity."[13]

At the New Orleans fair, the Texas state commissioner to the exposition tantalized visitors with a description of his state's resources: "With over 300 miles of mountains of metallic ores only awaiting the prospector with his pick to reveal to his 'Open, Sesame!' their hidden wealth, more fabulous than Ali Baba ever dreamed of in the cave, and which would have bade old Vulcan smile, the forge, the furnace and the factory can sustain in Texas a series of Sheffields and Birmingham[s]." After cataloging other resources, he asked: "Did I not say truly, then, that the story of her resources read like a Persian poem in an Eastern epic?" The federal government helped to nourish such claims at all of the fairs.[14]

For the Atlanta fair, Hoke Smith, secretary of the interior, promised that the Interior Department's display of natural wealth in the South "will be a revelation to the Northern and Western miners and capitalists, and will surprise even the best informed men of the South." Many northern businessmen journeyed to the fairs to see for themselves the economic possibilities of the South. Thus the directors of the Nashville exposition wined and dined numerous northern businessmen who visited Nashville's resurrection of the White City. Among these visitors were Stuyvesant Fish and John Jacob Astor, who expressed particular interest in the possibilities of making a round cotton bale. "There were more than $200,000,000 represented at that dinner," Killebrew later recalled. The New York Board of Commissioners to the Atlanta fair issued a report that lauded the "beauty, utility and economy of design and construction of the Exposition Buildings." The *New York Times* similarly noted that Atlanta's gala green-and-brown Romanesque exposition buildings had been built of inexpensive materials, especially of Georgia pine.[15]

Also generally understood was the estimate by Atlanta exposition officials that they had saved over $100,000 by using chain-gang labor to excavate "about a million yards of earth during the early months of construction." As one southern newspaper commented on the labor situation in the South: "It is very noticeable that while strikes are the order of the day at the north and many sections of the west, they are comparatively unknown in the south." "Investors," the newspaper added, "should not lose sight of this fact." Potential northern investors were also invited to notice the place of blacks in the political economy of the South as revealed in the Negro departments at each of the fairs.[16]

In his capacity as official historian of the Tennessee Centennial, Herman Justi explained that a Negro department was a "necessary feature" of the fair "because, in the first place, it determines [blacks'] industrial status." "This done," he continued, "we shall be able, with each succeeding exposition, to measure their strides and determine their progress." For the directors of the southern fairs, Negro departments were instruments of social control that would keep blacks in check by defining progress as self-improvement along industrial lines and by persuading blacks that builders of the New South would take their best interests to heart.[17]

For this reason many blacks rejected the expositions out of hand, believing that the fairs delimited too severely the possibilities for social change in the South. Other blacks, however, perceived survival as *the* issue facing them. The challenge for blacks sharing this viewpoint and agreeing to participate in the fairs was to define the issues confronting them within the symbolic social constructs the expositions presented. At the New Orleans exposition, survival and resistance were explicitly joined. By 1897, in contrast, black leaders who had taken charge of the Negro departments at the Atlanta and Nashville fairs were downplaying political resistance and elevating character building as the first step toward social change.[18]

Given the general exclusion of black exhibitors from the Philadelphia Centennial and the 1883 Supreme Court decision in the Civil Rights Cases sanctioning discrimination against blacks by individuals, many blacks regarded the Colored Department at the New Orleans fair as noteworthy for existing at all. Bishop Henry A. Turner told the audience present for the opening ceremonies of that department that, when he first heard that the exposition directors would permit displays organized by blacks, it "was so unexpected, so

marvelous, so Utopian, that we could scarcely believe it was true." For Turner
there was never any question about participating in the fair because "the Supreme Court had turned us over to the roughs on the public highways by virtue
of the decision in the civil rights cases." But the exposition directors, it
seemed to Turner, "have rebuked the Supreme Court for its decision, have
stretched out their hands to us, and have said: 'Come join us; we will treat
you right.' And they have kept their word. I have not been snubbed since
coming here. I cannot believe that I am in New Orleans. I am inclined to
think it must be all a dream. All honor, I say, to Director General Burke. All
honor to the managers of this Exposition. All honor to New Orleans." Turner's
enthusiasm was shared by J. J. Spellman, superintendent of the department.
Spellman believed that the Afro-American exhibit at the fair represented a
"new era" for blacks and that it was particularly fitting that this new beginning
occurred in the South, "where the greater part of us are identified with the
development and progress of its great natural resources." The exhibits by
blacks, he declared, "will demonstrate a capacity for all branches of industry
that will dispel all sentiment and interest as to the future."[19]

Praise for the exposition management from Spellman and Turner reflected
their perception that the Supreme Court decision had made the struggle
for survival a paramount issue for blacks in the South. But both of their
addresses and, even more strikingly, a speech by black attorney David A.
Straker of South Carolina stressed that survival by itself was not a sufficient
goal. Straker's address was remarkable. At one point he condemned the
"white piratic slave trader" while pointing to the existence of cultural contin-
uities between the African and Afro-American experience. He also expressed
his hope that the black exhibits at the exposition would bring all people "together in love, peace and unity, under equal laws, exact justice and common
privileges, so that the antagonisms of race, the hatred of creeds and parties,
the prejudice of caste and the denial of equal rights may disappear from
among us forever." Bishop Turner, during his address, which followed
Straker's, conceded that the existence of the Colored Department might lead
him to "somewhat modify my radical ideas." But even Turner insisted that
before he altered his radicalism, whites had to stop "maligning and misrep-
resenting us."[20]

To get this final point across, the blacks who participated in the Colored
Department at the New Orleans exposition made broad demands for political,
economic, and social justice. "Educated labor," as Straker termed it, was only
part of a broader plan for social and political change. "We need an education
of heart, of brains and of hands," he declared. The sixteen thousand exhibits
in the department, some from as far away as the Utah and Wyoming territories, reflected the same concerns. There were displays of mechanical inventions, scientific achievements, and an engraving entitled "Colored Chieftans"
that included portraits of white and black abolitionists. One of the most striking exhibits, however, was a divan embroidered by Sarah H. Shimm, a school-

teacher in Washington, D.C. Her silk embroidery told the story of Toussaint L'Ouverture's revolutionary success in Haiti. Over his head, in large red letters, she had sewed the motto: "The First of the Blacks."[21]

At the New Orleans World's Industrial and Cotton Exposition, blacks demanded many sweeping social, economic, and political changes. Director-General Burke, however, had a different conception of the Colored Department's purpose: "It was designed by the management of the Exhibition, through this exhibit, to reach out our hand to our brother in black; to shed upon that unfortunate race the sunlight of science and invention, and implant in him the desire to come out of the slough of ignorance and make a manly effort to occupy with us the improved farm, the workshop, and the factory." At the New Orleans fair, only the exposition directors sought to restrict opportunities for blacks to the fields and shops. A decade later, by contrast, the same message was delivered not only by the directors of a fair, but by the black commissioners as well. It was best articulated by Booker T. Washington, who in 1885 had protested the accommodations railroads provided for black passengers traveling to the New Orleans exposition by demanding that the separate passenger cars for blacks be truly equal with those provided for

Fig. 21. Ohio's Afro-American exhibit, New Orleans. Courtesy of Historic New Orleans Collection.

whites. "We can be as separate as the fingers," Washington wrote to a Montgomery newspaper, "yet one as the hand for maintaining the right."[22]

Washington's ideas were not unknown to Atlanta's segregation-minded businessmen. In 1893 he had traveled to the World's Columbian Exposition to participate in a session of the Labor Congress devoted to black workers. Washington's address focused on the southern sharecrop system, which, he argued, resulted in a form of labor resembling slavery. According to Washington, this system "could not exist but for the ignorance of the negro." The end of sharecropping, he suggested, would come through "manual training." Two months later, Washington journeyed to Atlanta to speak before a meeting of white Baptist leaders. The "dignity of labor" was his central theme.[23]

Businessmen in Atlanta planning the Cotton States and International Exposition were impressed by Washington's ideas. By early 1894 the directors agreed with prominent blacks in Atlanta to establish a Negro department at the fair. Although Washington was not involved in these initial negotiations for the exhibit, he was one of three black delegates the exposition's directors selected to appear with them before the Appropriations Committee of the House of Representatives on behalf of the exposition company's appeal for $200,000 in federal funds. These black ministers and educators were the final speakers heard by the committee. Yet in the few minutes allotted to them they had a decisive impact. Bishops Wesley J. Gaines and Abram L. Grant emphasized that whites and blacks in the South "understood each other," that blacks were "more interested in the culture and manufacture of cotton than in all other products put together," and that blacks could be relied upon never to engage in strikes. After the two bishops concluded, Washington spoke for less than ten minutes from notes jotted on an envelope. He began by telling the committee that "he had eschewed all participation in politics or political gatherings, and had advised his people to do the same." He also told the committee that his goal was to persuade blacks to aspire to "industry, thrift, intelligence and property," which would help them gain the respect of whites, and that the exposition would be an appropriate showplace. A congressional appropriation for the fair, he stressed, would demonstrate the government's concern for the South and for blacks.[24]

The importance of the addresses by Washington, Gaines, and Grant to the directors' drive to obtain federal support for the fair became apparent several months later during the final House debates on the bill. A representative from New York declared that the testimony by the black delegates before the committee had made him realize that "[i]nstead of being a hindrance to the prosperity of the South, [blacks] will furnish a body of workmen to be drawn upon for the development of the future enterprises of that section." Other members of the House were of similar mind and passed the appropriation for the fair. There was, however, one important amendment. Congress made the funds contingent upon the directors' establishing a separate Negro Building in lieu of placing the black exhibits in the Government Building as originally planned. The Atlanta Compromise occurred not on the exposition grounds, but during the previous year in the halls of Congress.[25]

I. Garland Penn, a black schoolteacher and attorney, headed the Negro department of the fair after Washington declined the post because of duties at Tuskegee. Penn, however, proposed inviting Washington "to represent the colored Race in the opening ceremonies of the Exposition." The president of the fair, Collier, was reluctant to agree to this proposal, preferring instead to give blacks a separate dedicatory exercise. Penn, however, prevailed on the six white businessmen who composed the committee in charge of the festivities to remind Collier of Washington's crucial speech on behalf of the fair before Congress. Collier's colleagues persuaded him to drop his opposition, and the exposition management extended an invitation to Washington to appear as one of the speakers at the opening ceremonies of the fair.[26]

When Washington spoke before the segregated audience gathered in the auditorium on opening day, he repeated ideas he had outlined in his 1885 letter to a newspaper and in his addresses at the Labor Congress, the Baptist conference, and before the Appropriations Committee. He spoke of the dignity of working, urging blacks to "cast down your bucket where you are," and promised whites that "in all things that are purely social, we can be as separate as the fingers, yet one as the hand in all things essential to mutual progress." "The wisest among my race," he further assured whites, "understand that the agitation of questions of social equality is the extremest folly." In addition to these long-remembered maxims, Washington also expressed his conviction that "No race that has anything to contribute to the markets of the world is long in any degree ostracized." With this key sentence, Washington pinned the alleviation of the social, economic, and political conditions of blacks squarely on America's expansion overseas, believing that new markets meant jobs for blacks, which in turn would enable them to earn the respect of whites. The day following his address, Washington explained the thrust of his message in a letter to a New York newspaper. "This is the year of Jubilee for the Negro," he wrote. "It is the beginning of a New Era—the heart of the New South is open today to the Negro as it has never been before—the greatest problem is now with the Negro himself."[27]

Even before Washington spoke, many blacks and their white supporters took exception to plans for a black exhibit at the fair. John C. Buckner, a black Illinois legislator, opposed the federal appropriation for the fair, expressing adamant hostility to any government aid for businessmen in the South until measures were taken to stop lynchings and to extend full constitutional rights to blacks. William S. Scarborough, a member of the National Philological Society, advised blacks to stay away from the fair because, he believed, their presence would lend tacit support to jim crow practices. Opposition also came from black Atlanta residents. At a public meeting in Big Bethel Church.

they voiced their objections to the "[l]ack of space for the colored exhibit, jim-crow cars and [to] convict labor at the grounds." In North Carolina, resistance to the planned black exhibit from the state was so strong that the state's commissioners to the fair had to inform interested fairgoers that a better display of achievements by North Carolina blacks could be found at the state's annual "colored fair."[28]

Once the fair got under way, these criticisms seemed prescient. Blacks were permitted to visit all the public buildings at the fair, but, as one newspaper noted, "they are not allowed to purchase refreshment in any of the buildings except the Negro Building." In the Auditorium, all audiences were segregated. Many private exhibitors, moreover, especially those with restaurant concessions, refused to admit blacks. And gatemen were reportedly more churlish to blacks than to whites. Such practices led the editor of the *People's Advocate*, a local black paper, to caution blacks:

> The Fair is a big fake . . . for Negroes have not even a dog's show inside the Exposition gates unless it is in the Negro Building. Many people have written, asking whether the exposition is worth coming to see. . . . If they wish to feel that they are inferior to other American citizens, if they want to pay double fare on the surface cars and also be insulted, if they want to see on all sides: 'For Whites Only,' or 'No Niggers or dogs allowed' if they want to be humiliated and have their man and womanhood crushed out, then come.[29]

Black supporters of the fair did their best to deny these charges and, with the aid of the *Constitution*, labeled critics of the fair "croakers," "demagogues," and "agitators." From the standpoint of the exposition directors, the hostility many blacks showed to the enterprise made it even more imperative to encourage black attendance. Thus the *Constitution* ran an editorial supporting efforts by the black commissioners to persuade white employers to give all black working people a day off to attend the dedicatory exercises for the Negro Building. Many employers seemed to have followed this advice, since the crowd in the auditorium was larger than for any other gathering, even the opening ceremonies. The keynote speaker for the dedication of the building was J. W. E. Bowen, a black educator, who, following Washington's line of reasoning, urged blacks to "have sense enough to stay in this country and contribute to the correct solution of the race question, until this Nation shall become in truth homogeneous in sentiment, though heterogeneous in blood." As was the case on opening day, blacks were told to accept segregation in return for a promise from whites to allow them to earn their livelihood, as industrial and agricultural workers in America's expanding economy. Buttressing these arguments were the displays in the Negro Building, which were drawn largely from the black industrial schools.[30]

At the opening of the Negro Building at the Tennessee Centennial, Charles

Fig. 22. Negro Building at Atlanta. Photograph from *Report of the Board of Commissioners Representing the State of New York at the Cotton States and International Exposition.*

W. Anderson, a black private secretary to the state treasurer of New York, delivered the main address. It came at the climax of the "most imposing colored parade ever seen in Nashville." Excursion trains and steamboats brought well over thirty thousand blacks to celebrate Negro Day at the fair. Thousands of black visitors, "the secret orders in the showy regalia, the military, the female societies, the school children in floats," joined together in a five-mile-long parade that led to the exposition grounds. Once there, several thousand paraders joined the audience of whites and blacks already in the exposition's auditorium. After a musical prelude and a welcoming address by Richard C. Hill, chief of the Negro Department, Anderson spoke. He was present at the ceremonies, he explained, because "we, as a race, do not fully appreciate the importance of industrial education." "Do not indulge in the pastime of throwing stones at the stars," he warned blacks. Instead, he counseled patience: "all things come to him who waits, if he hustles while he waits." "Learn to be practical," he added, telling blacks to acquire skills, cultivate character, and become useful citizens.[31]

As he sat on the speakers' platform, John W. Thomas undoubtedly was pleased by Anderson's speech. The exposition company had provided all the funds for constructing the Negro Building, free transportation for black exhibits, and free space to black exhibitors. Thomas, moreover, had personally offered ten free tickets apiece to any black person who helped organize excursions of blacks to the fair for Negro Day. When he was called to make a speech after Anderson concluded, Thomas modestly disclaimed any intention of delivering an address, but he did urge blacks to follow Anderson's advice, telling them, "You will make more material progress in the next five years than you have made in the last thirty." When the applause died down, Thomas continued and evidently warmed to the idea of making a speech. "I address you as fellow-citizens," he declared, "for though the colored race may have a different complexion and differ in intellectual attainments from the white race, we are still fellow-citizens of one great nation under one great flag (cheers)." Nostalgia then took hold and, according to a newspaper story, Thomas "went on to recall the memory of his 'black mammy' and, as he spoke of her devotion, the tears came in his eyes and in the eyes of others." Before the war someone offered to buy her, but, Thomas told the audience, he had informed the prospective buyer: "I would as soon sell my wife." After the applause calmed down, Thomas proceeded to recount the loyalty of his slaves—slaves who "had always been most faithful and true to their trust." This lesson of loyalty had practical application to the present: "For thirty years, I have been in the railroad business and during that time I have employed thousands of colored laborers and I say to you to-day that they have always given perfect satisfaction (applause). I will go further and say that the best laborer we have is the negro." The audience responded by giving Thomas a tremendous, "perfect ovation."[32]

The Nashville *Banner*, in an editorial on these speeches, set forth some of the ideas behind the directors' enthusiasm for black labor. European immigrants, according to the *Banner*, formed a "dissatisfied and dangerous element which opposes itself to the established order and tends to socialism and anarchism. The negroes, on the other hand, are a people that have respect for authority and are easily made content with their lot. The negroes are not dynamiters. With all their faults, with all their ignorance, as a race they are a tractable people that can be depended upon." Furthermore, the newspaper declared, blacks "can still be trusted, and the time may come when the negroes will be needed to join with the patriotic whites of the country in a common cause against the evils and dangers which are presaged by the continuous drift from the slums of Europe into this country. . . . This restless, dissatisfied, unassimilating population has not come to the South because the negroes have been in the way. And the negroes are more to be desired as laborers than the class they have kept away."[33]

For those who doubted that blacks could be easily controlled, the directors of the Atlanta and Nashville fairs added a "typical" antebellum scene to their entertainment avenues. Called the Old Plantation, the concession was owned by whites and managed by a former minstrel showman. Once inside, fairgoers were invited to observe "[y]oung bucks and thickliped [*sic*] African maidens 'happy as a big sunflower' dance the old-time breakdowns, joined in by 'all de niggahs' with wierd and gutteral sounds to the accompaniment of 'de scrapin' of de fiddle and 'de old bangjo [*sic*].'" At Atlanta, the concession received a tremendous promotional boost and implicit federal sanction when President Cleveland made it his only stop on the Midway. The Old Plantation, in short, did more than recreate the mythical past of the Old South. It created an impression that blacks would have a long road to travel before they would be considered equals. Like the villages depicting the Chinese, Japanese, and Mexicans, the Old Plantation conferred colonial status on its inhabitants.[34]

As contented, inferior beings, Judge Emory Speer suggested in his speech immediately following Washington's presentation at the opening of the Atlanta fair, blacks posed no threat to white civilization. He contended that there never had been and never would be any danger of "negro control" in the South. Those who thought otherwise were invited to "consider the imperious and commanding nature of the Anglo-Saxon race." In India, he claimed, "forty millions of dark-skinned men . . . were overcome by a handful of men of our race, and are wisely directed on all paths of modern progress by the English Government as readily as it controls a parish in Yorkshire or Kent." The English colonial model was especially applicable to the South, he intimated, because the South had "the largest percentage of the old Anglo-Saxon stock" of any region in the country. Furthermore, southerners were teaching blacks "to appreciate the dignity of labor" as a necessary step up the ladder of progress. The South, Speer firmly believed, not only had solved the "race question" but was well in front of the rest of the nation in shouldering the white man's burden.[35]

Collier made the same point for the readers of "Dixie," an Atlanta-based manufacturers' journal, and noted the universal implications of the Negro exhibit. "This will be a great object lesson in education, in sociology, and in government, to the whole world," he wrote. "The race question is not peculiar

Fig. 23. Old Plantation concession on Midway Heights, Atlanta. From Division of Prints and Photographs, Library of Congress.

to the Southern States. There is no continent, and hardly an important country, which does not have to face this problem in some form. In South America
it is almost identically the problem we have here. In Mexico, it is different,
but still difficult, and in India, where caste is entrenched behind centuries of
custom, the question is hardly less perplexing." In America, he asserted, the
situation was no better. "Even in our own country, other races are clashing
and at this moment the United States Government is wrestling with problems
arising from the cosmopolitan character of the exposition." Collier's veiled
reference to difficulties the management had encountered with immigration
legislation in trying to secure a Chinese Village concession did not detract
from his argument. Rather, it confirmed a central theme of the fair. "The race
questions of the world will show themselves in the folk and folklore of the
Exposition," he declared.[36]

Proponents of the New South were ready to apply the lessons of race management on a regional, national, and international scale. The *Nashville American* explained the intended message of the Negro Department to black Americans:

> It should rejoice him to know that he has those innate qualities which
> enable him not to suffer but to profit by contact with a stronger race and
> a race in a much higher state of development. Let the negro be
> consoled by the fate of other races who have gone down before the
> onward march of the Anglo-Saxon civilization, and take courage for a
> renewal of the fight for a higher development.

The place of blacks in the symbolic constellation of the New South further
crystallized at the Tennessee Centennial when Booker T. Washington, from
the steps of the Negro Building, delivered an Emancipation Day address on
the benefits that industrial education for blacks would confer on the South.
Washington's speech, commemorating the end of chattel slavery, located
blacks as part of an industrial and agricultural work force that would produce
raw materials and manufactured goods for American expansion into Latin
America. Appropriately, the Negro Building, backdrop for Washington's
speech, was designed in the style of the Spanish Renaissance. At Nashville,
as at Atlanta, Washington and the black commissioners assented to, rather
than challenged, the economic aims of the exposition directors.[37]

The eyes of the exposition directors were fixed on broadening America's
commercial horizons overseas as well as on developing the natural resources
of the South. The managers of the World's Industrial and Cotton Exposition
explained that New Orleans was the appropriate site for the fair because it
"was the gateway to and from Mexico, Central America and the West Indies,
the immense resources of which are now being so rapidly developed, while
their commercial interests are being so greatly expanded under the vigorous
influence of American enterprise; the building of railways, the establishment

Fig. 24. Negro Building at Nashville. From Herman Justi, *Official History of the Tennessee Centennial Exposition*.

of steamship lines, and the colonizing of commercial and industrial enterprises." Exposition president Collier expressed the similar aspirations behind the Atlanta celebration by never appearing in public during the exposition months without wearing in his lapel his *Busto del Liberador* pin. This miniature of Simón de Bolívar not only indicated Collier's interest in and identification with Latin America, but expressed his conviction that the ideas about progress embodied in the exposition he presided over would have a liberating effect on Latin America. With national attention riveted on the dispute between Great Britain and Venezuela over the latter's boundary, Collier and his business associates placed themselves in the role of liberating Latin America from European influence. From the Cotton States and International Exposition, they recast the net of the Monroe Doctrine over Latin America in order to establish an American commercial protectorate.[38]

The man most responsible for encouraging Latin American countries to participate in the fair was Isaac W. Avery. Over a nine-month period beginning in October 1894, he visited seven Latin American countries. Testifying to the national importance of his thirty-thousand-mile voyage were the letters he carried from Walter Q. Gresham, secretary of state, ordering the United States ministers to aid Avery in every way possible.[39]

Avery arrived in Brazil at a propitious time. The Brazilian government was unveiling a statue of James Monroe in Rio de Janeiro, and Avery was invited to deliver an address to mark the occasion. He took advantage of the opportunity to extol "our Exposition as a great commercial instrumentality to bind our two largest American Republics, mutually interested in preserving the integrity of our American soil, in a practical as well as sentimental brotherhood." "America for Americans" became the gist of his message to other Latin American government officials and businessmen as he urged them to establish exhibits at the Atlanta fair. While in Buenos Aires, he argued that an Argentine exhibit would aid in establishing "ties of brotherhood that will all help us to develop our commerce with each other to vast proportions, and also to develop your wonderful country to its full material power."[40]

In the same letter to Argentina's minister of foreign affairs, he spoke frankly of the anticipated impact on Latin America: "A special and important purpose of this Exposition is to establish United States Banks here with agencies in our states, and to have direct lines of home steamers under our own flags running between our countries, and it will be to our mutual interest for you to give every facility for doing these things." Avery's precision on this point caused someone to have second thoughts and to cross this sentence out of the letter. But there was no doubt that the exposition was intended to promote American capital investment in Latin America and to demonstrate its market potential for American surplus production. As Avery informed Mexico's President Porfirio Díaz, "Mexico needs everything that the United States manufactures. . . . And it is to the interest of the United States to join the development of Mexico's imperial advantage [i.e., its natural resources]." The governments of Mexico, Venezuela, Costa Rica, Argentina, and Chile responded to Avery's invitation and established official buildings devoted to the mineral and agricultural wealth of their countries.[41]

Shortly after Avery's return, the *New York Times* reiterated that the exposition would portray Latin America as a market for American products. The *Times* also confirmed that southerners were thinking in global as well as hemispheric perspectives. At the heart of their dreams lay the plans for the Nicaraguan canal that would open trade routes between southern ports and Asia. To help bring this dream closer to realization, the directors awarded a concession contract to the Maritime Canal Company to display in the Transportation Building a scale model of an isthmian canal set in a relief map showing the terrain of the proposed route. The point of the exhibit, the *Constitution* stated, was to "create a sentiment favorable to the building of the canal through government aid." Twenty years later, two California expositions would commemorate the completion of the canal not in Nicaragua, but across the isthmus of Panama.[42]

The display at Atlanta of Latin American resources was unmatched until the 1901 Pan-American Exposition in Buffalo. Yet visitors to the New Orleans and Nashville expositions also had the opportunity to study the resources of Latin America, especially the natural wealth of Mexico. At the New Orleans fair, the Mexican government set up exhibits in the Main Building as well as in a separate structure given over entirely to Mexico's mineral wealth. The centerpiece in this mineral exhibit was a molded two-and-one-half-ton silver mountain from the Chihuahua mines. So important were the market and re- source potentials of Latin America to the builders of the New South empire that even the Tennessee Centennial, which did not have official entries by foreign governments, offered visitors a separate Mexico Building, housing dis- plays provided for the most part by Frederick Starr, head of the University of Chicago's Department of Anthropology. Minerals, agricultural resources, and by-products again predominated. A local paper told prospective fairgoers to keep an eye out for an exhibit of the maguey plant "surrounded with forty different articles manufactured from it." A veritable cornucopia seemed to be overflowing south of the border.[43]

American investors responded. As a result of the Mexican displays at the New Orleans fair, one northern cotton-mill owner decided to move his entire operation to Mexico. At the time of Avery's journey to Latin America, the lure of Latin American markets also captured the attention of T. H. Martin, editor of "Dixie," who proposed that American manufacturers join together and, with the consent of Latin American governments, sponsor several expositions in South America and Mexico. Avery, enthusiastic about the idea, told the Ar-

Fig. 25. Mexican "pagoda" at New Orleans. Courtesy of Historic New Orleans Collection.

gentine government: "The benefit of such interchangeable Expositions can not be estimated. The results will be broad, valuable and far-reaching. The education in republican ideas, the growth of American fraternization, the increase of commercial and friendly bonds, and the exchange of differing civilizations will be a rich harvest of good, besides the trade and other substantial fruits." In the United States two thousand letters went out to American manufacturers asking if they would support such expositions, recognizing that a "leading feature" would be "an elaborate exhibit of our machinery and manufactured products." According to Martin, 735 questionnaires were returned, and "[s]ix hundred and sixteen heartily endorsed the suggested expositions and expressed their immediate readiness to co-operate with the movement." Of these manufacturers, 103 reported that they were ready to send exhibits on a moment's notice. The 112 who responded negatively did so because they believed their machinery "was not adaptable to the present needs of the Spanish-American countries." This overwhelmingly favorable response led Martin to approach leading manufacturing interests in Cincinnati, sponsors of the industrial expositions of the preceding decade, to plan for an exposition in Mexico City that already had the support of President Díaz. Businessmen from around the country met in Cincinnati in September 1895 and organized themselves into the National Association of Manufacturers. One of their first actions was to pass a resolution endorsing Atlanta's fair. Expositions at home and abroad, these businessmen hoped, would demonstrate the value of the United States commercial expansion to Americans of both continents.[44]

Not all Latin Americans were sanguine about the idea of increased commercial ties with the United States. The Venezuelan minister of production, while accepting Avery's invitation to establish an exhibit at the Atlanta fair, expressed his hope "that the Monroe Doctrine be translated into positive and cordial practices." Nor were responses to Latin American participation at the southern fairs altogether promising.[45]

Exposition directors at each of the fairs cordially received Latin American businessmen and government officials, and at Atlanta they went so far as to increase the number of awards to Latin American exhibitors who had displays considered important to American manufacturing interests. But manipulating awards to gain access to Latin American resources was only part of a larger picture of condescension and hostility toward Latin Americans that emerged at the expositions. At New Orleans, the management named a lake for the wife of the Mexican president, but it also bilked the Mexican band out of $800 in gate receipts. The band, moreover, was subjected to the verbal abuse of a local newspaper concerned about white women associating with band members. The Atlanta and Nashville fairs also left little doubt about the place of Latin Americans in the onward march of civilization. Along with selected "types" of Asians, Africans, and Afro-Americans, Mexicans and Cubans were put on view in villages on the entertainment avenues of the fairs that were also the areas of the exposition set aside for cheap thrills and monkey houses.[46]

Atlanta's Midway Heights and Nashville's Vanity Fair were the progeny of Chicago's highly successful Midway Plaisance. These amusement avenues, like the original Midway Plaisance, also served as cathartic respites from the social upheavals of the 1890s. "A night on Vanity Fair," the *Nashville American* asserted, "is a night to be marked with a white stone in the dreary desert of a life of care, business worry and labor and a catholicon for all ills that flesh and spirit are heir to." Furthermore, Midway Heights and Vanity Fair stressed interludes of equality in an increasingly class-divided society: "[T]he man whose name is worth much in the marts of the world came down the chutes with the reckless abandon of the younger man and enjoyed the sensation no less than the fellow on the back seat of the same boat whose note he had perchance turned down on the morning of the same day." Noting similarities with Chicago's Midway, an Atlanta exposition official observed that "Midway Heights possessed the features of the circus, the menagerie, the museum and the vaudeville, with an odd collection of strange nationalities forming a unique anthropological exhibit."[47]

Close resemblance of the entertainment avenues at Atlanta and Nashville to the Midway Plaisance was by no means fortuitous. Personnel and amusement features radiated out from Chicago to the southern expositions like the beams of an exploding star. At Atlanta and Nashville, Edmund A. Felder and Charles Maloney superintended the respective Departments of Admissions and Concessions. Felder, a secretary for various railroad companies by vocation, began his exposition work as Daniel Burnham's assistant in the Division of Works at the World's Columbian Exposition. When the Cotton States and International Exposition was in the planning stage, Collier invited him to take charge of the Midway attractions. Maloney's career intersected with Felder's at several points. Before his duties at the Tennessee Centennial, he too had served in the Admissions Department at Chicago and had worked as Felder's assistant at Atlanta.[48]

Not surprisingly, these two men replicated many of Chicago's successful Midway attractions for the two southern fairs. Visitors to Atlanta and Nashville could once again shoot the chutes, wind their way through various mirror mazes, and ogle the women who participated in the beauty shows or at the more daring exhibitions of flesh in various hootchy-cootchy dances. Some amusements underwent a gradual metamorphosis. On Midway Heights the Ferris wheel became a phoenix wheel. On Vanity Fair it was replaced entirely by a giant see-saw that illustrated "the nineteenth century evolution of the pine board and the rail fence."[49] Displays of human beings were changed to reflect the specific aims of the southern fairs. Thus, Afro-American, Mexican, and Cuban "types" highlighted a series of villages that also included Asians, Native Americans, and Africans. As at Chicago the entertainment avenues played an integral part in shaping the ideological content and impact of the Atlanta and Nashville expositions. With mechanical contrivances like the revolving wheels illustrating the compatibility of man and machine, the villages served to clarify the vision of the New South as a classless society of Anglo-Saxons, ready to lead the rest of the nation in the imperial duties of subjugation and uplift. The ethnological qualities attributed to these nonwhite villagers made the concessionaires' claims of verisimilitude more credible and gave apparent scientific standing to the separation of nonwhites from whites in the upward spiral of civilization. The claim by Walter G. Cooper, director of publicity and official historian of the Atlanta fair, that the "live subjects were nowise disconcerted" was untrue, but it reflected the general perception of Midway villagers as lesser human beings incapable of feeling humiliation or pain.[50]

A leading attraction on Midway Heights was the Indian Village organized by C. P. Jordan of the Rosebud Indian Agency. The exhibit recalled the events of the early 1890s that had culminated in the Wounded Knee massacre. Many of the Sioux put on display had been involved in the Ghost Dance movement and had fought United States troops. In the village they lived and were exhibited in the same lodges, transported to the Midway and re-created, that federal troops had riddled with Gatling gun fire at Wounded Knee. On display were a woman and her young son who had been shot—the infant twice—by Gatling gun rounds while asleep in their lodge. Their feelings at reliving these events at the fair were not recorded by Cooper, who simply observed: "This boy, known as 'Little Wound,' seems to be no worse physically for his early taste of war, and during the Exposition, showed all the lively and mischievous tendencies of a robust urchin."[51]

The Chinese fared similarly. Although congressional action exempted employees of the Chinese Village from the exclusion restrictions of the Geary Act, Treasury Department officials kept them under close scrutiny. The villagers also fell prey to the owners of the concessions. Georgia's Chinese residents, numbering only several hundred, lodged a protest against the concession at the Atlanta fair. They claimed that its organizers—Leong Lam, a vice-president of the Six Companies, and Kee Owyang, a member of the New York banking house of Aiello and Company—were reaping large profits from the illegal transportation of Chinese and from selling the women into prostitution. Whether these accusations were true—and it appears that most of the Chinese who were originally brought from China by Kee Owyang to the World's Columbian Exposition never returned to their homeland—the villagers had little control over their destinies while at the expositions. The hostility of the exposition environment made their experience even less tolerable.[52]

When Chinese bound for Midway Heights stepped off the train in Atlanta's depot, they were met by over twenty-five hundred curious onlookers whose comments, according to the *Constitution*, were typified by the following: "Dey're laundry dat's brought over for de exposition rush uv people," exclaimed one onlooker to his sidekick. "Easy dere, Pete!" "Get onto his pigtail's Sunday clothes, will yer? Dat's a woman wid de bloomers!" To promote the Tennessee Centennial, Anthony Gormon, proprietor of the wild animal show, took a Chinese child with him on an advertising swing by railway around the state. "The little ones are very 'cute,' to use a woman's word," the *Nashville Banner* reported, "and the little Chinaman is sure to attract a great deal of attention. He will be permitted to distribute the handbills that are used to advertise the Exposition, and will thus have an opportunity to circulate among the crowds in all the towns and be seen by all of them." In the early going, the Chinese were welcome advertisements for the exposition, but a group of off-duty soldiers were less than enthusiastic about their presence on Vanity Fair. Before the nearly two hundred troops left the village, they had tied together a number of Chinese by their hair and generally treated them "in a very rough manner."[53]

Brutality, ridicule, and commercial exploitation, however, did not preclude efforts to uplift the Chinese while they were at the fairs. The minister of Nashville's First Presbyterian Church made an effort to christianize Chinese youngsters so that they could spread the gospel in China. "When they return to that benighted country at the close of this Centennial," a Nashville newspaper wrote, "they will be able to teach many of their less fortunate brothers the Way, the Truth and the Light." Fairgoers were doubtless pleased when the Chinese children's chorus joined Innes's Concert Band and sang "Jesus Loves Me" in Chinese and "Up in the Sky" in English.[54]

The Mexican Village at the Cotton States and International Exposition was the work of James Porteus and his Mexican Village Exposition Company. Porteus, with the help of A. H. Smythe, former manager of the Cairo Street concession at Chicago, and J. B. Legg, a Saint Louis architect, built the three-acre attraction that was supposedly "a characteristic and picturesque representation of Mexican life." It offered visitors reproductions of famous ruins and missions as well as a working replica of a coffee plantation. The managers planned a bullfight, but protests against the anticipated cruelty to animals forced cancellation. Visitors, instead, had to rest content with "Mexican musicians, families of peons, and representatives of the higher classes" at work and play in an environment created by American showmen. The net effect of the village was to fix fairgoers' perceptions of Mexicans as fun-loving, generally inferior beings, incapable of managing themselves or their resources.[55]

One exhibit on Midway Heights, Buffalo Bill's Wild West show, summed up the intended effect of the ethnological attractions and confirmed the midway avenue as the end point on a continuum of racial and material progress stretching to the monumental Southern Railway Building with its sixty-foot statue of *Progress* as a spire. "At Chicago," according to the *Constitution*, Buffalo Bill's show had been "accepted as 'the key to all,' and was voted the most genuine of ethnological exhibits from its composition of so many races and nationalities." It had "divided honors with the 'white city by the lake,'" dealing as it does with primitive man (of all races) in his natural condition, making it groundwork for comparison of the past with the great advancement of the arts, sciences and mechanism as presented in our exposition." Nate Salisbury, Buffalo Bill's business manager, told an interviewer that a "negro village" would also be included in the concession and that it too would have "ethnological" value.[56]

Midway Heights and Vanity Fair, like the Midway Plaisance, offered concise digests of human "types" with professed ethnological significance. Although showmen, not anthropologists, controlled the exhibits along the avenues, the absence of direct involvement by ethnologists in the midway concessions was easily compensated for by exposition authorities. Scientific validation was as near as the Smithsonian Institution's exhibit in the United States Government Building. Cooper, for instance, wrote: "The visitor who had examined the series of figures from the Smithsonian Institution, representing the various types of man, could see many of them in very live flesh and blood and by taking a turn through the Midway." Once on the avenue of fun, Cooper recorded, visitors encountered a mirror, a "vanity fair," that revealed what "but for the grace of God everyone might be." The mirror held by Smithsonian scientists produced the same effect but gave ethnological substance to the mysterious workings of God's grace.[57]

In 1906 Walter Hough, curator of the USNM's Division of Ethnology, looked back at the New Orleans exposition and likened it to the Philadelphia Centennial. He thought that both fairs had been "a golden opportunity for ethnology," for both had resulted in sizable acquisitions for the Smithsonian. Robert Edward Earll, special agent in charge of installing the Smithsonian's display at New Orleans, commented to Otis Mason: "The work is pretty well along and heaps of nice things have been borrowed, begged, or stolen, from all parts of the Exposition. Mexico has panned out nobly, as, indeed, have many other exhibits, China alone excepted." The Chinese collection, to Earll's chagrin, went to the University of Michigan. By the mid-1890s Smithsonian scientists had to reconcile themselves to giving more than they received as acquisitions from the later fairs were less numerous. But the fairs that followed the World's Columbian Exposition remained prime opportunites for ethnologists to popularize their theories about human development and for Goode to introduce the museum idea to the South.[58]

In 1884 Mason issued a circular describing the Smithsonian Institution's planned ethnological exhibit at the upcoming World's Industrial and Cotton

Fig. 26. Chinese exhibit at New Orleans. Courtesy of
Historic New Orleans Collection.

Exposition. The exhibit, he explained, would "show, as far as it can be done
with objects and labels, the present state of anthropological inquiries." "Naturally," he wrote, "at the head of the list would come those investigations that
are being made concerning the origins of man." Eight other categories of interest to anthropologists followed: biology, the development of intelligence in
animals and humans, the divisions of mankind (illustrating the classification
schemes of Blumenbach and Huxley as well as various methods for examining
facial angles and measuring the cranium), linguistics, arts, social order, religious life, and the relation of human beings to their surroundings. The organizing principle for objects designed to illustrate the origins of man set the
tone for the remainder of the exhibit: "Whatever views we may hold respecting
the productive agencies involved," Mason affirmed, "all anthropologists agree
to work upon the hypothesis of evolution, to seek for the parentage of our race
in the lower species of animals, and to regard the delinquent and criminal
classes as in some manner the return to a primitive type." To shed light on
these Mason planned to include among his displays:

1. Crania, skeletons, and brains of the different species of apes and man arranged in a progressive series.
2. Crania of defective and delinquent individuals.
3. A series of embryos illustrative of the theory that the human foetus epitomizes the early life history of the lower orders. This may be done by a set of photographs.[59]

The association of apes, "lower orders" of humanity, and criminals took on an added dimension since the exhibit as a whole generally consisted of busts of Indian chiefs and artifacts collected from North American Indian tribes and from Eskimos. If criminals were savagelike, did so-called primitive man bear criminal characteristics? Mason left this corrollary unstated. But the idea was never far from the surface as a scientific rationale for the government's Indian policy.

More indicative of the prevailing conception of evolution at the Bureau of American Ethnology, under the direction of John Wesley Powell, were the photographs relating the human fetus to "primitives." Human evolution, from this perspective, involved struggle, but not necessarily a bloodbath. Primitive men, including Indians, were believed to exist in a condition that all men had passed through at an early point in their individual and collective lives. For whatever reasons—and Mason's exhibit suggested many explanations ranging from biological to cultural—"lower orders" of man had not advanced much beyond the very earliest stage of human development. They remained, Mason and Powell believed, in much the same condition as unborn infants, requiring protection and nurture. The effect of such a view was not altogether different from that of conceptualizing "savages" as criminals. At best, lower grades of humanity, if analogous to children waiting to be born, would be treated as wards of the nation. If more like criminals or animals, they possessed no rights and must be controlled by violence. Both perspectives vindicated the twin policies of uplift and extermination variously practiced by the government.[60]

In preparing their exhibits for Atlanta and Nashville, Smithsonian officials took frequent backward glances to their highly successful performance at Chicago. Just as the World's Columbian Exposition had inspired the Field Museum, so Goode hoped to "encourage the formation of public museums in the cities of the South." Furthermore, he regarded the southern displays as illustrating "the methods by which science controls, classifies, and studies great accumulations of material objects, and uses these as a means for the discovery of truth."[61] In practice, however, what was illustrated was not so much a process of discovery as a repetition of what was assumed to be true.

At the Cotton States and International Exposition, Smithsonian and United States government officials became embroiled in a controversy over the content of the anthropology display. A correspondent from the *Richmond Times* interviewed Charles W. Dabney, assistant secretary of agriculture and chairman of the United States government board in charge of the federal exhibit at the fair. The paper quoted Dabney as saying that the Smithsonian planned to offer fairgoers "a series of figures illustrating the evolution of the Negro from the earliest animals through the ape, chimpanzee and South African Bushman, down to the Negro as he is in this country." The black commissioners to the fair and the black press were outraged. Dabney wrote to Goode claiming that he had been misquoted and had actually told the reporter that the Smithsonian was planning an exhibit of anthropoidal apes, period. Goode called the story in the *Times* "ludicrous" and denied planning any such exhibit. After consulting with Goode, one of the government board officials wrote to the newspapers demanding a correction: "How could the evolution of the Negro be shown from the earliest animals without also showing the evolution of the Caucasian from the earliest animals? How could you attempt to show the characteristics of one branch of the human family without showing the characteristics of the whole human family?" A display illustrating evolutionary linkages, in other words, would require a breadth similar to Mason's exhibit at the New Orleans fair—an exhibit that encompassed, at least in theory, the evolutionary origins of all human beings, including but not limited to Afro-Americans.[62]

Ideas about human progress along evolutionary lines were not repudiated by Smithsonian officials planning the Atlanta and Nashville exhibits, but they were modified to reflect the Smithsonian's innovative cultural groupings at the World's Columbian Exposition. Groupings depicting grades of culture again predominated. W J McGee, ethnologist-in-charge of the Bureau of American Ethnology and future director of the anthropology department at the Saint Louis fair, described the Seri Indians, illustrated in one of the groups, as "probably the most primitive Indians remaining in North America." "By reasons of their warlike and treacherous character," McGee wrote, "the Seri Indians are little known to ethnologists." The Cherokees came across only slightly better in McGee's account: "While many of the articles are acultural (or affected by the influence of the higher race)," he explained, "many illustrate fairly the aboriginal ideas of the Indians of southeastern United States."[63]

Twelve life-size figures depicting various "types" of humanity supplemented the environmental groupings at Atlanta and Nashville. Mason had a hand in organizing the display of these figures, but his chief contribution at both fairs was the exhibit of "modern savagery" originally developed for the World's Columbian Exposition. He believed that the life-size figures representing Native American, African, and Polynesian women demonstrated the rule that "in the continual struggle called Progress or Culture men have played the militant part, women the industrial part." Mason's arrangement made clear that these women performed economic functions; it also fixed an impression that they labored in lower grades of culture and were best regarded as modern savages.[64]

Within the larger contents of the southern fairs, these hierarchical displays of race and culture furnished a scientific scaffolding for the emerging ideology of the New South. Seemingly backward "types" of humanity, including blacks, could legitimately be treated as wards of the factory and field until an indeterminate evolutionary period rendered them either civilized or extinct. This idea complex assumed worldwide proportions at the midways at the Atlanta and Nashville fairs. But the far-reaching consequences of ethnological ideas about race and culture were perhaps most vividly portrayed in the Government Building at the New Orleans exposition, where, in the section given over to the Department of State, a giant globe rose above all other exhibits. This fifty-foot-tall sphere had transparent crystal sides etched with outlines of the continents and stood on a low pedestal with a short flight of steps leading visitors to its interior. Inside, fairgoers saw alcoves containing displays from United States consulates around the world. Each exhibit was arranged with reference to the particular continent depicted on the diaphanous wall immediately behind. Included among the displays were items "typifying the religious faiths of heathen lands, and the exquisite handiwork of the semi-barbarian of the distant Orient." The globe, according to one account, "was a perfect textbook of the habits, modes of life, social and political, of the countries over the seas." If the State Department's globe put the rest of the world at America's beck and call, it rotated on a conceptual axis furnished by the ethnologists at the Smithsonian.[65]

President McKinley summarized the national significance of the southern expositions in an address at the Tennessee Centennial: "The lesson of the hour, then, is this—that whatever adverse conditions may temporarily impede the pathway of our national progress, nothing can permanently defeat it." Other leading educators, politicians, and businessmen lent legitimacy to the delineations of progress projected by the fairs. Daniel Coit Gilman, president of the Johns Hopkins University, who served as chairman of the jury of awards of the Altanta exposition, described the fair as "in the highest and best sense educative." Special trains brought the sponsors of the World's Columbian Exposition to the celebrations of Chicago Day at the Atlanta and Nashville fairs. Harlow N. Higinbotham, president of Chicago's fair, gave his seal of approval to both expositions:

We are here to testify by our presence and our spoken words our appreciation of the noble work in which you have been engaged. The best work of the Exposition is the bringing of the people into contact with each other. They very naturally exchange views, compare methods, laws, religions, ideas, habits of life and the best and strongest, the healthiest and most vigorous are sure to exert the most lasting and beneficial influence. The best, whether animate or inanimate, has an inspiring and elevating influence. Contemplation of the best elevates and ennobles. The inferior are lifted up by contact with the superior race. Expositions are proper agencies to mark epochs in history—milestones, as it were, on the highway of civilization.

Chicago Day at Atlanta and Nashville marked a laying on of hands as Chicago's businessmen sanctified efforts by the New South prophets to bring about a broad consensus on the meaning of progress. Ferdinand W. Peck, vice-president of the World's Columbian Exposition Corporation, congratulated the promoters of the southern fairs for their "great work in promoting national unity." The urgency of this task was no less in 1895 and 1897 than it had been in Chicago some years earlier. Chicago's business leaders, while exuding confidence, were accompanied to the Atlanta fair by the First Regiment of the Illinois National Guard. A similar message was expressed by a Nashville minister: "There is no room in Nashville for anarchy—not a flagstaff on which to hang the red rag of socialism. We have no homes for those who are at war with American institutions." Like their northern counterparts, the directors of southern expositions hoped their fairs would provide social order through cultural inspiration and fulfill the role Grady had assigned to them as "oligarchs leading in the popular movement."[66]

Masses of southerners, black and white, visited the expositions. The World's Industrial and Cotton Exposition in New Orleans attracted 1,158,840 fairgoers; 1,286,863 people traveled to the Cotton States and International Exposition in Atlanta; and the Tennessee Centennial Exposition recorded 1,779,074 entries. Over the span of slightly more than a decade, some four million fairgoers were introduced to a vision of the New South as reflecting and contributing to the national ideology of progress. Although none of the fairs earned a dividend for its stockholders and only the Nashville exposition made a profit, they offered substantial rewards to their backers. The Atlanta directors believed their exposition "stimulated business, increased the population, and caused a larger number of improvements, both of business houses and residences." The railroads profited from passenger and freight revenues. In the case of the Nashville fair, Thomas noted that "no less than one thousand families have settled on the line of our road" as a direct result of the Tennessee Centennial. No financial recompense, however, could match the benefits the directors of the fairs derived from the special days held in their honor—generally days that attracted the largest attendances. After John W. Thomas Day, a newspaper described the president of the Nashville affair as "an honest man, made in the image of God." On Sam Inman Day at Atlanta, crowds strolled around the fairgrounds singing: "What's the matter with Inman? He's all right! / Who's all right? / Sam Inman!"[67]

Even some of the rebellious Populists joined this litany. Although Alabama Populists had helped to defeat a bill providing for a state exhibit at the Atlanta fair, Tom Watson, leader of the Georgia Populists, supported the exposition: "I do not hesitate to declare my friendship to the enterprise and my hope that

the Cotton States and International Exposition may be a magnificent success."
Watson was echoed by the Georgia-based *People's Party Paper*, which concluded that the exposition's "conception was great, its execution brilliant" and
urged its readers to visit the Smithsonian's ethnological exhibit to "notice the
different races of men."[68]

The vision of progress along racial lines tapped deep roots in southern history and cut across class lines. Not all Populists were brought into the fold of
the New South as a result of the fairs, but the expositions of the 1890s posed
a cohesive world view at a time when Populists were badly divided over strategy. The Tennessee Centennial attracted a two-day conference of Populist
leaders, including Jacob Coxey and Ignatius Donnelly, who sought "to bring
about a solidification of the ranks." They were confronted, however, by another "organizing process" that had assumed monumental form in the White
City of Nashville's fair. Drawing on history, science, and art to validate the
dream of future progress, its cultural sway found symbolic expression in construction of the Parthenon, an exact replica of the original on the Acropolis.[69]

As the most lasting visible reminder of any southern fair, the Parthenon
still stands in Nashville's Centennial Park, visited annually by more than eight
hundred thousand tourists. Historian Nathaniel Stephenson described its significance at the time it was built. He wrote that the Parthenon "was no mere
accident, rather it is the symbol of a great recovery in American life, a rein-

Fig. 27. Parthenon, Nashville. Courtesy of Smithsonian Institution
Archives, Record Unit 95, Photograph Collection.

statement of Art as the Crown of Commerce." It humanized the machine. But this monument also had an explicit racial meaning. It embodied, according to Stephenson, "the Celtic notes" that "give to the Anglo-Saxon that delicate sensibility . . . which made it possible to produce Shakespeare. Without these notes in our racial character we might still be the greatest colonizers since the Romans, but we could not be, what is perhaps even greater to be, the most poetical race since the Greeks." This "gigantic museum with immense educational value" became a permanent tribute to the efforts by southern oligarchs to promote national unity around a cluster of ideas about progress defined as Anglo-Saxon racial superiority and international economic expansion.[70]

The vision of the New South manifested at the southern fairs was not a nostalgic retreat into myth, but a powerful explanatory ideology that shaped the national and world outlook of untold numbers of southerners and other Americans while embellishing the authority of the elites that fashioned this utopian vision. In the closing decades of the century, the southern fairs succeeded in reintroducing antebellum imperial dreams to millions of fairgoers. The distinction of celebrating the fulfillment of these imperial desires, however, went to the sponsors of the Omaha, Buffalo, and Saint Louis expositions.

4

The Trans-Mississippi and International Exposition, Omaha, 1898: "Concomitant to Empire"

The Exposition has become the instrument of civilization. Being a concomitant to empire, westward it takes its way—The Crystal Palace, the Centennial, the World's Fair, The Trans-Mississippi Exposition.

Opening address by John Baldwin, 1898

In deep black one beautiful ship is encased, the base of its case a catafalque. It is a ship very dear, sadly tragically dear, to America. Above its shapely form the government has printed, in clear type "Remember the Maine."

Harper's Weekley, 1898[1]

DURING THE SUMMER OF 1898, over two and one-half million people visited another White City, a "Little City of the Beautiful," two miles from downtown Omaha, on the bluffs overlooking the Missouri River. Through the Arch of States, fairgoers first entered the Grand Court. Monumental white buildings devoted to agriculture, mining, manufacturing, fine arts, liberal arts, machinery, administration, and the United States government lined the esplanade surrounding a half-mile-long lagoon. In whiteness and neoclassical design these structures resembled the Chicago World's Columbian Exposition of 1893, but the ivy-covered colonnades that joined "the isolated masses of the great exposition buildings into a whole as with the links of a richly decorated chain" only heightened the impression of the Omaha exposition's permanence.[2]

By relegating the state buildings and midway features to separate portions of the bluff tract and north tract, the exposition builders enhanced the overall symmetry of the fair. Rudolph Ulrich, a New York landscape architect, transformed the southern portion of the bluff, the area given to the state structures and to the Horticultural Building, from "corn stubble" into a flowering, tree-

Fig. 28. Omaha's White City. Courtesy of Smithsonian Institution Archives, Record Unit 95, Photograph Collection.

Fig. 29. Grand Court, Omaha. Courtesy of Smithsonian Institution Archives, Record Unit 95, Photograph Collection.

lined park. His arcadian creation, with the White City looming in the background, offered tangible evidence for exposition president Gurdon Wattles's declaration: "The Great American Desert is no more."[3]

Walking northward on the bluff, fairgoers left Eden behind and entered the Midway, a "[p]layground of all nations . . . with the accompanying pandemonium." Since most foreign nations had declined to participate because of doubts about Omaha's ability to hold a world's fair, the exposition's Midway concessions provided much of the substance for claims by the exposition directors to have international participation in their celebration. As visitors walked along the entertainment avenue, which made two sharp turns back to the White City, they saw the world presented as an amusing cabaret, as an odd assortment of "types" represented in villages or by restaurant concessions, with each building designed in an architectural form "peculiar to the nationality depicted."[4]

After exhausting the Midway attractions, fairgoers reentered the White City behind the Administration Building and saw the vistas of the palatial city that spread before them in sharp contrast to the "kaleidoscopic jumble of grotesque shapes and flaring colors along the Midway streets." Fairgoers, wrote a correspondent for Harper's Weekly, "see only that the buildings are a blinding, dazzling mass of white. I have seen men and women stand stupefied at the entrance of the Grand Court, blinded as they would have been by a flash of lightning." Most of the visitors, according to this account, were "hard-working people" who left the fair with "memories that will make all the rest of their lives brighter and more hopeful." Visitors arriving at the White City at dusk were treated to a slightly different visual spectacle as thousands of incandescent lights illuminated the fairgrounds and, in the process, dramatized the underlying unity of the exposition. The electrical decoration culminated each evening, according to the exposition's official historian, when "the ray of a powerful searchlight is seen shooting from the torch in the hand of the heroic statue of 'Liberty Enlightening the World,' which surmounts the Government building, and the picture of fairyland is made complete."[5]

This beacon for all the world to see signaled the imminent realization of earlier dreams about an American overseas empire. On 16 February 1898 the battleship *Maine* sank off the coast of Havana. Two months later, the United States embarked on a "splendid little war," which began auspiciously for the Americans with Admiral Dewey's victory over the Spanish fleet in Manila Bay. During the first six months of the year, the exposition nearly disappeared from public view as newspapers filled their columns with war news. But the fair concluded as the focal point for the national Peace Jubilee, which President McKinley sanctioned by his presence. Omaha's exposition provided more than a convenient site for the celebration. From the moment it opened in June, the fair provided ideological scaffolding for mass support for the government's imperial policies. Through a massive gathering of Indians into an ethnologically validated Indian Congress, located on a multiacre site adjacent to the Midway, the exposition's promoters explained past and future national and international expansion as the natural outcome of America's westward expansion and Anglo-Saxon racial development. In his opening day address John L. Webster, a prominent attorney, stated the central theme of the fair: "In the fulfillment of our destiny, and to hold trade and commerce within our grasp, we have to work out the problem of universal civilization." Sponsors of the fair attempted to make this task a shared cultural imperative.[6]

Just before opening day, a local clergyman inquired rhetorically of his congregation: "Did this exposition all come together by chance, by accident? Don't you know it was the result of design? So with the stars above." The exposition had several designers. Five railroads contributed large sums of money. Utility companies, banks, newspapers, breweries, stockyards, meatpacking houses, mercantile interests, and insurance companies also invested in the enterprise. The Union National Bank contributed more than cash; its first vice-president, Gurdon W. Wattles, a railroad investor and member of the executive board of the Omaha Commercial Club, served as president of the exposition corporation. These sponsors shared a common anxiety about the aftershocks of the 1893 depression, and like the backers of the Atlanta (1895) and Nashville (1897) fairs, had been deeply impressed by the economic and cultural successes of the World's Columbian Exposition.[7]

Lingering memories of the 1893 depression and subsequent outbursts of class violence coupled with the recollections of the many triumphs of the Chicago World's Fair sparked several midwestern businessmen's organizations into action. One was the Trans-Mississippi Commercial Congress, a league of

Fig. 30. Model of the *Maine* in United States Government Building.
Courtesy of Smithsonian Institution Archives, Record Unit 95, Photograph
Collection.

commercial leaders concerned with promoting the economic growth of the
West through industrialization and development of international markets. At
its eighth annual meeting, Dudley Smith, head of an Omaha grocery firm and
Nebraska commissioner to the San Francisco Midwinter Fair of 1894, drew up
a resolution urging the United States government to support a world's fair in
Omaha in 1898. William Jennings Bryan introduced the resolution to the convention, and it was unanimously endorsed. In Omaha, another businessmen's
association, the Knights of Ak-Sar-Ben, also gave its enthusiastic endorsement
to the exposition.[8]

An adjunct of the Omaha Commercial Club, Ak-Sar-Ben (an anagram for
Nebraska), had begun in 1894 as a businessmen's fraternity, complete with
secret rituals and initiations inspired by Washington Irving's account of Co-
ronado's quest for gold in the mythical kingdom of Quivera. The Knights
sought to provide a "soothing tonic to entertain and cheer a depressed people"
through pageants modeled after the Mardi Gras celebration in New Orleans.
In 1897 Ak-Sar-Ben's elixir combined with the plans for the upcoming fair in
a notable parade. "Twenty floats," according to the souvenir program, "designed and built in Omaha, at a cost of $20,000, covered with living figures
in superb costumes, escorted by mounted knights and ten bands, pass through
three miles of streets illuminated by strings of incandescent lights, making the

most beautiful fall festival in the United States." The procession of floats, recapitulating the fable of the Seven Cities of Cibola, illustrated Nebraska's wealth of natural resources and concluded with two tableaux depicting "Welcome Prosperity" and the "Trans-Mississippi Exposition." From the porticos of the float devoted to the fair, muses representing art, science, and literature tossed flowers to the throngs lining the streets.[9]

These expensive and intensive efforts to boost the fair suggested that support for the enterprise was not automatically forthcoming from all Nebraskans. Bryan's ardent advocacy of the exposition had little influence on many Populists in the state legislature, who mounted a concerted assult on the state's exposition appropriation bill that came up for discussion in early 1897. Populist leader Charles Wooster denounced the Trans-Mississippi Congress as "a 'job lot of politicians' who imposed the idea of an exposition on the people." He called attention to the fact that the exposition directors, with one exception, were from Omaha and expressed grave doubts about the benefits the fair would have for Nebraska's farmers. Instead of providing funds for an exposition, Wooster urged that the proposed appropriation be used to pay off the state debts accumulating from people's inability to pay taxes. "It seems to me," he observed, "that with the present condition of our people it is damnable to ask for money for that Omaha show."[10]

On a seventy-to-twenty vote, the legislators approved funds for the exposition, but Wooster succeeded in reducing the amount allocated for the fair. Opposition remained intense. Several months after the legislative battle, a supporter of the fair wrote from Wayne urging exposition officials to "commence a system of missionary efforts in the rural districts of this state among the masses of the people in the interests of the Exposition, or all hope so far as Nebraska is concerned will be lost." Hostility to the exposition "now fills the hearts and souls of three fourths of the common people of this state," the correspondent warned, and offered, for a $100 per month retainer, to proselyte on behalf of the fair in rural areas of the state. "Missionating" for the fair also became one of the projects of Nebraska women's clubs. "Pin on your walls illustrations of the grounds and buildings," urged one club member. "The colored views given in the different Nebraska journals are worthy of a hanging place in any room, and, if looked at often enough and through the right sort of eyes, will enable one to feel quite at home while at the exposition, especially while taking a lesure [sic] stroll through the grand court." The exposition also received advertising assistance from the federal government. The Post Office, following precedent established at the Philadelphia Centennial Exhibition of 1876, distributed commemorative postage stamps through approximately seventy thousand post offices across the country. This stamp issue, the *Omaha Bee* explained, "gives to the project the prestige of government recognition and support."[11]

The individual mainly responsible for advertising was Edward Rosewater, head of the exposition's Department of Publicity, owner of the *Omaha Bee*, and one of the largest individual stockholders in the fair. Just when other promotional activities were getting under way, Rosewater introduced a plan he believed would create a groundswell of interest in the exposition. In August 1897 Rosewater proposed "an extensive exhibit illustrative of the life, and customs and decline of the aboriginal inhabitants of the western hemisphere." "This grand ethnological exhibit, " he argued, "undoubtedly would be the last gathering of these tribes before the bronze sons of the forests and plains, who have resisted the encroachments of the white man, are gathered to the happy hunting ground."[12]

The idea appealed to the organizers of the fair. The following month the Knights of Ak-Sar-Ben unveiled a float entitled "The Vanquished Races," which appeared at midpoint in the same procession that included the exposition tableau. This float, according to the parade program, illustrated the lesson that "[t]he retirement of the Spaniards left the prairies for a century more to their Indian owners and vast herd of buffaloes, both destined to fade away before a mightier race." Before the same message was institutionalized in the Indian Congress at the Trans-Mississippi and International Exposition, it attracted the interest of ethnologists from the Bureau of American Ethnology (BAE) at the Smithsonian Institution.[13]

One month after Ak-Sar-Ben's parade, BAE ethnologist James Mooney arrived in Omaha for a conference with Rosewater about the Indian exhibit. Mooney's ethnological credentials were impressive. He had worked in the bureau since 1885, compiling data for John Wesley Powell's linguistic map. His interests included Native American religions, especially the Ghost Dance and the use of peyote in Native American worship. Mooney, moreover, was an expert in the matter of Indian exhibits at expositions. For the BAE displays at the Chicago and Nashville fairs, he had installed exhibits depicting Kiowa life, including his much-acclaimed miniature Kiowa camping circle at the Tennessee Centennial Exposition.[14]

When Rosewater first conceived the idea for an Indian exhibit, he acknowledged that its success depended on the support of BAE ethnologists. But he went one step further than simply requesting Mooney's advice. Rosewater asked him "to draw up an Indian plan" for the fair, and Mooney complied. The ethnologist's first step was to reduce the scope of Rosewater's initial plans. Where the newspaper publisher wanted Indian representatives from every tribe in North and South America to live around a gigantic Indian wigwam, Mooney suggested instead "a representation based upon house types" as part of a "giant relief map of nations" on the fifty acres of land set aside for the exhibit. Mooney believed that his plan would be more manageable but doubted that the exposition management would completely agree with his ideas because it was becoming increasingly apparent that the directors were

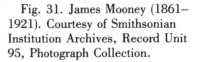

Fig. 31. James Mooney (1861–
1921). Courtesy of Smithsonian
Institution Archives, Record Unit
95, Photograph Collection.

hampered by "limitations of time, space and money." Mooney nonetheless
came away from his conferences with the exposition directors with a firm conviction that they wanted only "genuine presentations and not of the dime museum order." Rosewater impressed Mooney so favorably that he urged W J
McGee, ethnologist-in-charge at the BAE, to give Rosewater all possible assistance. Not since the Chicago World's Fair had exposition builders offered
ethnologists such a preeminent role. But as a United States Senate report
made clear, the importance the exposition promoters attached to ethnology
related to their imperial ambitions.[15]

In December 1897 Nebraska Senator William V. Allen placed Rosewater's
proposal for an Indian exhibit before the heads of the various executive departments that would have to approve the display. Following the position taken
by the government at previous fairs, Allen's letter noted the reciprocal benefits
to accrue to Indians and fairgoers from such "instructive" displays. Yet, rather
than stressing that the exhibit planned for the Omaha fair was similar to Native American exhibits at earlier fairs held in the United States, he emphasized that the Indian Congress would be modeled after colonial exhibits at
recent European fairs. "Foreign Governments," Allen commented, "which
have held or promoted great world's fairs in recent years—notably France and
Belgium—have made these the occasion of bringing from their remotest colonies and dependencies families, groups, and even whole villages of aborigines, and have found their profit in the educational advantages which strange
people mutually afford when brought into contact." Motives of educational
uplift notwithstanding, the Indian Congress would also have the effect of reminding white Americans that they were anything but newcomers to the imperial arena and suggest that the government's Indian policy was applicable
to "aborigines" abroad.[16]

Allen included his letter in the "Report from the Committee on Indian Affairs," which he offered to his congressional colleagues in support of the federal appropriation bill for the Indian exhibit. The report also contained endorsements from John Wesley Powell, head of the BAE, Cornelius N. Bliss, secretary of the interior, Herbert Welsh, secretary of the Indian Rights Association, and A. C. Tonner, acting commissioner of the Office of Indian Affairs. Powell found the plan meritorious because it would give fairgoers a chance "to understand more clearly the nature and characteristics of savagery and the problem which is presented to the Indian department in the endeavor to lift the aboriginal inhabitants of the country into the status of civilization." Welsh wrote that he could think of "no better means of reaching the popular mind, and touching the warm and true instincts of the American heart, than by such an object lesson as this." The "striking contrast between the original savage condition of the Indian" and the educated Indian in government schools, Welsh suggested, would demonstrate the value of private and governmental philanthropic efforts. Bliss and Tonner also endorsed the Indian Congress. Tonner, however, qualified his support by recommending that the entire display be supervised by an army officer. [17]

The Indian Congress seemed destined to be ready by opening day, until hostilities with Spain erupted in February. As Congress turned its attention to the war, all projects not directly related to military preparations went into abeyance, including the Indian Congress. A week before the fair opened in June, Rosewater pleaded with Allen to do everything in his power to expedite the congressional appropriation. "This is one place," the *Omaha Bee* sourly commented, "where the war and the exposition have come in conflict." Rosewater found the delays "very embarrassing," yet he clung to plans for the exhibit that he believed would become the "best drawing card" of the fair. If funding was the problem, Rosewater wrote to the secretary of interior, the exposition directors were prepared to use their own financial resources for the display. [18]

Throughout this period of waiting for congressional action, plans for the exhibit moved ahead. The War Department and Bureau of Indian Affairs selected army captain William A. Mercer, acting agent of the Omaha and Winnebago Agency, to oversee the Indian Congress. After consulting with Mercer, Rosewater completely abandoned his original intention of including representatives from all Indian tribes, because Indians "who had seldom come in touch with whites would prove a more attractive feature." While Rosewater awaited final word on federal funds, the Bureau of Indian Affairs sent a circular to its agents around the country explaining the proposed display: "It is desired that the encampment should be as thoroughly aboriginal in every respect as practicable, and that the primitive traits and characteristics of the several tribes should be distinctly set forth." [19]

On 30 June, one month after the exposition opened, Congress made $40,000 available for the Indian exhibit as part of the Indian Appropriation

Bill. Mercer hastily asked Indian agents "to invite" Indian delegations to participate. Most of the Indians declined, but this refusal did not deter the federal agents. "It was wholly a case of persuasion," according to one journalist. "The agents were instructed to send old men and head men as far as possible—typical representatives of the old-time Indian before the Government introduced its system of civilization."[20]

The Indian Congress opened for public inspection on 4 August. Captain Mercer began the festivities of "Indian Day" by taking 150 of "his children" to parade through the streets of Omaha and thence to the site just off the Midway set aside for the Indian Congress. Mercer had earlier requested a United States flag "of the largest size" for the occasion, noting that "[t]he desirability of having the U.S. flag floating over the Congress of American Indian tribes, when installed, can hardly be questioned." The Indian band played the "Star-Spangled Banner" as the flag was raised, while the Indians demonstrated their "mark of respect to the flag" by giving three loud cheers. After the band played "Yankee Doodle," Mercer adjourned the Congress for a dinner break, reminding the participants to reconvene for a parade through the exposition grounds later in the afternoon.[21]

This procession along the Midway avenues and across the Bluff Tract—but evidently not through the White City proper—represented one of the high points of the exposition. Thousands of spectators lined the streets as exposition police led the way from the encampment onto the Midway, followed by Indian musicians and hundreds of men and women on foot. Mercer, astride a horse, came next in the procession at the head of "150 reds [sic] mounted upon horses and dressed in war costumes." Many of the Indians on horseback "waved with great satisfaction great bunches of flesh, to which was attached hair, not human flesh and hair, but flesh and hair torn from a beef that had been slaughtered during the morning hours." When the parade eventually concluded back at the encampment, visitors, for a twenty-five-cent admission fee, could see the Indians "amuse and entertain" through athletic events, music, and dance. That evening, before the exhibit closed, fairgoers were informed that the following day the program would be different, including "a scalp dance . . . together with some horse races and ball games."[22]

During the two months until the fair closed in late October, fairgoers apparently could wander through the Indian encampment at will, beginning at eight in the morning. Pennants in front of the tents and tepees identified the tribal names of their inhabitants, and visitors could observe Indians living in family groups, preparing meals, performing religious ceremonies, and generally acting out their "aboriginality." The leading feature of the exhibit, however, was the sham battle between whites and Indians or, occasionally, between Native Americans themselves.[23]

The idea for this feature came from a fraternal organization of white businessmen, the Improved Order of Red Men. Several weeks before the Indian

Congress opened, a delegation from this group persuaded Mercer to allow the Native Americans under his charge to participate in a battle between cowboys and "friendly Indians" (i.e., the Improved Order of Red Men) on the one hand, and the Native Americans of the Indian Congress, "who were supposed to be hostile," on the other. Three hours before starting time, Mercer received a message from the Improved Order that most of their members would not arrive in time to participate. Thrown back on his own resources, he quickly drew up his own plans. He borrowed guns from the cadet team of an Omaha high school and bought a large number of blank cartridges. Frank Mattox and Rattlesnake Pete, proprietors of the Midway's Wild West show, responded to Mercer's urgent request to participate and bring their Indian entertainers into the fray. By six o'clock the captain had rounded up nearly seven hundred Indian and white performers. The sham battle would be outdoor theater on a monumental scale.[24]

Mercer himself held top billing as a renegade white man, "Wyoke Nicyople Tigurebli Acolthy, or Great Man Who Fights Them All," at the head of a group of Indians hostile to white settlers. The show opened with Mercer and his allies asleep in camp. A Brulé Sioux hurried into camp, waking Mercer with the news that they were about to be attacked. Mercer, with two other white renegades (his assistants from the Indian Office), grabbed binoculars and took stock of the cloud of dust rising beyond the exposition's Dairy Building. Several horsemen appeared in the distance, and Mercer roused his sleep-

Fig. 32. Sham battle. Courtesy of National Anthropology Archives.

ing comrades with a piercing war cry. He leaped on his horse and tore through camp to tell the Indians of the pending battle. The Indian men, "painted and bedecked with feathers," took the women and children a safe distance away and returned to prepare for battle. Mattox's forces descended on Mercer's allies, forcing the Indians to retreat to the forested area of the encampment. But Mercer rallied his ranks. "Uttering a war whoop that froze the blood of the spectators, they charged the whites and drove them across the field," noted the *Omaha Bee*'s correspondent.[25]

In the course of their retreat, many of Mattox's forces were "scalped or turned over to the squaws, who were following in the wake of the savages like so many vultures." The "piteous" cries of the captured whites created the impression that the women "tortured their victims in the most heartless manner." While the women took their captives back to the village, Mercer's renegades pursued Mattox to the Dairy Building and were just on the verge of victory when the United States army arrived on the scene and captured or killed most of the Indians. Mercer, however, slipped back to the Indian Village. Mattox, his numbers now substantially increased, decided to move on the village "and wipe out the entire savage outfit." As they approached the Indian Village, scalped and "horribly mutilated" comrades lay on the ground, and the screams of captured soldiers hailed the arrival of the troops. T. G. Maggarell, "one of the prominent Redmen" of Omaha, was one of several leading citizens tied to trees and surrounded by dancing Indians, "whooping and yelling, singing their war songs, while the squaws were plucking brands from the fires and pushing the burning ends into the sizzling flesh of the poor creatures." This was too much for Mattox. He led his men into the midst of the village, clubbing "savages" left and right until they finally released the captives. All of the Indians surrendered, but Mercer put up one last fight before finally giving in. For Wyoke Nicyople Tigurebli Acolthy the moment of truth finally arrived when Mattox told him that the battle had ended and his Indian followers had been nearly "wiped from the face of the earth." Confronted by this situation, Mercer promised "to quit his roving life and settle down and become [an] Indian agent, if given a chance." Mattox acceded to his request and proclaimed that Mercer would take charge of the Omaha Agency. The show concluded with Mercer leading the Indians to the reservation.[26]

Spectators were thrilled by the performance, and the *Omaha Bee* called the sham battle a "brilliant success." For the next two and one-half months it would be repeated many times before thousands of fairgoers. There was, however, a dissenting voice from a government employee.[27]

Shortly before the opening of the Indian Congress, James Mooney, temporarily transferred from the BAE to the Bureau of Indian Affairs to gather fair material, returned from Oklahoma with 106 Kiowas, their ponies, and selected artifacts, including a Wichita grass house. When he saw the state of affairs in the Indian Congress and heard about the proposed sham battle, his high hopes for ethnology dwindled. "This grass house & tipi & windbreak—for both of which the Exposition management paid—constitute about the only ethnology on the grounds as outlined in the original plans or in the circular from the Commissioner," Mooney informed McGee. The remainder of the Indian Congress, he lamented, "has degenerated into a Wild West show with the sole purpose of increasing gate receipts." Yet despite his difficulties with Mercer and his dejected comment to McGee that "in this place an ethnologist's time is wasted & his labor lost," Mooney commended the exposition management, especially Rosewater, for incorporating his suggestions wherever possible and for using exposition funds to pay many of the costs he incurred. Furthermore, far from totally repudiating the ethnological value of the Indian Congress, the BAE ethnologist wrote an article for the *American Anthropologist* in which he detailed the ethnological characteristics of various Indians who had participated in the exhibit and noted that the display had succeeded in increasing interest in anthropology. His own efforts, he suggested in passing, had enhanced the ethnological verisimilitude of the show. Not the least of his contributions were the performances of the Ghost Dance he organized and the foot races he arranged to measure the stamina of the Indians.[28]

Mooney did try to dissociate himself and the BAE from the sideshow aspects that prevailed in the Indian exhibit, but his attempts to find and create ethnologically redeeming features in the display served to confirm the widespread feeling that the exhibit was an authentic portrayal of Indian life. The Indian Congress, according to the *American Review of Reviews*, was "something genuine in a wilderness—a howling wilderness—of Midway fakes." Its "great charm," according to the *State* magazine, "is its genuineness. It rings true and is just what it was intended to represent—affording a scientific study of aboriginal race and tribe, and at the same time is spectacular in feature and vivid in color." Alice French, writing for *Cosmopolitan*, was even more emphatic: "It is not a Wild West show, but a serious ethnological exhibit."[29]

The exposition caught Indians between the goals of the scientific and entertainment professions. Three Native Americans died while the exhibit was open; one Indian woman attempted suicide. Geronimo, brought to the Congress along with twenty-one other Apaches as prisoners of war from Fort Sill, described the political reality of the exposition for Native Americans: "Right here at the exposition are enough people coming every day to put an end to every Indian in the world if they saw fit to do so. Then, besides this, the white men have all of the guns, powder and bullets. They have all of the big guns and they are the ones that count." "I am an old man," Geronimo told his interviewer, "and I want to see my people learn the ways of the whites. I want to see them raise corn and cattle and live in houses and I believe that the president and the big men at Washington will help my people if they will try to help themselves." Geronimo's faith, born of defeat, reflected one of two alternatives the exposition promoters offered Native Americans.[30]

The other was extinction. " 'Caesar, we who are about to die, salute you,' " was Alice French's rendering of the epic significance of the Indian Congress. The words from the traditional salute of the gladiators in the Roman games were apt, French wrote, because the "Indians who are dancing in the smiling Omaha fields . . . are doomed." To her poetic sensibilities, there was "something dramatic in this idea of a great meeting of a vanishing race."[31]

The dramatic counterpoint of the Indian Congress turned precisely on the relation of the ethnological exhibit to the exposition as a whole. According to Mary Alice Harriman, in the *Overland Monthly*, the Indian Congress testified to "the Indian as the Alpha of the alphabet of American history, as the exposition, with its wealth of accumulated inventions, of art, science, and culture, is its Omega." Fay Fuller put it more bluntly: "The object lesson of the Congress of American Indians in connection with the Trans-Mississippi Exposition is that of progress." It was a lesson many fairgoers internalized as historical time and space collapsed within the boundaries of the fair.

> From the primitive, crude, wigwams of the aborigines the visitor walks beneath the evening sky, star strewn and blue as Puget Sound, to gaze upon the Royal Court of the Grand Canal, the triumph of illuminating the masterpiece of the Exposition, and when he remembers that less than half a century ago the same docile Omahas, who are peacefully dozing to-night by their campfires within the Exposition gates, were waging the war of the tomahawk and bow on these very grounds, the heroic march of civilization and the progress of American development is told.

Reminding fairgoers of a heroically defined past, however, was also part of the directors' attempt to shape the future. "To see these ever formidable and hereditary enemies of the white man encamped together in a frame of architectural splendor erected by courage, manhood, and sterling integrity," the *Omaha Bee* observed, "will impress upon the growing sons and daughters a lesson which will bear fruit in years hence when the yet unsettled and uncultivated possessions of the United States shall have become jewels upon the Star Spangled Banner." On a more sober note, Rosewater wrote that "Uncle Sam's wards in Cuba and the Philippines are liable to be as intractable as his wards on the Indian reservations." Much of the rest of the world also seemed closer to "savagery" than "civilization" along the path to the White City from the Indian Congress blazing across the Midway.[32]

"At the Passing Show," Henry Wysham Lanier wrote for the *Monthly Review of Reviews*, "Moorish villages and Cairo streets, African savages and Southern darkies, with their cake-walks, songs, and varied old-time plantation activities, Chinese, Japanese, and other Eastern people—examples of all these help the Caucasian to a clearer understanding of the many races and civilizations besides his own, while European countries are almost without exception brought to the visitor's attention."[33]

A number of familiar shows appeared on the Midway at Omaha. The Afro-American Village, also called the Old Plantation, came straight from the 1897 Nashville fair. Managed by veteran showman Emmett W. McConnell, one portion of the village consisted of thirty-five to seventy-five "jolly, rollicking 'niggers' " living in slave cabins transported from the South. In another section of the exhibit were displays illustrating the "advancement" of black since emancipation. With Aunt Jemimah serving pancakes from a griddle in the Home Kitchen of the Manufacturing Building, the Omaha exposition promoters successfully consigned blacks to a class apart and introduced midwesterners to the paradigm of race relations advocated by the designers of the New South.[34]

The Chinese Village on the Midway, in connection with a separate display supposedly involving Chinese artisans, had an equally stark impact. Organized by Hip Lung, a Chicago merchant, with the help of Hong Sling, the Union Pacific Railroad's Chinese agent, the Chinese Village was modeled after similar villages at earlier fairs. The Wong Chin Foo Trading Company of Chicago initially promoted the artisans' exhibit to demonstrate the manufacturing capabilities of Chinese. Furthermore, as explained in the press, a collateral purpose of the exhibit involved demonstrating that Chinese from northern China, unlike the "lowest type" from the South, would make desirable immigrants to America and excellent workers. Wong's company, backed by wealthy Chinese in Chicago, New York, and Hong Kong, received permission from the United States government to bring 238 "artisans" to the fair. By the end of the exposition all of them had vanished.[35]

Wan Loy, one of the agents for Wong's company, explained that none of the Chinese brought to the fair ever intended to return to China and that the exhibit of artisans at work in various trades never materialized. Actually the display consisted only of a small curio store and served Chicago and New York trading companies as a front for circumventing the immigration restriction laws. The *Omaha Bee* commented on this turn of events at the fair in its headline: "HEATHEN CHINEE IS SMOOTH." This was the same message the backers of the Chinese Village had fostered over the preceding months with its advertisements for "opportunities for witnessing the sly tricks of the 'heathen Chinee.' " Racial stereotypes of the Chinese, in short, enabled the promoters of the exposition—the Union Pacific Railroad, significantly, contributed money both to the exposition and to the Chinese Village—to encourage visions of the fabled China market and to acquire an additional supply of cheap labor.[36]

Buffalo Bill arrived in Omaha in late August for a two-day show downtown and was honored with a special day at the fair. For the occasion the exposition

management organized an "ethnological parade" billed as "the greatest ethnological event in the history of the world." Cody headed the procession,
which included Cuban troops who had fought the Spanish, Midway villagers,
and Native Americans from the Indian Congress. This master showman, the
Omaha Bee declared, "has issued an educational supplement so to speak,
which will teach lastingly the splendid position held by Uncle Sam in the
council of powers of the earth."[37]

Other shows also stressed patriotic and imperial themes. Passengers on the
Scenic Railway saw "a representation of the BATTLE OF MANILA" on the walls
of the Giant Tunnel. Another amusement feature presented "a miniature bom-
bardment of Cuban forts." The popular showman Henry Roltair presented an
even more spectacular performance, complete with stereopticon slides, music,
and fireworks, depicting the passage of the battleship *Maine* from New York
to Havana, the destruction of the ship, and the funeral of the soldiers. "The
next picture," according to the *Omaha Bee*, "showed Uncle Sam ready to
avenge the destruction of the battleship." A flotilla of naval vessels and portraits of generals followed, and the show concluded with President McKinley's
portrait.[38]

Another show on the Midway brought home the immediate imperial gains of
the war in even more dramatic fashion. According to the exposition's official
historian, there was a Philippine Village on the entertainment street. This
village probably consisted of artifacts until late in the exposition season, when
George D. Steele brought "sixteen Manila warriors" to Omaha en route to
Washington, D.C. When Steele told a *World-Herald* correspondent that "a
portion of the party has cannibalistic proclivities," he confirmed an image of
the Filipinos as savages that had been building over the preceding several
months. As early as July the same newspaper had commended Admiral Dewey
for requisitioning sixty thousand pounds of soap for the Philippines: "Soap
and the Bible go hand in hand, figuratively speaking, in the development of
the backward races, and that cleanliness is next to godliness is a self evident
truth." Rosewater's *Omaha Bee*, on the other hand, put little credence in
either. "The fact is the Filipinos as a people are instinctively untruthful, dis-
honest, and insincere. Their faults are racial and are not due to Spanish treatment, though very likely this treatment has operated to more strongly develop
them." Where the promoters of future expositions would try to convince Americans of the value of possessing overseas territory, the directors of the Omaha
fair helped to ensure that the national debate over annexation would take
place in racial terms with national policy toward the Indians as the immediate
frame of reference.[39]

Ideas about racial hierarchy and progress permeated the Trans-Mississippi
and International Exposition, but they came into sharp focus during the Peace
Jubilee Week, particularly on the days set aside to pay homage to President

McKinley and to honor America's youth. McKinley's presence at the fair assured the success of the exposition in the immediate present; Children's Day
formed part of the attempt to ensure the fair's impact on the next generation.

McKinley received an awesome reception in Omaha. Thousands of people
jammed the city, only to find lodging wholly inadequate. On the morning of
the president's speech between seventy-five and one hundred thousand people
crowded into the Plaza on the Bluff Tract. Somehow, as the carriage bearing
McKinley and Wattles made its way through a path kept clear by a regiment
of Second Nebraska Volunteers, people managed to wave flags and handker-
chiefs, "while their voices united in a succession of tremendous cheers that
made the Plaza ring." Wattles fueled this patriotic fervor with his introductory
remarks: "All honor to the soldiers and their commanders who have so gal-
lantly planted the American flag where it will assure the blessings of liberty
and God. All hail to the chief who sent to a suffering people the humanity of
a mighty nation. All hail to our guest, our ruler, our president."[40]

McKinley graciously acknowledged the uproar that greeted him and responded with an address about America's progress. He compared the Omaha
exposition to the Philadelphia, New Orleans, Chicago, Atlanta, and Nashville
expositions. These others, he noted, "are now a part of the past, and yet in
influence they still live, and their beneficent results are closely interwoven
with our national development." American development reflected a universal
principle. "One of the great laws of life," McKinley declared, "is progress and
nowhere have the principles of this law been so strikingly illustrated as in the
United States." The quick victory over Spain confirmed America's divine or-
dination, McKinley added, but continued grace—and progress—entailed assuming "international responsibilities." He conceded that much remained unknown about the consequences of the war. Nevertheless, he assured
Americans: "Right action follows right purpose."[41]

As if to demonstrate his faith in this dictum, the president paid a visit to
the Government Building, with its mass of Spanish-American War relics, and
to the Indian Congress. He regarded the Indian Congress as so important that
he had informed friends before his arrival in Omaha that "this was the one
feature of the exposition that he did not wish to miss." Mercer planned an
extraordinary spectacle for the presidential visit and "fully impressed the Indians with the great honor of performing before the 'great father.' " As Mc-
Kinley proceeded to the viewing stands, the Indians stood by quietly while
many thousands of whites cheered wildly. Then, on a signal from Mercer, the
Indian band "blared forth a gay martial air," and the Indians joined in with a
"chorus of yells and chants." With over five thousand spectators watching,
Mercer introduced each tribe by name to McKinley, and the president "graciously doffed his hat in response to the greetings" of the Native Americans.
The "climax of the program" came with the sham battle.[42]

In contrast to the performance on the first day the Indian Congress opened to the public, the sham presented to McKinley involved Indians fighting each other, not whites. Mock burnings at the stake, scalpings, and mutilations again characterized the performance of the "fantastically or ridiculously attired Indians." Thus the show depicted both the "degeneracy" of Native Americans and the paternal role of government. Described as "alarming," full of "serious possibilities," it nonetheless left the impression that the federal government had the matter of "savagery" well under control. While the Indians pretended to destroy each other, McKinley, according to the *Omaha Bee*, "appeared to study rather than to take amusement out of the spectacle," and after the battle concluded he bowed "a kindly greeting to the redmen."[43]

The *Omaha Bee* perceived the ideological implications of these transactions in the following terms:

> Yesterday morning President McKinley received the homage of a
> hundred thousand representatives of a race that stands at the pinnacle

PRESIDENT McKINLEY AND PARTY ENTERING THE GRAND PLAZA

Fig. 33. President's Day at Omaha. From James B. Haynes, *History of the Trans-Mississippi and International Exposition of 1898.*

of the greatest civilization of the world's history and of a nation that in
the opinion of many statesmen is just commencing to play its great part
upon the stage of the universe. In the afternoon the president was
rendered honor by a thousand representatives of a passing civilization
that was in its way great and of a dying nation that acted within its
limitations as magnificent.[44]

And what of the future? Appropriately, the exposition's Peace Jubilee Week
concluded with a special day devoted to children.

Youth had long occupied the attention of the exposition promoters. As early
as March, the *Omaha Bee* had advised parents to bring their children to the
fair. Youngsters "are unusually impressionable," Rosewater wrote, "and the
exposition will be to most of them a revelation of the wonders of the world.
They will carry through life the mental picture of the new White City . . .
comprehending the whole exposition as typical of the advancement of the human race" and as "an invaluable school." Women's clubs endorsed this viewpoint and encouraged women to do their part in driving these lessons
home: "The mother can so trend the mind of her boy and girl that, when
passing through Machinery Hall, the wonderful engines will mean to them not
simply iron and steel and noise; but, beyond all that they will realize a something almost akin to human, which gives to the machine a personality second
only to that of its inventor." But to get the most from the experience, children
must be prepared in advance. "Special, previous, mind culture is the thing
that will get it best and quickest." The exposition directors pressed the same
theme with a campaign in the public schools urging that pupils raise money
to purchase exposition stock. Schoolchildren also contributed funds for a Boy's
and Girl's Building—an edifice that women's clubs around the state decided
to place in the White City in lieu of a Woman's Building. Just before the
exposition opened, moreover, the *Omaha Bee* mobilized children in Omaha to
clean the streets of the city in anticipation of thousands of visitors—and prospective residents.[45]

Through the summer, children visited the fair in large numbers. On Children's Day, held at the end of Jubilee Week, they were admitted free. "As
was to be expected," the *World-Herald* observed, "there was a larger number
than usual of the more poorly clad children and some of them after a long ride
reached the grounds chilled and shivering." "Everybody noticed the little people and seemed trying to take pains that they should have a good time," the
paper reported. "The distributors of advertising cards and booklets were especially kind to them, and few children there were who did not soon possess
a load of brightly printed stuff or have hanging about them gaily colored
cards." Advertising cards, however, were only one of many memories. Before
wandering about the grounds, many children who visited the fair in groups
were expected to memorize—and sing—"The Trans-Mississippi Ode for Girls
and Boys":

> All honor to the men of brain,
> Who first proposed to build it.
> And those who followed in their train
> Whose energy fulfilled it.
> The great Trans-Mississippi States
> Deserve congratulations,
> They've opened wide the Western gates
> To commerce of the nations.
>
> For boys and girls, some day, you'll see
> The Pillars of the Nation,
> But never will forgotten be,
> This day of Jubilation.
> And to our Father, good and great,
> We offer this petition,
> God bless our Flag: God bless our State
> And bless our Exposition.[46]

"Who said Omaha could not 'swing' a great exposition?" the *World-Herald* crowed on the final day of the fair. The Trans-Mississippi fair lived up to and perhaps even surpassed the most optimistic expectations of its sponsors. Not only did it attract 2,718,508 visitors, but it returned a 92.5 percent dividend to its stockholders.[47] So great was its success that Omaha businessmen reopened it the following July under a new name: the Greater America Exposition. The sponsors announced that the purpose was "to exploit the wonders of the colonial possessions." Plans for advertising the colonies included "novel and attractive exhibits of the material resources, products, industries, manufactures, architecture, art, types of native people, and illustrations of the present state of civilization of the islands of the sea recently acquired by the United States."[48]

To complement their overseas emphasis, the promoters mobilized another Indian encampment and placed it under the direction of P. E. Iller, owner of the Willow Springs Distillery. The Greater America Exposition, using many of the same structures built for the 1898 fair, managed to stay open for three months before it "fizzled out" as "a huge joke and failure."[49] The main problem apparently was nonparticipation by the federal government. In the immediate aftermath of the Trans-Mississippi and International Exposition, the most urgent need of federal funding was for the exploration and administration of the newly acquired territories rather than for continuing the Omaha fair. The government, however, never objected to the idea of a colonial exhibition per se. Consequently, in view of the intense debate beginning over annexation, it was only a matter of time before federal authorities turned to the exposition mode to demonstrate the centrality of colonialism to continued American progress. This effort culminated at the Saint Louis Louisiana Purchase Exposition of 1904, when the federal government and Saint Louis civic leaders put nearly one thousand Filipinos on exhibit in the so-called Philippine Reservation and juxtaposed this display to a living ethnological exhibit of Native Americans. But the Buffalo Pan-American Exposition of 1901 set the stage for the Saint Louis spectacle. At the Buffalo exposition aesthetics and ethnology interlocked to form perhaps the most powerful visual design of American progress ever presented by a world's fair held in this country. Owing in large measure to the success of the 1898 Omaha fair, the exposition movement would continue to be a "concomitant to empire" well into the future.

5

The Pan-American
Exposition, Buffalo:
"Pax 1901"

The Exposition must be at base philosophic, on the surface theatric. An understanding of the philosophy of the Pan-American is material for its fullest enjoyment.

Atlantic Monthly, 1901

Never in the history of expositions has there been a more carefully conceived and wrought-out fundamental plan than that of the Pan-American Exposition.

John Milburn, in an address before the American Institute of Architects Convention at the Exposition, 1901[1]

SHORTLY BEFORE THE PAN-AMERICAN EXPOSITION opened, the *Buffalo Evening News* reminisced about the Crystal Palace Exhibition fifty years earlier: "It was as if Darwin had pictured in panoramic view his 'Origin of Species' for the enlightenment of mankind." That simile, however, better suited the Buffalo fair. At the Pan-American Exposition evolutionary ideas about race and progress dictated the arrangement of buildings, the selection and placement of sculptural forms, and, above all, the color scheme that gave the exposition the name "Rainbow City" and inspired Richard Watson Gilder, editor of *Century Magazine*, to compose an ode to the "CITY OF LIGHT." On the exposition's midway, officially named the Pan, a show called the Evolution of Man, or the Connecting Link, joined the honky-tonk amusements, restaurants, and ethnological villages. As Eugene Richard Wright of the *Atlantic Monthly* observed, this was an exposition where "nothing was done fortuitously."[2]

Through the Pan-American Exposition, America's ruling elites initiated Americans into the twentieth century with a utopian fantasy about peace and progress that forecast "the spiritual synthesis of the far future." According to one guidebook, the "dominant purpose" of the fair was to "illustrate progress during the century just closed and lay a strong and enduring foundation for international, commercial and social unity in the world." Exhibits of people, artifacts, and natural resources came primarily from the Western Hemisphere, but Secretary of State John Hay stressed the universal importance of the proceedings: "The benignant influences that shall emanate from this great festival of peace shall not be bounded by oceans nor by continents." Pax 1901, how-

Fig. 34. General view of Pan-American Exposition. Courtesy of
Smithsonian Institution Archives, Record Unit 95, Photograph Collection.

127

ever, was interrupted by the assassination of President McKinley in the Temple of Music in early September.[3]

The idea for holding an international exposition in Buffalo originated at the American Exhibitors Association banquet at the Atlanta Cotton States and International Exposition of 1895. On that occasion, a Buffalo railroad speculator, John M. Brinker, produced a map showing that forty million people lived within a twelve-hour train ride of the city he represented. That consideration, coupled with the presence of Niagara Falls as a major tourist attraction and electrical power source, persuaded the Exhibitors Association to sanction Brinker's plans to hold another fair to foster visions of Pan-American harmony. True to its origins, Buffalo's exposition emphasized access to new markets and resources in Latin America.[4]

At century's turn, however, acquiring Latin American markets and resources meant overcoming heightened mistrust in these countries over the foreign policy objectives of the United States, in view of the explicit imperial consequences of the Spanish-American War. The exposition, its promoters hoped, would teach Latin Americans "that their gigantic northern neighbor is a comrade and friend, and not a potential tyrant or oppressor; and the inhabitant of the United States must learn that his nation's size and strength and wealth do not make unnecessary or unworthy the serious efforts of Latin and Teutonic communities to the south of us to build American institutions of their own." As evidence of their friendly intentions toward Mexico, Central America, and South America, the exposition directors decided to construct the exposition buildings in the style of the Spanish Renaissance. The *Nation* suggested that the architectural style atoned for America's commercial neglect of Latin America: "To-day our repentance assumes the form of architectural beauty at Buffalo." A United States naval representative to the exposition shed further light on the imperial subtleties that inspired the fair. As a result of the fair, Captain Richard Pearson Hobson explained, "the sister republics of the Western Hemisphere would come to know our flag better; and to know it would be to love it; to know that it represents all that is highest in human government and human civilization." The exposition directors underscored his point in promising that the twentieth century would be "an age of American dominance in international affairs."[5]

From the outset of the undertaking there never was the slightest doubt that the goal of international hegemony would have its domestic corollary. "Expositions," a promotional publication asserted, represent "an efficient means of instruction for the people . . . and serve as a basis for study and consideration to the busy workers who have contributed to make these expositions possible." The *Pan-American Herald*, official journal of the exposition, added that the fair would be "in the truest sense of the term, an exposition of the people, by the people and for the people," citing as proof that eleven thousand people, including "millionaires" and "laborers in the most humble positions in life,"

Fig. 35. "Senorita South America makes goo-goo eyes
at Uncle Sam." Cartoon from Thomas Fleming, *Around
the Pan with Uncle Hank.*

had subscribed to exposition stock. In actuality, however, this fair, like its
predecessors, resembled a corporate autarchy. A railroad advertisement in
The World's Work titled "How the Railroads Built the Exposition" contained
more truth than fiction. Led by the Vanderbilt Lines, railroads had contributed
substantial sums to the fair. Buffalo bank directors, moreover, collectively
chose the board of directors for the exposition from among businessmen who
subscribed to at least $300,000 worth of bonds. Among those selected were
Charles W. Goodyear, lumberman and railroad magnate, John M. Brinker,
who owned a coaling operation in addition to his railroad interests, George
Urban, Jr., a banker, Herbert P. Bissel, lawyer and future Supreme Court
justice, and Harry Hamlin, president of American Grape Sugar Company.[6]
   This group, which included other prominent bankers, lawyers, and industrialists, in turn selected as president John M. Milburn, an eminent attorney,
trustee of Columbia and Barnard colleges, director of American Express Com-

pany, and a board member of Chase National Bank. To assist in overseeing the operations of the fair, the directors named William I. Buchanan as director-general. Buchanan possessed outstanding credentials. His success in the early 1890s with the Sioux City Corn Palace Exposition Company had led to his appointment as superintendent of agriculture at the World's Columbian Exposition. President Cleveland subsequently appointed him United States foreign minister to Argentina—a post that enabled him to assist Isaac W. Avery's efforts to generate Latin American interest in the Atlanta fair. Buchanan's considerable knowledge about Latin America and his exposition pedigree—testified to by Harlow N. Higinbotham's endorsement—perfectly suited the needs of the corporate interests sponsoring the Pan-American Exposition.[7]

Buchanan, moreover, was only one of many former exposition makers to lend support to Buffalo's undertaking. When the directors deadlocked on selecting a site for the fair, they called in Daniel Burnham and Frederick Law Olmsted, Jr., to help resolve the issue. Other exposition specialists sped to Buffalo after the close of Omaha's two expositions. Luther Stieringer, the electrical engineer who had designed the lighting effects for the Trans-Mississippi Exposition, created electrical illumination for the Pan-American fair. Another figure from the Trans-Mississippi Exposition, landscape architect Rudolph Ulrich, supervised the landscaping plans for the 1901 fair.[8]

Buffalo's exposition promoters also selected Frederick W. Taylor, renowned horticulturist and head of the Horticultural Department at the 1898 fair, to take charge of the exhibits and concessions at Buffalo. Soon after assuming his position, Taylor stated that ethnology would be a central concern of the fair and proposed an Indian Congress for the midway—ideas that Edward Rosewater enthusiastically supported when he met with the managers of the Pan-American Exposition in late 1899 to share his insights about running an exposition. The knot linking earlier fairs and the Buffalo exposition tightened in the ensuing competition for the Indian Congress concession as Antonio Apache, one of Frederic Ward Putnam's assistants at Chicago, and Frederick Cummins, manager of the Indian Congress at the Greater America Exposition of 1899, emerged as front runners. When Cummins received the concession because of stronger financial backing, which he received from the Citizens Bank of Buffalo, the directors secured a proven show and another experienced showman for their fair.[9]

Relying on experienced exposition hands offered clear advantages to the sponsors of the Pan-American Exposition. But in another sense the overflow effect from previous fairs—especially from the World's Columbian Exposition and its City Beautiful satellites—presented the problem of novelty. Too much continuity with preceding expositions threatened loss of public appeal. Could new forms be devised to convey the message of imperial progress without altering the fundamental purposes of the exposition?[10]

The answer was affirmative and startling. Rainbow colors replaced the pervasive whiteness of earlier City Beautiful fairs in an all-encompassing evolutionary design of the world's progress. As they entered the fairgrounds, visitors to the Pan-American Exposition stepped into a carefully crafted allegory of America's rise to the apex of civilization. The color mosaic presented by the fair told the story of the nation's successful struggle with nature and forecast a future where racial fitness would determine prosperity. Inside the exposition, ethnological displays and midway attractions with ethnological attributes gave this historical and utopian narrative a basis in received scientific and pseudoscientific wisdom. But fairgoers first encountered the evolutionary message

Fig. 36. High-stepping tourist at Pan-American Exposition. Photograph by Frances Benjamin Johnson, Division of Prints and Photographs, Library of Congress.

of the exposition in the mutually reinforcing effects of the architecture, the colors of the buildings, and the outdoor sculpture. This intermeshing visual panorama resulted from close collaboration among artists, architects, and the exposition management.[11]

To design the exposition buildings, the directors selected architects R. S. Peabody, James Knox Taylor, George Cary, August Esenwein, Edward B. Green, George F. Sheply, John G. Howard, and Walter Cook and placed them under the supervision of John M. Carrère, who had submitted the winning plan for the fair in the architectural competition. Carrère's plan emphasized "formality picturesquely developed," with "a logical arrangement and significance in the groupings of the buildings." Carrère also drew up his plan with particular reference to the approaches to Delaware Park, site of the fair. He virtually eliminated all secondary entrances to the exposition "so that the intended first impression, which is always the most lasting," would be commonly shared by the majority of fairgoers. "It was possible to paint this picture at Buffalo," he explained, "with a definite view point, placed at the Triumphal Bridge, and to make the principal approach through the park, so that the spectator, as he approaches the Exposition, will see it develop gradually until he reaches the Bridge, when the entire picture will appear before him and almost burst upon him." Across the bridge, Carrère placed the main exposition buildings in a progressive series along a broad north-south axis with several intersecting secondary axes. He devoted the first structural grouping to natural resources and to the United States Government Building, thereby planting the national identity firmly in the conquest of nature and the development of natural resources. The next cross-axis juxtaposed the Temple of Music to the Ethnology Building in an effort to mark a transitional point in the march from savagery to civilization. Buildings devoted to technology and to the "genius of man" found their home in the final secondary axis in Carrère's plan, which centered on the Court of Fountains—a courtyard highlighted by the heroically proportioned Fountain of Abundance and an enormous Electric Tower. To enhance the continuity of this general plan, the architects and directors agreed to "highly color the Exposition Buildings" and to style them in the fashion of the Spanish Renaissance.[12]

In the spring of 1900 Carrère, as chairman of the Board of Architects, extended an invitation to the National Sculptors Society and the National Society of Mural Painters to nominate two individuals to supervise the sculptural work of the fair and to take charge of the coloring process. These organizations selected Karl Bitter and Charles Y. Turner. Neither arrived in Buffalo as a novice in the exposition business. Turner had worked as Frank Millet's assistant in painting the World's Columbian Exposition, and Bitter had modeled statuary groups for several buildings at the same fair. By the time they received their appointments, the architects and management had started working out the details of Carrère's plan. Exactly how color, sculpture, and architec-

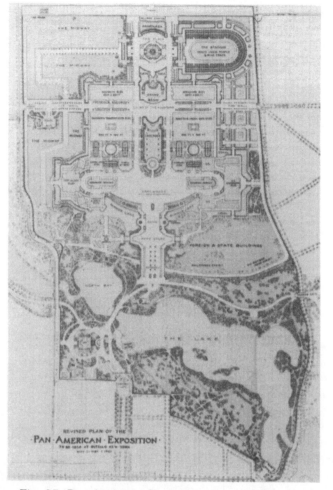

Fig. 37. Pan-American Exposition map. From Buffalo
and Erie County Historical Society.

ture would relate to one another, however, remained unclear. Responsibility
for the color scheme clearly lay in Turner's hands, but after an initial meeting
with the Board of Architects he returned to his New York City studio uncertain
how best to proceed. Meanwhile, as exposition president Milburn later described it, Bitter had "an inspiration."[13]

At a meeting of the National Sculptors Society, Bitter proposed considering
the sculpture for the fair "as a decorative feature forming a part of the entire
artistic scheme of the composition." Rather than treating sculptural pieces as
isolated works of art, Bitter stated his intention of having them designed with
particular reference to the physical landscape of the fair, to the contents of

the buildings, and to the overall purpose of the exposition. As Turner sat in the audience and listened to Bitter fill in the specifics, he concluded that Bitter's idea was "ingenious." Turner provided a full account of Bitter's proposal in a subsequent report to the exposition management:

> He proposed to treat the sculptural groups about the Government
> Building in such a manner as to suggest man in his primitive state, and
> the Horticultural group as the natural resources of the earth. Here the
> battle of life, which man has ever waged with elements, begins. We
> find as we progress up the grounds, the result of his labors in the
> Machinery and Transportation and Electricity Buildings shown on one
> side, and the Liberal Arts and Agricultural on the other suggesting the
> result of his struggles. The Restaurant and the entrances to the Midway
> and the Stadium should suggest amusements and games. The Electric
> Tower, the crowning achievement of man, could be dedicated to the
> great waterways and the power of Niagara which is utilized to generate
> the current which runs the Exposition.[14]

Finding Bitter's proposal a "logical and proper treatment," Turner determined on "a similar course" to make the use of color part of the "general scheme which was indicated in the plan of the grounds, buildings and sculptural arrangement." Visitors crossing the Triumphal Bridge, Turner wrote, "would come upon the elementary conditions, that is, the earliest state of man suggested on one side and primitive nature on the other." Consequently, "the strongest primary colors should be applied here," while farther up, "the colors should be more refined and less contrasting, and the Tower which is to suggest the triumph of man's achievement, should be the lightest and most delicate in color." He could thus capture "the emerald green hue of the water as it curls over the crest of Niagara Falls," Turner claimed and he would "carry this color on some portion of every building," thereby giving a sense of continuity to the entire coloring plan.[15]

The overall design so impressed the exposition directors that they rushed a descriptive pamphlet into print: "The whole group of buildings has been treated as one picture, and the colors made to harmonize, not only with one another, but with the foreground of green grass and water and the background blue of the sky." "Further," the pamphlet stressed, "an ethical significance is aimed at, in the chromatic arrangement as in the architectural plan; the whole symbolizing progression from a less civilized stage to a higher. Thus the strongest, crudest colors are nearest the entrances." Gradually, the colors evolved "from warm buff and ochre walls, with terra cotta roofs, through more refined and brilliant hues, to the Electric Tower at the head of the Court of Fountains, striking the highest and finest note of all in ivory white, delicate blue, green, and gold."[16]

By all accounts, the visual impact of the fair overpowered visitors. "Such beautiful displays of man's thoughts are far more to the world than any form of dogmatic religion," wrote the correspondent for the *Arena*, "for they show in which way man is tending. And, believe me, it is always upward." The entire artistic production reminded George H. Daniels, general passenger agent for the New York Central Railroad, of "an immense oil painting" with an effect "somewhat like a sunrise." A local schoolteacher, Mabel E. Barnes, who pedaled her bicycle to the fair on thirty-two separate occasions and recorded her experience in a three-volume diary and scrapbook, stated: "As the sculpture symbolizes the progress of the race, the coloring represents in epitome the growth of the color sense." For future reference, she also copied down, almost verbatim, the official description of the artistic plan of the fair from the pamphlet first issued by the exposition directors. Other visitors applauded the "magic" quality of the fair and its "architectural somersaults." Claude Bragdon, in *American Architect and Building News*, complimented Turner for his "highly psychological and philosophic" coloring scheme and proclaimed the Electric Tower "the high C of the entire architectural symphony." For other spectators, the 375 foot tower possessed an alluring sexuality. "The shaft of the Electric Tower," Julian Hawthorne wrote, "at the further extremity of this interminable space, assumes a magical aspect, as if it had been summoned forth by the genius of our united people . . . and it makes a

Fig. 38. Night view showing the Electric Tower. Courtesy of Smithsonian Institution Archives, Record Unit 95, Photograph Collection.

tender nuptial with the sky and seems to palpitate with beautiful life." Maurice F. Newton offered a similar perspective in the *American Architect and Building News:* "The Electric Tower is the climax. . . . It is the altar at the head of the aisle of increasing brilliance, spread with the cloth of white and illumined by golden candles—and that is the key." Amos K. Fiske, writing for *Harper's Weekly*, declared that the entire exposition culminated in the "cream and gold" of the tower top.[17]

Despite the phallic implications of the Electric Tower, most journalistic discussion focused on the use of color. "If there is a touch of the fanciful in this endeavor to suggest the evolution of man by means of a scheme of color," Hamilton Wright Mabie confided to the *Outlook*'s readers, "the general effect is rich and striking, and the eye which loves color finds delight in the warm tones modulated over great space with a harmonious sense of values." Writing in the *Architectural Record*, Herbert Croly, architectural critic and emerging spokesman for Progressivism, criticized the fair's excessive ornamentation, yet praised the designers for having successfully created "stimulating surroundings" that "embody something like the best ideals and training of American art." In contrast to Croly's modest praise for chromatic effects, a *New York Times* correspondent insisted that Turner had been too conservative. "But," the reporter conceded, "perhaps it is too much to expect from the staid white of North America that he should dare to be a Moor—someone might mistake him for a 'nigger' and that, bless his heart! would cut him to the quick." Like the artists and architects who had conceived the notion of color-coding the fair, this journalist linked perception of color to perceived racial qualities. "Color," the correspondent wrote, "is the most immediate speech that the outer world utters to our mind, for we see color before we detect term. . . . Color is in fact the primal language for the child as for the immature races."[18]

At the Pan-American Exposition, rainbow colors linked to displays with ethnological messages produced an unforgettable image of American progress that helped structure those messages for the eight million people who visited the exposition. Outside the Government Building, Carrère placed a Fountain of Man adorned with statuary created under Bitter's guidance, illustrating the struggle of man against nature. Inside the building visitors found Smithsonian exhibits delineating grades of Indian cultures in North and South America as well as a large display of cultural artifacts and natural resources from the Philippine Islands. Art and ethnology intersected more dramatically in the Ethnology Building. Since Carrère had placed this building at the center of the exposition grounds, Turner arranged its exterior colors "halfway between crudity and artistic refinement." According to the Buffalo *Enquirer*, the colors also moved in an ascending pattern: "In accordance with the general color scheme, which placed the harsh, bright colors at the southern end of the grounds and in the lower part of the buildings, red will predominate near the base, gradually merging toward the top with a pale yellow and then to bright

Fig. 39. Tourists resting against the Fountain of Man. From Division of Prints and Photographs, Library of Congress.

ivory." The Ethnology Building housed artifacts arranged geographically, together with oil paintings of various racial types set against a pyramidic backdrop of colors decorating the interior walls. "On the inside," the *Enquirer* commented, "the gradual change from an earthy red at the base to an ethereal blue at the top at once satisfies the artistic sense and prompts the analogy between it and the ascent of man from savagery to civilization."[19] To ascend the spiral staircases to the galleries was thus presumably to follow the course of human development through evolutionary stages. A sign in the building told visitors that these lessons about racial progress continued on the midway, where ethnological villages formed "an integral part of the educational exhibits." Turner reinforced this link between the Pan and the overall design of the fair by treating the color of midway structures more liberally, thereby linking midway features with primitive passions and the lower orders of mankind.[20]

Ethnological exhibits reinforced the artistic presentation of racial gradations. To organize the exposition's Ethnology Department, the directors selected A. L. Benedict, who held the "chair of physiology and digestive diseases" in the dental department at the University of Buffalo. An archaeologist by avocation, Benedict described his own role in the fair as "Editor of scientific work." In working out plans for the displays in his department, he solicited suggestions from "nearly every scientific anthropologist," including William Henry Holmes, Otis T. Mason, and W J McGee at the Smithsonian Institution and Frederic Ward Putnam at Harvard. With their aid, Benedict drafted plans to bring together "an exposition of the living natives of Pan America" encompassing "only the aboriginal races of the Western Continent and the islands geographically or politically associated with it."[21]

Benedict's grand plan, however, ran headlong into several problems, which he discussed in some detail in his final report. First, he noted that the cost of the plan proved much too high. Additionally, Benedict worried about preserving "discipline and sanitation in a large population of uncivilized tribes, each possessing its own peculiarities and religious prejudices." Finally, he anticipated difficulties in finding "untainted native stocks [and] keeping the inmates of the proposed colony from acquiring rapidly the clothing and customs of their surroundings."[22]

The net result of these problems was that when the exposition opened all that remained of Benedict's original plan was a "hexagonic stockade which enclosed Iroquois dwellings." Inside this enclosure he had hoped to have the Indians stage their religious celebrations, "but the execution of the plan was prevented by fear of competition with the Indian Congress on the Midway." Apparently Benedict accepted these setbacks philosophically and came to regard the ethnological villages along the Pan as offering the best solution to the problems he had encountered in trying to include live exhibits in his own department. On the midway, he observed, "the financial management and the discipline are adapted to the particular conditions, while criticism on the third point [the matter of representing 'untainted' racial stocks] is obviated by disclaiming all scientific responsibility on the part of the exposition." The midway area, in other words, permitted Benedict and the exposition directors to have their ethnological cake and eat it too by affirming or denying the scientific accuracy of the various ethnological villages to suit their needs. The beauty of the midway, once again, was that it made science and entertainment interchangeable.[23]

With living specimens of nonwhites relegated to the Pan, Benedict contented himself with organizing artifacts depicting aboriginal modes of manufacture and warfare along geographical lines—exhibits that Turner enveloped with a panorama of colors depicting evolutionary development. Despite the absence of live aborigines, visitors poured into the Ethnology Building. Attendance figures showed that "on any average day about 75% of the visitors to the exposition were represented in the Ethnology Building." But from the vantage point of the exposition management, the presence of large crowds in the building underscored their feelings that the Ethnology Department's exhibits should have been better. Buchanan considered the results of the department "far from satisfactory," primarily "because no commercial motives exist on the part of anyone for making such an exhibit." In his opinion the Ethnology Department had wandered far from its original purpose and assumed a strong archaeological bent that had failed to convey the explicit commercial lessons that permeated the displays devoted to the Philippine Islands in the Government Building and the villages on the midway.[24]

Early in the organization of the fair, the Philippine Islands emerged as the most important part of a planned exhibit depicting the newly acquired "outlying possessions." In the fall of 1899 exposition officials had written to the federal government's exposition board suggesting "the desirability of . . . a special governmental display of Exhibits from Cuba, Puerto Rico, Alaska, the Hawaiian and Philippine Islands, showing not only the products, resources and possibilities of these possessions, but also and particularly the ethnological features available." Such a display would satisfy the "intense interest felt by our people to learn all about the people and territories which have come under our charge and there has not been so good an opportunity as will present itself to reach the many million expected to visit us, as will be afforded at our exposition." In a second letter the exposition management promised that "[t]he exhibits would form the dominant feature of the Exposition," and emphasized that the government should "absolutely reproduce typical scenery . . . and [bring to] the Exposition grounds houses actually used in the respective countries." The plan included "bringing of 100, more or less, natives, housing and maintaining them during the Exposition period."[25]

"This is the first and best opportunity we have had," Director-General Buchanan had written in December 1899 to J. H. Brigham, chairman of the government exposition board, "to justify, by means of the most available object lessons we can produce, the acquisition of new territory; to demonstrate, as I am sure can be done, that the results to be obtained promise to be for us all ample compensation for the sacrifice already made, and, for the burdens yet to be assumed." The colonial exhibit at the exposition, in short, would generate support in the United States for maintaining and extending America's colonial empire. The undertaking was crucial, Buchanan stressed, "because of the influence it can be made to exert upon interests reaching beyond the scope of the Exposition; it may be made of so much effectiveness that it will come to be beneficial as a guide for our people in their consideration of our Government policy in the Islands—the shaping of which will be more largely influenced by the Agricultural and Mineral wealth such an exhibit will show existing therein than by any other medium." Financing the display, Buchanan explained, could easily be arranged without additional government expense, since "surplus" revenues generated by the islands were "presumably to be expended for the betterment of the Islands and in their best interest." He concluded by repeating that "no more advisable or beneficial use could be made of such funds than the exhibit we talked over."[26]

Buchanan's carefully articulated argument received a sympathetic hearing from the government board's Subcommittee on Outlying Possessions, headed by Frederick W. True of the Smithsonian Institution, but their hands were tied by the terms of the congressional appropriation for federal participation in the fair. Two days before Buchanan's last letter arrived, attorneys for the Treasury Department, responding to the exposition directors' proposal about government funding for colonial villages, declared that the appropriation from Congress would not permit the use of federal funds for a display of "natives from outlying possessions."[27]

This legal opinion, coupled with reservations over the projected cost of establishing the villages, led the government board to restrict direct federal financial support for the colonial display to material artifacts and natural resources from the colonies. Nevertheless, this decision met the exposition management more than halfway: the board had guaranteed a federally funded colonial exhibit at the fair and left open the possibility for the management to finance villages along the midway—an option exposition officials exercised. The government board complied with the directors' request in yet another way by determining to focus the exhibit from America's imperial acquisitions on the Philippine Islands, giving relatively little attention to Hawaii, Guam, Cuba, and Puerto Rico. As a memorandum from the board explained, its members were "desirous of complying with the wishes of the Management, and in view of the fact that the Philippine Islands would furnish the most valuable collecting field, the Chairman was authorized to employ a suitable per[son] or persons to make as full a collection as possible from these Islands; the necessary funds for this purpose to be set aside."[28]

In January 1900 the government board appointed Frank F. Hilder, employed as a translator by the Bureau of American Ethnology, to travel to the Philippines and gather material for the United States government exhibit at the Pan-American Exposition. Hilder's ethnological field research, along with his military and business background, amply fitted him for the job. Born in Hastings, England, in 1836, he had attended English military schools and served in the British army in India and Africa. After emigrating to America, he spent fifteen years as an international representative of Remington Arms Company, traveling around the world. Throughout his military and business careers, Hilder had actively pursued extensive ethnological, geographical, and archaeological research in Asia and the Americas. In the United States he became a popular public speaker on the "remote regions" of the earth and published many articles in the *Forum* and *National Geographic*. The BAE recognized his contributions to ethnology by appointing him to the position of ethnologic translator in 1898 and granted him leave to act as special agent for the government board to make the third and final trip of his career to the Philippine Islands.[29]

The government board explained Hilder's mission in a directive sent to him shortly before he left for the Philippines in January 1900: "The object of sending a special agent to the Philippine Islands, is to obtain such articles and information as will illustrate the natural resources of the Islands, the characteristics and mode of life of the inhabitants, and the principal features and methods of government, past or present." Hilder carried letters of introduction authorizing him "to collect by purchase, gift, or loan, articles of interest pertaining to each department of the Government, to be exhibited at the Pan-American Exposition."[30]

Hilder also received explicit instructions from William Henry Holmes, curator of the Department of Anthropology in the United States National Museum, to keep the long-range interests of the United States National Museum in mind while gathering exhibits for the Buffalo fair: "It is the desire of the Anthropological Department of the National Museum to secure from the Philippines materials that will illustrate the peoples and culture in a permanent way in the Museum and that at the same time will afford means of preparing effective groups of exhibits for the Buffalo Exposition." Holmes went on to explain that what he had in mind were "a series of *lay-figure groups* representing the native peoples, and the first object of the collector should be to secure data and collections for this purpose." The central aim, as Holmes put it, was "to give a complete idea of the character and culture of the people," adding that he preferred centering attention on "the more primitive peoples such as the Negritos, the Moros and the Igoroti [*sic*]."[31]

Hilder did everything in his power to accommodate the heads of the various government departments composing the government board, despite the shortage of time and difficult conditions in the Philippines. Aided by United States military personnel, merchants, journalists, and Catholic clergy, Hilder succeeded in gathering, cataloging, and shipping more than five hundred cultural artifacts as well as "a series of photographs of representative groups of different tribes, also of individual pictures with all anthropological details, measurements, etc." He amassed "a number of statistical schedules of labor, wages, etc. for the Department of Labor" and information about Philippine currency for the Treasury Department. On his return to San Francisco after a month of intensive effort in the Philippines, he informed the *San Francisco Chronicle* that "the greatest and most profitable industry of the future in the Philippines will be connected with the marketing of the magnificent timber that covers the island." In his final report to the government board, Hilder rated his expedition to the Philippines "successful." But Hilder never saw the final fruit of his labors. Five months before the Buffalo exposition opened, this unsung soldier-scientist and apostle of Anglo-Saxon imperialism died suddenly after a brief illness.[32]

Rather than distributing the materials he had gathered to the separate departmental alcoves of the Government Building at the fair, the government board decided to keep the Hilder collection intact, to supplement it with commercial exhibits from the Philippines provided by importers in New York and Boston, and to give it a separate place in the north wing of the government structure. There, according to *World's Work*, the display "probably attracted more spectators than other parts of the federal exhibit," which included the War Department's display of Spanish-American War relics, newly invented dum-dum bullets and smokeless powder, and the display by Smithsonian eth-

nologists of twelve lay-figure groups of Pan-American aboriginal types "designed to show the status of various native races as regards culture." Even the
Biograph motion pictures of military drills, shown by the Bureau of Education
in the government's first public use of this new medium, drew smaller crowds
than the "object lesson of the character and customs of the strange people"
from the Philippines.[33]

Minutes of the government board meetings matter-of-factly expressed satisfaction with the exhibit, noting that it evidenced "compliance with the desire
of the Exposition Management that the Government present an exhibit from
the Islands." F. W. Clarke, Interior Department representative on the board,
applauded the efforts that went into the display: "Everything," he wrote, signified "the work of trained intelligence." "After all," another commentator
pointed out, "the Government hasn't an equal in the show business."[34]

The government, however, had stopped short of completely satsifying the
exposition promoters. When the government board refused to fund the proposed village of Filipinos but left the door open for exposition backers to
arrange one on their own, the management acted quickly. Knowing that all
roads at the fair would eventually lead fairgoers to the midway, they relegated

Fig. 40. Hilder's Philippine exhibit. Courtesy of Smithsonian Institution
Archives, Record Unit 95, Photograph Collection.

the Filipino Village to the Pan. Buffalo businessmen invested $40,000 in the projected show and guaranteed any additional money necessary to complete the display of what a contemporary newspaper termed America's "somewhat reluctant citizens." E. W. McConnell, an experienced showman, received the contract for the concession and added the Filipino Village to his Red Star Route of seven other features he managed along the Pan. McConnell designated "Pony" Moore as his agent to travel to the Philippines to gather material and people for the attraction. Moore, a Naval Academy graduate, Omaha newspaperman, and theatrical press agent who had formerly managed the short-lived Philippine Village at both Omaha expositions, returned to Buffalo with one hundred Filipinos.[35]

The Filipino Village consisted of an eleven-acre enclosure loosely modeled after photographs of an actual village in the Philippines and embellished with many imperial touches added by McConnell. The village gateway somewhat resembled the fortifications at Manila Bay that had yielded to American assault and, as an added touch of realism, a detachment of United States soldiers was "on parade at the entrance at all times." Inside the compound, visitors found a colonial adventure awaiting them. Carts pulled by water buffalo provided free transportation among thatched huts, a lake complete with war canoes, a Catholic church, museum, and theater. It "is almost as good as a trip to the islands," the *New York Times* reported. The concession as a whole impressed anthropologist Frederick Starr from the University of Chicago as "really good." Like most other visitors, Starr was fascinated by the Filipino people and especially by "Buchanna," the Filipino girl who was born at the fair and christened after the director-general of the exposition. The theater Starr found especially noteworthy, for there "a sombre faced juggler did some tricks neatly and the [Filipino] band played the national anthem—*The Star Spangled Banner!*"[36]

Assessing the nature of the Filipino people and the part they would play in the American empire became a popular pastime at the fair. An article in the *Pan-American Herald*, the journal produced by the exposition management, quoted a British report about the Philippines to make a point about "the natural indolence of the Filipino." "They have no idea of putting energy into any of their pursuits," the report stated, "and have no commercial instincts; they care little for money, loss or gain being to them apparently a matter of indifference." Like the Afro-Americans and Native Americans on display in other villages on the midway, Filipinos appeared to require American tutelage in managing their future—a future the exposition depicted as inexorably linked to the production of raw materials and consumption of finished American products. The task, as Richard Barry suggested in his popular sketch of the Pan, was not hopeless, because the Filipinos "have earnestness and they have modesty, and better than all else they are clean, wholesome and somewhat diffident."[37]

The chief problem confronting American interests, the exposition management realized, involved teaching the Filipinos to be willing subjects. When Emilio Aguinaldo, leader of the Philippine resistance to the United States occupation, was captured in April 1901, the thought crossed several minds to put him on display in the Filipino Village, but the idea was dismissed as "not practical." The villagers already on display, however, seemed likely candidates for spreading the news of American power to other Filipinos upon their return to the Philippines. As they prepared to leave the Pan at the conclusion of the fair the Buffalo *Courier* commented: "the tidings of the goodness and greatness which [the Filipinos] will take back will be a great help in the furtherment of the United States Government's policy there." The next day the same newspaper noted approvingly that several Filipinos began crying as they left the midway. Yet their experience had not been altogether a positive one. Late in October, a twenty-five-year-old woman died in the hospital after contracting tuberculosis in the village.[38]

Doubtless many Filipinos left without being persuaded of the benefits to be derived from being wards of the United States. To correct that situation the federal government, in cooperation with the management of the planned 1904 exposition for Saint Louis, began laying the groundwork for a larger and more spectacular Philippine colonial display. At the Pan-American Exposition, the various Philippine exhibits and additional ethnological villages along the Pan provided ample precedent to draw on.

"I tol ye wanst," Finley Peter Dunne's Mr. Dooley insisted, "that f'r wan man that goes to a wurruld's fair to see how boots is made, they'se twinty goes to see th' hootchy-kootchy an that's where th' wan lands fin'ally." The backers of the Pan-American Exposition never underestimated the magnetic power of the midway. Local capitalists, in conjunction with showmen who could finance their own ventures, invested between two and three million dollars in the midway shows for the Pan-American fair. For their money they expected the results to be instructive, entertaining, and profitable. According to the director of exhibits, Frederick W. Taylor: "The organization and bringing together of the features now known under the generic name 'Midway,' for the amusement, edification, and instruction of the public, has become so great a factor in Expositions that nowadays that department is considered one of the most important and requires many months of strenuous labor in order that satisfactory results may be worked out." The concessionaire played a critical role in making a given show a success. "He must be a social philosopher," explained Mary Bronson Hart in *World's Work*. "Nothing short of a close study of the people at play will teach him what will 'take.' " Rarely, however, did the management completely rely on the showman's perceptions of social reality, much less his philosophy. Especially in the case of the ethnological villages, the exposition sponsors carefully shaped the social theory that informed the attractions by specifying the content of the shows in the contracts awarded to the various showmen. As Taylor put it: "it is more than likely that no single phase of the Exposition in architecture, exhibits, or concessions will leave a more lasting impress than will the ethnological features of the various villages." With this thought in mind, the contracts for the ethnological villages emphasized exhibits of alleged racial characteristics as part of the overarching demonstration at the fair of the need for Anglo-Saxon domination of the nonwhite world. "Great effort has been made to have [the ethnological] features correct in every way," Taylor assured fairgoers.[39]

After turning down one proposal to construct an African slave market on the Pan, Taylor awarded the concession for an African Village to French explorer-scientist Xavier Pené. This imperial entrepreneur had supplied African labor for the construction of the Pan-American Railroad in the 1880s and had managed the Dahomeyan Village at the World's Columbian Exposition. The contract he received for the African Village at the Pan-American Exposition stated that "the ground plan in a general way consists of groups of typical huts of at least twenty-five different races or tribes of Africa south of the Senegal River, the Desert of Sahara, and Egypt." The African people selected for display in the village, according to the contractual arrangement with the exposition directors, were expected "to present the racial peculiarities and customs . . . subject to the approval of the Director-General." Pené, with sup-

Fig. 41. The Pan—the "Evolution of Man" show stands immediately to the right of the "Trained Wild Animals" show. From Division of Prints and Photographs, Library of Congress.

port from the Buffalo Society of Natural Sciences as well as from the geographical and anthropological societies of France, obtained permission of the various European powers controlling Africa to make the planned expedition. "The original purpose of the expedition," according to the souvenir guide to the village, "contemplated chiefly an ethnological and anthropological exhibit, to specially include those race types of African natives known to us hitherto only by the descriptions of Moffat, Livingston, DuChaillu, Stanley and others." Pené realized, however, "that an added popular interest would be given to the exhibit if the natives could be shown in their natural surroundings and living entirely in the native way."[40]

Advertised as "REAL AFRICAN LIFE IN A REAL AFRICAN VILLAGE" and as being "In the Midway but not of it," Pené's Darkest Africa included ninety-eight Africans living amid "the occasional chatter of the monkeys and the constant screaming of the flock of African parrots giving a final touch of local color to the scene." Above all, the show's promoters asserted, "the scientific features of the exhibit of Darkest Africa differentiate it altogether from the common Midway show." Visitors would be instructed and entertained by "those incidental features springing out of the peculiarity of native habits and customs, the childishness, humor and love of frolic inherent in the African race, and as strongly marked in the descendants of those who have enjoyed a century of civilization in America, as it is in these who represent the savage ancestry of our colored population." Even before she saw the show, Minnie J. Reynolds informed readers of the *New York Times*: "I felt sure that the darkest inhabitants came from somewhere south of Mason and Dixon's line." Another visitor observed: "[Africans] adopt customs rapidly, and the most rapid acquisition they have made has been the inborn attribute of the colored gentleman of the palace car, whose remote ancestors they suggest; they can solicit a tip on the slightest provocation."[41]

Across the street from Darkest Africa, the Old Plantation cemented the impression of racial continuity. Elmer "Skip" Dundy, another emerging amusement industry magnate, had received the Old Plantation concession. In the contract he agreed to exhibit fifty "genuine negroes"—twenty men, twenty women, and ten children—who lived in the South. Richard Barry explained the importance of having southern blacks in the show: "It is easy to pick up the colored people of the North and draught them into the show business, but the darkies of the South do not take as kindly to the public rogue box." "They all love the beat of a bass drum and a limber-jointed abandon of a cake-walk," Barry continued, "but the Southern negro is a stay-at-home darkey, not so much through dislike for publicity as through the inherent laziness that will not run the risk of nomadic life." In addition to affording "more of the real ginger of genuine enjoyment," Barry wrote, a show consisting of southern blacks gives "more correctly a picture of real Southern life."[42]

The picture, however, was slanted from the start, since many of the blacks selected for the show had first attended a performance school in Charleston run by Fred McClellan, another blossoming midway showman. What the Old Plantation correctly depicted was the ideology of racial reconciliation and subordination promulgated by the promoters of the New South. In the concession blacks appeared as "jocular, careless serfs, who in the South before the war gave slavery the deceptive hue of contented and oft-times happy dependence." Barry invited whites who visited the attraction to recall the "pitiful history" of blacks and to remember equally well that Afro-Americans had been graced with "cheerful" qualities that would enable them to endure hardship and survive despite their alleged racial limitations. Miniature cotton bales for sale as souvenirs served as a not-so-subtle reminder of how blacks would fit into the economic structure of the Pan-American utopia forecast by the exposition's directors. Equally telling was the offer made to Jim Parker, the black Atlanta waiter who aided Secret Service agents in subduing McKinley's assassin, to join in an unnamed midway attraction. Parker refused; but the attempt to caricature a black hero as mock-heroic stood, nevertheless, as a monument to an ideology that sharply delimited the social roles open to blacks.[43]

As in the case of Africans, Afro-Americans, and Filipinos, the exposition also locked selected Latin Americans into villages with predetermined ideological contours. "In general," the contract for the Mexican Village concession read, "the 'Streets of Mexico' is to be a realistic reproduction of the architec-

Fig. 42. Concessionaire Frederic Thompson (1873–1919). From Richard H. Barry, *Snap Shots on the Midway of the Pan-American Exposition*.

Fig. 43. Concessionaire E. S. "Skip" Dundy (1862–1907). From Richard H. Barry, *Snap Shots on the Midway of the Pan-American Exposition*.

of different cities and villages of Mexico, and the general entertainment is to
be a display of the racial customs and characteristic street scenes of the Mexican people with the presentation of the Mexican sports and pastimes common
to Mexican routine daily life." H. F. McGarvie, former director-general of the
San Francisco Midwinter Exposition of 1894 and publicity director for the
Trans-Mississippi fair, raised the capital for the show by forming a joint-stock
company with several "responsible" Buffalo businessmen. Before he received
the contract, however, the exposition management asked the Mexican government for its approval of the attraction. President Díaz gave his permission for
the show on two conditions: "first—that the concession should not in any way
bring ridicule upon Mexico, her inhabitants or buildings; and, secondly, that
the concessionaire should guarantee to return to Mexico all Mexicans employed in the concession." Once assured that these provisions would be met,
Díaz enhanced the semiofficial nature of the concession by agreeing to provide
the show with a troop of *rurales*. In actuality, however, the location of the
attraction on the Pan and the exposition management's insistence on a display
of Mexican "racial customs" made compliance with Díaz's demand for respect
a remote possibility at best. McGarvie's concession romanticized the Spanish
influence in Mexico, emphasized the potential for American investment in the
Mexican economy, and stressed the inferiority of the Mexican people.[44]

The village, with its bullfights, dancers, archaeological and ethnological
artifacts, and restaurants, alternately appealed to and repulsed visitors. "The
laziness of the place is pleasing, and its rosiness attractive," Barry decided.
"The life of Mexico is shown," he noted, and is complete with "the peons, the
diminutive burros, and ever present bazaars, and the girls who dance with the
abandon of the Midway and languor of Old Spain." Another fairgoer found the
village utterly unbelievable, especially the symmetry of the architecture: "A
Mexican has no such ingenuity. He is absolutely lacking in mechanical
skill."[45]

Other ethnological villages provided opportunities for comparison. Uncle
Hank, the character in Thomas Fleming's novel about the Pan, for instance,
commented favorably on the commercial possibilities evidenced in the Cuban
Village and fully expected "Uncle Sam . . . [to] take [Cuba] to his heart and
make her one of his beloved daughters by adoption." Apparently the only
obstacle was the seemingly lackadaisical nature of the Cubans. "They need a
little Yankee blood down thar," Uncle Hank observed. "Hustle ez a good
word, a heap sight bettern Manany." Fairgoers came away from the Eskimo,
Hawaiian, and Japanese villages convinced that the "slant-eyed" Eskimos living in papier-mâché igloos were basically harmless, that Hawaiians were "el-
emental," and that the Japanese were the "Yankees ov ther orient" who would
soon "heve a Monroe doctrine ov ther own" and "give them Rooshins and
Germans something to think about."[46]

The same blend of affection and racial antipathy that characterized the popular response to the Streets of Mexico surfaced in the Indian Congress when Vice-President Theodore Roosevelt visited the concession and named a new-born Native American baby Pan-Anna. An official guidebook to the exposition underlined the didactic value of the Indian Congress: "No such lesson in history can be gleaned from books as is here shown by 'Native Americans'—long haired painted savages in all their barbaric splendor." A sketch in the Buffalo *Express* captured the image of Indians as presented by the show. According to the caption: "A wild Western Indian, at the Exposition, was observed absorbed in contemplation of a wolf. It was like meeting an old friend in the strange East. The wolf's howl, too, seemed to carry with it a note of recognition." With its sham battles and famous "living heroes," including Geronimo and a variety of United States military scouts, the Indian Congress left an indelible imprint on visitors, especially children. Mrs. William Jennings Bryan, for one, endorsed the attraction as "a school of instruction, a school-house of information, a happy, merry playground for little children." "Every man, every woman, every child in the Union should see it," she declared. A local kindergarten class apparently followed her advice. Two days after seeing the entire fair, the teacher asked the children to find illustrations of their favorite exhibits. Pictures of the Indian Congress outnumbered all others.[47]

The ethnological villages on the Pan presented a variety of human types and cultures. One exhibit in particular, The Evolution of Man, linked the variety of human types to the greater evolutionary lessons about progress as presented by the exposition as a whole. This attraction, brainchild of Frank

Fig. 44. Entrance to the Indian Congress. From Division of Prints and Photographs, Library of Congress.

Fig. 45. "Caught in the middle." Showman Frederic
Cummins *(left)* and William Jennings Bryan *(right)*.

Bostock, manager of the Zoological Garden, presented visitors to the Wild
Animal Show with the "missing link" to Darwin's evolutionary chain in the
form of a well-trained chimpanzee. "Here the Darwinian theory of evolution is
very completely illustrated," claimed the official exposition guidebook. "The
successive stages of development by which the 'genus homo,' of the present
day was evolved from its primaeval progenitors is shown by numerous well-
selected examples, from the lowest type of Simian development to the 'missing
link' or educated chimpanzee, Esau, who all but talks, and from the lowest
savage to the polished gentlemen of today." Whether any human beings were
actually displayed in the same show with Esau is uncertain, but the presence
of the "missing link" in the larger setting of the midway only reinforced the
lessons of racial hierarchy that saturated the artistic dimensions of the fair and
the living ethnological shows.[48]

If the midway colonies and related attractions reflected the imperial ambitions of the exposition promoters, the villages also evidenced an important
concomitant to imperial expansion—disease. Tuberculosis hit the Filipino Village. Furthermore, the director of the exposition's medical department, Roswell Park, reported that eleven cases of measles appeared in the Eskimo Village and in several instances advanced to pneumonia. Park also recorded an
outbreak of mumps in the Hawaiian Village and eight cases of tuberculosis in
the Indian Congress. But despite quarantines imposed on several villages for
varying lengths of time, visitors generally remained oblivious to these aspects
of village life. Many fairgoers, like Uncle Hank, found the villagers "all rich
in mirth-provoking possibilities."[49]

As Americans stepped gingerly into the twentieth century, they found that

the Pan offered an atmosphere of joy and gaiety where education and entertainment waltzed hand in hand. They discovered that all the world was a fair
and found even the far reaches of the universe on display for their amusement
and edification. Swaddled in the comfortable security of the exposition's utopian promises, many exposition visitors simply let themselves go when they
hit the Pan. "Serious-minded clergymen cheer on the bloodless bull-fight,"
Mary Bronson Hart wrote about the midway, and "portly ex-senators run races
on oriental donkeys several sizes too small for them, and timorous maiden
ladies explore the awful mysteries of the Darkness and Dawn Under-World."
This last concession initially horrified midway pleasure seekers with "seas of
fire," the sudden "appearance of brown-suited young men wearing painted
skeletons," and a confrontation with a likeness of Satan himself. Visitors,
however, wrestled only briefly with the darker recesses of their psyches, for
darkness soon gave way to the "Grotto of Dawn," a heavenly city of "soft
lights," "flowing fountains," and "walls of jasper." At the conclusion, "the
mist-like forms of floating angels" pointed the way back to the thoroughfare of
the Pan. Once back on the midway, tourists alternated taking turns on the
giant see-saw and rotating aero-cycle, which afforded sweeping panoramas of
the Pan-American grounds. Another popular concession, Frederic W. Thompson's Trip to the Moon—with effects so realistic that many in the audience
suffered from motion sickness—caused one journalist to exclaim: "There! you
see, not satisfied with exhausting the earth, [showmen] have already begun
upon the universe. Behold, the world is a sucked orange."[50]

Throughout the summer visitors continued their revelry in the shadows of

Fig. 46. Esau, "the connecting
link." From Richard H. Barry, *Snap
Shots on the Midway of the Pan-
American Exposition*.

the displays devoted to American progress. As 5 September, President's Day, approached, the swell of self-congratulation grew. What the directors intended as the consummating moment of the fair, however, miscarried. The day after delivering one of the most memorable speeches of his career, while shaking hands with the crowd in the Temple of Music, President McKinley was shot by Leon Czolgosz, a reputed anarchist. The shooting triggered the arrests of anarchists and socialists across the country and, since Czolgosz was the son of recent Polish immigrants, escalated nationwide demands for immigration restrictions on European populations perceived as undesirable. McKinley's death—which occurred in the home of exposition president John Milburn eight days after the shooting—exposed the ethnic and class rifts in American society; it also underscored the fundamental importance of the exposition for maintaining a shared cultural faith in American progress at a time of acute political crisis.[51]

In his President's Day address McKinley praised expositions as "time-keepers of progress," extolled industrial growth as the guarantor of progress, and charted the course to future utopia through the establishment of "reciprocal" commercial relations with Pan-American countries. Expositions played an important part in this process, McKinley explained, because "[t]hey record the world's advancement. They stimulate the energy, enterprise, and intellect of the people and quicken human genius. They go into the home. They broaden and brighten the daily life of the people." The force of McKinley's

Fig. 47. McKinley's entrance. From Division of Prints and Photographs, Library of Congress.

statement about the impact of expositions on everyday life received added weight in the aftermath of the shooting as souvenir prices on the grounds skyrocketed. "The demand for souvenirs with a picture of the Temple of Music or of the President was tremendous," the *Express* commented. "Little trays, ornamented with pictures of the Temple of Music, went like hotcakes." Such keepsakes would enliven memories of the assassination of McKinley and of the life of the fair.[52]

"Do Not Neglect the Fair," the *Express* editorialized after McKinley's death. "The Exposition is recognized now as an enterprise of national importance to a greater extent than it ever was before." The same newspaper admonished its readers "to have faith in [the exposition], to admire it, to praise it to their friends." Between the first week of September and the first week of November, when the fair closed its gates, weekly attendance figures increased as nearly two million people visited the exposition. The experience of one elderly man was not untypical. As he and his wife entered the fairgrounds a local newspaper reporter observed that the old man burst into tears when he "spied an American flag flying on a tall flagpole" in the Esplanade. "Thank God, it's there yet!" the reporter heard him cry out. On Railroad Day, well over one hundred thousand people traveled to the fair, and many crammed the Temple of Music to hear Senator Chauncey Depew recite the accomplishments of American railroads and eulogize McKinley as "a Christian and a patriot." At the conclusion of the speech, the crowd sat motionless and silent. Then deafening applause broke out, the band struck up the "Star-Spangled Banner," "and the audience arose, waving flags, [with] the Senator waving a flag and virtually leading the audience." Two days later the spirit of political authority infused the cultural sovereignty of the fair in yet another way as a likeness of McKinley mysteriously appeared on the floor of the Temple of Music near the spot where he was assassinated. No one ever discovered the origin of the design, but it had the same import as the remark by Governor Benjamin Odell on New York Day at the fair: "Our Government still lives, and as we turn from the bier of our martyred President let us resolve to be more earnest in our devotion." McKinley's death, in short, increased the stature of the exposition as a visible reminder of cultural and political continuity in a society wrenched by disturbing signs of class conflict.[53]

As the Pan-American Exposition moved to conclusion, another effort to inspire patriotic devotion to imperial visions of progress through a world's fair was well under way in Saint Louis. Like the directors of the Buffalo exposition, the civic leaders sponsoring the celebration commemorating the one hundredth anniversary of the Louisiana Purchase understood that the "true function of an exposition is education" and that the "purpose and end of all its ministrations should be the development and ripening of each soul which comes within the scope of its influence." The directors of the Louisiana Purchase Exposition, however, did more than merely try to influence the souls of men. They sought to gain the world as well.[54]

6

The Louisiana Purchase Exposition, Saint Louis, 1904: "The Coronation of Civilization"

So thoroughly does it represent the world's civilization that if all man's other works were by some unspeakable catastrophe, blotted out, the records here established by the assembled nations would offer all necessary standards for the rebuilding of our entire civilization.

David R. Francis, 1904

Meet me in St. Louis, Louis,
Meet me at the fair,
Don't tell me the lights are shining
Any place but there;
We will dance the Hoochee-Koochee
I will be your tootsie wootsie
If you will meet me in St. Louis, Louis,
Meet me at the fair.

"Meet Me in St. Louis, Louis," 1904[1]

FOR THE BETTER PART OF 1904, the Louisiana Purchase Exposition, an ivory-tinted city of vast proportions, served as the cultural touchstone for the nation as over nineteen million "open-eyed" and "open-souled" visitors, many armed with notebooks, thronged through its gates. Exhibits included a floral clock, one hundred feet in diameter and powered by machines hidden in a shaft beneath the flowers, that measured time in thousandths of a second. Reflecting the national cult of strenuous living, or "the gospel of muscles" as it was called at the fair, the exposition included a Department of Physical Culture that presented the first Olympic Games ever held in the Western Hemisphere. Displays of airships and automobiles—the latter introduced to Americans three years earlier at the Buffalo fair—excited popular expectations for a better way of life in the twentieth century. A series of international congresses brought leading scientists and men of letters from around the nation and world to the fair, including Max Weber, Henri Poincaré, William Rainey Harper, and Hugo Münsterberg, to address audiences on topics ranging from the social and natural sciences to philosophy and mathematics. Few fairgoers would ever forget their first experience with an ice cream cone, a novelty introduced at this exposition by an enterprising concessionaire who rolled up a waffle and topped it off with a scoop of ice cream. Yet the taste sensations, scholarly gatherings, transportation innovations, athletic competitions, machines in the gardens, and monumental exhibit halls were only isolated aspects of the overarching effort by local and national elites to issue a manifesto of racial and material progress and national harmony that would equal the far-reaching effects of the utopian decree laid down at Chicago a decade earlier.[2]

"Remember," *Harper's Magazine* predicted as the fair got under way, "that such a Fair as this that St. Louis offers leaves no intelligent visitor where it found him. It fills him full of pictures and of knowledge that keep coming up in his mind for years afterwards. It gives him new standards, new means of comparison, new insight into the conditions of life in the world he is living in." William F. Slocum, president of Colorado College, elaborated on the educational value of the exposition for the masses. According to Slocum, the fair embodied "as perfect an illustration as has been seen of the method of the 'University of the Future,' which is to exchange pictures and living objects for text-books, and to make these, with the aid of laboratory work, the means whereby instruction is given and individual development [is] obtained." Slocum compared the Saint Louis fair to the Crystal Palace Exhibition, the Centennial, and especially the World's Columbian Exposition, noting that "[i]t is the same kind of people that learned most there that will be the greatest gainers here—the great mass of unlearned, if not unlettered, people whose first really wide outlook is to come to them now, and that other class possibly as large, who have never known the widening influence of travel, but have learned from their reading the fact that here much that the ordinary traveler may fail to see is made accessible to them." With an initial capitalization of

Fig. 48. Opening day before the Column of Progress at the Louisiana Purchase Exposition. From Division of Prints and Photographs, Library of Congress.

$15 million (ironically, the same amount of money that the United States originally paid for the Louisiana Territory), the directors of the Saint Louis fair turned this portrait of the world into an anthropologically validated racial landscape that made the acquisition of the Philippine Islands and continued overseas economic expansion seem as much a part of the manifest destiny of the nation as the Louisiana Purchase itself.[3]

The directors of the exposition formed a notable court. Heading the enterprise was David R. Francis, a former grain broker who had served as mayor of Saint Louis, governor of Missouri, and secretary of the interior in Grover Cleveland's second administration. At a meeting of the Saint Louis Businessmen's League in 1896, Francis won acceptance of the idea, first proposed by the directors of the Missouri Historical Society, to hold an exposition commemorating the centenary of the Louisiana Purchase. During the ensuing eight years, Francis was instrumental in gaining support for the fair from leading bankers, exporters, railroad directors, corporate lawyers, wholesalers, mining tycoons, and university presidents. He also included in the roster of world's fair officials many former exposition builders. Frederick J. V. Skiff, director of Chicago's Field Museum and widely acclaimed authority on expositions, was selected as director of exhibits. The immigrant German sculptor Karl Bitter again arranged the sculptural ornamentation into a series of heroic allegories about America's progress. Frederick W. Taylor, who had just finished his tenure as director of exhibits for the Pan-American Exposition Company, journeyed to Saint Louis to take charge of the Horticultural Department. Together with many other experienced exposition hands, these individuals lent their personal talents and collective dreams to the success of the Saint Louis fair.[4]

The magnitude of their vision translated directly into the sheer size of this fair—the largest international exposition the world had ever seen. Its total acreage nearly doubled the 664 acres of the World's Columbian Exposition. Total exhibit space exceeded the 82 acres at Chicago by more than one-third. "Any of the principal exhibit palaces at St. Louis covers virtually as much space as was occupied by all of the exhibit buildings of the Pan-American Exposition," boasted the official catalog of exhibits. The Saint Louis fair was so vast that Dr. Charles H. Hughes, professor of neurology and dean of Barnes Medical College in Saint Louis, urged his colleagues in the medical profession to do everything in their power to prevent patients diagnosed as neurasthenic from visiting the exposition because its dimensions would surely lead to their collapse. Hughes also admonished his fellow doctors to encourage "specially brain-fagged businessmen" and other mentally fatigued "men of affairs" to make their visit "a recreative, diverting, restful, sight-seeing tour" lasting at least several weeks or months in order to avoid the almost certain breakdown that would result from a hurried visit.[5]

Fig. 49. Sunken garden. Courtesy of Smithsonian Institution Archives,
Record Unit 95, Photograph Collection.

His advice was not without merit. Ambulances, according to visiting British
architect H. Phillips Fletcher, were kept busy transporting overweary visitors
to first aid stations and hospitals. "The fatigue entailed in seeing the Exhibition was simply enormous," he reported, "and the glare of the buildings rendered smoked glasses an absolute necessity." After a day of sightseeing, Saint
Louis author Kate Chopin, whose most recent book had met with neglect and
unfavorable reviews, collapsed and died. Many years later Thomas Wolfe,
through the semiautobiographical protagonist of Look Homeward, Angel, recalled that visiting the exposition had exacted an enormous mental toll. "His
mind," Wolfe wrote, "gave way completely in this Fair." For most fairgoers,
however, fascination with the exhibits and buildings tempered the mental and
physical exhaustion occasioned by crisscrossing the expansive exposition
grounds and studying the exhibits. "Sally," Pa Detwiler exclaimed in a magazine story about the fair, "so long as I've lived on God's green earth I never
looked to see nothin' like this! It's fine!" Postcards sent from the fair reported:
"We are enjoying every minute." "Weather perfect. . . . Crowds are coming

in to St. Louis," noted one visitor. "Hello Gladys, I wish you were here," said another. "Buildings are now light up [sic]. Beautiful beyond description," observed a third exposition enthusiast. Writing in the *National Magazine*, Joe Mitchell Chapple summed up the experience of many exposition visitors when he wrote: "The Fair is a succession of mental shocks, cumulative and educative." Nothing, he added, impressed him more than "the deep, far reaching, ethical, and educative import of the Universal Exposition in St. Louis."[6]

The person who classified the exhibits for the fair, F. J. V. Skiff, explained the meaning of this cumulative education on opening day: "The scene which stretches before us to-day is fairer than upon which Christian gazed from Delectable Mountain." Continuing, he explained: "over and above all [the fair] is the record of the social conditions of mankind, registering not only the culture of the world at this time, but indicating the particular plans along with which different races and different peoples may safely proceed, or in fact have begun to advance towards a still higher development." As Skiff understood it, the exposition was "designed to teach all—but primarily and distinctly . . . the expert working citizenry of the country and the world—in all lines of human activity." Over two hundred strikes directed against the exposition company during the course of construction gave a special sense of urgency to Skiff's classificatory mission. As he explained the social importance of his exposition classification scheme to the graduating class at Colorado College:

Capital and labor must be classified; classified and correlated. A spade is of no value except in its employment, and it cannot be properly employed except directly or indirectly in the work of development in the line of progress. Progress depends upon unity, upon harmony. Common labor is the seed of progress. But the harvest must be gathered, and science must be the husbandman.

A scientific classification, Skiff believed, gave purpose to people's lives, shaped their methods of analysis, and created "a properly balanced citizen capable of progress."[7]

To create this ideal citizen, Skiff developed a twofold classificatory arrangement for the exposition that refined classification schemes developed for earlier fairs. In the first place, he organized exhibits in "a sequential synopsis of the developments that have marked man's progress." But he subsumed this portrayal of "the evolution and development of individuals in certain environments" within a broader synchronic arrangement illustrating an ideal, "composite type of man." This composite portrait consisted of sixteen categories that corresponded to the exposition's departments. The departments of Education, Art, Liberal Arts, and Applied Sciences (including Manufactures, Machinery, Electricity, and Transportation) headed the classification, Skiff noted, because they "equip [man] for the battle and prepare him for the enjoyments of life." Next came departments devoted to displays of raw materials—Agriculture, Horticulture, Mining, Forestry, and Fish and Game—that "show how man conserves the forces of nature to his uses." Three departments concluded the classification: Anthropology, representing the study of man; Social Economy, "where man considers the welfare of communities"; and Physical Culture, "where it is demonstrated that a sound mind and moral character demand a healthy body." Skiff regarded each of these categories as important, but he left no doubt about which he considered the cornerstone for the rest. "A universal exposition," he told the graduating seniors at Colorado College, "is a vast museum of anthropology and ethnology, of man and his works." This observation reflected the reality of the Saint Louis fair and the importance assigned by the directors to the Anthropology Department in their attempt to create that "properly balanced citizen."[8]

The Louisiana Purchase Exposition featured the most extensive Anthropology Department of any world's fair. The directors expressed their intent to establish "a comprehensive anthropological exhibition, constituting a Congress of Races, and exhibiting particularly the barbarous and semi-barbarous peoples of the world, as nearly as possible in their ordinary and native environments." These plans received enthusiastic endorsement from leading anthropologists around the country, including Frederic Ward Putnam, former head of the Department of Anthropology at the World's Columbian Exposition, who tendered the directors his "hearty approval" for their plans. To head the department, the directors turned to W J McGee, who had become one of the nation's preeminent anthropologists during his tenure at the Bureau of American Ethnology before charges of financial irregularity forced him to resign.[9] His reputation was blemished, but by no means demolished. He regarded the exposition as an opportunity not only to maintain his stature in the anthropology profession, but to fashion the national identity out of his own well-developed theory of racial progress.[10]

McGee had organized the substance of his theory about progress into two 1899 addresses: "The Trend of Human Progress," delivered at the Washington Academy of Sciences, and "National Growth and National Character," one in a series of lectures on national expansion sponsored by the National Geographic Society. In "The Trend of Human Progress," McGee developed a broad overview of human history, observing the existence of a "trend of vital development from low toward the high, from dullness toward brightness, from idleness groveling toward intellectual uprightness." The driving forces behind this upward movement, he explained, were "cephalization"—the gradual increase in the cranial capacity of different races—and "cheirization"—the regular increase of manual dexterity along racial lines. The proof, he believed, was self-evident: "It is a matter of common observation that the white man can *do* more and better than the yellow, the yellow man more and better than the red or black." As a consequence of cheirization and cephalization, the "advance of culture" proceeded along lines of racial achievement:

Classed in terms of blood, the peoples of the world may be grouped in several races; classed in terms of what they do rather than what they merely are, they are conveniently grouped in the four culture grades of savagery, barbarism, civilization, and enlightenment.[11]

This division of humanity into racially based cultural grades did not signify a static universe for McGee. Far from it. He saw the turn of the century as a time when "perfected man is over-spreading the world." By "perfected man" he simply meant "the two higher culture-grades—especially the Caucasian race, and (during recent decades) the budded enlightenment of Britain and full-blown enlightenment of America." Caucasians, he argued, were ushering in a new era in world history when "human culture is becoming unified, not only through diffusion but through the extinction of the lower grades as their representatives rise into higher grades." The net effect of this process was "that the races of the continents are gradually uniting in lighter blend, and the burden of humanity is already in large measure the White Man's burden—for, viewing the human world as it is, white and strong are synonymous terms."[12]

McGee elaborated on the specific role of the Anglo-Saxon as burden bearer in "National Growth and National Character," a spirited exhortation to Caucasian race pride and action:

it is the duty of the strong man to subjugate lower nature, to extirpate the bad and cultivate the good among living things, to delve in earth below and cleave the air above in search of fresh resources, to transform the seas into paths for ships and pastures for food-fishes, to yoke fire and lightning in chariots of subtly-wrought adamant, to halter thin vapors and harness turbulent waters into servile subjection, and in all ways to enslave the world for the support of humanity and the increase of human intelligence.

McGee scoffed at "pessimists, doubters, and cowards among the highest races who shudder at the figment of Wall Street and the phantom of monopoly; they forget that the multi-millionaire's daughter becomes an angel of mercy . . . and that the best organized monopoly founds a university whence a thousand students go forth annually to diffuse higher knowledge." For McGee, progress demanded unity of purpose as much as racial fitness.[13]

All in all, McGee's two lectures vindicated American national experience and synthesized the works of leading evolutionary thinkers including Darwin, Powell, and Spencer. The lectures offered a vision of racial progress that made cultural advance synonymous with increased industrial expansion. By stretching humanity out on an anthropological rack that highlighted racial "grades," moreover, McGee distinguished between "enlightened" and "civilized" whites, thus broadening his racial theory to include various white ethnic populations just when national concern was mounting about the racial "fitness" of southern and eastern Europeans immigrating to America.[14]

McGee admitted that his theoretical apparatus suffered to the extent that much of the anthropological data on which he based his argument was unpublished, and perhaps unpublishable. The necessary pieces of evidence, he assured his listeners, existed in abundance, "but they overflow the poor work-sites of savage skin-dressers and ancient arrow-makers,· the simple laboratories of barbaric stone-workers and semi-barbaric smiths, the mines and mills of civilization, and the elaborate manufactories of enlightenment—they are far too voluminous for books, yet within the constant sight of all whose eyes are open."[15]

This matter of evidence, however, could not be dismissed so easily. The credibility of his theory depended in large measure on assembling for public view "types" of various people acting out their traditional cultural pursuits. McGee's interest in international expositions followed accordingly. He had been involved with Smithsonian preparations for the Atlanta, Nashville, Omaha, and Buffalo fairs but had been disappointed over their failure to incorporate wide-ranging living ethnological displays under the direct supervision of anthropologists. After receiving assurances that the management of the Louisiana Purchase Exposition planned to make anthropology the heart of their fair, McGee left his troubles at the BAE behind and eagerly accepted the directors' offer to take charge of the Anthropology Department.[16]

When McGee arrived in Saint Louis in August 1903, he made it clear that he would fashion the exhibits in his charge into an exemplum of his theory of racial progress. "The aim of the Department of Anthropology at the World's Fair," McGee stated, "will be to represent human progress from the dark prime to the highest enlightenment, from savagery to civic organization, from egoism to altruism." "The method," he added, "will be to use living peoples in their accustomed avocations as our great object lesson," with particular emphasis on "Indian school work, America's best effort to elevate the lower races." As the exhibits took shape, McGee noted that the Anthropology Department would also contribute "a moral motive" to the overall education offered by this "university of the masses." That moral dimension involved teaching exposition-goers "something of that upward course of human development beginning with the Dark Ages of tooth and claw and stone and tools, and culminating in the modern enlightenment illustrated in the great Exhibit Palaces and the International Congresses." This constant upward spiral, McGee emphasized, left some people by the wayside:

> So every advanced nation has its quota of aliens through ill-starred birth and defective culture, who can be lifted to the level of its institutions only through a regeneration extending to both body and mind, both work and thought—they are the mental and moral beggars of the community who may not be trusted on horseback but only in the rear seat of the wagon. In truth, standards are rising so rapidly that the lower half find it hard to keep up.

McGee's metaphor aptly summed up the idea of progress that took visible form on the fairgrounds at Saint Louis. For his efforts to implement this vision, a local newspaper dubbed him "overlord of the savage world."[17]

By opening day, though his appropriation had been substantially cut, McGee had converted the western portion of the exposition grounds into a field research station for the study of nonwhite "types." Groups of pygmies from Africa, "Patagonian giants" from Argentina, Ainu aborigines from Japan, and Kwakiutl Indians from Vancouver Island, as well as groups of Native Americans gathered around prominent Indian chiefs including Geronimo, Chief Joseph, and Quanah Parker, were formed into living ethnological exhibits. They were supplemented by an adjoining United States government exhibit of nearly one thousand Filipinos and by separate ethnological concessions along the Pike. McGee assembled the nonwhites directly under his charge into a "logical arrangement" of living "types" stretched out between the Indian School Building and the Philippines display.[18]

The department also contained anthropometry and psychometry laboratories "so that the race-types and culture-grades assembled on the grounds may be brought within the range of comparative study." Sections devoted to archaeology and history illustrated respectively "the successive states of advancement during prehistoric times" and "the later development of a vast territory from a savage wilderness to the family of the great commonwealths of which the seat of the Exposition is the metropolis." With its offices, museum space,

Fig. 50. W J McGee (1853–1912): "Overlord of the savage world." From Mark Bennitt, *History of the Louisiana Purchase Exposition*.

and laboratories located in Cupples Hall No. 1, a permanent building belonging to Washington University, McGee's department possessed implicit academic stature that made its role as the scientific foundation of the exposition all the more convincing. [19]

Scientific prestige and credence also accrued to the department as a direct result of several other anthropologists' contributing advice and collections of material. For advice on the laboratories, McGee turned to Franz Boas at Columbia and Aleš Hrdlička, newly appointed head of the Department of Physical Anthropology at the United States National Museum. Until his appropriation from the Smithsonian failed to materialize, Hrdlička had planned to participate in the administration of the anthropometry section. As it stood, the laboratories were placed under the direction of two Columbia University psychologists, Robert S. Woodworth and his student Frank Bruner, whom Boas had nominated for their positions at the fair. [20]

McGee made clear what he expected of these laboratories in a prospectus he submitted to Woodworth for approval before sending it to the exposition's publicity division. The laboratories, McGee explained, would make "customary measurements" and "introduce tests of strength, endurance, etc., in order that the results may indicate—so far as measurements may—the relative physical value of the different races of the peoples" involved in the fair. Psychological measurements, he added, would involve testing "sensitiveness to temperature, delicacy of touch and taste, acuteness of vision and hearing, and other sense reactions, together with power of coordination as expressed in rapidity and accuracy of forming judgement, etc., in the different races and cultural stages, in order to determine the relative prevalence of sense defects." In its first month of operation, McGee noted with satisfaction that over twenty-five thousand people had visited the laboratory and that well over one hundred measurements had been taken. Various juries of awards were equally impressed. One jury, composed of James Cattell, Hugo Münsterberg, and E. B. Tichener, believed that the results obtained from the laboratories "will be a real contribution to science." Yet, if the published results of the psychometry measurements were any indication, rather than serving the cause of science the laboratories served to quantify the impressions visitors received from the remainder of the anthropology exhibits and from the fair in its entirety. According to Bruner's report, "the racial superiority of whites was manifest in their heightened sense of hearing" as opposed to the hearing ability of "inferior races," while intelligence testing demonstrated that the Pygmies were "dense and stupid." Anthropologist Clark Wissler commented favorably on these findings, noting that Bruner had left little doubt that "racial differences exist." Most fairgoers left the laboratories with the same idea firmly ingrained in their minds. [21]

Boas and Hrdlička, particularly the latter, regarded the Anthropology Department in its entirety as a valuable source for field research, especially "for acquiring some interesting racial anatomical material." The basis for this brainstorm was Hrdlička's suspicion—confirmed by McGee—that deaths were inevitable "among the Filipinos and other tribes" gathered for display. Two Filipinos, in fact had already died en route to the fair when, despite freezing weather across the western states, train crewman shut off heat to their cars. What to do about this expected loss of life at the fair? Hrdlička approached Boas and George S. Huntington at Columbia as well as Livingston Farrand at the American Museum of Natural History about formulating "some arrangement by which all of us would benefit from such cases." Since the bodies would be lost to various cemeteries, Hrdlička, after discussion with Boas, proposed obtaining as many corpses as he could lay hands on and dividing the bodies in such a way that Columbia and the American Museum would receive "the soft parts" and skeletons while the United States National Museum would receive the brains. The response by Columbia officials is unknown, but Farrand presented this idea to Hermon Bumpus, director of the American Museum. According to Farrand, the publicity-conscious Bumpus declared that, "while he is personally entirely in sympathy with the idea he feels it is better not to participate formally." Farrand was "sorry," he told Hrdlička, "for I should like to see the stuff come here," but reminded Hrdlička that "it makes no difference to science in which institution the results are placed." Hrdlička certainly agreed, for shortly after the close of the exposition three Filipino brains from Saint Louis augmented the collections of the Smithsonian Institution.[22]

Fig. 51. Aleš Hrdlička (1869–1943). Courtesy of National Anthropology Archives.

The didactic value of the Anthropology Department also engaged the attention of a perennial fairgoer and frequent contributor to past exhibitions, Frederick Starr, professor of anthropology at the University of Chicago. At the behest of the exposition management and McGee, Starr became a special commissioner to Japan and returned with several Ainus, aboriginal inhabitants of northern islands in the Japanese archipelago, for display in the Anthropology Department. Starr's contributions to the department continued far beyond the completion of his expedition to Japan. He also received permission from McGee and from the University of Chicago "to give a definite and systematic field school work at St. Louis, using the living ethnological material there gathered." Starr's plans included "definite class lectures, practical talks, and direct work with material, living and not." Regularly enrolled students at the University of Chicago could take an examination at the conclusion of the three-week session at the fair and receive course credit in their major fields. The course, appropriately titled "The Louisiana Purchase Exposition Class in Ethnology," attracted approximately thirty "society" coeds from the University of Chicago as well as a number of Saint Louis schoolteachers. Beginning on 1 September, the members of the class heard Starr deliver two daily lectures on a variety of topics extending from "cannibalism" and "physical characteristics of race" to art and sculpture. Starr's educational venture, just as McGee predicted in letters to concessionaires along the Pike requesting free admission for Starr and his students, delighted the local press and generated a great deal of publicity for the exhibits that were visited. The Saint Louis *Post-Dispatch* headlined a front-page article "Chicago Co-eds Who Hitched Their Wagon to Prof. Starr Are Finding Anthropology a Live Study at World's Fair." The pun was telling, since the living exhibits along the Pike, in the Philippines exhibit, and in the Anthropology Department proper formed the nucleus of the course.[23]

The efforts of Starr, Boas, and Hrdlička combined to give the Anthropology Department an important aura of legitimacy as a valid educational undertaking. McGee also considered it his duty to instruct as many people as possible. Consequently he jumped at the suggestion by John E. Sullivan, head of the Amateur Athletic Union and of the Department of Physical Culture, to arrange an Anthropology Day at the track stadium to help promote the Olympic Games. "The object of the contests," McGee told the superintendents of the Native American and Filipino exhibits, "will be to obtain for the first time what may be called interracial athletic records." Many nonwhites from the Pike villages, Anthropology Department, and Philippine exhibit participated in the show, but because of poor advance publicity the turnout of spectators was disappointingly small. McGee, however, remained undaunted and proceeded to lay plans for another competition in September that "will give the audience a chance to see the pick of the primitive tribes contesting in modern and native games of strength, endurance, and agility." To promote the competition, McGee joined an "Emergency Exploitation Committee" that generated publicity for the event and attempted to raise money for prizes. He also tried to shift the site for the event to the main plaza area of the exposition and retitled the contest an "anthropology meet." Although he had to use the parade grounds instead of the plaza and had to forgo plans to give monetary prizes, the meet attracted thirty thousand spectators. Albert W. Jenks, head of the anthropology section of the War Department, awarded the winners of the various events American flags as trophies. A local newspaper summed up the results: "The meeting was a grand success from every point of view, and served as a good example of what the brown men are capable of doing with training."[24]

Training, as McGee understood it, was part and parcel of the imperial mission. "One of the gravest tasks of any progressive nation," he wrote for the *World's Fair Bulletin*, official journal of the exposition, "is that of caring for alien wards, i.e., bearing the 'White Man's burden,' as told by Kipling, or performing the Strong Man's duty, as felt by the most modern statesmen." McGee condemned much of America's historical treatment of the Indians but praised Indian schools as "a boon to the survivors of our passing race." The Indian School building, however, was "designed not merely as a consummation, but as a prophecy; for now that other primitive peoples are passing under the beneficent influence and protection of the Stars and Stripes, it is needful to take stock of past progress as a guide to the future." On the other side of Arrowhead Lake, McGee noted before the fair opened, "will stand the Filipino, even as against the Red Man on the continent, just beyond the Pacific, stands the brown man of the nearer Orient; and it is the aim of the Model Indian School to extend influence across both intervening waters to the benefit of both races." As a result of careful planning by Skiff and McGee, the encampments of living Native Americans that stretched between the Indian School and the lake made explicit the connection between America's imperial past and imperial future. As one official exposition publication noted: "the time is coming when the purchase and retention of the Philippine Islands will seem as wise to our descendants as does the Louisiana Purchase seem to us who live today." To make the juncture between past, present, and future airtight, the Department of Exploitation, in charge of publicity for the Philippine Island exhibit, widely advertised the display from the islands as the "Philippine Reservation."[25]

The Philippine Reservation, according to William P. Wilson, chairman of the United States government's Philippine Exposition Board, constituted "an exposition within an exposition; the greatest exhibition of the most marvelous Exposition in the history of the world." With nearly twelve hundred Filipinos living in villages on the forty-seven-acre site set aside for the display, the exhibit climaxed the efforts of earlier exposition promoters to establish, under federal government auspices, a large-scale exhibit of the people and resources of the Philippine Islands. But the size of the exhibit at

Saint Louis far exceeded the wildest dreams of the directors of previous fairs. It was also unique in having the full support of the federal government at the outset.[26]

The directors' hopes for government participation in the planned Philippine showing received an early endorsement from William Howard Taft while he was civil governor of the islands. According to the *World's Fair Bulletin*, Taft believed that the proposed exhibit would have a "moral effect" on the people of the islands and that "Filipino participation would be a very great influence in completing pacification and in bringing Filipinos to improve their condition." President Theodore Roosevelt and Secretary of War Elihu Root supported Taft's position and encouraged his efforts to organize "as comprehensive an exhibit as possible of the products and resources, manufactures, art, ethnology, education, government of the Philippine Islands, and the habits and customs of the Filipino people."[27]

Responsibility for the success of the undertaking centered on William Powell Wilson, Taft's appointee to direct the Philippine Exposition Board. At the time of his selection, Wilson had a national and international reputation as the founder and head of the Philadelphia Commercial Museum—an institution that wedded science to the interests of American business expansion overseas. The Commercial Museum came into existence as a direct result of Wilson's visit to the World's Columbian Exposition while he was still chairman of the School of Biology at the University of Pennsylvania. The exhibits at the Chicago fair so impressed him that he returned to Philadelphia and persuaded many of the city's political and commercial leaders of the value of "preserving and enlarging such collections."[28] He received guarantees of private and public support and purchased many of the foreign displays as the nucleus for a museum in Philadelphia. In 1894 Wilson was elected director of the museum, a position he held for the next thirty-three years. Under his leadership the institution became an information clearing house, providing American businessmen with data about economic conditions abroad, and a vehicle for public education as well. The museum opened formally in 1896 with a Pan-American Congress inaugurated by President McKinley. Two years later the museum hosted the National Export Exhibition, which drew more than one million visitors to displays devoted to the possibilities for American economic expansion abroad. By the time of his appointment to the Philippine Exposition Board, in short, Wilson, had a considerable reputation as a scientist with America's business interests at heart.[29]

One of Wilson's first steps as head of the Philippine Exposition Board was to recommend that his associate at the Commercial Museum, Gustavo Niederlein, be appointed director of exhibits for the board. Like Wilson, Niederlein was a naturalist and scientist devoted to the advance of Western imperialism. His international reputation was such that at the Paris Exposition of 1900 he participated in a number of congresses, including those pertaining to

Fig. 52. William Powell Wilson (1844–1927). From Mark Bennitt, *History of the Louisiana Purchase Exposition*.

"commercial geography," botany, and "colonial sociology." He so impressed the French government with his contributions to the Paris exposition that government officials asked him to classify exhibits for a permanent colonial museum in Paris. For his work there he received half the collection for the Commercial Museum in Philadelphia. He subsequently joined the secretary-general of the French colonies on an expedition to the colonies and was in the process of advising him on exhibits for the Hanoi exposition of 1902 when the United States War Department appointed him to Wilson's staff in the Philippines. As Wilson described him, Niederlein was "a thoroughly trained scientific and business man."[30]

In late 1902 Niederlein and Wilson put their scientific and business talents to work in the Philippines. With the cooperation of several prominent Filipinos and numerous United States colonial officials—including Clarence R. Edwards, chief of the Bureau of Insular Affairs, Albert E. Jenks, former ethnologist at the Bureau of American Ethnology and head of the War Department's Ethnological Survey of the Philippine Islands, Daniel Folkmar, anthropologist and lieutenant-governor in charge of the Philippine civil service, and Pedro A. Paterno, president of the Philippine senate—they proceeded to arrange material for the colonial exhibit at the Louisiana Purchase Exposition. Simultaneously, in accordance with the congressional act authorizing establishment of the Exposition Board, Wilson and Niederlein collected materials for a permanent commercial museum in Manila and for a preliminary exposition that would show Filipinos the exhibits that would be sent to Saint Louis. The museum, intended primarily to provide American business interests with commercial data about the economic possibilities of the islands, opened in February 1903 but closed in May when it became apparent that the exhibits would be needed to complete the display for Saint Louis. The preliminary exposition never materialized for the same reason. Yet the motives behind the Manila exposition and museum informed the plans for the exhibit at Saint Louis and revealed the overall goal of the government to institutionalize American colonial rule, to bring to the Philippines "the impelling power of modern civilization," as Niederlein termed it, and to show the Filipinos how America would aid the development of the islands through "the consumption of the raw material of this archipelago in [America's] well developed and increasing industries."[31]

To emphasize to Filipinos the long road they would have to travel before achieving the capacity for self-rule, the short-lived museum included a division of ethnology illustrating "tribal and racial exhibits in every detail" and "showing the state of culture and growth of civilization" on the islands. This ethnological feature not only reappeared in the exhibit at Saint Louis, but dominated the Philippine Reservation to such an extent that McGee, as early as November 1903, informed the *New York Times* that the display from the islands would be "to all intents and purposes ethnological in character." When the experienced midway organizer Edmund A. Felder joined the board as an executive officer in March 1904, it became clear that the Exposition Board would draw upon the decade-long tradition of midway ethnological concessions as well as upon received scientific wisdom en route to establishing what amounted to a federally sanctioned ethnological village on the site of the reservation.[32]

Under the primary direction of government-appointed scientists, the reservation affirmed the value of the islands to America's commercial growth and created a scientifically validated impression of Filipinos as racially inferior and incapable of national self-determination in the near future. No exhibit at any exposition better fulfilled the imperial aspirations of its sponsors. As David R. Francis observed at the official dedication of the million-dollar exhibit in mid-June, the display from the Philippines alone justified the expense and labor that went into the entire fair. From start to finish he believed it was the "overshadowing feature" of the exposition. Francis noted, moreover, that ninety-nine out of a hundred fairgoers visited the reservation.[33]

The pervading imperial message of the reservation was inescapable and apparent from the moment visitors set foot on the forested acreage set aside for the display. The moss-covered Bridge of Spain, the main entrance to the reservation, conveyed visitors into an immense War Department exhibit in the Walled City—a replica of the fortification around Manila—where fairgoers could relive the recent military triumphs by the United States.[34]

Beyond the Walled City, the Philippine Exposition Board engineered the circular ground plan of the reservation into a series of three cultural spheres depicting the civilizing influence of the Spanish past, the current ethnological state of the islands, and the beneficent results that Filipinos and Americans alike could expect from the United States takeover. At the center of the reservation the board established a "typical" Manila plaza, surrounded by four large Spanish-style buildings. These structures, consisting of an upper-class residence, a government building, an educational building, and a reproduction of the commercial museum in Manila, reminded visitors of the Spanish legacy on the islands and at the same time laid out the attributes of civilization—social and political order, education, and commerce—that the federal government considered essential to the future well-being of the islands.[35]

Radiating from the central plaza were a series of ethnological villages, often placed adjacent to exhibit buildings depicting the wealth of natural resources on the islands. The villages portrayed a variety of Filipino "types," including Visayans, "the high and more intelligent class of natives," Moros, "fierce followers of Mohammed," Bagobo "savages," "monkey-like" Negritos, and "picturesque" Igorots. In the third cultural sphere, at the farthest outreach of the reservation and concentrated behind the Igorot and Negrito villages, the board located encampments of Philippine Scouts and Constabulary—collaborationist police forces enlisted by the American military to aid in suppressing the ongoing insurrection in the islands against the United States. The function of these units at the fair extended beyond policing the reservation. As one official guide to the reservation explained, the Constabulary and Scouts were juxtaposed to the Igorots and Negritos to bring out the "extremes of the social order in the islands." Numbering nearly seven hundred, or over half the total number of Filipinos on the reservation, these paramilitary forces were intended to illustrate the "result of American rule" and to suggest the possibility for cultural advance under America's colonial administration of the islands.[36]

This possibility was also the subject of an ethnological museum situated on the reservation. Directed by Albert Jenks, this institution, "with cloisters like a convent," contained exhibits devoted to "an interpretation of the habits and life of the Philippine tribes." Jenks concentrated on the Igorots, Moros,

Fig. 53. Negrito Village, with White City looming in background. From National Archives.

Bagobos, and Negritos and declared that they were "true savages." Jenks, however, stressed that they "represent only about one-seventh of the entire population of the Archipelago, and their culture is almost entirely of their own development."[37]

Their relative numerical insignificance in the islands and at the fair notwithstanding—there were 38 Bagobos, 41 Negritos, 114 Igorots, and 100 Moros—the exhibits of the "wild tribes" became the most popular displays on the reservation. From the start of the fair, the Igorot and Negrito villages, especially the former, caught the fancy of fairgoers and of the nation to a degree unsurpassed by any exhibit at any fair since the summer of 1893 when Fatima had danced the hootchy-kootchy on the Midway at the World's Columbian Exposition. The perceived simplicity of Igorot life doubtless accounted for part of their appeal and made some fairgoers long for a less complicated way of living than that represented by the monuments to industrialization contained in the White City palaces. But the immediate impetus to see the Igorot exhibit stemmed less from preindustrial longings than from a powerful mixture of white supremacist sexual stereotypes and voyeurism.[38]

Nothing propelled the Igorots and Negritos into prominence more rapidly than the controversy that erupted in June, shortly after the opening of the exhibit, over what one visitor termed "their dusky birthday robes." With a presidential campaign under way and with anti-imperialists in the Democratic party on the verge of including a plank in the party's platform stating that the Filipinos were "inherently unfit to be members of the American body politic," the Roosevelt administration became concerned that local press reports emphasizing the absence of clothing on these Filipinos would undermine the government's efforts at the fair to show the possibilities for progress on the islands. On 23 June Taft wired Edwards to avoid "any possible impression that the Philippine Government is seeking to make prominent the savageness and barbarism of the wild tribes either for show purposes or to depreciate the popular estimate of the general civilization of the islands." In a follow-up telegram, Taft suggested "that short trunks would be enough for the men, but that for the Negrito women there ought to be shirts or chemises of some sort." Taft also ordered: "Answer what you have done immediately. The President wishes to know." Edwards lost no time in cabling his response, telling Taft that the Negritos "were until recently dressed up like plantation nigger[s], whom they diminutively represent, recently . . . [the] men have discarded these clothes and put on their native loin cloth." Furthermore, Edwards informed the secretary of war, signs had been put up showing the low number of "wild tribes" relative to the overall population of the Philippines. The administration, however, remained unsatisfied. The following day Taft's private secretary wired Edwards: "President still thinks that where the Igorot has a mere G string that it might be well to add a short trunk to cover the buttocks and front." Taft, moreover, instructed Edwards to obtain a written statement

Fig. 54. Igorot Village—note spectator with opera glasses seated on bench. Stereoscope card from Division of Prints and Photographs, Library of Congress.

from the Board of Lady Managers, an adjunct to the general directorship of the exposition, assuring the administration that the appearance of the Igorots and Negritos was unobjectionable. In the meantime Edwards ordered Niederlein to have Truman K. Hunt, former lieutenant-governor of the Lepanto-Bontoc province and manager of the Igorot village, put breechclouts on the Igorots and "allow no child to go naked."[39]

The government's efforts at overnight civilization provoked much mirth, brought an outcry from anthropologists, and generated a great deal of publicity

Fig. 55. Igorot dance. Stereoscope card from Division
of Prints and Photographs, Library of Congress.

for the exposition. The Saint Louis *Post-Dispatch* carried a cartoon showing
Taft carrying a pair of pants, in hot pursuit of an Igorot clad only in a G-
string. The editor of the same newspaper dispatched a letter to the "Department of Exploitation" at the reservation, declaring: "To put pants on [the
Igorots and Negritos] would change a very interesting ethnological exhibit
which shocks no one into a suggestive side-show." An irate Frederick Starr
seconded these thoughts in a memo to Wilson: "The scientific value of the
display is unquestionably great. Such value would be completely lost by dressing these people in a way unlike that to which they are accustomed." Starr
also added that clothing might actually kill the Igorot and Negrito villagers,
given the heat of the Saint Louis summer. By mid-July the Board of Lady
Managers concurred in the need for maintaining the apparent genuineness of
the exhibits, and the Roosevelt administration abandoned its plans to compel
the Igorots and Negritos to wear bright-colored silk trousers.[40]

Authenticating these villagers as "savages," however, left the administration with the original problem. If fairgoers perceived the villagers as utterly
backward and incapable of progress, the displays would actually buttress the
racist arguments used by anti-imperialists to oppose annexation of the islands.

Fig. 56. "Missing Link." Photograph by Gebhardt Sisters, from Division of Prints and Photographs, Library of Congress.

But the Philippine Exposition Board had already circumvented this dilemma by driving an ethnological wedge between the Igorots and Negritos. The Negritos, according to various official descriptions of their village, were "extremely low in intellect," and "it is believed that they will eventually become extinct." To reinforce this idea, one of the Negritos was named Missing Link. The Igorots, on the other hand, were judged capable of progressing. "Scientists," according to an official souvenir guide, "have declared that with the proper training they are susceptible of a high stage of development, and, unlike the American Indian, will accept rather than defy the advance of American civilization." Igorot women, one American official hastened to point out, "are the most expert ore-sorters" in the world. The possibility for uplift was highlighted when Roosevelt visited the reservation and a missionary schoolteacher led her class of Igorots in a chorus of "My Country 'Tis of Thee." The *Globe-Democrat* recorded the president's satisfaction. "It is wonderful," Roosevelt declared. "Such advancement and in so short a time!" In conceding that the Igorots might be capable of cultural advance, however, the government did not suggest that they were capable of achieving equality with Caucasians. Rather, the schools in operation on the reservation suggested that the place of the Igorots and other members of the "wild tribes" in the American empire would closely resemble the place mapped out for Native Americans and blacks in the United States.[41]

With the exception of the Negritos, who were placed on the road to extinction by government ethnologists, the Philippine Exposition Board crowded other "grades" of Filipinos into the wagon of progress—to borrow McGee's metaphor—without permitting them to ride horseback. As several members of the Scouts and Constabulary discovered, any attempt to cross the forward limits of the racial hierarchy imposed on the riders down the road to utopia would meet with serious consequences. Members of the Scouts and Constabulary who accepted the invitation of young white women schoolteachers from Saint Louis

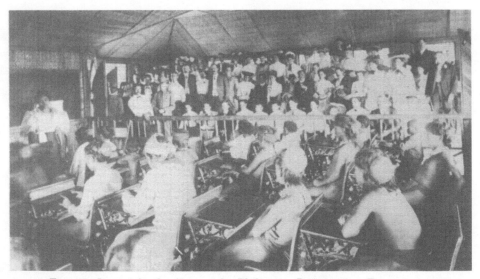

Fig. 57. Imperial schooling on the Philippine Reservation. From National Archives.

Fig. 58. Visayan theater. From National Archives.

to accompany them on tours of the fairgrounds and of the city were taunted as "niggers." When taunts failed to halt the promenades, several United States Marines, with the active cooperation of the exposition's police force, known as the Jefferson Guards and composed largely of southern whites, took matters into their own hands. As couples walked around the grounds, a contingent of Marines and guards—the latter had been issued slingshots "heavily loaded with lead" in lieu of revolvers—threatened to arrest the white women and kicked their Filipino escorts to the ground. When the Scouts returned to their camp, an even larger group of Marines arrived on the scene determined to show the Filipinos that the lynch law was not limited to southern blacks. They charged the Filipinos, shooting revolvers into the air and shouting, "Come on boys! Let's clean the Gu-Gus off the earth!" Edwards deplored the racial clashes, "in view of the fact that there are none of the negro blood in the Scouts or Constabulary." But the outburst of violence against the "highest grade" of Filipinos represented on the reservation underscored the success of the exhibit in confirming the impression that Filipinos were savages at worst and "little brown men" at best.[42]

On the occasion of Philippine Day at the fair, held to commemorate the surrender of Manila, "a great step in the diffusion of freedom over the globe," a local paper summarized the overall meaning of the reservation: "For the sake of the Filipinos and for the credit of our own country we retained control of the Philippines, with the determination to educate their people into the nearest approach to actual independence which they can have with safety to themselves." As the reservation made clear, that "nearest approach to actual independence" entailed instructing Filipinos in the ethnological limitations operating to hamper their progress—limitations that in turn mandated that

Filipinos be willing workers and consumers in the burgeoning overseas market being established by American commercial interests. "The Filipinos themselves learned from their St. Louis experience that they were not ready for self-government," the *Portland Oregonian* reported on the eve of the Lewis and Clark Centennial Exposition, which also would include an exhibit of Filipinos. Americans, the newspaper added, "who talked with [the Filipinos] and studied the tribesmen disabused themselves of any impression that the natives could take care of themselves." The newspaper conceded that "[t]here are intelligent Filipinos. But the majority are comparatively helpless. They are children. . . . Burdened with a problem of government, they would be hopelessly lost." Two home missionaries who visited the exhibit similarly commended the government officials in charge for "a grand affair—wisely planned, well adjusted to enable Americans to see the several tribes in their various stages of development and to note the capabilities and possibilities of the race." The reservation, they continued, "has strengthened our confidence in the widsom of our government's general policy respecting the Philippines and their people, and in the hopeful outlook for the Filipinos under American jurisdiction." The missionaries, moreover, promised to do everything in their power to advertise the exhibit as they traveled around the country on the National Home Mission lecture circuit. It remained for the *New York Post* to sum up: "There probably was never such a colonial exhibit gathered in the world."[43]

The exhibits in the Anthropology Department and on the Philippine Reservation provided fairgoers with an anthropologically calibrated yardstick for measuring the world's progress. In important respects these two areas of the fair served as the scientific proving ground for the lessons about comparative racial progress that pervaded the entire exposition, especially the amusement street, the Pike.

According to Thomas R. MacMechen, press agent for the Department of Concessions: "The Pike is a living color page of the world, and pictures speak louder than words." With its total cost exceeding five million dollars, MacMechen stressed that the Pike "is not a jumble of nonsense. It has meaning just as definite as the high motive which inspired the exposition. It mirrors the lighter moods of all countries." Norris B. Gregg, Saint Louis businessman and director of the Department of Admissions and Concessions, explained that the meaning of the Pike lay in its "ethical origin." The exposition management, Gregg wrote, intended "to make the lighter field of entertainment a pleasant vehicle of academic impression, producing its lesson in a lasting manner by direct appeal to the imagination, the most active and retentive faculty of the mind." Entertainment, in other words, became a vehicle for instruction about the world's progress. As Gregg declared:

Through the guise of amusement, therefore, lives and manners of peoples may be contrasted with our own, thus establishing by the most striking comparison, true ethnological values. The industries of many races, as they will be plied on the Pike, give us a keen lesson in economics. Their ways of living offer suggestions along the lines of sociology.

The Pike, in short, reflected the imperial vision of the exposition's promoters and was intended to shape the way fairgoers saw the world.[44]

"To See the Pike Is to See the Entire World," the *St. Louis World* headlined an article about the L-shaped street with its ethnological villages, wild animal shows, mechanical amusements, and sham battles. The same newspaper provided a brief synopsis of the Pike, explaining how its location complemented and underlined the importance of its purpose: "The original idea of giving the amusement section a strong educational value by having its general tone reflective of the manners and customs of the whole world, has been carried out in its conspicuous location, especially in relation to the exhibit division of the great show." The exposition's directors purposefully arranged the Pike "between two grand entrances to the Exposition, with an additional entrance from the outside, in the very center of the amusement street." For the first time, the *World* noted, "a street of concessions becomes the earliest impression of the visitors."[45]

The impression of humanity that the exposition management intended the exhibits along the Pike to convey crystallized on the opening day of the fair in a parade of "Pike types," with Frederick Cummins, head of the Wild West show, serving as grand marshal. Shortly before the fair opened, one newspaper "estimated that about 2,000 natives of the various races will be seen in the parade and that several hundred animals will add to the barbaric picture." In actuality, close to nine thousand people, whites and nonwhites, participated in the caravan as it wound around the exposition grounds. Immediately after Cummins, at the head of the parade, came the "aristocracy of the Pike"— Hale's firefighters, "a crack organization of American fire laddies with their modern apparatus"—followed by "a hodge-podge of all nationalities" drawn from Cairo Street, Mysterious Asia, Empire of India, Fair Japan, the Chinese Village, the Tyrolean Alps, the Moorish Palace, the Irish Village, the Old Plantation, and the Boer War Exhibit.[46]

Over the course of the fair, the distance between the Pike "aristocracy" and the "descendants of races which have at least left thumb-prints on the records of civilization" came into sharp focus in the Boer War Exhibit. Twice daily, British and Boer troops, including several wartime heroes from both sides, reenacted battles of the recently ended war against a backdrop of "a village of Zulus, Swazies and other South African tribes" that also formed part of the concession. This conflict between white Europeans over the domination of

South Africa, Walter Wellman wrote in *Success* magazine, "compels the pity that such valor and endurance as the heroic Boers displayed might not have been exerted in behalf of progress rather than in a futile effort to block its way." Wellman concluded that this exhibit, as much as any other, complemented the general lesson of the fair: "As this is a story of progress, the lesson is that it is imperious, irresistible, and universal. Nothing, whether prejudice, or error, or selfishness, or tradition, or bigotry, or habit, or pride, can stand before it."[47]

This same law of racial and material progress dictated that the Japanese be represented at the Louisiana Purchase Exposition by official displays in the White City and in Fair Japan—a concession on the Pike. Unlike the Chinese at the fair, who were "measured by the Bertillon system, put on record by the thumbprint process and . . . tagged with a card bearing a number, which was recorded by government representatives, and which will be worn so long as the Chinamen are in this country," the Japanese were comparatively well received. With Japan's victories over Russia in the Russo-Japanese War sharing headlines with the opening of the fair, the Japanese exhibits became, in Wellman's words, "the sensation of the Louisiana Purchase Exposition." Particularly noteworthy, he remarked, was the progress shown by the Japanese in the decade since the World's Columbian Exposition. "At Chicago," Wellman recalled, "the Japanese appeared as interesting and picturesque makers of toys and knicknacks and articles of virtue of characteristic form but limited range—a sort of half-developed, peculiar people, with a hazy past not far

Fig. 59. Boer War concession. From David R. Francis, *The Universal Exposition of 1904*.

removed from actual savagery and with an uncertain future. At St. Louis they appear as one of the first nations of the world." It was precisely this rapid rise to military and industrial prominence, however, that occasioned concern and required explanation. One place to turn for an answer was the Anthropology Department.[48]

When asked about Japan's sudden military triumphs by a reporter from the *Post-Dispatch*, McGee replied: "It's the complexity of the blood. The more strains of blood a nation has in its veins, the greater and more powerful it becomes . . . and in the instance of the [Japanese] anthropologists find that they are the most complex nation of the Orient, just as the Anglo-Saxons, through the waves of successive populations that swept over the continent, were made the most complex nation of the Occident." McGee admitted that anthropologists knew little about the Japanese except "that they constitute a distinctively composite assemblage of more primitive types than any other Oriental nation." But part of the answer to the dramatic appearance of the Japanese as "The Greeks of the East," McGee believed, lay with the Ainu aborigines on display in the Department of Anthropology. According to McGee, the exhibit of the "occupations and handiwork" of the eight Ainus presented fairgoers with "some of the most significant stages in industrial development known to students—germs of some of those material arts which in their perfection have raised Japan to leading rank among the world's nations."[49]

In McGee's eyes, moreover, the Ainus magnified the racial characteristics that underlay Japanese progress. "Ainu men," McGree noted, "have skins as white as Europeans, and in facial appearance they often resemble the Greeks, but among the women there is always the heavy, coarse features and dark-hued complexion that characterizes the lower order of Mongolians." This ethnological profile was not unlike the description of the Japanese offered by Finley Peter Dunne's Mr. Dooley: "Th- Japs ar-re Chinymen well-done." Indeed, this split ethnological personality that McGee attributed to the Ainus, and by extension to the Japanese people as a whole, reinforced the ambiguity that ran throughout the popular response to the Japanese at the fair. The title of Grace Griscom's newspaper article about the Japanese exhibits perhaps shaped as much as it reflected the popular perceptions of the Japanese: "Some Quaint Little Ways of the Quaint Little Japs." Admiration for the Japanese, in short, was tempered, as it had been at Chicago, by the view that Japanese were "little brown people"—this phrase was Wellman's—and by the conditions, noted by the *Globe-Democrat*, that the Japanese maintain the Open Door in China and otherwise contribute to the ongoing Anglo-Saxon domination of the world. These considerations would continue to determine the evaluation of the Japanese at subsequent expositions held on the Pacific Coast over the next ten years.[50]

Similar commercial motives buttressed by claims of ethnological authenticity animated the bazaars along the Pike that represented the Near and Middle East. In the Mysterious Asia concession, street scenes depicting Calcutta,

Rangoon, and Tehran, populated with Indians, Burmese, and Persians, created the impression that these portions of the world were simply vast marketplaces peopled with "exotic types." The same effect was achieved by the separate concessions devoted to Jerusalem, Constantinople, and Cairo. Together these exhibits left few visitors in doubt about the Near and Middle East as a marketplace in which Americans could play at will.[51]

The precise relation between the White City and the various ethnological features along the Pike, in the Anthropology Department, and in the Philippine Reservation hinged on the contrast between "savagery" and "civilization." Contrasted with the grades of culture illustrated in the ethnological shows, the vision of America's racial and material progress embodied in the White City burned bright. Most visitors basked in the glow.

The success scored by the exposition directors became most apparent in the exhibit established by the American Federation of Labor as part of the Department of Social Economy. A souvenir catalog of this exhibit, issued by the AFL, reminded fairgoers that "it was the council of the American Federation of Labor, acting in conjunction with the chiefs of the railway brotherhoods, which refused in the face of immense pressure to participate in the great strike on the railroads centering in Chicago in 1894, and thus averted a bloody and disastrous conflict with the military forces of the United States." The AFL, the catalog continued, "in refusing to affiliate with the Central Federation in New York, with its 59 local unions and some 18,000 members because it included a branch of the Socialist labor party, struck the keynote of resistance against the dangerous delusion that the emancipation of the working class can be achieved by placing in the hands of shallow politicians the business enterprises now conducted by private persons." Fairgoers were also told that the AFL had spearheaded the drive in which "the programme of the common ownership of all the means of production and distribution was declared alien to the trade union movement." By informing exposition-goers that "the spirit of the trade union is essentially conservative, and that in the measure of its conservation it has become the most valuable agent of social progress," the AFL leadership left little doubt that it embraced the vision of utopia projected by the exposition's promoters. Participation by the AFL, of course, did not signify an endorsement of this blueprint for progress by all members of the working class. But the presence of this exhibit suggested that the exposition had gone a long way toward becoming what exposition president Francis termed "an incomparable seminary of ideas and inspirations for people of all classes and avocations."[52]

In the minds of the directors of the Louisiana Purchase Exposition, the fair had succeeded as an inspirational force. "It is evident," Saint Louis Mayor Rolla Wells told the closing day audience, that the exposition "has not lived in vain, but has been a joy and a benefit to all who may have been so fortunate as to have been within its sway." On that same occasion, Francis expressed confidence that the "compensation will continue to flow for at least a generation to come." When, at the close of his remarks, the exposition band struck up "Hail to the Chief" and the "primitive" people assembled at the fair marched around the central plaza in a gesture of apparent tribute, the fulfillment of the directors' imperial aspirations seemed near. But what about their efforts to implant their values in American culture? What did fairgoers remember from the Saint Louis world's fair?[53]

Testimony gathered by the Missouri Historical Society for the seventy-fifth anniversary of the exposition substantiated the directors' faith in the fair's abiding influence. The persons interviewed for this occasion had been young—between the ages of six and twenty—when they saw the fair. And they remembered eating their share of ice cream cones and hot dogs and getting lost on the Pike. Like the tenant farmers in John Steinbeck's *Grapes of Wrath*, some still treasured souvenir soapstone carvings purchased at the fair. Such lasting sentiments for the fair were important because they formed a reservoir for other memories as well. When asked specifically about exhibits that still stood out in their minds, respondents almost invariably recalled the ethnological displays, particularly villages of Filipinos, Indians, and Pygmies. "There," one former fairgoer emphasized, "are memories that do not fade."[54]

Above all, the Louisiana Purchase Exposition gave a utopian dimension to American imperialism. So great was the fair's success that it fired the imaginations of commercial and political leaders in the Pacific Northwest. Gripped by world's fair fever, exposition promoters in Portland and Seattle actively sought and willingly received from their Saint Louis peers the task of keeping visions of empire before the American people. "The king is dead. Long live the king," proclaimed the *Post-Dispatch* in an article about the relation of the Saint Louis exposition to the Portland fair planned for 1905. At the close of the Louisiana Purchase Exposition, the scepter of cultural sovereignty passed into the hands of commercial and political leaders in the Pacific Northwest.[55]

7

The Expositions in Portland and Seattle: "To Celebrate the Past and to Exploit the Future"

Speaking for the War Department, I will say that we are in the exposition business now. We have a Government exhibit that we can really almost put on wagons and transport from one place to another.

William Howard Taft, 1908[1]

"THIS EXPOSITION LOGICALLY FOLLOWS the great Exposition which commemorated the Louisiana Purchase," Charles Fairbanks, vice-president of the United States, told the opening day crowds at Portland's Lewis and Clark Centennial and American Pacific Exposition and Oriental Fair of 1905. The Saint Louis and Portland fairs, he explained, both took their inspiration from Thomas Jefferson's expansionist vision for America. Then, striking the central theme for the exposition movement in the Pacific Northwest, Fairbanks predicted: "The future has much in store for you. Yonder is Hawaii, acquired for strategic purposes and demanded in the interest of expanding commerce. Lying in the waters of the Orient are the Philippines which fell to us by the inexorable logic of a humane and righteous war. We must not underrate the commercial opportunities which invite us to the Orient." Four years later railroad magnate James J. Hill reiterated the same message in his opening day address at Seattle's Alaska-Yukon-Pacific Exposition: "If the star of empire in history has moved westward, it followed rather than led those bold spirits by which empires are made and upheld." "This exposition," he added, "may be regarded as the laying of the last rail, the driving of the last spike, in unity of mind and purpose between the Pacific coast and the country east of the mountains." That unity centered on "a vision of Oriental trade." Visitors, he concluded, would "carry away with them along with recollections of new possibilities of wealth, new methods, new markets and new trading peoples, a fund of new ideas and old ones recast in a larger mold." Fundamentally designed as imperial theme parks (Seattle's fair was crisscrossed with streets named after America's colonies and their inhabitants), the exposition utopias reared in Portland and Seattle focused national attention on the possibilities for economic growth through the development of trans-Pacific markets while providing the region and nation with visions of racial progress.[2]

The official emblems of the fairs made the point of the expositions clear. In the symbol of the Lewis and Clark Centennial, as described by a contemporary trade journal,

> [t]hree striking figures compose the spirited group in the foreground of the picture, facing the blazing sun as it sets in glory in the Pacific. The two buckskin-clad explorers, each with a powder horn and gun, have raised their hands in salutation. Between them, with a hand on the shoulder of each, moves Progress, a woman draped in the Stars and Stripes. The whole symbolizes confidence, energy, trust, and solemn wonder, and well illustrates the well-known and appropriate sentiment on the stately colonnade at the main entrance of the exposition grounds: "Westward the course of empire takes it way."

The design for the official seal of the Alaska-Yukon-Pacific Exposition, generally referred to as the A.-Y.-P., was equally explicit. Three women, representing Japan, Alaska, and the Pacific Northwest, cradled respectively a

Fig. 60. Main entrance to Lewis and Clark Exposition—note motto above colonnades: "Westward the Course of Empire Takes Its Way." From Division of Prints and Photographs, Library of Congress.

steamship, a gold nugget, and a railroad engine, thereby suggesting the drive by the exposition promoters to link increased industrialization with expanding markets and to develop new sources of natural wealth.[3]

Beauty, not size, became the main concern in building and promoting these fairs. In Portland the drive for aesthetic effect led to the design of a special smoke filter for the city crematorium, which stood less than a thousand feet from the Guild Lake location of the fair. A small matter by itself, the smoke screen was part of the larger transformation wrought in the Guild Lake tract itself. "Where once was wilderness," the *Oregon Daily Journal* recorded,

Fig. 61. Seattle's Alaska-Yukon-Pacific Exposition—overview. From Department of Special Collections, Library, California State University, Fresno.

"now blooms paradise . . . , a mighty monument to American energy and heroism." This "full grown Eden," with its Renaissance revival exhibit halls constructed in the parklike environment designed by John C. Olmsted, had a powerful effect. "Beauty," wrote one enthusiastic sightseer, "affects me like julep or electricity—makes my fingers 'all pins and needles.' It is mental intoxication that brings its after-ache—the knowledge that strive as you may, no cunning of words can ever paint in the lack-luster black and white rhetoric a thousandth part of the charm that man's hand can spread in God's colors for the eye!" Advertised as the "World's Most Beautiful Exposition," Seattle's A.-Y.-P., built next to the University of Washington, set in an evergreen forest again landscaped by the Olmsted brothers' firm, evoked similar praise for its

Fig. 62. Alaska-Yukon-Pacific Exposition official seal. Postcard courtesy of Department of Special Collections, Library, California State University, Fresno.

artistry. "Beauty in civil life means health, economy, comfort and happiness," stated the *Portland Oregonian*. "Beauty implies conscience in plan and execution. It means honesty. It means love of home and country. Beauty in our civic structures means beauty in our civic life. . . . Love your country; this is the great lesson of the Fair, and build your cities and your lives to show your love." The *Oregon Daily Journal* was more succinct: "to behold is to become a better American." These concerns by the builders of both expositions were rooted in the imperial aspirations of the exposition directors and in the social origins of the fairs.[4]

The Lewis and Clark Centennial took form against the backdrop of class antagonisms that had carried over from the economic depression of the 1890s, and the drive behind Seattle's fair escalated with the Panic of 1907. Despite the assertions by their promoters, neither exposition was popular in origin or organization. Instead, these imperial dream cities represented concerted efforts to root out what Hill, in his opening day remarks in Seattle, termed "that most hateful and corroding element in a republic that is called class consciousness."[5]

The idea for the Portland fair originated in 1895 with dry-goods merchant Dan McAllen, who traced the stimulus for this plan to San Francisco's Midwinter Fair of 1893–1894 and the economic hardships experienced during those years. Over the next five years, with Portland's economy remaining in a pronounced depression, McAllen's proposal received support from the city's most prominent and influential citizens. Among the early advocates of the idea were Henry L. Pittock and Harvey W. Scott, respectively owner and editor of the *Oregonian*, and, most important, Henry W. Corbett.[6]

Corbett, described in the official history of the exposition as a "conspicuous and masterful man of affairs," controlled a corporate empire that extended from banking and insurance to real estate and railroad holdings. He had twice served as Oregon's United States senator. He subscribed to one-tenth of the initial $300,000 stock issue for the exposition, personally nominated the directors in advance of the shareholders' first meeting in the Oregon Mining and Exchange Building, and in turn was elected president of the board by his appointees. Corbett died in 1903, but the chain of command he initiated remained intact. After a brief tenure by Scott, the presidency passed to the exposition's director-general, Henry W. Goode, head of the Portland General Electric Company. One of Goode's smaller contributions to the fair was a 110 by 30 foot electrical sign that he donated to the exposition cause. Placed at the summit of one of Portland's hills, "1905" could be seen for over thirty miles.[7]

While the Lewis and Clark Centennial was still under way, the exposition spirit seized Seattle's business community, and members of the city's Alaska Club—an adjunct of the Chamber of Commerce—began to lay plans for a fair that would celebrate and advertise the resources of Alaska. Initial proposals to limit the focus of the fair to exhibits of Alaskan Indians and Alaska's natural wealth rapidly fell by the wayside, however, after Henry E. Reed, secretary of the Portland exposition corporation, addressed club members and pointed out the benefits that would accrue to commercial interests in the Northwest by including Pacific markets in the purview of their exposition. Seattle's business leaders incorporated their fair as the Alaska-Yukon-Pacific Exposition and appointed him director of exploitation. They also drew on Reed's expertise to devise a "system of management" for the exposition, but that task required little innovation. As Reed explained to a congressional committee considering an allocation of funds for a colonial exhibit for the fair: "The general plan of organization conforms to that adopted by the St. Louis and Portland expositions. All work is initiated by the directors of divisions . . ., in conjunction with the proper subcommittees of the board of trustees, and carried out, subject to the supervision of the executive committee." At the helm of this group of businessmen stood John E. Chilberg, vice-president of several banks and a mining company and president of the Century Company, a Seattle investment firm. His exposition associates included John H. McGraw, a Seattle real estate investor, Richard A. Ballinger, attorney and soon to be secretary of the interior, and A. S. Kerry, a prominent lumber baron. Ira A. Nadeau, vice-president of the Chamber of Commerce and former general agent for Hill's Great Northern Railroad, was elected director-general of the exposition. With railroads, including the Great Northern, banks, and newspaper firms providing financial support, the directors proceeded to build an exposition that would educate fairgoers about the nature and direction of national and international progress. Their plans, like those of the Portland exposition promoters, encountered a groundswell of opposition that underlined the urgency of their self-appointed cultural mission.[8]

Opposition to the construction of the Lewis and Clark Centennial was sparked by what the *Portland Labor Press* termed a "breach of faith" by the exposition management on the issue of the closed shop. In 1902 and 1903, agents appointed by the directors of the fair solicited subscriptions to the exposition stock issue from the city's trade unions. For their subscriptions, the *Labor Press* claimed, the unions received promises that "all work on the grounds would be done under union conditions with union men, whose homes and interests were in the City of Portland and the State of Oregon." But in April 1903, after the state legislature had appropriated $500,000 for the fair, the management implemented an open shop policy, denying that any promises to the contrary had ever been made to organized labor. To support their contention, the directors cited the policy of lumber mills and building contractors in Portland to refuse to sell lumber to strictly union jobs.[9]

This turn of events drew a quick response from the painters' and carpenters' unions, following the path taken the month before by a group of Albany farmers. Farmers in Albany, upset by the failure of the state legislature to pass legislation taxing the state corporations, had demanded that Oregon's one-year-old referendum amendment to the state constitution be applied to the $500,000 exposition appropriation bill and had organized a Referendum League to gain signatures on petitions. Toward the end of April, in the wake of the open shop decision, O. N. Pierce, business agent for the carpenters' union, similarly insisted that a referendum vote be taken on the fair. Amid reports that rents in Portland were already rising on two or three days' notice as a result of real estate speculation brought on by the expected increase in property values because of the fair, members of the painters' union began circulating petitions demanding that the exposition be put to a vote of the people.[10]

Portland's Board of Trade, the most powerful commercial body in the city, which numbered most of the exposition's trustees as members, issued a declaration stating that "in the opinion of this board a resolution asking the members of labor unions to burn down the public buildings would be quite as justifiable." The Board of Trade requested a meeting with a committee from Portland's Federated Trades Council to work out an agreement. Sketchy details of this meeting were later provided by Henry Kundert, editor of the *Labor Press*, to George Shaver, Oregon's delegate to the American Federation of Labor's 1904 convention, where a proposal to condemn the fair by resolution was under consideration. According to Kundert, the basis for an accord at the meeting called by the Board of Trade had existed in the perception of a common "enemy" by the exposition promoters and conservative trade unionists. As Kundert acidly described the organizers of the referendum drive: "It is needless to say that these men are Socialists."[11]

According to Kundert, Harry Rogers, chairman of the labor committee, returned from the conference and reported to the Trades Council "that they had been assured that if the attempt to use the referendum on the Fair was dropped, an agreement could be secured with the Fair management that would unionize every job on the Grounds." Rogers, moreover, tried to persuade the Council that "[t]he people . . . and the citizens demanded the Fair, and [that] it would be a great mistake for organized labor to oppose it." Socialists, however, "controlled the Council," Kundert wrote, and refused to accept this compromise, voting instead to lend the support of the Trades Council to the petition drive. Several weeks later socialists carried the referendum issue to a vote in the State Federation of Labor convention, where it narrowly passed. But, as Kundert's report made clear, a rift had developed between socialists and those trade unionists who supported the fair. Many union members who owned property in Portland or who worked in service trades that stood to benefit from the influx of fairgoers came out against the referendum. Coupled with the publicity campaign launched by the exposition management, this split in the labor movement proved fatal to the referendum drive, and socialists and farmers failed to gain enough signatures on petitions to qualify the appropriation bill for a statewide ballot.[12]

In 1904, with tensions between the socialists and their trade union opponents running high, Kundert concluded his letter to Shaver—a letter Kundert wrote after consulting with Henry Reed—by urging "that the A. F. of L. exhibit be sent from St. Louis to Portland" as part of the campaign by conservative trade unions in Portland "to reclaim the [labor] movement to where it was three years ago."[13]

In the meantime the exposition directors did not miss a trick. Had the labor unions accused the management of breaking faith on the closed shop issue? Once the referendum drive got under way, it was Reed's turn to cry foul, claiming that the Federated Trades Council had "rejected any promise made or implied" at the meeting with the Board of Trade "by proceeding to demand the referendum on the LEWIS AND CLARK appropriation." The directors responded by advertising employment on the fairgrounds in major daily newspapers across the country. Several months before the exposition opened, the *Labor Press* noted that one Portland businessman had received a letter from his brother, a brick contractor living in Canada, asking about an advertisement for one hundred bricklayers at the fair. But, as the newspaper bluntly told its readers: "It is a well-known fact that not a brick is being laid on the fairgrounds." By 1905 similar advertisements had caused Portland to be "flooded with men for whom there is no work at all," while those who did find work discovered that "the wages paid are less than enough to live decently." Wages and working conditions became so intolerable that in March a strike effectively shut down construction for several days and forced the directors to make some concessions to the workers' demands for an eight-hour working day. Ironically, given their nationwide labor recruitment crusade, the management blamed this latest round of labor discontent on "outside agitators" from Saint Louis.[14]

The "systematic plan of discrimination" prevailing against union labor at the Lewis and Clark Centennial also characterized the Seattle fair. "In the winter of 1907," the Seattle *Socialist* recalled on the eve of the exposition's opening, "in order to have the buildings constructed at less cost without sacrifice of profits, in the midst of financial panic in which thousands of working men hungrily tramped the streets, a number of our 'best citizens' caused notices to be placed in Eastern papers announcing that work was plenty and help scarce in the world's fair city—in all lines, but especially in the building trades. By this means they were able to inaugurate the open shop at the A.-Y.-P." Terming the exposition a "scab fair" on the "skirmish line" of class struggle, the socialist newspaper warned workers: "If you have any idea of coming to see the show, better take your button off. To the class conscious Seattle wage worker, it stands a great fantastic monument to the brutal avarice of the capitalist class." Unlike the situation in Portland, where socialists and many trade unionists disagreed about the appropriate response to the fair, unionists in Seattle and throughout the state of Washington concurred in putting the A.-Y.-P. Exposition on the unfair list. "This enterprise," the *Seattle Union Record* wrote of the exposition in 1908, "for the good of organized labor everywhere and for the good of Seattle, deserves to be a frost, and we ask our friends to bend every energy to that end." By opening day, criticism of the fair in the *Union Record* became increasingly bitter. "Ours comes as the final cup of tarantula juice in the last period of a prolonged debauch," wrote one union member.[15]

In both exposition cities, the language and action of class resistance that marked the construction period of the fairs spurred the directors to find ways of attracting workers to the completed products in hopes that they would learn the lessons of progress embodied in the exposition cities. Directors of the Lewis and Clark Centennial approached industrial concerns throughout the region, calling attention "to the manifold educational advantages" of the fair, noting that the exposition "is a line of welfare work heartily approved and advocated by the great National Civic Federation." Industrialists desiring to send their employees on excursions to the fair were promised "a day in honor of the event" as well as "a suitable meeting place on the Fair Grounds for appropriate exercises" and "a band of music" for the occasion.[16]

The directors, moreover, set aside one entire day, 2 August, as Workingmen's Day and reduced the general admission charge to twenty-five cents. The *Oregon Daily Journal* explained the reasoning behind this special day: "The working people and their families need to see the exposition at considerable length. It will do them good." Observing that "some of Portland's largest and most patriotic business houses gave their employees the privilege of leaving benches and tools to visit the exposition" for this occasion, a newspaper recorded that the 10,282 people who entered the turnstiles before noon made Workingmen's Day the largest morning gathering to date at the fair.[17]

In Seattle the directors attempted to make the fair the focal point for celebrating the national Labor Day holiday. But as 6 September approached, the *Union Record* admonished its readers: "If your boss is willing to buy you tickets and give you a holiday on some other day than the one set aside as a tribute to the toilers of this state and nation, then there might be a reasonable excuse for the presence of a 'union member' on the grounds of the unfair Alaska-Yukon Exposition." Labor Day, in fact, brought the ongoing tension between the workers and the directors to a climax.[18]

To attract a larger crowd, the directors designated the holiday as Seattle Day at the fair and promoted a bogus labor newspaper to build up working-class support for the civic celebration. Employers, meanwhile, mixed offers of free passes with threats that workers would not be given the day off unless they visited the exposition. When it became apparent that the union would hold an independent Labor Day celebration in a city park, city officials re-routed their parade and even removed selected streetcars from service in an attempt to discourage the workers' gathering. Nevertheless, between twelve and fourteen thousand people gathered at Woodland Park to show their solidarity with union opposition to the fair. Their sentiments surfaced when the parade to the park came to the triumphal exposition arch erected downtown by the fair's directors. "By way of showing their disapproval of the methods said to have been employed in the construction of this arch," the *Union Record* noted, "several members of the Plasterers, Painters and Carpenters refused to walk under it." Instead, they walked around and "rejoined the parade on the other side of the arch."[19]

The two years of resentment toward the exposition management that culminated in the Woodland Park gathering did not signify that Seattle's workers had wholly escaped the influence of the exposition's lessons about American progress. Etched into the vocabulary of union resistance to Seattle Day were indications that the lessons of living ethnological concessions at the fair were inscribed on the consciousness of a labor movement already laden with anti-Asian feelings. In what was intended to be the crowning epithet hurled at the directors for their efforts to subvert organized labor's celebration by blocking the paraders' right-of-way permit, the *Union Record* declared: "The way in which the fair is conducted would bring the blush of shame to the cheeks of the Igorrote and their last act should make even the A.-Y.-P.-E. commission hide their heads in shame." At the Alaska-Yukon-Pacific Exposition, as at the Lewis and Clark Centennial, the appeal of the Filipino Village and other village concessions along the midways—named the Trail at Portland's exposition and the Pay Streak at Seattle's fair—continued to cut across class lines.[20]

In October 1904 Henry Dosch, Oregon's commissioner to the Saint Louis fair and later director of exhibits at Seattle's exposition, reminded Goode about the popularity of the Philippine Reservation at the Louisiana Purchase Exposition. "In fact," Dosch declared, "it is of so much interest, as you well know, that I do not see how we can get along without it." Several hurdles, however, stood in the way. The War Department had promised Filipinos on display at the Saint Louis exposition that they would be returned to their homes once the fair concluded. Furthermore, the War Department had exceeded its appropriation for the reservation, thus making department officials wary about incurring any additional expenses. In response to the request for a Philippines exhibit from the promoters of Portland's fair, the only offer forthcoming was a "dead exhibit" of artifacts on display at Saint Louis. But even this proposal initially ran into opposition as William P. Wilson, head of the Philippine Exposition Board, expressed his fear that the artifacts, if sent to Portland, would be returned to the Philippines instead of going to the Philadelphia Commercial Museum as planned.[21]

Confronted with the likelihood that a government-sponsored Philippines exhibit, if it materialized at all, would not include Filipinos, Dosch informed Goode that it was imperative to finance a Philippine Village concession. To find willing concessionaires, Dosch did not have far to look.[22]

While the Saint Louis fair was still under way, several individuals—including Samuel M. McGowan, assistant head of the Anthropology Department of the Saint Louis fair and superintendent of the Indian Industrial and Agricultural School at Chilocco, Oklahoma, Truman K. Hunt, manager of the Igorot Village in the Philippine Reservation, and Edmund A. Felder, long-standing midway showman and advisor to the Philippine Exposition Board—joined forces and organized a firm called the International Anthropological Exhibit Company for the purpose of exhibiting Filipinos around the country. By November 1904 the directors of the Portland fair negotiated a tentative agreement with this firm for a "Philipino Exhibit" that would consist of Igorot, Visayan, and Negrito villages and be situated on the Trail. After reaching this understanding, Hunt and his partners requested permission from the government to bring Filipinos to America to replace the ones returning after 1904. Felder, who drafted the letter to the War Department, explained the goals of the firm: "It would be my idea to arrange for their stay in this country for about two years, exhibiting them at the Portland Exhibition, at Coney Island, or other amusement centers, and at the larger State Fairs." Rather than paying the Filipinos, Felder proposed putting the money into the improvement of trails in the appropriate provinces in the islands. Schooling, Felder promised, would be provided for all the people who participated in the exhibit. Taft approved of this plan, and Clarence Edwards, head of the Bureau of Insular Affairs, added his endorsement, albeit only after following a finely drawn line of imperial reasoning. "I really see nothing against it," Edwards wrote, "but at the same time I rather deprecate the idea of taking these people to Coney Island and giving the people of the United States the idea that the majority of the people of the Philippines are similar to the Igorrots and Negritos, in the same way as I would rather deprecate the idea of having Apachee [sic] Indians travelling around to represent Americans." But, Edwards hastened to add, "I must admit that [Indians] have done so, with Buffalo Bill, and it has not hurt us abroad, and possibly might do no harm in the case of the Filipinos."[23]

By early 1905 the stage appeared to be set for a display of Filipino villagers, which would be supplemented by an exhibit of products and resources from the islands, furnished by the federal government. But for unknown reasons the International Anthropological Exhibit Company split into rival firms. Hunt organized the Igorot Exhibit Company and tried to persuade Goode to accept an Igorot village in lieu of the three villages initially agreed to. Felder, meanwhile, organized the Filipino Exhibition Company with his newfound partner Richard Schneidewind. A former private in the medical corps during the Spanish-American War, Schneidewind had been fired in 1901 from his position as a postal clerk in Manila because of alleged "complicity in a smuggling scheme." He found a job with Gustavo Niederlein cataloging exhibits for the Philippine Reservation and received the cigar concession on the reservation, which in turn brought him into contact with Felder. Once Felder and Schneidewind formed their own company, they quickly countered Hunt's proposal to the directors of the Lewis and Clark Centennial. Whereas Hunt offered the directors a show composed solely of Igorots, Felder and Schneidewind proposed a village of Visayans, Negritos, and Igorots. From the directors' point of view, the comparative drawing power of the suggested villages was the critical factor. Goode noted that the Negritos and Visayans were considered to be "a sort of heavy weight to the proposition" and "would not be the moneymakers the Igorrote exhibit would be." But there were other considerations as well. Hunt already had his troupe of Igorots organized, while Felder still needed government permission to carry out his plans. Bearing these thoughts in mind, Goode informed Hunt that his offer would satisfy the management. Hunt, however, accused the directors of double-dealing and refused to come to terms. He proceeded to sign a contract with the Benevolent and Protective Order of Elks in which he agreed to establish his Igorot village at various Elks' carnivals around the country.[24]

The directors then turned to Felder and Schneidewind, who promised "an installation of not less than twenty-five (25) Igorrotes, and also such other and additional representatives of other Philippine Tribes as may prove to be possible." But just when the concession seemed to be in hand, another problem arose. Taft apparently was having second thoughts about permitting any more Filipinos to participate in privately operated concessions. With the Lewis and Clark Centennial already under way, a frantic Goode cabled the secretary of war: "Exposition widely advertised Igorotee [sic] village as ethnological and educative feature. . . . [U]nderstand you have cabled Manila Government doubting wisdom permitting people to come. Sincerely trust you will reconsider and withdraw opposition so informing Manila." Goode concluded his plea by stating: "We are anxious to keep faith with our visitors." Ultimately, so was Taft. He relented and permitted Felder's agents to fulfill their mission.[25]

Although only six weeks remained of the Portland exposition when the Philippines exhibit finally opened on the Trail, it instantly became one of the most popular attractions at the fair, helped along by accounts such as the following in the *Portland Oregonian:*

> See the Igorrote. You do not have to look through any opaque Sartorial
> Adornments to see him. He is visible to the Naked Eye. The Igorrote is
> a very happy Individual. He ought to be Happy. He does not have to
> pay Two Bits every four days to get his Pants creased. In that way he
> saves $22.75 per annum. When he has saved up for forty years he can
> buy an Automobile on Time Payments. He also economizes by not

Buying pocket knives, because he has no Pocket in which to put
Knives. But the Igorrote never worries about not Owning an Auto. His
motto is "Sufficient unto the day is the Evil thereof." He lives the
Simple Life. All he requires is his Pipe and his Pup. He smokes his
Pipe and boils his Pup, and he is not particular about the Pedigree of
the Pup. If you or I ate Pup we would insist upon well-bred Poodle or
dainty Water Spaniel. To the Igorrote a Dog with any other name will
taste as Sweet. His only requirement is that it be Dog. After the
Igorrote gets hold of a dog it is Dog-Gone.

The response of one fairgoer to the village was typical. "We saw the dog-
eaters," she confided to her diary, "and had just lots of fun."[26]

Goode recognized the value of the show and wrote Felder a letter of commendation: "The representation of primitive man as exhibited in the Igorrote
Village has not only been a distinct drawing card at this Exposition, but has
been justly regarded as a fine anthropology and ethnological display, of a high
educative and scientific value." The jury of awards, moreover, conferred gold
medals and certificates of merit on the show in the areas of anthropology,
ethnology, education, and manufactures.[27]

The significance of Goode's praise and of the awards increased over the
next year. In 1906 Felder and Schneidewind took the Filipinos from Portland
to amusement parks in California and Illinois. At Chutes Park in Los Angeles,
broadsides advertised the Igorot Village as "The Call of the Wild," boasted of
the awards received at Portland, and recalled that at the Saint Louis fair the
village had been visited by distinguished people from around the world.
"WHY? Because it was the most interesting and instructive educational exhibit
portraying primitive man ever made, and was so pronounced by press and
clergy." Similar claims entered the promotional literature issued for the show
at Riverview Park in Chicago. These endorsements, however, not only sought
to lure visitors, but reflected the efforts by the concessionaires to deflect the
inquiries by officials of the federal government into the treatment of the Filipinos in these shows.[28]

When a federal agent—a military recruiting officer—questioned the Igorots
in Chutes Park, the Filipinos were "unanimous in their desire to return" to
the Philippines. Their evident discontent threatened the continuation of the
show and moved Schneidewind to send a written report to the War Department, reminding federal officials of the praise the exhibit had received at the
Lewis and Clark Centennial. Schneidewind appended to his report a copy of
Goode's letter of commendation and another letter written by the exposition
president noting that the Igorots had been happy with their treatment in Portland. But to prevent a mutiny in the village, Felder and Schneidewind increased the Igorots' wages—which the concessionaires held in trust—and the
Filipinos agreed to accompany the ethnological road show to Chicago.[29]

Shortly after they arrived at Riverview Park, Felder and Schneidewind were dismayed to discover Truman K. Hunt's Igorot Exhibit Company digging in for an engagement at the cross-town Sans Souci amusement park. Concerned about a sizable loss of revenue from the competition, Felder and his partner turned their recent experience with the War Department to their advantage. They reported that conditions in Hunt's village were deplorable and requested an inspection of his operation, purportedly to keep their own from acquiring a bad reputation. Self-interest loomed large in Felder's and Schneidewind's request for an investigation of Hunt's company, but the latter's operation was patently corrupt. By the following year Hunt was in a Memphis jail on charges of embezzling the Igorots' wages and was facing similar charges in New Orleans. For the time being Felder and Schneidewind were more careful, but not necessarily much better. In 1913, while the Igorot village was on tour of Europe, Schneidewind, apparently running the show by himself, was also accused of embezzlement. In the meantime Felder and Schneidewind were awarded the Philippine Village concession on the midway, or Warpath, at the 1907 Jamestown Tercentennial Exposition. Although the Bureau of Insular Affairs received word that the forty new Filipinos on their way to the fair "were quartered in steerage, poorly clothed [and] fed, the children naked," the government took no action. By 1909 both men reappeared in the Pacific Northwest, holding the concessions for the Igorot Village at the Alaska-Yukon-Pacific Exposition, where it was "commandingly located at the head of the South Pay Streak."[30]

Unlike the centrally located Trail at the Lewis and Clark Centennial, Seattle's Pay Streak was situated along the boundaries of the exposition grounds, just inside the main entrance, and integrated with the rest of the exposition through its architectural style, dubbed "Jap-Alaskan." Totem poles connected by strings of Japanese lanterns lined the thoroughfare leading to the midway avenue. At the entrance, an archway supported by eight totem poles presented a frieze with the exposition seal in the center and a "swastika fret, the Alaskan good luck symbol," extending in both directions. Once on the Pay Streak, visitors could hardly miss the Igorot Village, which the official guidebook described as "the most extensive, interesting and amusing exhibit at the exposition."[31]

Even before the exposition opened, the Igorots constructing their village attracted the attention of more than sixteen thousand schoolchildren on a tour of the fair. "Swarming about the Igorrote women, who were seated on the ground peacefully weaving reeds," the Seattle Post-Intelligencer observed, "the youngsters picked up the bundles of Filipino straw and inadvertently became somewhat annoying." The women responded by chasing the children away, while the young people "shrieked with delight" and shouted: "My ain't they wild." Well into the summer, University of Washington students added only a touch of sophistication to the same pattern of behavior. "See the simple Igorots," a student newspaper correspondent wrote about two Igorots paid by

Fig. 63. Igorot Village on the Pay Streak. Sign in upper right reads
"Igorotte Village—Barbaric Tribes." Stereoscope card courtesy of
Department of Special Collections, Library, California State University,
Fresno.

the newspaper staff to pose for a photograph dressed in suits and smoking
cigars, "all y'clad in hats and coaties barbarism now despised, they are ultra
civilized." A final gibe brought out the didactic value of the Igorot show.
"Though right simple seems their smile, think not they have lost their guile:
for this picture the expense was per [fifty cents]. What an adjunct they would
be to our un-i-ver-si-tee!"[32]
    Similar thoughts had already crossed the mind of University of Washington

administrators. Following the precedent established by the University of Chicago at the Saint Louis fair, they invited noted Cambridge anthropologist Alfred C. Haddon to offer a summer-school course in conjunction with the exposition. As the registrar explained: "It was our purpose in bringing Dr. Haddon here this year to use the different races on the fair grounds as a living laboratory. The exposition affords a fine museum of the peoples of the borders of the Pacific." Haddon proved to be an invaluable asset to the exposition promoters. His course, "The Growth of Cultural Evolution around the Pacific," sanctioned the exposition as an educational undertaking, while his endorsement of the Igorot Village helped the concessionaires and exposition officials refute the charges made by a group of visiting Filipino sailors that the attraction was "indecent." "I have taken a keen delight in the study of these strange people," Haddon said when asked by a reporter to comment on the charges. "I spend much of my time at the exposition village and everyone who will do so will profit." For Haddon, as for the exposition promoters, the village was "a vital issue in living bronze."[33]

While Filipino villages proved to be highlights at both expositions in the Pacific Northwest, other village attractions along the midways also contributed to the world view designed by the builders of the fairs. The Trail—under the charge of veteran showman John A. Wakefield—numbered among its shows Fair Japan, the Streets of Cairo, and an Eskimo Village. Other features included the Old Plantation, "peopled by a colony of southern negroes of different ages," a Haba-Haba Man show, consisting of one Harry L. Blitz, who had learned his trade as a Zulu dancer while employed by P. T. Barnum, and a Vaudeville Theater where blackface minstrels regularly performed. Along the Pay Streak, in addition to Japanese and Chinese villages and the perennial Streets of Cairo, the directors determined "to have the largest Eskimo village ever presented at a world's fair." Arthur W. Lewis, formerly in charge of the Boer War concession at the Saint Louis fair and director of concessions for the Seattle exposition, awarded this contract to an Arctic trader, A. M. Baber. Baber gathered thirty-four Siberians as illustrations of the lowest "stage of civilization" in Alaska. For a while before the exposition began, Baber housed the native Alaskans in a Seattle cold storage plant. Then he took them on an exhibition swing to various western cities. By the time the exposition opened the Eskimo village had expanded to include other native Alaskans "who are partly educated," and others "who can conduct our business affairs, operate mills and canneries and who have reached an advanced stage of civilization." When seen in conjunction with the federal government's exhibits of natural resources on display in the Alaskan Building—which was built "to show the world that Alaska is no longer a place where only the Eskimo and Indian can live"—the Eskimo Village created the impression that for these people progress would be judged by their racial attributes and by what and how much they contributed to the economic growth of America's commercial empire.

This same vision of racial and material progress girdled the entire trans-Pacific region as it was depicted at both expositions.[34]

"The United States is the only white power of any consequence which fronts on the Pacific," a trade journal told its readers in an article about the Portland fair. "The 800,000,000 of Asiatics, half of the population of the entire world at this moment, will, when they wake up after the Russo-Japan war, contribute to the world's commerce in a degree undreamed of now. The day when the Pacific shall be transformed into an American lake will come even earlier than Seward's prophetic vision grasped." In Seattle, exposition president Chilberg was no less enthusiastic: "Alaska-Yukon-Pacific! What an appeal to the imagination these three words make! What dreams of commercial and industrial development they inspire!" At both fairs, exhibits supplied by the United States government from America's colonial possessions in the Pacific suggested that the transformation of the Pacific into an American lake was well under way, while displays devoted to the development of markets in Japan and China made the development of an American commercial empire throughout Asia seem inevitable.[35]

At each fair the federal government built separate buildings for displays devoted to the commercial possibilities of America's overseas possessions. De-

Fig. 64. The Trail at Portland's Lewis and Clark Centennial. Courtesy of Department of Special Collections, Library, California State University, Fresno.

spite William P. Wilson's objections, the government sent to Portland's fair many artifacts from the Philippines that had been gathered for the Louisiana Purchase Exposition, but the exhibit paled by comparison with the display sent to Seattle four years later. Where the Lewis and Clark Centennial had a main government building with one annex structure devoted to colonial exhibits, the Alaska-Yukon-Pacific Exposition boasted a main government building and three adjacent structures given over to exhibits from Alaska, the Philippines, and Hawaii. For the Seattle exposition, moreover, the Smithsonian Institution's appropriation and amount of display space was nearly double what it had received to establish a smaller version of its Saint Louis exhibit at Portland's fair. At the A.-Y.-P. Exposition, the Smithsonian provided the historical and ethnological footings for the imperial vistas laid out elsewhere in the government complex and on the exposition grounds.[36]

The general guidelines for the Smithsonian display at Seattle, as at all the expositions, were set forth in the congressional appropriation bill authorizing the federal government's participation in the fair. In May 1908 Congress mandated that for the Seattle exposition the Smithsonian provide "such articles and material of an historical nature as will impart a knowledge of our nation's history, especially that of Alaska, Hawaii, and the Philippine Islands and that part of the United States west of the Rocky Mountains." In the course of preparing their exhibit, Smithsonian officials—headed by USNM administrative assistant W. de C. Ravenel, William H. Holmes of the BAE, and Walter Hough, acting head curator of the anthropology division of the USNM—determined "to present an outline of our national achievements and progress."[37]

Along with 190 portraits of "eminent persons" in United States history (ranging from Columbus to Bret Harte to Emilio Aguinaldo) and maps showing the history of the nation's territorial expansion, the exhibit included models of churches, showing the impact of different religious groups on the Far West, models devoted to the history of transportation designed to show "the advance of civilization," and a display devoted to the history of photography. Lay-figure family groupings typifying selected nonwhites who had been subjugated over the course of America's westward expansion formed the core of the exhibit. "Before leading into an exhibit of the peoples of the Pacific coast and of our island possessions," wrote an unidentified Smithsonian official in a description of the exhibit for the Seattle Post-Intelligencer, "a group of models give some idea of the way certain prehistoric Americans of the southwest lived." From the artifacts, photographs, and family lay-figure arrangements depicting Zuni and Pueblo Indians, visitors followed America's westward expansion into a display area depicting the Native Americans of the Pacific Coast, ranging from the Hup Indians of California to the Eskimos of Alaska. The collapse of historical time and geographical distance continued in even more dramatic fashion as visitors moved past the lay-figure groups of Hawaiians, Samoans— "robust and happy as a race," according to the Smithsonian account—and

Guamanians. But the capstone of the Smithsonian's ethnological display consisted of representations of Filipinos.[38]

Surrounded by artifacts drawn in part from Frank Hilder's collection on behalf of the Buffalo exposition of 1901, the Filipinos appeared as "not merely one native people but a collection of different tribes of different peoples as far apart in habits and mode of living as scattered bits of different branches of races can be in one general locality." The spectrum of racial/cultural "types" extended from the Negrito—described as "cheerful, intelligent, peaceable and moral . . . strong, marvelously agile, and his black, wizened, dwarfish frame is capable of incredible endurance"—to the Igorot—portrayed as being "of cheerful disposition, strong, a good worker and inclined to peaceful pursuits" and to the Moro—"a step farther advanced towards civilization."[39]

The reason for characterizing Filipinos as racially inferior but as willing workers became more evident in the War Department's Philippines Building, which, on the average, attracted nearly five thousand visitors each day of the fair. Immediately inside the door, War Department ethnologists also arranged lay-figure groupings and photographs chronicling the same stages of racial/cultural advance that characterized the Smithsonian's display. But unlike the exhibit in the main United States Government Building, the War Department's display in the Philippines Building carried the history of the islands into the present and the years ahead. Exhibits of straw hats, cigars and cigarettes, hemp, wine, and beef, according to one government report, "suggested that the future prosperity of the Philippine people is to be limited only by the great productive capacity of the islands." That prediction alone made the Philippine Islands—depicted as resource-rich in terms of raw materials and humanity—a valuable colonial asset in the present.[40]

With the exhibition of America's Pacific colonies at both fairs fixed largely in the hands of the federal government and concessionaires, the directors concentrated much of their attention on securing exhibits that would illuminate the market possibilities of Asian countries, especially Japan and China. In 1902 Dosch traveled to Japan's Osaka exposition with a mercantile and industrial display organized by Portland businessmen, in hopes that the Japanese government would respond in kind with an exhibit for the Lewis and Clark Centennial. During his stay in Japan Dosch approached numerous Asian exhibitors about sending displays to Portland and, by his own account, "advocated the exhibiting of the various industries of these countries by actual operating, working exhibits by the natives themselves, clad in their native costumes, living in their own houses, showing their modes of life, work and play." But whatever expectations Dosch had for effecting this plan were shattered by the experience of Asian exhibitors at the Louisiana Purchase Exposition. As the Saint Louis fair drew to a close, Dosch informed Goode that he was having difficulties attracting foreign exhibitors to Portland because "these

Foreign and Oriental people have received such bad treatment here, that they are not only discouraged, but thoroughly disgusted with all Expositions." Even D. R. Francis, head of the Saint Louis enterprise, conceded that the Chinese at the Saint Louis fair had suffered many affronts.[41]

Difficulties with foreign governments notwithstanding, the directors of the Lewis and Clark Centennial gave substance to their dreams of linking Asian markets to America's Pacific empire by persuading many private exhibitors at the Saint Louis fair to send their exhibits to Portland for installation in the Oriental Exhibits Building. Within this edifice, the directors constructed an elaborate visual fantasy about the future of Asian-American relations by decorating the interior balconies with red, white, and blue bunting and American flags, while placing an emblematic American eagle over the main entrance. "The idea one received immediately," noted the *Oregon Daily Journal*, "is 'America looking toward the orient.' Below are the nations of the orient with their old ideas and customs, while above, looking over the whole, is America, extending to these countries her civilization through the medium of education."[42]

What made education an imperative was the prospect of rapid industrial growth in Asia. As Benjamin Ide Wheeler, president of the University of California, explained in an address before the Lewis and Clark Educational Congress: "If the enormous force of trained industrial patience of China shall be on a sudden armed with modern steel weapons, i.e., machinery, engines, dynamos, rails, it means, of course, for the world an industrial cataclysm, an economic revolution and upturning from the depths." The real problem, he stressed, was racial: "Chinese patience in toil is not a personal acquisition of individuals; it is trained into the bone of the race, and the quality and quantity of it combine to give China a latent working force, an industrial power far exceeding that of all the nations added together." The only way to avoid certain catastrophe, Wheeler argued, was to instill in the Chinese, before it was too late, a set of Victorian truths: "initiative and a sense of control and the modern sciences whose development rests upon these qualities of mind." Wheeler suggested that Japan would be a model for China to emulate, noting that "it was from America Japan received its impulse toward the adoption of the modern equipment of life." Wheeler's description of an "oriental Japan of occidental veneer," however, betokened uneasiness over Japanese progress. Industrializing Japan, after all, had fought a war with Russia—and won.[43]

Yet if the metamorphosis of Japan "from an island power to a power encircling the Sea of Japan" gave some promoters of a trans-Pacific American empire pause for thought, it also prodded them to redouble their efforts to develop closer commercial bonds with Japan in the belief that Japan held the key to the untapped market potential of China and the rest of the Asian continent. Promoters of the Alaska-Yukon-Pacific Exposition recast the interlocking concerns of trade and race that had characterized the portrayal of Japan at earlier fairs into a vision of commercial harmony that the *Seattle Post-Intelligencer* characterized with the slogan "hands across the sea."[44]

The metaphor was grounded in the reality of the exposition. Not only did the Japanese government establish an official exhibit at this fair, thus becoming the only Asian government to do so, but a delegation of Japanese business and civic leaders visited the fair and toured the country as guests of the federal government and the Associated Chambers of Commerce of the Pacific Coast. Headed by Shibuzawa Eiichi, president of the First Bank of Japan and "the man who financed the war with Russia," the Japanese commissioners came to the United States as "ambassadors of commerce" and exemplars of "the best and most progressive element of the most remarkable people of the Orient." They were received accordingly. When James J. Hill's steamship *Minnesota* landed at the Great Northern docks in Seattle, a large crowd of Seattle business leaders and many residents of Seattle's "Japanese colony" turned out to greet them. Over the course of their five-day stay, they toured many industrial and commercial establishments and exchanged with Seattle's business leaders innumerable speeches "brimming over with expressions of good will between America and Japan." To honor their guests, the directors set aside 4 September as Japan Day, and nearly seven thousand Japanese residing in the Northwest turned out for the occasion.[45]

These expressions of goodwill represented nothing less than the fruition of the principles underlying the Gentlemen's Agreement of 1907 and of the Root-Takihara Agreement of 1908, whereby the Japanese government had agreed to curtail the emigration of Japanese workers and maintain the open door policy in China. As Eiichi told Seattle businessmen, emigration restriction was a "good thing." "Owing partly to the growth of our industry at home," he informed the readers of *Pacific Northwest Commerce*, "but more largely to the exodus of our emigrants to various foreign countries, there has been a strong tendency toward the appreciation of wages which naturally threatens those who have direct interests in our industrial undertakings." He elaborated further on the nature of the "mutual interest" that existed between the commercial interests of the two countries:

> Moreover, demand for our labor has been constantly growing, as it has come to pass that we have become responsible for the development of Korea, where we need a great deal of our labor. In Formosa, where we are fast subjugating wild tribes, a great deal of our labor is in demand. Hokkaido, in the northern part of our country, which is but thinly populated, needs to be developed. Above all, Japan itself has to grow as an industrial country. As a business man, therefore, I regard the sending out of our cheap labor to this or any foreign country, will prove a great disadvantage to our home industry [*sic*].

As far as the directors of the fair were concerned Eiichi's goals were compatible with their own, especially since the virtual completion of Hill's railroad empire in the Pacific Northwest had made it unnecessary to increase the force of Japanese railroad laborers.[46]

From the directors' perspective, the real problem lay with the tide of anti-Japanese hysteria and violence that had swept the Pacific Coast over the course of the decade. Only one year before the exposition opened, the first meeting of the International Convention of the Asiatic Exclusion League of North America had convened in Seattle, and an AFL delegate had announced "the fact (and the history of the Oriental races or Asiatic races proves it) that any country touched by these people is blighted as the grasshopper used to blight the crops in Kansas and Colorado." Confronted on the one hand with a desire to promote commercial intercourse with Japan and on the other with widespread racial hatred for the Japanese, the exposition promoters, through the Seattle Commercial Club, issued a resolution appealing for an end to violence: "We therefore urge upon our fellow citizens of Seattle the great importance of showing their civilization and good manners at all times in dealing with our transpacific neighbors; of frowning upon any expression of blind race prejudice, and endeavoring to promote good feelings, confidence and extensive trade relations."[47]

The precise meaning given by the exposition directors to the concept of "good feelings" had been succinctly expressed by exposition vice-president J. H. McGraw two and a one-half years before he stood on the docks to receive the Japanese trade delegation. "While we all admire the Japanese," McGraw had said, "we can not for a moment approve of their becoming citizens of the republic." Seen in this context, "hands across the sea" meant exactly that. Japanese were welcomed as customers, but they were still regarded as "little brown men" who were expected to make Asia safe for democracy and capitalism. This view of Japan at the Alaska-Yukon-Pacific Exposition rounded out the picture of that country that had been built into every exposition held in the United States since the Philadelphia Centennial of 1876.[48]

Fairgoers, the *Portland Oregonion* wrote in an article summing up the significance of the Lewis and Clark Centennial, returned to their homes "knowing as they never knew before what Tennyson meant by his 'Better fifty years of Europe than a cycle of Cathay.' " "Every fireside," the newspaper explained, "is a little Cathay, where we vegetate and tend to relapse into barbarism. A great stimulus like the Fair, when it calls us away from routine and stagnation, is in a deep and true sense regenerative. It makes us all over again." Before the gates closed on the world's fairs in the Pacific Northwest, 4,354,543 fairgoers had left their firesides and paid to gain entry to these extravaganzas. Doubtless most of them had read about the earlier fairs, and some had even been inundated with souvenir postcards sent by family and friends, but there was nothing quite like actually touring an exposition and seeing the evidence of American progress firsthand.[49]

As a steamer from Astoria made its way toward Portland on the last night of the fair, a young woman standing next to a reporter on the deck of the ship saw the lights of the fair off in the distance and began sobbing. "It was unconscious, and of course unforced," the newspaperman wrote, "and it added the final element. She had seen the Fair but a few times and was an alien, but so great was her simple tribute to the beauty of a man-made paradise that I longed for the woman's prerogative of tears and envied her." Another correspondent admonished fairgoers: "Away with melancholy details. Let us all go to the Fair once more, to leave our tears with the scenes which we shall behold no more—the Trail, that motley medly of music and mirth . . .; the art gallery, harbor of long-haired men and short-haired women—we shall leave our tears with these, I say, but we shall carry home with us a memory to be bequeathed as a rich legacy to our children's children." First and foremost among those memories was the lesson "that America is not an aggregate of little semi-hostile communities antagonistic in feeling and welfare, but that we belong to a united and homogeneous Nation, one in aspiration, one in feeling and one in interest." "There are no bad Americans," the *Portland Oregonian* concluded. "We are all good; and the better we are acquainted the more we like each other."[50]

The Portland exposition did more than build self-esteem. It also built Portland's economy and several private fortunes. On the eve of San Diego's exposition of 1915, Portland businessmen sent letters of encouragement to the directors of the Panama-California Exposition and related the benefits that had accrued to them as a result of the Lewis and Clark Centennial. Theodore Wilcox, a prominent Portland grain and flour exporter, noted that "the exposition at Portland increased his fortune two million dollars." In an effort to preserve the cultural legacy that had helped to make such financial rewards possible, Portland's civic leaders organized an annual Rose Festival that persists to this day. But the most important monument to the exposition was the Guild Lake region of Portland, which would become the industrial center of the city. Although the exposition buildings were generally destroyed or removed to other areas of the city, and though the natural marshland reclaimed the landscaped gardens after the fair closed, the gradual transformation of the exposition site into a hub of industrial activity represented less the destruction of Eden than the consummation of empire.[51]

The legacy of Seattle's world's fair assumed a different form. Numerous exposition buildings and a sizable portion of the landscaped grounds became part of the University of Washington campus. Before the exposition ended, the Seattle Chamber of Commerce also endowed the university with a bronze tablet—still embedded in a stone monument on the campus—"as testimonial to those citizens of Seattle who, from a sense of civic loyalty and at great personal sacrifice, created and carried to success an exposition of lasting benefit not only to this city, but to the entire Northwest." "Such men," the inscription concluded, "are the proudest possession of any community and the surest guarantee of its prosperity and greatness." By the close of the exposition, "such men" were also hard at work in San Francisco and San Diego, striving to extend the web of America's international expositions to California and the Southwest.[52]

8

The Expositions in San Francisco and San Diego: Toward the World of Tomorrow

In these days of stifling struggle our people need something to bring back to them the heritage, not only of the combat of immediate fathers in the upbuilding of the West, but also to bring to the people that they have a heritage of race.

[Herbert C. Hoover] to Charley Field, 29 April 1912

California has treasured the missions long. Those who have seen them have carried their inspiration away, yet left it strong to inspire others. It is an inspiration and an appeal that can never die. The soldiers and the adventurers are remembered. The priest-civilizer still lives.

"Prospectus of the 1915 Exposition in San Diego"[1]

IN AUGUST 1914 THE PANAMA CANAL WAS COMPLETED and Europe went to war. Designed to commemorate the opening of the canal, San Francisco's Panama-Pacific International Exposition of 1915 and San Diego's Panama-California Exposition of 1915–16 stood out as colorful oases in a world that had suddenly become much smaller and more terrifying.

Nearly nineteen million people passed through the turnstiles of the Panama-Pacific show, and over three and one-half million visited the more regionally oriented Panama-California Exposition. The author of a children's book about the San Francisco fair captured the essence of its appeal: "There was the beautiful tower of Jewels, smiling and twinkling its shiny eyes at us, and saying, 'Come in, children; come in, and walk under my beautiful blue arches, and through my magic courts, and my sheltered gardens, and be happy, and love each other and all the children of the world. Peace I offer you, and Plenty, and Harmony, and Beauty. Here you are safe, and here you are welcome.'" The mission-revival architecture of the San Diego fair offered a similar illusion of security to anxious pilgrims. According to the directors, a typical visitor to the Panama-California Exposition—built on a mesa that had been converted into Balboa Park—entered "the rose trellised gateway and—presto! . . . He has stepped backward three or four centuries, full into a city of Old Spain, sprang [sic] by magic, domed, towered, castellated, from the top of the mesa." If "dark-eyed Spanish girls" and "gaily-clad cabelleros" strolling alongside "somber-clad monks" added historical romance to the San Diego fair, it was no more quixotic than its San Francisco counterpart. The San Diego fair "will be a comparison of the old with the new," declared a publicity release in advance of the opening, "and, best of all, it will show how the old came to pass away and how the new came into existence." At both expositions the directors made it plain that the mechanism directing this process of change was natural selection.[2]

Inside the "storied walls" of these fairs, elaborate racial fantasies about California's history were intertwined with predictions of continued national progress. "This is not an exposition," according to the San Diego Union, "it is . . . the expression of an idea." The idea, as one columnist made clear, was a Darwinian struggle between the races:

> Then westward the tide sets along the respective parallels of latitude marking the domain of the Saxon and Latin. Still in the north and the south the old world conquered the new until the restless hordes met and mingled on the California coast—here in San Diego in the beginning of this later and latest history of the moving ideas of men. And the weaker was absorbed by the stronger; but with the passing of the weaker they left a legacy of their art and culture, which the survivor has gladly possessed to beautify and decorate his own. They left us their tradition, their romance, and their musical nomenclature. . . . We have received this tradition gladly; we have made of this romance the background of

PANAMA PACIFIC
INTERNATIONAL
EXPOSITION
SAN FRANCISCO 19

our own history . . . in this fair port of San Diego and on this golden coast of California.

A similar concept of racial struggle and progress stirred the imagination of the promoters of the Panama-Pacific International Exposition. Before the opening, Herbert Hoover, international mining engineer, future president, and San Francisco's exposition representative in England, proposed to the directors that a pageant be held in San Francisco to dramatize the racial history of westward expansion:

> If you start with the innumerable conflicts of the Northern and Southern
> branches of the Aryan race over the Continent of Europe, the spread of
> the northern branch into England, whose people assumed the burden of
> contention with the Latin races, who had divided the Western world
> amongst themselves by Papal Bull, and the ultimate culmination of this
> great racial struggle in the defeat of the Armada. These are all events
> not disassociated with California. Drake touched its coasts and
> eventually California formed the last great conflict of these races for the
> actual possession of the land. There the meekly religious Southerner
> vanished like a mist before the more virile Northerner.

Although the pageant itself never materialized, this conception of racial progress permeated the San Francisco fair. Around the Fountain of the Psychology of Life, for example, sculptural groupings—variously titled *The Dawn of Life, Natural Selection,* and *Survival of the Fittest* or *Development of the Militant Spirit*—told the story of "primitive man." "On these primitive people pass through life," a guidebook explained. "You can see them if you look up on the Tower. On they march, in that upward climb of civilization." This sculptural construct gave form to the message Winston Churchill had delivered two years earlier during his preexposition tour of California. "All progress," he had declared, "is primarily a matter of race."[3]

Both expositions were crafted by well-tried exposition hands. Lyman Gage, first president of the World's Columbian Exposition and former secretary of the treasury, had retired to San Diego but surfaced as one of the directors of the Panama-California fair. Frederick J. V. Skiff, who also traced his world's fair lineage back to the Chicago fair, assumed the post of director-in-chief for the Panama-Pacific Corporation. John C. Olmsted and Frederick Allen, the landscape architects responsible for creating the parklike sites for the Portland and Seattle fairs, journeyed to San Diego and turned a chaparral-studded plateau overlooking the city into a verdant setting for the Panama-California fair. Another experienced exposition craftsman, Karl Bitter, plied his sculptural

---

Fig. 65. *(opposite)* "The thirteenth labor of Hercules"—parting the Isthmus. Poster courtesy of Department of Special Collections, Library, California State University, Fresno.

Fig. 66. Night illumination of Panama-Pacific International Exposition.
Courtesy of Department of Special Collections, Library, California State
University, Fresno.

talents at the Panama-Pacific International Exposition—just as he had at the
Buffalo and Saint Louis fairs—before losing his life in a San Francisco automobile accident. Architects from the New York–based firm of McKim, Meade,
and White, along with architects from its crosstown rival Carrère and Hastings, continued their practice of designing selected exposition structures by
creating respectively the Court of the Universe and the Tower of Jewels at the

San Francisco fair. A host of well-known midway showmen once again received contracts for numerous concessions on the entertainment avenues of these fairs—streets that were named the Isthmus at the Panama-California Exposition and the Joy Zone at the Panama-Pacific fair in keeping with the motif celebrating the opening of the canal. Following the pattern of earlier expositions, scientists from the Smithsonian Institution also joined these showmen, artists, and architects and helped to design the California expositions along the lines laid out by their directors and financial backers.[4]

Since the engineering triumph of the canal was the occasion for the celebration, it was appropriate that an engineer, Charles C. Moore—president of one of the nation's largest hydroelectrical engineering firms as well as a director of numerous banks and railroads—headed the Panama Pacific International Exposition Corporation. A veritable dynamo and Corliss engine rolled into one, he was surrounded by equally notable and powerful figures. In addition to Herbert Hoover, he drew on the services of Franklin Delano Roosevelt, appointed by President Woodrow Wilson to the exposition's national commission. At the time of the fair, however, several directors of the exposition were even more distinguished than these future heads of state.[5]

The board included William H. Crocker, son of one of the builders of the transcontinental railroad, president of Crocker Bank, vice-president of Pacific Telephone and Telegraph, and a regent of the University of California. Other directors included corporate attorneys, railroad executives, bankers, and labor leader Patrick Henry McCarthy—the mayor of San Francisco and head of the State Building Trades Council, who was instrumental in persuading organized labor in San Francisco to subscribe to exposition stock and to accept prevailing open-shop conditions on the exposition grounds in return for oral assurances that only union labor would be employed in the excavating work. Two names absent from the exposition's board of directors were newspaper publisher William R. Hearst and sugar king Rudolph Spreckles. But both men had subscribed to large amounts of exposition stock. Hearst, moreover, had exerted a decisive influence in the campaign to bring the Liberty Bell to both fairs. Spreckles, on the other hand, had remained aloof, and an exposition official complained that "the trouble with Rudolph Spreckles is that he is not quite sure whether God made him or whether he made God."[6]

In San Diego the exposition builders regarded themselves as "priest-civilizers." In addition to Lyman Gage, vice-president of the exposition corporation, the directorship included Ulysses S. Grant, Jr., son of the former president and owner of San Diego's most fashionable hotel; Albert G. Spaulding, sporting goods magnate, real estate developer, and head of a securities company; and, John D. Spreckles, Rudolph's brother and a "multimillionaire, with over twenty-five million invested in San Diego alone, the owner of steamships, railways, newspapers, hotels, factories, office buildings, etc." Also contributing their financial support and managerial skills to the enterprise were George W. Marston, merchant, railroad promoter, land developer, and benefactor of several universities; Harry O. Davis, automobile builder and motion picture producer; and G. Aubrey Davidson, president of a local bank and later head of the Bank of America in the San Diego region. Together they selected David C. Collier—a lawyer, real estate investor, and railroad builder—to serve as president of the exposition. Before it was over, Collier had invested between $100,000 and $500,000 of his own money to make the fair a success.[7]

The individuals who financed and directed the Panama-Pacific International Exposition and the Panama-California Exposition stood atop the pinnacle of wealth and power in their communities and in the state as a whole. Their stature made the rivalry that developed between them all the more intriguing.

The idea to mark the opening of the Panama Canal with an international exposition originated with San Francisco businessmen in 1904. They drew their inspiration from President Theodore Roosevelt's decision in that year to create a commission to oversee the construction of the Isthmian passageway and were further stimulated by the opening of the Louisiana Purchase Exposition. Plans for the San Francisco celebration moved ahead over the next year and a half as the city's business leaders gathered pertinent records from the directors of the Saint Louis fair. When the earthquake and fire of April 1906 leveled a substantial portion of San Francisco, exposition enthusiasts barely paused to catch their breath before deciding to make the fair the rallying point for rebuilding the city. By the fall 1906 the city's exposition promoters had persuaded members of the state legislature to draft a constitutional amendment suspending pertinent stockholders' liability laws in the instance of the exposition stock issue. After the state voters approved the amendment, the exposition boosters proceeded over the next three years to organize the Portola festival to sustain mass support for their undertaking and lobbied successfully for a special state tax to support their efforts. They were not a little chagrined when, in 1909, the business leaders of San Diego announced their intention of celebrating the canal's completion with a world's fair of their own.[8]

Like their counterparts in San Francisco, civic leaders in San Diego were engaged in a process of city- and culture-building. Throughout the 1890s and the first years of the twentieth century, men like Collier, Marston, and Spreckles were attempting to escalate the value of their real estate holdings, to increase the population of the city, to promote the agricultural and industrial development of the American Southwest, and to open markets and extract resources in Latin America. With the opening of the Panama Canal imminent,

---

Fig. 67. *(opposite)* San Diego's Panama-California Exposition. Cover from *The Official Guide and Description Book, Panama California International Exposition.*

THE OFFICIAL
GUIDE
and Descriptive Book
Panama California International Exposition
SAN DIEGO 1916

it became obvious that the realization of these goals would be hastened considerably if the commercial traffic through the canal could be routed via San Diego. But it was equally obvious that augmenting the economic growth of the city and the region would require a broad political and cultural consensus—something that plainly did not exist in the first decade of the century. In the 1904 national elections, Republican Theodore Roosevelt had won the majority of San Diego votes, but among the runners-up socialist Eugene Debs had outpolled Democrat William Jennings Bryan. The socialist presence in San Diego remained strong throughout the prewar period and provided a constant reminder of the lack of agreement concerning the future course of American society. Against this backdrop of imperial ambition and political opposition, the idea for the Panama-California Exposition was born at a meeting of the Chamber of Commerce.[9]

Once San Diego's business leaders announced their intention of holding a world's fair and seeking congressional recognition for their exposition, the "tournament of cities" began in earnest. And then, to the dismay of exposition promoters throughout the state, agricultural and business interests in the Deep South, excited by the rift developing in California, announced that New Orleans would be "the logical point" for a fair commemorating the completion of the canal. This unexpected development in the exposition competition spurred the Los Angeles Chamber of Commerce to action. Realizing that California's

Fig. 68. Avenue of Progress at the Panama-Pacific International Exposition. From Prints and Photographs Division, Library of Congress.

businessmen would stand little chance of securing any exposition if the state's congressional delegation was divided between San Diego and San Francisco, Joseph F. Sartori, a Los Angeles banker, suggested that before Congress took up the exposition matter it would be prudent for business organizations throughout California to convene in Santa Barbara to decide which exposition city to endorse. At that convention, held in March 1910, San Francisco, with its larger population and greater financial resources, was the overwhelming choice.[10]

This decision, however, did not bind the San Diegans. Only in May 1910, as a result of much consultation between California's congressmen and exposition promoters in the two cities, did the San Diego businessmen agree to suspend their demand for a world's fair and to support the San Franciscans. In return for their cooperation, however, San Diego's exposition planners elicited assurances from their northern cohorts that, once San Francisco received federal recognition, its businessmen would support federal recognition for a more limited exposition in San Diego that would focus on exhibits from Latin America and the American Southwest and on "a synopsis of man's evolution through a demonstration of the myriad processes which mark the present acme of civilization, and embody the history of man."[11]

With this compromise in tow, California's congressmen concentrated on beating back the challenge from New Orleans. In February 1911, after dragging out the matter of the as-yet-unpaid federal loan that had been necessary to bail out the exposition held in New Orleans in 1885, California's representatives obtained federal sanction for the Panama-Pacific International Exposition in San Francisco. Six months later the House voted to bestow federal recognition on the more narrowly defined Panama-California Exposition in San Diego. But the House bill also required Senate approval. Late in the year, Collier and Moore sat down with their congressmen to map out strategy. Just to be absolutely certain he had the support of the San Franciscans, Collier yielded to their demand that San Diego's exposition sponsors refrain from using the word "international" in advertising their fair. At the conclusion of the meeting, federal support for the San Diego fair seemed a certainty. But in January 1912 a Senate committee killed the House measure.[12]

Exposition builders in San Diego accused the backers of the San Francisco fair of an outright double-cross compounded by political sabotage. The San Franciscans, Collier and his associates charged, had made a secret deal with President Taft in which they agreed to support his renomination drive against Theodore Roosevelt in return for the president's pledge to quash the San Diego exposition bill in the Senate. Whether or not these allegations had any foundation in reality, the Senate committee's decision had the effect of strengthening the determination of the San Diego boosters to hold a fair, even if they had to get along without federal recognition. As a first step in this direction, Collier sold a portion of his real estate holdings to finance his own promotional

Fig. 69. Panama-California Exposition—central court.
From Prints and Photographs Division, Library of
Congress.

and display-gathering trips around the United States and Latin America. But
a series of rapidly unfolding political events in Mexico, Nicaragua, and San
Diego made this strategy increasingly unrealistic and led Collier and his colleagues to renew their drive for federal sanction of the exposition.[13]

In 1912 the revolution in Mexico that had swept Porfirio Díaz from power
the year before was still under way, and United States Marines intervened in
Nicaragua to protect American investments from the political turbulence shaking that country. Closer to home, open violence erupted in San Diego as vig-
ilante groups attempted to suppress the Free Speech Movement that had been
launched by the Industrial Workers of the World. Violence directed against
the Wobblies reached such intensity in San Diego that the state's attorney
general threatened to use troops to restore order if the city police force was
unable to do so. By the end of the year, with both the domestic and the
international political fabric splitting at the seams, federal support for the
exposition acquired greater significance than ever before in the eyes of the
city fathers. Not only would congressional support aid their efforts to extend
American influence in Latin America, but it would validate the legitimacy of
their local political authority as well.[14]

Once the Wilson administration assumed office, William Kettner, the newly
elected congressman from San Diego, quietly introduced a bill authorizing the
establishment of a federal warehouse on the exposition grounds. By the time
San Francisco's exposition interests realized that this measure would lay the
basis for federal recognition of the San Diego fair, it was too late. Despite a
last-ditch attempt by San Francisco businessmen to have the bill tabled, Kettner's exposition measure passed both houses of Congress and, in May 1913,
was signed into law by Woodrow Wilson.[15]

Lingering bitterness persisted between the rival exposition forces, but this "tournament of cities" continued to be fought out in an arena of shared ideological assumptions about American progress. Consequently it was relatively easy for the directors of the two corporations to declare a truce—capped off in 1916 when many of the international exhibits from the San Francisco fair were sent to San Diego and the exposition there was rechristened the Panama-California International Exposition. Shortly after the San Diego exposition first opened in 1915, San Francisco banker William H. Crocker expressed approval. "Personally," he remarked, "I am so delighted with this Exposition, with its beauty, originality, and perfect taste, that I am going to make it part of my business to send people down here. I am going to pound it into them that they must come to San Diego, and that if they go back to their homes without coming to San Diego, they will have missed half the show." That peace ultimately prevailed among the civic-minded deities and "priest-civilizers" of both cities was not surprising. After all, the directors of both fairs sought to preserve the people's faith in the idea of progress—with all its interlaced connotations of technological advance, material growth, racism, and imperialism—and to reshape that faith with particular reference to the challenges posed by domestic and international turmoil. The directors, moreover, projected a mutually reinforcing view of the world carved out of the same ideological mold as earlier fairs. At California's fairs, however, the vision of utopia rested squarely on the application of scientific racial categories to selected white and nonwhite populations alike.[16]

When Crocker described the much smaller Panama-California Exposition as "half the show," he paid the San Diego fair only its due. Acting largely on the advice of Frederick Skiff, Crocker and the other directors of San Francisco's Panama-Pacific International Exposition had decided that the cost of establishing a separate anthropology department in keeping with the scale of the fair would be prohibitive. Consequently they followed the route taken by the directors of several earlier fairs and conveyed the message of evolutionary national and international progress through art, ethnological concessions, and a relatively small lay-figure display of Native Americans provided by the Smithsonian Institution. The promoters of the Panama-California Exposition, however, decided to make the "science of man" their central focus and to offer a "New Deal in Education and the humanization of science." These different emphases made the San Diego and San Francisco fairs distinctive, but by no means antithetical.[17]

The decision to make anthropology the linchpin of the Panama-California Exposition originated with its president. "In searching for a theme for the San Diego, Cal. exposition which would teach the visitor something worth knowing and therefore leaving a lasting and useful impression," the *San Diego Union* reported, "President Collier hit upon the plan of a synopsis of man's evolution through a demonstration of the myriad processes which mark the present acme of civilization, and embody the history of man." To implement this idea Collier first sought out "the highest scientific authority" he could recruit to serve as director of exhibits for the exposition and settled on Edgar L. Hewett, head of the American Institute of Archaeology in Santa Fe, New Mexico. "It is the purpose of the Panama California Exposition. . . ," Collier informed Hewett, "to illustrate, as has never been done before, the progress and possibilities of the human race. You will appreciate the large part that archaeology and ethnology must take in such a scheme."[18]

In addition to assuring Hewett that a minimum of $100,000 would be available for the ethnology and archaeology exhibits, the exposition president pledged that the collections assembled for the fair would be placed in a permanent museum in San Diego. Collier next enlisted the publicity and organizational talents of Charles F. Lummis—librarian, amateur ethnologist, and founder of the Southwest Museum in Los Angeles—who had dedicated his life to the proposition that "the California frontier offered an environment wherein the educated Anglo-Saxon might bring into fruition his latent potential to attain Herculean accomplishments." In a letter to Collier, Lummis expressed his delight with the fair and told the president that he found the exposition especially appealing because "you have mixed Science with business so splendidly that it becomes really a man's game." Before long the exposition's carousel of scientists and businessmen also included anthropologists from the Smithsonian Institution.[19]

Almost from the moment Hewett became director of exhibits in late 1911, he began soliciting the advice of anthropologists William Henry Holmes and Aleš Hrdlička of the United States National Museum. By January 1912 they had jointly worked out a detailed plan for the Department of Ethnology—an outline of which Collier submitted to Charles D. Walcott, secretary of the Smithsonian Institution, along with a request that Holmes be permitted to assemble a stone-art exhibit for the department and that Hrdlička be allowed to serve as head of the department's division of physical anthropology. The overall plan for the department, as Collier explained it to Walcott, called for the exposition corporation and Smithsonian Institution to sponsor several expeditions to different countries for the purpose of gathering artifacts in three broad categories: "the Physical Evolution of Man," "the Evolution of Culture," and "the Native Races of America." This far-reaching project appealed strongly to Smithsonian anthropologists, especially Hrdlička.[20]

When Hewett and Collier approached him about participating in the Panama-California Exposition, Hrdlička—by this time a curator at the USNM and solidly established as one of the foremost physical anthropologists in the world—leaped at the opportunity to popularize the findings of physical anthropology and to increase the collections of the Smithsonian. "The plan of making a representative exhibit in [physical anthropology] is a most commendable one," Hrdlička declared, "and if this exhibit can be realized on the proper scale, it is bound to prove, on the one hand, of the greatest interest and instructive value to the public, and on the other, of much importance to the standing and progress of physical anthropology in this country." The models of "well chosen racial types," he continued, "will be directly in line of developing the exhibits of our Institution and advancing research." Finally, he observed that, since the "San Diego exhibits will be made under the auspices of the Smithsonian Institution, or the National Museum, their success will in a large measure be to the credit of these." Having been thwarted in his desire to set up a physical anthropology exhibit at the Saint Louis fair in 1904, Hrdlička set out to make up for lost time.[21]

As soon as he received Walcott's permission to proceed, Hrdlička put Smithsonian modelers to work on busts of selected "racial types" and organized field research for himself and other anthropologists drawn from a variety of institutions in Europe and America. European anthropologists Jindrich Matiegka, A. Rutot, and Kazimierz Stolyhwo canvassed central and southeastern Europe collecting "skeletal remains of ancient man" for the exposition. Hrdlička personally explored Siberia, Mongolia, and Peru and traveled to various European museums to make plaster casts of selected craniums. Frank Mička and Riley Moore of the USNM undertook separate expeditions to study the Eskimos and the Sioux Indians. Meanwhile Philip Newton, an anatomist at Georgetown University, journeyed to the Philippines to study the Negritos and surreptitiously desecrated graves in the search for cranial and skeletal material for the fair. Another anthropologist, Voltjetch Schuck of Prague, traveled to Africa to photograph and gather anthropometric data about the Pygmies, Zulus, and Bushmen as part of a long-range comparative study of Africans and Afro-Americans that Hrdlička was planning to conduct. When World War I began Schuck was arrested and imprisoned in British-controlled East Africa, but not before he had measured and photographed numerous Africans.[22]

As results from the various expeditions poured into San Diego, Hrdlička's assistant, United States naval surgeon Joseph Thompson, followed instructions from Hrdlička and Hewett and installed the exhibits in the California Building, the Science and Education Building, and the Indian Arts Building. "Housed in Buildings of Beautiful Spanish-Colonial Architecture in a Gorgeous Setting of Tropical Verdure," the displays provided an easily understood classification of mankind along racial lines. No exhibit was more crucial to this categorization than the physical anthropology display, which filled five adjoining rooms in the Science and Education Building. These displays told the "first chapter" of the story of man's progress toward perfection as revealed by the exposition.[23]

Visitors to the physical anthropology section first entered a room illustrating "Man's Evolution." The "Evolution Room," as it was sometimes called, consisted of ten busts "representing man at different stages of his evolution," ten reconstructed skulls, and "accurate casts of the most important skeletal remains of Early Man thus far discovered." Furthermore, "a series of original crania showing in general a progression from lemur to man" helped to demonstrate the central lesson Hrdlička sought to convey, namely that "the facts now in the possession of science make it clear that the views of Darwin, Wallace and Lamarck regarding man's ascension from lower forms were substantially correct. It is ascertained that the further we go back along the course of man's physical progress, the more simple appears his intelligence, the more primitive, the less human, his features." In sum, Hrdlička noted, this particular roomful of exhibits "illustrates, in something like ascending biological order, the species that now connect man with the rest of the animal kingdom."[24]

With ideas of the evolutionary process fresh in their minds, visitors next moved into a room that illustrated the development of the human body from the moment of birth to death. "All these vital processes," Hrdlička wrote in a description of the exhibits, "progress under definite and very fixed laws . . . [that] show nevertheless racial and environmental variations." To illuminate these variations, Hrdlička put on display one hundred facial molds gathered from the various expeditions. "The backbone of the exhibits," he explained, were "three series of true-to-nature busts, showing definite age-stages, from birth onward and in both sexes, the principal races of this country, namely the 'thoroughbred' white American (for at least three generations in this continent on each parental side), the Indian, and the full-blood American negro." Supplemented by exhibits of portions of the human anatomy, especially of the brain, as well as by comparative data about apes, the exhibits in the second room left little doubt that man's physical development through time had resulted in variations that were fundamentally racial.[25]

This emphasis on racial variation formed the basic theme for the third room of the display as racial portraits, charts, busts, and body casts divided humanity into "the main races and the sub-races of man." The "main races," Hrdlička explained, "may be defined as the main physical streams of humanity; the secondary races are the important tributaries of these streams; and the types are the main affluents of these tributaries." "There are," he continued, "three great main races, the White, the Yellow-Brown, and the Black" which, in turn, were "divisible into a number of secondary races, and each of the latter into two or more types." Conceding that this system of racial classification, "based on the most obvious characteristic of man, his skin-color," was imperfect, Hrdlička nevertheless justified its value on the grounds that it was "the simplest." Precision in racial categorization, however, was not at all impossible in Hrdlička's book. Elsewhere in this exhibit hall, displays of skulls were arranged according to the quantitative and genetic typology of the cephalic index—a mathematical system for computing cranial capacity—thus suggesting that whites and nonwhites could be subdivided into different races with some degree of scientific exactness.[26]

The two remaining galleries devoted to the physical anthropology exhibit consisted of a model anthropology laboratory and a hall containing displays relating human pathology and senility to racial variation. These exhibit halls gave added substance to the image of human beings as higher animals who had been tiered into identifiable races and subraces as a result of an ongoing and endless process of evolution. What made this presentation so striking in 1915 was not simply that Hrdlička linked the concept of race with biology and presented this equation to fairgoers as scientific truth, but that he did so four years after Franz Boas had leveled his "critique of racial formalism" in *The Mind of Primitive Man*. Over the long run, Boas and his students would deeply influence the intellectual contours of the anthropology profession and make many of the evolutionary props for popular racial attitudes untenable. At the Panama-California Exposition, however, it was the anthropology of government science and the evolutionary racial doctrines espoused by Hrdlička that reached the public. His exhibits won praise from lay visitors and scientists alike.[27]

Importantly, Hrdlička did not stop at classifying mankind into racial categories. He defined physical anthropology so as to include within its purview "man's evolution in the future, with its possible regulation or control." Hrdlička, in short, created the impression that physical anthropology could substantiate the existence of evolutionary racial change and that physical anthropologists might be able to "regulate" the course of that change, thus becoming utopian agents in their own right. Newspaper columnist James Wilkinson dramatized the impact of these lessons in an article about the physical anthropology exhibit at the fair. "The inevitable result of the spread of the doctrine of evolution," Wilkinson wrote, "will be that man will strive more and more to control the forces of nature and make them work for his lasting welfare. There will be an enlightened program favoring courageously the survival of the fittest human beings and the gradual development of a sturdy public opinion that will refuse to tolerate industrial and social conditions that tend toward the debasement and deterioration of the race." "Protoplasm," he concluded, "will be held sacred only insofar as it gives promise to worthy spiritual expression." As Wilkinson's account made clear, Hrdlička's interest in eugenics—which the anthropologist defined as "the science of improving the human stock"—glimmered through the physical anthropology exhibit. It dovetailed perfectly with the promise of progress that the directors of the San Diego exposition sought to instill in fairgoers.[28]

To implant a similar faith in the possibility for achieving racial perfection in the future, the directors of the San Francisco fair relied less on anthropologists than on eugenicists themselves. In the tradition of earlier expositions, the directors decided to convene a series of congresses and conventions on significant issues of the day and dedicate the meetings to the idea of "service." Eugenics did not dominate, or even enter into, all 948 congresses, but the subject of race betterment crept into several papers at the International Purity Congress and the Education Congress and formed the basis for the National Conference on Race Betterment that was organized by David Starr Jordan, former president of Stanford University and a leading voice in the eugenics movement.[29]

At the opening session of the Race Betterment Congress, John H. Kellogg, cereal producer and founder of the Race Betterment Foundation in Battle Creek, Michigan, welcomed delegates by announcing his intention to create "a eugenic registry through which [the foundation] hoped to establish an aristocracy of health." Edgar L. Hewett, who traveled up from San Diego for the occasion, spoke on the "Mexican situation" and confided his belief that Mexicans "imperil in some measure the health of the race in its onward march." After hearing a lecture from a San Francisco physician about the need to muzzle dogs to bring about an end to rabies, the audience listened to an appeal for another form of prophylaxis: the prevention of "ill-fit and improper intermarriages." Two days later, Luther Burbank stood before the assemblage and emphasized that people "are like plants and . . . will not prosper without proper selection any more than vegetables would if indiscriminately planted." "There are two distinct lines in the improvement of race," Burbank declared. "One is by favorable environment; the other, ten thousand times more important, is by selection of the best individuals through a series of generations." That same evening the Race Betterment Foundation dramatized these points in a theatrical "masque," entitled "Redemption." This allegory of "man's struggle with the agencies of race deterioration, disease and war" revealed "how mankind, boastful, disregarded the warning of the Great Unseen Spirit and under the influence of scoffers followed Pleasure until the Neglected Child fell ill and died, despite the efforts of Art, Science and Religion." All was not lost, however. After one character—named "Fortunate" because of the careful upbringing he had received from his family—lost his life as a result of war, "Mankind and Womankind, enlisting the services of Science, Faith and Enlightenment, overcame war and began a new race upon the solid foundation of physical perfection and mental enlightenment." In an effort to perpetuate these lessons in racial improvement, the Race Betterment Foundation made copies of the script available to social service clubs in communities around the country.[30]

The relevance of the Race Betterment Conference to the overarching concept of "service" that lay behind the world's congress movement at the fair surfaced in the *San Francisco Chronicle*. Probably timed to coincide with the last day of the conference, a column by Henry Smith Williams, the former director of the Randall Island Hospital in New York City, stressed that "the problem of immigration is essentially a problem in eugenics." "It is not merely our right," Williams asserted, "it is our duty to ask ourselves these questions: What is likely to be the effect upon our national civilization, upon the prospects of our descendants, of this greatest migration in the history of the world? Is the traditional American type worth preserving, and shall we take steps to preserve it?" Earlier in the exposition year, Williams provided some of the answers to these questions in another newspaper column in which he offered statistics "to suggest very strongly the prevalence of brains of a doubtful or undesirable quality among the immigrant population. And no student of heredity can doubt that the future of civilization of America is thereby gravely endangered."[31]

In the lingering atmosphere of concern over race suicide left by the Race Betterment Conference, the Education Congress convened and provided additional support for the assumptions underlying the eugenics movement. "Probably the most significant single feature of the congress," Frank Morton Todd, the exposition's official historian, later related, "was its reflection of the movement, then beginning, toward the scientific estimation of individual intelligence through the Binet-Simon test, a movement that promised the ultimate grading or selecting of pupils according to their capacity to receive education." Lewis Terman, one of the leading proponents of the IQ test, addressed the congress on "The Stanford Revision and Extension of the Binet Scale" and doubtless alerted educators in the audience to the findings presented in his forthcoming book, that a definite correlation existed between intelligence and race. By introducing the Stanford revisions of the intelligence quotient test at a scholarly gathering held in conjunction with the fair, Terman firmly identified the IQ test with the forces of progress. Its import was enormous. As the exposition's historian noted, the IQ test "enabled the teacher to tell how [students] should be classed and classified to get the best intellectual and economic result."[32]

As important as these congresses were for lending the weight of scientific and educational authority to the eugenics drive, an exhibit in the Palace of Education established by the Race Betterment Foundation had greater significance for popularizing the message of eugenics. "One of the exhibits that caught the eye of every visitor," wrote Todd, "was the Race Betterment booth, representing the eugenics movement in the thought of the time. Here were large plaster casts of Atlas, and Venus, and of Apollo, Belvedere type, to advertise the human race at its best, and get that race interested in its glorious past and possible future." On the walls of the booth, pictures of the foundation's supporters—among them Harvard president Charles W. Eliot, conservationist Gifford Pinchot, and judge Ben Lindsey—gave the exhibit an added measure of credibility. Printed notices around the booth informed fairgoers about the goals of the foundation:

To present the evidence of race deterioration, to show the possibility of
race improvement, to emphasize the importance of personal hygiene and
race hygiene, or eugenics, as methods of race improvement. The Race
Betterment movement aims to create a new and superior race through
euthenics, or personal and public hygiene, and eugenics, or race
hygiene.

Highlighting the urgency of the task were "four 'live' people . . . who sat on
vibrating chairs and were agitated physically by [an] electric motor, and usu-
ally looked resentful of the past and careless of the future, and as though they
thoroughly needed the good shaking they were getting." But could the human
race be improved? To answer this question, the exhibit also included "examples of what man has done, through selection and breeding, to improve the
dahlia, the cactus, corn, and various kinds of animals." In its totality, Todd
recalled, the booth devoted to eugenics "was so admirably arranged that you
didn't have to ask many questions; all you had to do was just to look, to see
the necessity for its work."[33]

An exhibit established by the United States government made this necessity
seem even more apparent. In the United States Department of Labor exhibit,
situated in the Palace of Mines and Metallurgy, an electrical diagram illustrated "the wave of immigration between 1820 and 1914, flashing by years."
The exhibit, moreover, furnished spectators with "statistical facts for 1914 as
to races of alien arrivals; occupations of those admitted; routes of entry followed by admitted aliens; distribution of persons admitted; causes of exclusion; and arrests and deportations by classes." Supplemented by a motion
picture about the Ellis Island receiving station, the display made it clear that
the composition of the white ethnic population of the United States was changing. Eugenicists left no doubt that it was changing for the worse.[34]

Through California's expositions, in short, numerous exposition-goers became aware of the work of physical anthropologists and eugenicists in the area
of race classification and race betterment. With the classificatory emphasis of
scientific racists unmistakably broadening to include selected white ethnic
groups, the popularization of these racial categories had profound consequences. In the first place, the exhibits afforded fairgoers a scientific explanation for evolutionary racial progress that could easily encompass events in
the not-so-distant past when one group of whites, Anglo-Americans, wrenched
land titles away from another group of whites, the Californios, or "native born
Californians of Spanish-speaking parents." In the second place, these exhibits
went a long way toward providing the intellectual underpinnings for mass support for the immigration restriction laws of the 1920s, which placed limits on
European immigration, fixed racial quotas on other immigrant groups, and, by
1927, excluded Asians altogether. Within the neo-Mediterranean and Spanish
Renaissance walls of these expositions, anthropologists and eugenicists played
an indispensable role in charting the course to a future utopia in which the

Fig. 70. The Joy Zone. From Prints and Photographs
Division, Library of Congress.

lamp of human perfection burned ever whiter. For many nonwhites, as villages
on the Joy Zone and Isthmus made apparent, the meaning of the utopia forecast by the exposition directors connotated "no place" and underscored the
pressing need for alternative visions for the future.[35]

With their well-tested formulas for midway shows firmly in hand, such noteworthy impressarios as Frederic Thompson, Arthur W. Lewis, Frederick Cummins, Emmett W. McConnell, and Fred McClellan traveled to California,
where they, along with local businessmen, invested millions of dollars in stage
sets that continued to cast entertaining and didactic spells for entranced fun
seekers. Two enormous toy soldiers standing guard at the entrance to Toy-
land—one of Thompson's many concessions—gave substance to the prospect
of finding pleasure, while a ninety-foot-tall wooden caricature of a banner-
waving, drum-beating suffragist—dubbed "Little Eva" because the directors
feared "Panama Pankaline Imogene Equalrights" would offend women—suggested the reality of distortion.[36]

For his Panama Canal concession, McClellan originally planned to build a
model of the canal large enough to allow visitors to ride in boats through a
system of locks, but it proved too expensive. His scaled-down show was a hit
nonetheless. A moving walkway conveyed people around a working model of
the waterway, while recorded descriptions of the canal's operations were
played through a system of telephone receivers. Elsewhere on the Zone, the
Union Pacific Railroad constructed a reproduction of the Old Faithful Inn at
Yellowstone Park and set it against a backdrop of "burlap-and-stucco mountains" and erupting geysers. Not to be outdone, the Santa Fe Railroad constructed a three-dimensional rendering of the Grand Canyon, complete with
the Daughters of the American Revolution headquarters, a pueblo containing

Hopi Indians, and a Navajo blanket concession managed by famous restaurateur Fred Harvey. This Indian Village left no doubt that much of the recreation found along the amusement street derived from the re-creation of racial stereotypes and the lessons of racial progress.[37]

Numerous village concessions dotted the Zone. With the help of motion picture star G. M. Anderson, otherwise known as "Bronco Billy," Captain A. W. Lewis built the Tehuantepec Village—a gaudy reconstruction of a Mexican village, complete with a restaurant and theater, gardens, and Mexicans "working at characteristic handicrafts." According to one description, the village embodied "a complete and typical reproduction of an aboriginal community." Richard Schneidewind, who had made a name for himself exhibiting Filipinos at earlier expositions, appeared on the Zone with a Samoan village. The *San Francisco Examiner* promised prospective visitors that it "will amuse you with the primitive ways of its semi-naked citizens. Weird, too, are their dances, and one gets a glimpse of the life of a race thousands of years behind civilization." An African village was intended to convey a similar impression with its "community of thin, black, and hollow-cheeked wanderers from Somali land," but even with one villager, spear in hand, doing a war dance on the ballyhoo stand, sightseers found the "savages too tame," and the directors agreed. Within weeks of the show's opening, the Africans were deported by United States immigration officials.[38]

Other shows along the Zone caricatured people from Asia and the Asian subcontinent. Villagers in the Mysterious Orient concession had performed at previous fairs dating back to the World's Columbian Exposition, but a newspaper correspondent assured fairgoers that the Turks and Arabs "retain . . . all the old-world customs and manners, for the Occidental speed and restless activity makes little impression upon blood imbued with centuries of languor and the leisure pace when factories and steam and automobiles were not." Japan-Beautiful—the Japanese Village—was hard to miss. A huge golden Buddha, rising 120 feet above the Zone, marked the entrance to a series of bazaars and shooting galleries that composed the show. Termed "a junk shop" by one exposition official, this trivialization of Japanese culture—accomplished by Yumeto Kushibiki, who had run similar villages at earlier expositions—offset the impressions of Japanese progress created by the official Japanese buildings on the main exposition grounds. The Chinese, at first glance, seemed to fare somewhat better. As a result of objections raised by members of the local Chinese business community and by the Chinese consul, the directors agreed to close one portion of the Chinese Village—the Underground Chinatown concession, operated by theater executive Sid Grauman, which depicted a "chamber of horrors" including opium dens. The decision to close this concession rested largely on the belief that closure would hasten the realization of closer economic ties with the new Republic of China.[39]

China, the *San Francisco Chronicle* proclaimed, "has declared for modern ways." Hovering in the background of this assessment was the nationalist revolution in 1911, the subsequent creation of the Republic of China, and the expressed willingness of the new Chinese government to court American capital, as evidenced by the nature of its official participation in the fair. Few buildings attracted greater notice than the structures constituting the Forbidden City. This complex stood in the main portion of the exposition grounds and housed the bulk of the Chinese exhibits sent to the fair under the auspices of the new Chinese government. The buildings were prefabricated in China and reassembled on the exposition grounds by Chinese laborers "who wore American clothes" and "who did their work effectively with ineffective tools—the best test of good workmen."[40]

This reminder that the Chinese were good laborers suggested many possibilities for the future development of China, especially in light of the plan unveiled by the Chinese government in the Transportation Palace for constructing a railroad line between Peking and Constantinople. "What this might mean in world commerce," Todd exulted, "in gathering up the product of the mineral resources of one of the most heavily mineralized regions on the globe, manufactured by modern industrial organization with the potencies of disciplined Chinese labor, and pouring it into the trade of the Mediterranean and western Europe, is staggering to the imagination." Little wonder, Todd noted, that the Chinese commissioners to the fair—several Chinese businessmen from China and from the United States including financier Kee Owyang, who had held the concession for many Chinese villages at previous fairs—received a twenty-one-gun salute from the nearby Presidio army base, even though the United States government had yet to recognize the Republic of China.[41]

Given these circumstances, neither was it surprising that the exposition directors closed the Underground Chinatown concession after the Chinese protested. The official Chinese exhibits projected an eminently serviceable image of the Chinese as willing workers and China as a land ripe for American investment. Eliminating the offensive concession, however, did not free the Chinese from ridicule. The Chinese Village continued to operate on the Zone for the duration of the exposition, and before long it included a new concession called Underground Slumming. Although this new show contained no Chinese entertainers, it conjured up fantasies of finding illicit amusement in the Chinese Village—a village that stood out as just one more nonwhite ghetto among many others on the outskirts of the utopia planned by the exposition directors.[42]

Plenty of possibilities for ethnological slumming also existed along the Isthmus at the San Diego exposition, where at one point fairgoers dressed in Native American costumes and danced the "Indian Rag." Long before the exposition opened, publicists began whetting the public's appetite for "live" midway shows. The author of one publicity release aroused the people's expectations in a particularly imaginative way by adopting the persona and rhythmic inflection of a midway spieler giving joy seekers a tour of the Isthmus. He began in classic fashion: "And a jaunt for joy it is ladies and gentlemen, every inch of the way you will observe." After pointing out the primitive life-style of the inhabitants of the fictitious Aztec City, he turned sightseers' attention to the fanciful Conquest of Peru show and explained how "baffled" scientists were by the Incas. In response to a series of questions from his rapt audience, the ballyhooer raised the significance of the Isthmus from the level of the honky-tonk to the more rarefied stratum of pseudoscience: "Why yes, it happened to be my privilege to take a prominent part in one of the leading expeditions to these parts. Our researches and discoveries at that time has proven invaluable to—er—many scientific societies throughout the civilized globe. What's that the little boy says? Were the Incas black? Certinly, my son, inky—that's why they call them the Incas." Intended to caricature the ballyhooer as well as the Isthmus, this vignette also suggested that the essence of the "spiel" at the San Diego fair entailed more than simple exaggeration; it also involved strengthening the claims that ethnologists made for their anthropology exhibits.[43]

The gap between science and pseudoscience narrowed considerably as a result of efforts by the exposition directors to integrate the shows along the Isthmus with the didactic thrust of the fair as a whole. An early newspaper account explained that scientists from the Smithsonian Institution would provide displays devoted to "forgotten peoples," while the directors of the fair would organize a display of "their descendants" consisting of "barbarous and semi-civilized tribes, living their own lives in their tents, huts or other native habitations, and engaged in typical occupations such as weaving blankets, making spears or arrows, shaping pottery or whatever arts and crafts they may excel in." Among the so-called descendants of man's prehistoric forebears put on display on the Isthmus as illustrations of "stages of progress" were the Japanese living in the Oriental Joy Garden; the Chinese inhabiting Underground Chinatown; Afro-Americans residing in the Southern Plantation; Singhalese working on Sir Thomas Lipton's model Tea Plantation; and Native Americans living in the Painted Desert.[44]

Financed entirely by the Atchison, Topeka and Santa Fe Railroad, the Painted Desert—consisting of several pueblos constructed by members of southwestern Indian tribes under the supervision of Fred Harvey—stood out as an ethnological colony par excellence. From the moment of its inception, the directors of the exposition and of the railroad intended this concession to furnish fairgoers with "something of an education, something partaking of the nature of the ethnological exhibit away at the other end of the grounds." To give exposition-goers "a little sermon" about progress, the directors, moreover, located this exhibit across the street from the Model Farm—a working, fully mechanized farm financed and operated by the International Harvester Company. In the overall context of this "exposition with a purpose," the con-

trast between these two exhibits pushed across the lesson that continued progress toward the ultimate realization of the California dream depended on continued racial and technological advance. Motion pictures and newsreels—in
widespread use at both fairs—drove the lesson home. [45]

Motion picture studio concessions on both the Isthmus and the Joy Zone
signaled the blossoming of film as a powerful medium for shaping cultural
values under the aegis of entertainment. "To a degree never seen before,"
observed newspaper columnist Ben Macomber about the San Francisco fair,
"the moving picture has taken a place in this exposition as an exhibition
adjunct." Lewis J. Selznick, vice-president of the World Film Corporation,
showed promotional films of the Panama-Pacific International Exposition in
over 3,500 theaters across the United States and Canada, while seventy-seven
movie theaters in the various palaces on the fairgrounds bombarded fairgoers
with films on topics ranging from immigration to city planning to state politics. [46]

Equally enthralling were the movies actually produced at the fairs. Film
crews from Universal Films traveled to the Panama-California Exposition to
produce *The World to Come*, a tale of "Count Rabboni who seeks to change
the lives of people from the age of commercialism to that of more idealistic
living conditions." The count, one newspaper reported, "builds what will appear in the motion picture as the San Diego exposition for his paradise on
earth and the characters begin their lives there. As the story unfolds the life
and the results of life in such ideal surroundings are shown." The climax of
the film occurred with an outdoor wedding featuring sixty beauty-contest winners supplied by the president of the studio, Carl Laemmle. Not to be outdone, William Randolph Hearst featured his leading actress, Grace Darling,
in a feature-length film about the San Francisco fair. "Her adventures,"
Hearst's *San Francisco Examiner* informed readers, "should be filled with absorbing interest for all the world-weary people who cannot get away from the
problems of life" and should transport them "back into the land where enthusiasm and joy and love of life bubble from every roadside spring." Grace
Darling, the *Examiner* asserted, "is going to prove that the fairy tales of today are a thousand times more splendid than the fairy tales we read about in
the storybooks."[47]

Another film producer also had his eyes on the Panama-Pacific extravaganza. During an interview at the Saint Francis Hotel in downtown San Francisco, David W. Griffith praised the fair as "the grandest thing the world has
known." Consequently, he continued, "it would be a crime to let the exposition come and go without perpetuating it in photography. I don't mean ordinary photography, but something stupendous. . . . I mean, in short, a film
drama that will mark another forward leap as great as that of 'The Birth of a
Nation.'" Griffith's plans to produce an exposition epic on the same scale as
his film about the redemption of the South by the Ku Klux Klan seem not to

have materialized. Nevertheless, his idea to perpetuate the image of the exposition through the medium of film—together with the actual accomplishments of Hearst and Laemmle along these lines—indicated the value of this
new cultural form for perpetuating the hegemony of the nation's ruling classes
and for transmitting their cultural values to communities around the nation.
Yet, even without the contributions by filmmakers, California's world fairs left
a formidable cultural legacy.[48]

"For 288 days," the official historian observed of the San Francisco fair,
the fair had been the answer to "the prayer of the dying Goethe for 'More
Light!'" On the evening of 4 December 1915, nearly half a million people
stood silently in the Court of the Universe "expecting the hour of fate—the
termination of an epoch in the history of every soul there present. . . . [O]ne
heard a half-stifled sob, forced by the anticipated craving for the return of
what could never be again." Exposition President Charles Moore delivered the
eulogy:

> The end of a perfect day, the beginning of an endless memory! We
> know now more than ever how through all the trying months God's
> blessing has been ours. We have assembled here, we builders of the
> Exposition, for the last rites before official closing. Through it all, good
> friends, keep a smile on your faces, though there be tears in your
> hearts. . . . We are here to perform the final act of putting out the
> lights that we hope have burned brightly, to good purpose. These lights
> must now be dimmed. . . . The time approaches. If the reverential
> prayer of a layman is permissible, let me quote those inspired words,
> ages old: "The peace of God, which passeth all understanding, keep
> your hearts and minds in the knowledge and love of God, now and
> evermore." Friends, the Exposition is finished. The lights are going out.

Moore's funereal tone underscored the significance of the exposition as a sacred event in the cultural life of the nation.[49]
    "But I did love it," one visitor to the Panama-Pacific International Exposi-
tion recalled in 1960. "I wish I could tell it, now, how much I love it; that it
is one of the many affectionate messages to the dead I would like to send."
These same sentiments had long since been institutionalized. When the exposition closed, Hubert Eaton, director of what would become Forest Lawn
Cemetery in Los Angeles, purchased the much praised bronze *Duck Boy* for
his theme park and decided to highlight the cemetery with a modified version
of the Tower of Jewels. His idea for turning a burial ground into an exposition
flowed directly from the ritualistic nature of the world's fair that had culminated in the last rites on the final day of the fair.[50]
    The legacy of the Panama-California Exposition was even more enduring for
the simple reason that it never ended. Many of its mission revival buildings
had been designed as permanent exhibit halls to adorn Balboa Park. One

basilica in particular stood out in the directors' plans for immortalizing their enterprise. At the close of the San Diego fair they presented the California Building—a domed structure with a two-hundred-foot campanile and churrigueresque frontispiece detailing the history of San Diego—to the San Diego Museum Association as a display space for many of the ethnological and archaeological materials gathered at the exposition. "San Diego's museum of man is unquestionably today the most convincing presentation to be found anywhere on the subject of man's evolution," a San Diego resident wrote in 1925. "An entire fireproof building is filled with the collections, systematically arranged in such plain and logical sequence as to be comprehensible to observers of any age. While strictly scientific in its plan, the museum is developed for popular use." Through the museum, the other permanent structures, and the park itself, the exposition builders fashioned a permanent utopian construct that still shapes the cultural values of visitors to Balboa Park. The directors summed up the exact meaning of their bequest—and the cumulative legacy of the exposition movement as a whole—in a short inscription high on the walls of one of the permanent fair buildings. It reads: *"Ordem e Progresso."*[51]

Conclusion

BETWEEN 1876 AND 1916, a network of international expositions spanned the nation, putting the world on display and shaping the world view of millions of Americans. Without exception, these expositions were upper-class creations initiated and controlled by locally or nationally prominent elites.

What were the motives for creating these fairs? However much large investors hoped for an immediate return on their subscriptions to exposition stock, it became increasingly apparent that expositions rarely returned a dividend. For large investors, however, the goal was not immediate profit, but long-range gain for their regional, national, and international economic interests. On another level, exposition promoters also saw the fairs as vehicles for maintaining, or raising, their own status as regional or national leaders and for winning broad acceptance across class lines for *their* priorities and *their* decision-making authority.

To achieve these ends, the directors turned to the federal government for assistance, thus continuing to cement the alliance between federal power and industrial capitalism that had been institutionalized in the United States since the 1860s. For each of the expositions, Congress appropriated funds, thus assuring the exposition directors of exhibits from various government departments and of the participation of government specialists to oversee the installation and arrangement of displays. Without the aid of the Bureau of Indian Affairs and the Bureau of Insular Affairs, for example, the Indian Congress at the Omaha exposition and the Philippine Reservation at the Saint Louis fair would never have existed.

The continuing involvement of experts from the Smithsonian Institution in providing exhibits, advice, and display classifications also confirmed the intermeshing of upper-class purpose and federal power. Such eminent Smithsonian scientists as Spencer F. Baird, Otis Mason, G. Brown Goode, W J McGee, and Aleš Hrdlička were not industrial capitalists. But they were immersed in the ethic of industrial capitalism; they were its high priests. Their labors produced an intellectual scaffolding for the cumulative symbolic universe under construction at the fairs.

This symbolic construct centered on the interpenetration of Darwinian theories about racial development and utopian dreams about America's material and national progress. Central to the presentation of this constellation of ideas as a valid interpretation of social reality were ethnological exhibits furnished by both reputable anthropologists and well-financed showmen. Anthropological attractions—consisting of cultural artifacts, lay-figure groupings of "primitive types," and selected nonwhites living in ethnological villages along the midways—charted a course of racial progress toward an image of utopia that was reflected in the main exposition buildings.

The role of the midway at these fairs should not be underestimated. The very existence of the Midway Plaisance as a planned adjunct to the World's Columbian Exposition represented a significant shift in the attitudes of elites toward popular culture. After all, only seventeen years had lapsed since Philadelphia exposition authorities had persuaded city officials to condemn and burn many of the honky-tonk amusements built immediately outside of the fairgrounds by showmen well versed in the traditions of the popular museum, freak show, and diorama. At the 1893 World's Columbian Exposition, if the physical layout of the grounds is any indication, the loathing seen at Philadelphia gave way to ambivalence about popular shows. What is more important—and it is here that historians miss the point in debating the symbolic significance of only one fair out of the many held between 1876 and 1916—is that less than a decade after the Chicago fair, ambivalence gave way to outright endorsement. By 1904 exposition promoters sponsoring the Saint Louis world's fair incorporated the midway into the main exposition grounds. By century's turn, in short, midway entertainments had come into their own, which is to say, more precisely, that they simultaneously gained legitimacy and offered legitimacy to a particular view of the world—one that was avowedly imperialistic.

Were the world's fair midways just for fun? Hardly. Their development into integral components of the expositions reflected the growing efforts by the upper classes, threatened by class conflict at every turn, to influence the content of popular culture. Their centrality to American culture and to the efforts by American elites to establish their cultural hegemony is certain. World's fair midways constituted "living proof" for the imperial calculations by exposition sponsors. Their anthropologically validated racial hierarchies served several purposes. They legitimized racial exploitation at home and the creation of an empire abroad. Carefully designed exhibits of nonwhites left little doubt that the same set of ideas that had been used to justify the political and economic repression of Native Americans, Afro-Americans, and Asian-Americans were being used to validate American imperial policy overseas. The emphasis on white supremacy as a utopian agency, moreover, muted class divisions among whites, providing them with a sense of shared national purpose.

That all the fairs were intensely nationalistic was not surprising, for nationalism coincided with racism in obscuring class divisions within white society. Largely as a result of the expositions, nationalism and racism became crucial parts of the legitimizing ideology offered to a nation torn by class conflict.

The class warfare that exploded in America with the railroad strikes of 1877 continued with varying degrees of intensity through the First World War and formed the immediate social background for the creation of the expositions. The thrust of the expositions was to defuse the perception of class domination, and evolutionary ideas about race played a key role in this process. Scientific racism, if accepted by the lower classes, meant acquiescence in the power relations of the status quo as necessary to progress and therefore as legitimate and right. Thus the intense propagation of scientific racism at the fairs served to reinforce the implicit acquiescence by lower-class whites in the conclusions reached by the upper class about the proper organization of American society. Such acquiescence may have been far less than total. But for America's lower classes, regardless of race, the possibility of constructing alternative visions of progress became increasingly hemmed in and attenuated.

The influence of America's international expositions permeated the nation's arts, political system, and economic structure. Far from simply reflecting American culture, the expositions were intended to shape that culture. They left an enduring vision of empire.

Notes

Introduction

1. John Allwood, *The Great Exhibitions* (London: Studio Vista, 1977), 179–85.

2. General histories of the fairs include Kenneth W. Luckhurst, *The Story of Exhibitions* (London: Studio, 1951); Richard D. Altick, *The Shows of London* (Cambridge: Harvard University Press, 1978); and Burton Benedict et al., *The Anthropology of World's Fairs: San Francisco's Panama-Pacific International Exposition, 1915* (Berkeley: Scolar Press, 1983).

3. Peter L. Berger and Thomas Luckmann, *The Social Construction of Reality: A Treatise in the Sociology of Knowledge* (New York: Anchor Books, 1967), 92–108.

4. Quinton Hoare and Geoffrey Nowell Smith, eds., *Selections from the Prison Notebooks of Antonio Gramsci* (New York: International Publishers, 1971), 12. Important discussions of hegemony include Eugene D. Genovese, *In Red and Black: Marxian Explorations in Southern and Afro-American History* (New York: Pantheon Books, 1968), 339–442; Aileen S. Kraditor, "American Radical Historians on Their Heritage," *Past and Present*, no. 56 (August 1972): 136–53; David Brion Davis, *The Problem of Slavery in the Age of Revolution, 1770–1823* (Ithaca: Cornell University Press, 1975), 349–50; and Jerome Karabel, "Revolutionary Contradictions: Antonio Gramsci and the Problem of Intellectuals," *Politics and Society* 6 (1976): 123–72. Also important are many works by Raymond Williams. See especially *Marxism and Literature* (New York: Oxford University Press, 1978). Ronald T. Takaki links the concept of hegemony to the study of race and culture in *Iron Cages: Race and Culture in Nineteenth Century America* (New York: Alfred A. Knopf, 1979). See also T. J. Jackson Lears, *No Place of Grace: Anti-Modernism and the Transformation of American Culture, 1880–1920* (New York: Pantheon Books, 1981).

5. Quoted in [Richard Rathbun?], "Expositions in General," typescript, 1, Smithsonian Institution Archives (cited hereafter as SIA), Record Unit (cited hereafter as RU) 55, Assistant Secretary in Charge of USNM, box 19, folder 9.

6. Henry Adams, *The Education of Henry Adams* (Boston: Houghton Mifflin Company, 1961), 465. Originally published 1907.

7. H. W. Waters, *A History of Fairs and Expositions* (London: Reid Brothers, 1939), 5.

8. Norman Holland, *Poems in Persons: An Introduction to the Psychoanalysis of Literature* (New York: W. W. Norton, 1973), 148.

9. Robert H. Wiebe, *The Search for Order, 1877–1920* (New York: Hill and Wang, 1967); Francine Curro Cary, "Shaping the Future in the Gilded Age: A Study of Utopian Thought, 1880–1900" (Ph.D. dissertation, University of Wisconsin, 1975); and Kenneth M. Roemer, *The Obsolete Necessity: America in Utopian Writings, 1888–1900* (Kent, Ohio: Kent State University Press, 1976).

10. "President McKinley Favors Reciprocity," *New York Times*, 6 September 1901, 1. See also chapter 5.

11. See, for instance, "The World's Columbian Exposition," *World's Columbian Illustrated* 1 (February 1891):2.

12. This definition was originally suggested to me by Professor Alexander Saxton. See his "Review Essay," *Amerasia* 4, no. 2 (1977):141–50, and his "Historical Explanations of Racial Inequality: A Review Essay," *Marxist Perspectives* 2 (Summer 1979):146–68. See also George M. Fredrickson, *The Black Image in the White Mind: The Debate on Afro-American Character and Destiny, 1817–1914* (New York: Harper Torchbooks, 1971); and his *White Supremacy: A Comparative Study on American and South African History* (New York: Oxford University Press, 1981). Also useful is John W. Cell, *The Highest Stage of White Supremacy: The Origins of Segregation in South Africa and the American South* (London: Cambridge University Press, 1982).

13. See, for instance, Richard Hofstadter, *Social Darwinism in American Thought* (Boston: Beacon Press, 1955); Thomas F. Gossett, *Race: The History of an Idea in America* (New York: Schocken Books, 1965), 144–75; and Takaki, *Iron Cages*. Lately some historians have questioned the pervasiveness and legitimating function of Darwinian ideas. See Robert Bannister, *Social Darwinism: Science and Myth in Anglo-American Social Thought* (Philadelphia: Temple University Press, 1972).

14. Frank M. Turner, "The Victorian Conflict between Science and Religion: A Professional Dimension," *Isis* 69 (1978):356–76.

15. John Higham, *Strangers in the Land: Patterns of American Nativism, 1860–1925* (New Brunswick: Rutgers University Press, 1955); and Mark Haller, *Eugenics: Hereditarian Attitudes in American Thought* (New Brunswick: Rutgers University Press, 1963).

16. There is a growing body of literature on the ideological function of American popular entertainment. Especially important are Neil Harris, *Humbug: The Art of P. T. Barnum* (Boston: Little, Brown, 1973); John F. Kasson, *Amusing the Millions* (New York: Hill and Wang, 1978); Robert Toll, *Blacking Up: The Minstrel Show in Nineteenth Century America* (New York: Oxford University Press, 1974); and Alexander P. Saxton, "Blackface Minstrelsy and Jacksonian Ideology," *American Quarterly* 27 (1975):3–28. For the circus, see Phyllis A. Rodgers, "The American Circus Clown" (Ph.D. dissertation, Princeton University, 1979). For the Wild West show, see William E. Deahl, Jr., "A History of Buffalo Bill's Wild West Show, 1883–1913" (Ph.D. dissertation, Southern Illinois University, 1974). Zoos have also received critical attention. See Helen L. Horowitz and William Bridges, *Gathering of Animals: An Unconventional History of the New York Zoological Society* (New York: Harper and Row, 1974); and two articles by Horowitz: "Animal and Man in the New York Zoological Park," *New York History* 57 (1975):426–55, and "Seeing Ourselves

through Bars," *Landscape* 25, no. 2 (1981):12–19. Another informed account is Jeffrey R. Stott's "The American Idea of a Zoological Park: An Intellectual History" (Ph.D. dissertation, University of California at Santa Barbara, 1981). A suggestive study of popular recreation is Hugh Cunningham's *Leisure in the Industrial Revolution* (London: Croom Helm, 1980). An important review essay is Neil Harris's "Cultural Institutions and American Modernization," *Journal of Library History* 16 (Winter 1981):28–47.

17. Quoted in Paul H. Oehser, *Smithsonian Institution* (New York: Praeger, 1970), 15; see also [Rathbun?], "Expositions in General," 7, 9–11. Two important studies of the Washington scientific community are Curtis M. Hinsley's *Savages and Scientists: The Smithsonian Institution and the Development of American Anthropology* (Washington, D.C.: Smithsonian Institution Press, 1981); and Michael James Lacey's "The Mysteries of Earth-Making Dissolve: A Study of Washington's Intellectual Community and the Origins of American Environmentalism in the Late Nineteenth Century" (Ph.D. dissertation, George Washington University, 1979), 284–342. I am also indebted to T. Dale Stewart for sharing his insights with me.

18. Walter Hough, "Historical Sketch of the Division of Ethnology [United States National Museum], 1906," MS, National Anthropology Archives.

19. G. Browne Goode, "Smithsonian Institution *Annual Report,* 1893," in [Rathbun?], "Expositions in General," 25.

20. [Wilbur O. Atwater], "What the Exposition May and Ought to Be," n.d., 4, SIA, RU 70, Exposition Records of the Smithsonian Institution and United States National Museum, 1875–1916, box 19.

21. Thomas G. August, "Colonial Policy and Propaganda: The Popularization of the Idée Coloniale in France, 1919–1939" (Ph.D. dissertation, University of Wisconsin, 1978); Michael R. Godley, "China's World Fair of 1910: Lessons from a Forgotten Event," *Modern Asian Studies* 12 (1978):503–22; Richard D. Mandell, *Paris 1900* (Toronto: University of Toronto Press, 1967); William Schneider, "Colonies at the 1900 World's Fair," *History Today* 31 (1981):31–34; Debora L. Silverman, "The 1889 Exhibition: The Crisis of Bourgeois Individualism," *Oppositions* 8 (1978):71–91; and Kenneth Walthew, "The British Empire Exhibition of 1924," *History Today* 31 (1981):34–39.

Chapter One

1. "The Day We Celebrate," *The American Centennial Fourth of July Memorial* [4 July 1876?], City Archives of Philadelphia (cited hereafter as CAP), Record Series (cited hereafter as RS) 230.6, United States Centennial Commission, Centennial Scrapbooks (cited hereafter as USCC Centennial Scrapbooks), 37; "The Great Exhibition," *New York Times,* 6 June 1876, 1; and William Phipps Blake, "Previous International Exhibitions," in *Journal of the Proceedings of the United States Centennial Commission at Philadelphia, 1872* (Philadelphia: E. C. Markley, 1872), 63.

2. John Maass, *The Glorious Enterprise* (Watkins Glen, N.Y.: American Life Foundation, 1973), 129–30.

3. *New York Times,* editorial, 11 May 1876, 6; Dee Brown, *The Year of the Century: 1876* (New York: Charles Scribner's Sons, 1976), 113–37; J. S. Ingram, *The Centennial Exposition, Described and Illustrated, Being a Concise and Graphic*

Description of This Grand Enterprise Commemorative of the First Centennary of American Independence (Philadelphia: Hubbard Brothers, 1876); and Charles Hirschfeld, "America on Exhibition: The New York Crystal Palace," *American Quarterly* 9 (1957):101–16.

4. "Things at Philadelphia," *New York Times*, 5 March 1876, 1; Dorothy E. C. Ditter, "The Cultural Climate of the Centennial City: Philadelphia, 1875–1876" (Ph.D. dissertation, University of Pennsylvania, 1947), 9, 298; "Centennial Notes," *Press*, 13 March 1876, 6; *The Proceedings of the Dedication of the John Welsh Memorial, 23 June 1887* (Philadelphia: Allen, Lane, and Scott, n.d.), 10, in Historical Society of Pennsylvania (cited hereafter as HSP).

General accounts of the economic, social, and political contours of America at the end of Reconstruction are provided by Fred A. Shannon, *The Centennial Years* (Garden City, N.Y.: Doubleday, 1967), and by Robert H. Wiebe, *The Search for Order, 1877–1920* (New York: Hill and Wang, 1967), 1–43. In addition to Ditter's study, several other works locate the fair in the maelstrom of American culture. Among these works are Christine Hunter Donaldson, "The Centennial of 1876: The Exposition and Culture for America" (Ph.D. dissertation, Yale University, 1948), and John Henry Hicks, "The United States Centennial Exhibition of 1876" (Ph.D. dissertation, University of Georgia, 1972). The entire issue of the *Hayes Historical Journal* 1 (1977):159–222 is devoted to the Centennial Exhibition.

5. Birdsley Grant Northrup, *Official Bulletin of the International Exhibition: Educational Number* (Philadelphia: International Exhibition Company, 1877), 59, Smithsonian Institution Archives, Record Unit 70, Exposition Records of the Smithsonian and the United States National Museum, box 3 (cited hereafter as SIA, RU 70); "The World's Fair," *Philadelphia Inquirer*, 27 September 1876, 2. For an in-depth discussion of these issues consult Donaldson, 65–81.

6. "The Nation's Centennial: The Great Exhibition Opening," *New York Times*, 11 May 1876, 1; "The Exposition," *Press*, 11 May 1876, 12; and Ingram, 73–116.

7. Ingram, 95–96; James D. McCabe, *The Illustrated History of the Centennial Exhibition Held in Commemoration of the One Hundredth Anniversary of American Independence* (Philadelphia: National Publishing Company, 1876), 320–29.

8. Dorsey Gardner, ed., *United States Centennial Commission: International Exhibition, 1876, Grounds and Buildings of the Centennial Exhibition, Philadelphia, 1876* (Philadelphia: J. B. Lippincott, 1878), 24, 143–55; Ingram, 680–711; and "The Nation's Centennial," *New York Times*, 14 May 1876, 1.

9. McCabe, 320–29; Ingram, 680–711; and *Independent* 27 (6 July 1876):8, quoted in Donaldson, 30.

10. "The Nation's Centennial: Review of the Opening Events," *New York Times*, 12 May 1876, 1; "The Multitude Admitted," *Press*, 11 May 1876, 2, 4; H. C., "The Great Exhibition: Scenes in Fairmount Park," *New York Times*, 23 May 1876, 4; and William Dean Howells, "A Sennight of the Centennial," *Atlantic Monthly* 38 (July 1876):97.

11. D. Otis Kellogg, "The Rev. Mr. Kellogg's Impressions," *Press*, 11 May 1876, 1; and *Press*, editorial, 10 May 1876, 4.

12. Ingram, 73–98; Sidney Lanier to Dudley Buck, 15 January 1876, Duke University, Perkins Library, Sidney Lanier Papers; and McCabe, 287–88.

13. McCabe, 294–95; Ingram, 86–87; Maass, *Glorious Enterprise*, 41–43.

14. Howells, "Sennight of the Centennial," as quoted by Rodney Reid Badger, "The World's Columbian Exposition: Patterns of Change and Control in the 1890s" (Ph.D. dissertation, Syracuse University, 1975), 51; Joaquin Miller, "The Great Centennial Fair and Its Future," *Independent*, 13 July 1876, clipping in the Claremont Colleges, Honnold Library, Special Collections Department, Joaquin Miller Papers.

15. Guy Stanton Ford, "Expositions, International," in *Encyclopedia of the Social Sciences* 6 (London: Macmillan, 1932):23–27; "The World's Epitome," *Philadelphia Inquirer*, 13 May 1876, 1; and "Centennial Stock Certificates," *Evening Star*, 23 February 1874, clipping, USCC Centennial Scrapbooks, 24:193.

16. Maass, *Glorious Enterprise*, 28; McCabe, 167–69; McCabe gives joint credit to Campbell, Charles B. Norton, and M. Richards Mucklé for originating the idea. Ingram, 41, 745–46, gives credit to Campbell, as does S. Edgar Trout, *The Story of the Centennial of 1876: Golden Anniversary* (n.p., 1929), 193. See also Ingram, 739–40; and Philip D. Spiess, II, "Exhibitions and Expositions in Nineteenth Century Cincinnati," *Cincinnati Historical Society Bulletin* 28 (1970):171–92.

17. Ingram, 740; and Centennial Board of Finance to George Clarkson et al., 30 January 1875, HSP, William Bigler Papers, 1875–80 box, January 1875 folder.

18. "List of Voters at the Election Held on April 20 [1876], Election of Directors," in CAP, RS 231.2, Centennial Board of Finance, Election Materials, box A-541, 1876 folder. The complete list of subscriptions are in Centennial Scrapbooks 27:53–56, and 44:64–68. See also "To Our Employees," circular, n.d., *Documentary Record of the Centennial Celebration*, 1, HSP, Centennial Collection.

19. William Phipps Blake to Alfred T. Goshorn, 26 November 1872, CAP, RS 230. 2, USCC Correspondence and Papers, box A-1502, William Phipps Blake Copybook, 386–89.

20. A. T. Goshorn, "The Scope of the Exposition of 1876," National Archives, Record Group 48 (cited hereafter as NA, RG), Centennial Exposition Letterbook, 32–36; and Peter Cooper, William M. Evarts, Cyrus W. Field, et al., *The Centennial Celebration and International Exhibition: Address to the People of New York by Prominent and Influential Citizens* (New York: New York Evening Post Steam Presses, n.d.), in HSP, *Documentary Record of the Centennial Celebration*, 4.

21. [Address by William Bigler], 22 April 1873, in CAP, RS 231.1, Centennial Board of Finance, Annual Reports box, Organizational Meeting folder; *Georgia Telegraph and Messenger* quoted in "Awakening: The Southern States and the Centennial," *Journal of the Exposition* 1 (15 November 1873):73–74, USCC Centennial Scrapbooks, 14:18–19; and, William Bacon Stevens to [members of the clergy], 14 February 1873, HSP Centennial Collection, box 1, folder 10.

22. Rossiter W. Raymond, "Biographical Notice of William Phipps Blake," *Transactions of the American Institute of Mining Engineers* (November 1910), 749–62, clipping, SIA, RU 7230, Department of Geology, Biographical File, box 2, folder 18. See also Maass, "Who Invented Dewey's Classification?" *Wilson Library Bulletin* 47 (December 1972):337.

23. Raymond, 754; *Report on the Classification Presented at the May Meeting of the Commission, 1874, by the Committee on Classification*, 3 (cited hereafter as *Report on Classification*) in HSP *Documentary Record of the Centennial Celebration*, 5; *Report on Classification*, 5–6; W. P. Blake and Henry Petit, *Reports on the Vienna*

Universal Exposition, 1873, 22, in USCC Centennial Scrapbooks, City Archives of Philadelphia. Cf. Maass, "Who Invented Dewey's Classification?" 537; and *Report on Classification*, 9; *United States Centennial Commission, System of Classification, Philadelphia, 1874*, circular, in SIA, RU 70, box 3; "The Centennial," *New York Times*, 4 March 1876, 2.

24. McCabe, 193; *System of Classification*; Maass, "Who Invented Dewey's Classification?" 335–41.

25. *New York Times*, 4 March 1876, 2.

26. "City Affairs," *American and Gazetteer*, 20 May 1875, USCC Centennial Scrapbooks, 66:166–67.

27. Gardner, 51–52; and "At the Exhibition," *Sunday Herald and Weekly National Intelligencer*, 23 July 1876, USCC Centennial Scrapbooks, 31. See also Neil Harris, "All the World a Melting Pot? Japan at American Fairs, 1876–1904," in *Mutual Images: Essays in American Japanese Relations*, ed. Akira Iriye (Cambridge: Harvard University Press, 1975), 28.

28. Quoted in [Richard Rathbun?], "Expositions in Which the National Museum Has Participated," typescript, SIA, RU 55, Assistant Secretary in Charge of the USNM, 1897–1917, Records, box 19, folder 8; [Gar], "The Centennial: The Government Exhibition," *New York Times*, 29 March 1876, 1. See also H. Craig Miner, "The United States Government Building at the Centennial Exhibition, 1874–1877," *Prologue* 4 (1972):203–18.

29. Curtis M. Hinsley, Jr., *Savages and Scientists: The Smithsonian Institution and the Development of American Anthropology, 1846–1910* (Washington, D.C.: Smithsonian Institution Press, 1981), 74; T. D. A. Cockerell, "Spencer Fullerton Baird and the U.S. National Museum," *Bios* 13 (1942):6–7, clipping, SIA, RU 7098, Biographical Information File, A–B folder; Robert A. Trennert, "A Grand Failure: The Centennial Indian Exhibition of 1876," *Prologue* 6 (1974):118–29; and Judy Braun, "The North American Indian Exhibits at the 1876 and 1893 World Expositions: The Influence of Scientific Thought on Popular Attitudes" (M.A. thesis, George Washington University, 1975), 31–52.

30. Spencer Fullerton Baird, "Appendix to the Report of the Secretary," *Annual Report, Smithsonian Institution, 1875*, 67, cited by Braun, 32, 35.

31. Trennert, 120–21; Braun, 41; Otis T. Mason, *Ethnological Directions Relative to Indian Tribes of the United States* (Washington, D.C.: Government Printing Office, 1875), 3–5, cited by Trennert, 123; Baird, "Appendix to the Report of the Secretary," cited by Trennert, 127; and Baird to Lyford, 23 March 1876, House Executive Document 148, 32–36, quoted in Trennert, 127. For a discussion of Klemm's work and its impact on Mason see Hinsley, 281–89, and Marvin Harris, *The Rise of Anthropological Theory* (New York: Thomas Y. Crowell, 1968), 101–2.

32. Hinsley, 87–91; Baird, "Appendix to the Report of the Secretary," 69; Charles Rau, "The Happy Age," MS, n.d., National Anthropology Archives, Private Papers of Charles Rau, pp. 24–27; and "Centennial Notes," *Philadelphia Inquirer*, 26 July 1876, 2.

33. Braun, 44–45.

34. James L. Dale, *What Ben Beverly Saw at the Great Exposition* (Chicago: Centennial Publishing Company, 1876), 69–70; and Howells, "Sennight of the Centennial," 103, portions cited by Trennert, 127. An exception to the generally

hostile attitude toward Indians was Marietta Holley, *Josiah Allen's Wife as a P.A. and P.I.: Samantha at the Centennial* (Hartford, Conn.: American Publishing Company, 1877).

35. J. Q. Smith to Secretary of Interior, 29 April 1876, NA, RG 48, entry 86, Letters Sent concerning the Centennial, 1876–77, 58–60, cited by Trennert, 127; and Indian Office Circular, 3 February 1876, NA, RG 75, cited in Trennert, 126.

36. Griest to J. Q. Smith, 18 April 1876, NA, RG 75, Office of Indian Affairs, Letters Received, Centennial Exhibition, 1876–77, Records of the Office of Indian Affairs, cited in Braun, 38; Smith to Charles Ewing, 21 June 1876, NA, RG 48, entry 86, Letters Sent concerning the Centennial, 1876–77, 69–70; "The Indians Here," *Press*, 3 April 1876, 6; and *Magee's Centennial Guide of Philadelphia* (Philadelphia: R. Magee, 1876), 173.

37. "Reports on Awards, 1876," SIA, RU 70, box 1, awards folder; Brown, 292–97.

38. Philip S. Foner, "Black Participation in the Centennial of 1876," *Negro History Bulletin* 39 (1976):533–38. See also Brown, 120; and Hicks, 74–79, 176–177.

39. " 'The Sex' on Colored Equality—A Centennial Side-Show," *Sunday Mercury*, 20 April 1873; "Women's Centennial," *Philadelphia Inquirer*, 13 May 1873, clippings, in USCC Centennial Scrapbooks, 44:161, 210; Foner, 534.

40. "Our Colored Citizens," *Press*, 15 May 1876, 6.

41. *Centennial Exposition Guide* (Philadelphia: G. Lawrence, [1876?]), UCLA, Special Collections, Expositions and Fairs Collection, 344/M, box 1; Joaquin Miller, "Song of the Centennial," in *Frank Leslie's Illustrated Historical Register of the Centennial Exposition, 1876* (no imprint), 128; and Howells, "Sennight of the Centennial," 93.

42. "Foreign Trade and the Exposition," *Public Record*, 16 May 1876, 2; "Eastern Asia and the American Centennial," *Press*, 9 July 1873, clipping, USCC Centennial Scrapbooks, 23:69; and "Our Trade with Oriental Nations," *Philadelphia Inquirer*, 2 August 1873, clipping, ibid., 104.

43. [E. V. Smalley?], "Japan," *Letters about the Exhibition: New York Tribune Extra*, no. 35, ([New York], 1876), 28; "Our Japanese Visitors," *Press*, 21 April 1876, 2; Dale, 84; *Official Catalogue of the Japanese Section* (Philadelphia: W. P. Kildare, 1876), 114; "Exhibition Notes," *Philadelphia Inquirer*, 5 September 1876, 3; and "A Centennial Catalogue: A Stroll through the Nave," *New York Times*, 8 May 1876, 4–5.

44. "The Centennial Exposition," *Public Record*, 5 October 1876, 4; Ingram, 581; "Notes from Philadelphia: Various Centennial Matters," *New York Times*, 30 July 1876, 7; and "The Chinese Problem," *Philadelphia Inquirer*, 9 June 1876, 4.

45. Jonathan Goldstein, *Philadelphia and the China Trade, 1682–1846: Commercial, Cultural, and Attitudinal Effects* (University Park: Pennsylvania State University Press, 1978); Su Cheng Chang, "Contextual Framework for Reading Counterpoint," *Amerasia* 5 (1978):118; and "The Centennial Exhibition and the Oriental Nations," *American and Gazetteer*, 28 July 1873, clipping, USCC Centennial Scrapbooks, 23:93–94.

46. Northrup, 62–64; and, George Fredrickson, *The Black Image in the White Mind* (New York: Harper Torchbooks, 1971), 61.

47. [E. V. Smalley?], "The Orange Free State," in *Letters about the Exhibition*, 29; Ingram, 550–54; D. S. Cohen [Daisy Shortcut] and H. B. Sumner [Arry O'Pagus], *One Hundred Years a Republic. Our Show: A Humorous Account of the International Exposition* (Philadelphia: Claxton, Remsen, and Haffelfinger, 1876), 38; Charles B. Norton, ed., *Treasures of Art, Industry, and Manufacture Represented in the American Centennial Exhibition at Philadelphia, 1876* (Buffalo: Cossact, 1877).

48. United States Centennial Commission, *International Exhibition, 1876: Reports of the President, Secretary, and Executive Committee Together with the Journal of the Final Session of the Commission* (Philadelphia: J. B. Lippincott, 1879), 2:14.

49. Circular quoted in "Our Workmen and the Centennial," *Evening Bulletin*, 18 April 1874, clipping, USCC Centennial Scrapbooks, 28; "Our World's Fair," *Philadelphia Inquirer*, 26 May 1876, 8; and "Skilled Mechanics at the Exposition," *Public Record*, 28 June 1876, 2.

50. "The Workmen and the Centennial," *Philadelphia Inquirer*, 25 April 1876, 4; "Poor Man's Day at the Exhibition," ibid., 8 September 1876, 4; and A. P., "Machinery Hall," *New York Times*, 5 June 1876, 2.

51. "The Exposition," *Philadelphia Inquirer*, 15 August 1876, 2; "Centennial Excursionists," ibid., 25 August 1876, 4; "The Exposition," ibid., 18 July 1876, 2; "Centennial Notes," ibid., 21 July 1876, 2; "Poor Man's Day at the Exhibition," ibid., 8 September 1876, 4; Howells, "Sennight of the Centennial," 106–7; and J. K. Brennan et al., "Expositions and Progress," in *The World's Work*, vol. 10, *The Delphian Society* (New York: Doubleday, Page, n.d.), 93.

52. McCabe, 302–15.

53. "Visiting the Centennial," *Public Record*, 8 August 1876, 2; Richard D. Altick, *The Shows of London* (Cambridge: Harvard University Press, 1978).

54. Kennard H. Jones, "Fourth Annual Report of the Chief of Police of the City of Philadelphia," in *Fifth Annual Message of William S. Stokley, Mayor of the City of Philadelphia . . . October 11, 1877* (Philadelphia: E. C. Markley, 1877), 167, in CAP, RS 60.1, Annual Messages and Reports of Departments. See also "Shantytown," *Sunday Dispatch*, 24 September 1876, 2; "Shantytown Doomed," *Press*, 20 September 1876, 6; "They Must Come Down," *Press*, 21 September 1876, 2; Suzanne Hilton, *The Way It Was: 1876* (Philadelphia: Westminster Press, 1975), 195–96; Ditter, 280; Edo McCullough, *World's Fair Midways: An Affectionate Account of American Amusement Areas from the Crystal Palace to the Crystal Ball* (New York: Exposition Press, 1966), 48; and Hicks, 127–29.

55. Ingram, 760–70; McCabe, 819–44.

56. McCabe, 829–30.

57. Miner, 203; and *Catalogue of the Centennial Loan Exhibition* (Philadelphia: J. B. Lippincott, [1875]), 26–27, in CAP, RS 230.3, USCC Bureau of Fine Arts, Official Catalogue, Department of Art, 1876, box A-1527, Centennial Loan Collection folder.

58. John Welsh in *Memorial to the Honorable the Senate and House of Representatives of the United States* (Philadelphia: Allen, Lane, and Scott's Printing House, 1882), 14–16; McCabe, 830.

59. "John Welsh Testimonial: Correspondence of the Committee and Letters from the Subscribers, Philadelphia, 22 February 1877" [arranged and bound by J. B. Lippincott], HSP, John Welsh Collection; and Ingram, 45.

60. John Maass, "The Centennial Success Story," in *1876: A Centennial*

Exhibition, ed. Robert Post (Washington, D.C.: National Museum of History and Technology, Smithsonian Institution, 1976), 23.

61. Henry May, *The End of American Innocence* (Chicago: Quadrangle Books, 1964), 30–51; and Francis A. Walker, *The World's Fair* (New York: A. S. Barnes, 1878), 39.

Chapter Two

1. Robert Herrick, *The Memoirs of an American Citizen* (Cambridge: Belknap Press of Harvard University Press, 1963), 147. Originally published 1905.

2. Useful histories of the fair include David F. Burg, *Chicago's White City of 1893* (Lexington: University of Kentucky Press, 1976); Rodney Reid Badger, *The Great American Fair: The World's Columbian Exposition and American Culture* (Chicago: Nelson-Hall, 1979). See also Badger's "The World's Columbian Exposition: Patterns of Change and Control in the 1890s" (Ph.D. dissertation, Syracuse University, 1975); Robert Knutson, "The White City—The World's Columbian Exposition of 1893" (Ph.D. dissertation, Columbia University, 1956); Bessie L. Pierce, *A History of Chicago, 1871–1893,* 3 vols. (New York: Alfred A. Knopf, 1957); Maurice F. Neufeld, "The Contribution of the World's Columbian Exposition of 1893 to the Idea of a Planned Society in the United States" (Ph.D. dissertation, University of Wisconsin, 1935); J. M. Weimann, *The Fair Woman* (Chicago: Academy Press, 1981); and Virginia Grant Darney, "Women and World's Fairs: American International Expositions, 1876–1904" (Ph.D. dissertation, Emory University, 1982), 65–124. See also Justus D. Doenecke, "Myths, Machines, and Markets: The Columbian Exposition of 1893," *Journal of Popular Culture* 6 (1973): 535–49; Larzer Ziff, *The American 1890s: The Life and Times of a Lost Generation* (New York: Viking Press, 1966); John Cawelti, "America on Display, 1876, 1893, 1933," in *America in the Age of Industrialism,* ed. Frederic C. Jaher (New York: Free Press, 1968), 317–63; Alan Trachtenberg, *The Incorporation of America* (New York: Hill and Wang, 1982), 208–34; and Robert W. Rydell, "The World's Columbian Exposition of 1893: Racist Underpinnings of a Utopian Artifact," *Journal of American Culture* 1 (1978): 253–75.

3. Quoted from "Goodbye to the Fair," *Chicago Tribune,* 1 November 1893, 4, in Harold M. Mayer and Richard C. Wade, *Chicago: Growth of a Metropolis* (Chicago: University of Chicago Press, 1969), 196. Frances Hodgson Burnett, *Two Little Pilgrims' Progress: A Story of the City Beautiful* (New York: Charles Scribner's Sons, 1895), 9.

4. "Testimony of H[arlow] N. Higinbotham," in *The Reports of Committees of the House of Representatives for the First Session of the Fifty Second Congress, 1891–1892,* no. 3047 (Washington, D.C.: Government Printing Office, 1892), 362 (hereafter cited as *Reports of Committees);* Horace G. Benson Diary, 7, University of Colorado, Boulder, Western Historical Collections, Horace G. Benson Papers; Charles M. Stevens [Quondam], *The Adventures of Uncle Jeremiah and Family at the Great Fair* (Chicago: Laird and Lee, 1893), 46.

5. William Dean Howells, "Letters from an Altrurian Traveller," *Cosmospolitan Magazine* 16 (1893): 219–32. See also Howells, *Letters of an Altrurian Traveller,* ed. Clara M. Kirk and Rudolf King (Gainesville, Fla.: Scholar's Facsimiles and Reprints, 1961), v–xii, 13–34.

6. Frederick Starr, "Anthropology at the World's Fair," *Popular Science Monthly*

43 (1893): 621. Architectural dimensions of the fair are discussed by Thomas S.
Hines, *Burnham of Chicago: Architect and Planner* (New York: Oxford University
Press, 1974); David H. Crook, "Louis Sullivan, the World's Columbian Exposition,
and American Life" (Ph.D. dissertation, Harvard University, 1963); and Helen
Lefkowitz Horowitz, *Culture and the City: Cultural Philanthropy in Chicago from the
1880s to 1917* (Lexington: University of Kentucky Press, 1976); George Alfred
Townsend, "People and Impressions of the World's Fair," MS, in the Chicago
Historical Society, Manuscript Division, George Alfred Townsend Papers.

7. Francis L. Lederer, II, "Competition for the World's Columbian Exposition: The
Chicago Campaign," *Journal of the Illinois State Historical Society* 45 (1972):365–81;
Robert D. Parmet, "Competition for the World's Columbian Exposition: The New
York Campaign," *Journal of the Illinois State Historical Society* 45 (1972):382–94;
Badger, 86–195; Knutson, 8–15; and the *United States Centennial Commission
Reports* as cited by John Clarke Lathrop, "The Philadelphia Exhibition of 1876: A
Study of Social and Cultural Implications" (M.A. thesis, Rutgers University, 1936),
9–16.

8. [William E. Cameron, Thomas W. Palmer, and Frances E. Willard], *The
World's Fair: Being a Pictorial History of the Columbian Exposition* (Philadelphia:
National Publishing Company, 1893), 132, 232; Knutson, 14–15; Telegram to
Lyman Gage, 8 March 1890, in Chicago Historical Society, Manuscripts Division,
Samuel Waters Allerton Collection; Lyman Gage, *Memoirs of Lyman J. Gage* (New
York: House of Field, 1937), 80; Parmet, 381; and Charles H. Baker, *Life and
Character of William Taylor Baker* (New York: Premier Press, 1908), 157.

9. Lyman Gage, *The World's Columbian Exposition: First Annual Report of the
President* (Chicago: Knight and Leonard Company, 1891), 22.

10. [Richard Rathbun?], "Expositions in General," Smithsonian Institution
Archives (cited hereafter as SIA), Record Unit (cited hereafter as RU) 55, Assistant
Secretary in Charge of USNM (Rathbun), 1897–1916, box 19; Robert Earll to Edwin
Willits, 26 March 1892, SIA, RU 70, Exposition Records of the Smithsonian
Institution and the USNM, 1875–1916, box 10 (cited hereafter as SIA, RU 70).

11. Samuel Pierpont Langley, "Memoir of George Brown Goode," in *Annual Report
of the United States National Museum: Year Ending June 30, 1897* (Washington,
D.C.: Government Printing Office, 1898), 58; G. Brown Goode, "Museums and Good
Citizenship," *Public Opinion* 17 (1894):758.

12. Langley, "Memoir of George Brown Goode," 41–61; "George Brown Goode,"
National Academy of Science, clipping, SIA, RU 7098, Biographical Information File
E–G; Curtis M. Hinsley, Jr., *Savages and Scientists: The Smithsonian Institution and
the Development of American Anthropology, 1846–1910* (Washington, D.C.:
Smithsonian Institution Press, 1981), 91–94.

13. George Brown Goode, "The Museums of the Future," in *Annual Report of the
United States National Museum: Year Ending June 30, 1897* (Washington, D.C.:
Government Printing Office, 1898), 243–62.

14. George Brown Goode, "First Draft of a System of Classification for the World's
Columbian Exposition," 656, 650–52, SIA, RU 70, box 37; Badger, 187; "Professor
Goode in the City," *Chicago Post*, 1 October 1890, *Chicago Herald*, 3 October 1890,
clippings, SIA, RU 7050, George Brown Goode Collection, 1798–1896, box 27
(cited hereafter as SIA, RU 7050); "Called on Professor Goode," *Chicago Tribune*, 1

October 1890, "Professor Goode in the City," *Chicago News*, 1 October 1890, *Chicago Post*, 2 October 1890, *Chicago Herald*, 3 October 1890, clippings in SIA, RU 7050, box 27. See also William H. Dall, "Science," *Nation* 57 (14 September 1893):186–87; "Science at the Columbian Exposition," *Popular Science Monthly* 44 (1893):124; "Department of Organization," *World's Columbian Exposition Illustrated* 1 (June 1891):20.

15. G. Brown Goode, "America's Relation to the Advance of Science," *Science*, n.s., 1 (4 January 1895):8–9.

16. Thomas W. Palmer, "Presentation of the Buildings," in *Memorial Volume: Dedicatory and Opening Ceremonies of the World's Columbian Exposition* (Chicago: A. L. Stone, 1893), 159; Knutson, 55–56; "National School Celebration of Columbus Day: The Official Program," *Youth's Companion* 65 (8 September 1892):446–47; Annie Randall White, *The Story of Columbus and the World's Columbian Exposition . . . Designed for Young Folks* (Chicago: Monarch Books Company, [1892]), 288, 355–56.

17. Henry Adams, *The Education of Henry Adams* (Boston: Houghton Mifflin, 1961), 342. Originally published 1907.

18. Knutson, 246; and Frederick Jackson Turner, "The Significance of the Frontier in American History," in *The Significance of the Frontier in American History*, ed. Harold P. Simonson (New York: Frederick Ungar Publishing Company, 1963), 1.

19. Clarence A. Buskirk, "The Pageant of the Centuries from the Dawn of the New Light to the Triumph of the Full Day: A Vision of Strong Manhood and Perfection of Society in Columbia's Future," Chicago *Daily Inter Ocean*, 26 April 1893, supplement; Mariana G. van Rensselaer, "At the Fair," *Century Magaine* 46 (1893):12–13; Potter Palmer in the *Chicago Tribune*, 21 October 1892, clipping, UCLA, Department of Special Collections, Expositions and Fairs Collection, 344/2, box 2 (cited hereafter as UCLA, 344/2); and Burnett, 98.

20. *Daily Inter Ocean*, 27 September 1893, supplement; J. S. Norton, "Blessings of American Liberty," *Chicago Tribune*, 5 July 1893, 2; Walter Besant, "A First Impression," *Cosmopolitan Magazine* 15 (1893):536–37; *Chicago Tribune*, 2 May 1893, clipping, UCLA, 344/2, box 2; "The People Opened the Fair," *Chicago Tribune*, 12 May 1893, 2.

21. *A Week at the Fair Illustrating Exhibits and Wonders of the World's Columbian Exposition* (Chicago: Rand McNally, 1893), 162, 168, 239; Ben C. Truman, *History of the World's Fair* (Philadelphia: Mammoth Publishing Company, 1893), 427–37; Hubert Howe Bancroft, *The Book of the Fair*, 2 vols. (New York: Bancroft Books, 1894), 2:679–85; Gozo Tateno, "Japan," *North American Review* 156 (1893):42. A recent account is Neil Harris's "All the World a Melting Pot? Japan at American Fairs, 1876–1904," in *Mutual Images: Essays in American Japanese Relations*, ed. Akira Iriye (Cambridge: Harvard University Press, 1975), 24–54.

22. "Freaks of Chinese Fancy at the Fair," *Chicago Tribune*, 24 September 1893, 33; and *Oriental and Occidental: Northern and Southern Portraits. Types of the Midway Plaisance* (Saint Louis: N. D. Thompson Publishing Company, 1894). For an account of anti-Chinese feelings in the United States see Richard A. Thompson, "Yellow Peril, 1890–1924" (Ph.D. dissertation, University of Wisconsin, 1957).

23. Harris, 24–54, offers a provocative interpretation of America's fascination with Japan. Quotations are from *Daily Inter Ocean*, 20 September 1893, supplement;

Delano W. Eastlake, "Moral Life of the Japanese," *Popular Science Monthly* 43
(1893):348; Stevens, 100; and *Midway Types: A Book of Illustrated Lessons about the
People of the Midway Plaisance* (Chicago: American Engraving Company, 1894).

24. *Daily Inter Ocean,* 20 September 1893, supplement; Truman, 201.

25. *Midway Types; Chicago Tribune,* 23 July 1893, reprints Eastlake's article. See
also Truman, 566.

26. *Sunset City and Sunset Scenes, no. 2, May 14, 1894* (San Francisco: H. S.
Crocker, 1894); and *Official History of the California Midwinter International
Exposition* (San Francisco: Press of H. S. Crocker Company, 1894).

27. "Freaks of Chinese Fancy," *Chicago Tribune,* 24 September 1893, 33;
Bancroft quoted in Jacobus tenBroek, Edward N. Barnhart, and Floyd W. Matson,
Prejudice, War, and the Constitution (Berkeley and Los Angeles: University of
California Press, 1954), 11; Bancroft, *Book of the Fair,* 2:873.

28. Stevens, 163–64; and *Harper's Weekly: A Journal of Civilization* 37 (7 July
1893):629.

29. The *Cleveland Gazette,* quoted in Elliot Rudwick and August Meier, "Black
Man in the 'White City', Negroes and the Columbian Exposition, 1893," *Phylon* 26
(1965):354. My discussion of Afro-Americans and the fair owes much to this article.
See also Ann Massa, "Black Women in the White City," *Journal of American Studies*
8 (1974):319–37; "The Women and the World's Fair," editorial, *New York Age,* 24
October 1891, 4; M. W. Caldwell, "World's Fair Commissioner," *New York Age,* 14
February 1891.

30. Frederick Douglass and Ida Wells, *The Reason Why the Colored American Is
Not in the World's Columbian Exposition* (no imprint, 1893), 4; Alfreda M. Duster,
ed., *Crusade for Justice: The Autobiography of Ida B. Wells* (Chicago: University of
Chicago Press, 1970); Frederick Douglass, "Inauguration of the World's Columbian
Exposition," *World's Columbian Exposition Illustrated* 3 (March 1893):300; Badger,
248–51; *New York Age,* 27 June 1891; and "Testimony of George R. Davis," in
Reports of Committees, 476.

31. "The Jubilee Day Folly," *Indianapolis Freeman,* 2 September 1893; "The
World in Miniature," *Indianapolis Freeman,* 2 September 1893.

32. *Oriental and Occidental.*

33. Rudwick and Meier, 357; and *Harper's Weekly* 37 (15 July 1893):681; (23
September 1893):914; (19 August 1893):797; (4 November 1893):1059.

34. Otis T. Mason, "Summary of Progress in Anthropology," in *Annual Reports of
the Smithsonian Institution for the Year Ending July 1893* (Washington, D.C.:
Government Printing Office, 1894), 605; Judy Braun, "The North American Indian
Exhibits at the 1876 and 1893 World Expositions: The Influence of Scientific
Thought on Popular Attitudes" (M.A. thesis, George Washington University, 1975),
53–80; William H. Dall, "Anthropology," *Nation* 57 (28 September 1893):226.

35. Mason, "Report on the Department of Ethnology in the U.S. National Museum,
1890," MS, p. 10, SIA, RU 158, Curators' Annual Reports, 1881–1904, box 3,
folder 10.

36. Debora L. Silverman, "The 1889 Exhibition: The Crisis of Bourgeois
Individualism," *Oppositions* 8 (1978):77–80; *Congrès Internationale d'Anthropologie et
d'Archéologie Préhistoriques: Compte rendu de la dixième session à Paris, 1889* (Paris:
Ernest Leroux, 1891), 33–35; Mason, "Report of the Department of Ethnology in the

U.S. National Museum, 1890"; and Mason [notes for Chicago exhibit], in
Anthropology Correspondence, 1891–92, in National Anthropology Archives, USNM
Division of Ethnology, Manuscript and Pamphlet files, box 2, folder 20 (cited
hereafter as Mason, [notes for Chicago exhibit]).

37. Samuel P. Langley and G. Brown Goode to Secretary of the Treasury, 12
March 1890, 10, SIA, RU 70, box 27.

38. Badger, 188.

39. George W. Stocking, *Race, Culture, and Evolution: Essays in the History of
Anthropology* (New York: Free Press, 1968), 278; *Chicago Tribune*, 31 May 1890,
quoted by Ralph W. Dexter, "Putnam's Problems Popularizing Anthropology,"
American Scientist 54 (1966):316; "Suggested Attractions for the Exposition," *World's
Columbian Exposition Illustrated* 1 (February 1891):18; and "Ethnology and
Archaeology at the Exposition," ibid. 1 (June 1891):9. Dexter's article is the best
account of Putnam's activities at the fair.

40. Dall, 225–26; Harlan Ingersoll Smith, "Man and His Works: The
Anthropology Building at the World's Columbian Exposition," *American Antiquarian*
15 (March 1893):115–17, quoted by Joan Lester, "A Museum's Eye View," *Indian
Historian* 5 (Summer 1972):31.

41. Mason, "Report on the Department of Ethnology in the U.S. National Museum,
1892," SIA, RU 158, box 3, folder 12; "Testimony of O. G. [sic], Mason," in *Report
of Committees*, 639–40, 643–44; Mason, [notes for Chicago exhibit].

42. Mason, "Ethnological Exhibit of the Smithsonian Institution," in *Memoirs of
the International Congress of Anthropology*, ed. C. Staniland Wake (Chicago: Schute
Publishing Company, 1894), 210.

43. Mason, [notes for Chicago exhibit]; Mason to Goode, 8 July 1890, attached to
Goode to Mason, 11 July 1890, SIA, RU 70, box 33.

44. Braun, 75–77; Mason, "Ethnological Exhibit of the Smithsonian Institution,"
211–12; Hinsley, 316–20.

45. Mason, "Summary of Progress in Anthropology," 606. Dall was one scientist
who easily made this transition between lay figures and the living villagers of the
Midway. See Dall, "Anthropology," 225. Mason followed suit in "Anthropology," in
*Report of the Committee on Awards of the World's Columbian Commission: Special
Reports upon Special Subjects or Groups (1901–1902)*. House Report no. 4373,
154:319–22.

46. "Is a New Paradise," *Chicago Tribune*, 30 April 1893, supplement; Bancroft,
Book of the Fair, quoted in Edward Wagenknecht, *Chicago* (Norman: University of
Oklahoma Press, 1964), 14–15; Rao Telang, *A World's Fair Souvenir: Impressions of
the World's Fair and America in General* (San Francisco: Pacific Press Publishing
Company, 1893); and "Wonderful Place for Fun," *New York Times*, 19 June 1893, 9.

47. "Within the Midway Plaisance," *The World's Fair Special Number: Illustrated
American*, n.d., 59, Chicago Historical Society; *Report of the President to the Board
of Directors of the World's Columbian Exposition* (Chicago: Rand, McNally, 1893),
85–86, cited by Horowitz, 99; Rossiter Johnson, ed., *A History of the World's
Columbian Exposition*. 4 vols. (New York: D. Appleton, 1898), 2:315–57; and *A
Week at the Fair*, 230. See also Putnam to George R. Davis, 17 October 1893, in
Harvard University Archives, Frederic Ward Putnam Papers, World's Columbian
Exposition Correspondence, A–D, box 31, folder D (cited hereafter as Putnam

Papers). Putnam did try at first to keep the North American Indian display off the
Midway. See "Indian Office Exhibit . . .," transcript, 1 February 1892, ibid., box
34. I wish to express my thanks to Ralph W. Dexter and the authorities of the
Harvard University Archives for permission to consult this collection.

48. Horowitz, 99; John F. Kasson, *Amusing the Millions* (New York: Hill and
Wang, 1978), 11–28; Badger, 188–90; Sol Bloom, *The Autobiography of Sol Bloom*
(New York: G. P. Putnam, 1948), 107–40; Johnson, 2:316. See also John A.
Kouwenhoven, "The Eiffel Tower and the Ferris Wheel," *Arts Magazine* 54
(1980):170–73; and Barbara Rubin, "Aesthetic Ideology and Urban Design," *Annals
of the Association of American Geographers* 69 (1979):339–61.

49. Bloom, 106, as cited in Badger, 189.

50. Frederic Ward Putnam, in *World's Columbian Exposition: Plan and
Classification* (Chicago: Chicago World's Columbian Exposition, Department of
Publicity and Promotion, 1892), 8–9.

51. *New York Times*, 8 October 1893, quoted by Dexter, 327; Frederic Ward
Putnam to the Commissioner of Indian Affairs, 29 September 1893, 2, in Putnam
Papers, box 34, Indians folder; and duplicate of undated Putnam memorandum in
ibid., box 33, folder T. Some years later R. H. Pratt, head of the Carlisle Indian
School, wrote of the Chicago and Saint Louis fairs: "In some cases the ethnologists
who managed had to show the Indians how to build and dress because none of the
present generation in such tribes knew." See Pratt to Franklin K. Lane, 21 August
1913, National Archives, Record Group 75, Records of the Indian Office, Indians for
Show and Exhibition Purposes, folder 5–70.

52. *Midway Types*.

53. *Chicago Tribune*, 21 October 1892, clipping, UCLA, 344/2, box 2; and Amy
Leslie, *Amy Leslie at the Fair* (Chicago: W. B. Conkey Company, 1893), 13.

54. Leslie, 99.

55. "Scientific Teaching in the Colleges," *Popular Science Monthly* 16 (1880):558,
cited by Richard Hofstadter, *Social Darwinism in American Thought* (Boston: Beacon
Press, 1955), 5; Stocking, 278; Ralph W. Dexter, "The Impact of Evolutionary
Theories on the Salem Group of Agassiz Zoologists," *Essex Institute Historical
Collections* 115 (1979):144–71; and Putnam, in *Oriental and Occidental*. Putnam
wrote the introduction for this volume, apparently before seeing the pictures or
captions. On the back cover he was connected with the editorial work, but such was
not the case. See N. D. Thompson to Putnam, 19 June 1894, in Putnam Papers, box
33, folder T.

56. Julian Hawthorne, "Foreign Folk at the Fair," *Cosmopolitan Magazine* 15
(1893):568, 570.

57. Denton J. Snider, *World's Fair Studies* (Chicago: Sigma Publishing Company,
1895), 237, 255–57; "Through the Looking Glass," *Chicago Tribune*, 1 November
1893, 9.

58. *Oriental and Occidental*; Edward B. McDowell, "The World's Fair
Cosmopolis," *Frank Leslie's Popular Monthly* 36 (October 1893):415; John C.
Eastman, "Village Life at the World's Fair," *Chautauquan* 17 (1893):602–4; Dall,
225; and *Midway Types*.

59. McDowell, 412–14. "The American public," according to a promotional

pamphlet, "are now able to judge of the Javanese art and industry in this village and the syndicate that brought it over expects . . . that American capital and commerce may combine to develop commercial relations between Java and the Great Republic." See *The Javanese Theatre, the Java Village, Midway Plaisance: World's Columbian Exposition, Chicago, 1893* ([Chicago]: Java Chicago Exhibition Syndicate, n.d.).

60. *Daily Inter Ocean,* 14 June 1893, supplement. E. E. Packer, *The White City, Being an Account of a Trip to the World's Columbian Exposition at Chicago in 1893* (San Diego: n.p., 1933), 54, notes that South Sea Islanders concluded their shows by singing "America."

61. Starr, 619; and Clara Louisa Burnham, *Sweet Clover* (Chicago: Laird and Lee, 1893), 201.

62. This aspect of American racism has been discussed by Winthrop D. Jordan, *White over Black: American Attitudes towards the Negro, 1550–1812* (Baltimore: Penguin Books, 1968); Joel Kovel, *White Racism: A Psychohistory* (New York: Vintage Books, 1971); Michael P. Rogin, *Fathers and Children: Andrew Jackson and the Subjugation of the American Indian* (New York: Alfred A. Knopf, 1975); and Peter Loewenberg, "The Psychology of Racism," in *The Great Fear: Race in the Mind of America,* ed. Gary B. Nash and Richard Weiss (New York: Holt, Rinehart and Winston, 1970), 186–202.

63. Burnham, 201–2; and "Captain Jack at the Fair," *Chicago Tribune,* 10 September 1893, supplement.

64. Kenten Druyvesteyn, "The World's Parliament of Religions" (Ph.D. dissertation, University of Chicago, 1976). See also Neufeld, 260–79; Johnson, 4:414–15, 444, 480–84; and Adams, 343.

65. Hines, *Burnham of Chicago;* Carl S. Smith, "Fearsome Fiction and the Windy City; or, Chicago in the Dime Novel," *Chicago History* 7 (1978):2–11; Imre Kiralfy, "America," in California State University, Fresno, Department of Special Collections, vertical files. For an account of the scale model of the White City constructed by Ferris, designer of the Ferris wheel, consult "Exposition Notes," SIA, RU 70, box 40, folder 1. For other reactions, see Louis H. Sullivan, *The Autobiography of an Idea* (New York: W. W. Norton, 1926), 325; Sinclair Lewis, *Babbitt* (New York: Harcourt, Brace, 1922), 305; and Joe Mitchell Chapple, "Affairs at Washington," *National Magazine* 21 (1904):4. The museum is discussed by Horowitz, 149–50; and by Regna Diebold Darnell, "The Development of American Anthropology, 1879–1920: From the Bureau of American Ethnology to Franz Boas" (Ph.D. dissertation, University of Pennsylvania, 1969), 195–206.

66. "Testimony of F. J. V. Skiff," in *Reports of Committees,* 299; and Frederick J. V. Skiff, et al., *An Historical Account and Descriptive Account of the Field Columbian Museum.* Field Columbian Museum Publication no. 1 (Chicago, 1894), quoted by Darnell, 199; Dorsey, quoted by Darnell, 205; Ralph W. Dexter, "The Role of F. W. Putnam in Founding the Field Museum," *Curator* 13 (1970):21–26; and Phyllis Rabineau, "North American Anthropology at the Field Museum of Natural History," *American Indian Arts Magazine* 6 (1981):30–37.

67. "Association Welcomes Japan's Exposition Envoys to Europe and to the United States," *Chicago Commerce* (16 April 1909), 5–11, 28–34, in Colorado Heritage Center, Frederick J. V. Skiff Scrapbook, no. 573, 3.

68. Ibid.

69. Frederick F. Cook, "An Eloquent Article on the Scene in Jackson Park," *Halligan's Weekly World's Fair* 3 (December 1893):713.

Chapter Three

1. Booker T. Washington, "The Standard Printed Version of the Atlanta Exposition Address," 18 September 1895, in *The Booker T. Washington Papers*, ed. Louis Harlan (cited hereafter as *BTW Papers*), 7 vols. (Urbana: University of Illinois Press, 1972), 3:586.

2. The starting point for understanding the southern fairs is C. Vann Woodward's observation thirty years ago that these "solemn circuses" that "promoted sectional reconciliation in the name of Progress" offered substantial "food for reflection." Consult C. Vann Woodward, *Origins of the New South, 1877–1913* (1951; reprinted [Baton Rouge]: Louisiana State University Press, 1974), 124–25. Few studies have pursued Woodward's insight, and only the New Orleans and Atlanta fairs have received adequate treatment. See Donald Clive Hardy, "The World's Industrial and Cotton Centennial Exposition" (M.A. thesis, Tulane University, 1964); Mary Roberts Davis, "The Atlanta Industrial Expositions of 1881 and 1895: Expressions of the Philosophy of the New South" (M.A. thesis, Emory University, 1952); Norman Shavin, "The Great Cotton Exposition of 1895," *Atlanta Magazine* 5 (October 1965):32–37; Sharon M. Mullis, "Extravaganza of the New South: The Cotton States and International Exposition, 1895," *Atlanta Historical Bulletin* 20 (Fall 1976):17–36; and Carl Abbot, "Norfolk in the New Century: The Jamestown Exposition and Urban Boosterism," *Virginia Magazine of History and Biography* 85 (January 1977): 86–96. The standard works about the expositions are the contemporary official histories: Herbert Fairall, *The World's Industrial and Cotton Centennial Exposition* (Iowa City: Republican Publishing Company, 1885); Walter G. Cooper, *The Cotton States and International Exposition and South Illustrated* (Atlanta: Illustrator Company, 1896); and Herman Justi, *Official History of the Tennessee Centennial Exposition* (Nashville: Brandon Publishing Company, 1898).

3. Cooper, *Cotton States and International Exposition and South Illustrated*, 210–11; "Looked Like Real War," *Nashville American*, 15 August 1897, 1; Fairall, 361–78; "The Liberty Bell Goes South," *New York Times*, 24 January 1885, 4; "The Liberty Bell in Atlanta," editorial, *Atlanta Constitution*, 6 October 1895, 16; " 'Tis Children's Day," *Constitution*, 7 October 1895, 5; and "Our Bell Now," *Constitution*, 9 October 1895, 1.

4. Speeches quoted in Cooper, *Cotton States and International Exposition and South Illustrated*, 104, 134–35.

5. Joaquin Miller, "La Exposición," *Chicago Times*, 21 December 1885, clipping in Claremont Colleges, Honnold Library, Department of Special Collections, Joaquin Miller Collection; and Cooper, 29.

6. On the origins of the fairs, see Hardy, 1–30; Alfred C. Newell, "The Birth of the Exposition," *Constitution*, 15 September 1895, 40; Justi, 3–41; Davis, passim; and Jack Blicksilver, "International Cotton Exposition of 1881 and Its Impact upon Economic Development of Georgia," *Cotton History Review* 1 (1960):175–94.

7. Talmadge quoted in Hardy, 31; "The Great International," [news release] 14 January 1895, in Smithsonian Institution Archives (cited hereafter as SIA), Record

Unit (cited hereafter as RU) 70, "Incoming Correspondence," Assistant Secretary USNM, Cotton States and International Exposition (cited hereafter as CSIE), box 39; and Justi, 14.

8. Henry Grady, "The New South," in *The New South and Other Addresses by Henry Woodfin Grady*, ed. Edna Henry Lee Turpin (New York: Charles F. Merrill Company, 1904), 37–38. See also Paul M. Gaston, *The New South Creed: A Study in Southern Mythmaking* (New York: Alfred A. Knopf, 1970); and John Cell, *The Highest Stage of White Supremacy: The Origins of Segregation in South Africa and the American South* (London: Cambridge University Press, 1982), 82–191.

9. Hardy, 12–18; and Joy J. Jackson, *New Orleans in the Gilded Age: Politics and Urban Progress, 1880–1896* (Baton Rouge: Louisiana State University Press, 1969), 31, 41, 217.

10. Cooper, *Cotton States and International Exposition and South Illustrated*, 143, 154, 206; [Isaac W. Avery], *City of Atlanta: A Descriptive Historical and Industrial Review of the Gateway City of the South, Being the World's Fair Series on Great American Cities* (Louisville, Ky.: Inter-State Publishing Company, 1892–93), 114–16; Alfred C. Newell, "Men Who Made the Exposition," *Constitution*, 15 September 1895, 38; and "The Cotton States and International Exposition to Be Held in Atlanta, Georgia, September 18–December 31, 1895," *New York Times*, 8 June 1895, 17. See also Walter G. Cooper, "The Growth of a Great Exposition," *"Dixie"* 11 (May 1895):32.

11. Edgar Jones to John W. Thomas, 25 May 1897, Tennessee State Library and Archives, Tennessee Centennial Exposition Collection (cited hereafter as TCE), box 4, folder 10.

12. "Report of the Director General," 9 November 1897, in Minutes of the Board, 70, TCE, box 8, folder 2; "Palaces on Wheels," *Nashville American*, 9 October 1897, 10; and A. G. Brown, "Railroads and the Centennial," *Nashville Banner*, 19 July 1897, 6. See also Samuel Boyd Smith, "Joseph Buckner Killebrew: Tennessee Spokesman for the New South" (M.A. thesis, Vanderbilt University, 1960), 187–200; and Jesse C. Burt, "History of the Nashville, Chattanooga and St. Louis Railroad, 1873–1916" (Ph.D. dissertation, Vanderbilt University, 1950), 188–95.

13. "Atlanta's Hustling Lesson," *New York Times*, 7 December 1895, 16; "The South—Vast Resources, Rapid Development, Wonderful Opportunities for Capital and Labor," *New York Times*, 8 June 1895, 17.

14. Fairall, 282–83.

15. "Exposition Notes," 5 May 1895, SIA, RU 70, "Incoming Correspondence," Assistant Secretary, CSIE, box 40; "Atlanta's Great Show," *New York Times*, 19 September 1893, 5; Joseph Buckner Killebrew, "Recollections of My Life: An Autobiography," [1898], MS., p. 334, Tennessee State Library and Archives, Joseph Buckner Killebrew Papers; and *Report of the Board of Commissioners Representing the State of New York at the Cotton States and International Exposition* (Albany: Wynkoop Hallenbeck Crawford Company, 1896), 34.

16. Cooper, *Cotton States and International Exposition and South Illustrated*, 29; and *Thomasville Times*, quoted in *Constitution*, 31 January 1895, 4.

17. Justi, 193.

18. Accounts of the Negro departments can be found in each of the official

histories of the fairs. See also Ruth M. Winton, "Negro Participation in Southern Expositions, 1881–1915," *Journal of Negro Education* 16 (Winter 1947): 34–43; and William Ziegler Schenck, "Negro Participation in Three Southern Expositions" (M.A. thesis, University of North Carolina, 1970). Two additional contemporary accounts are useful: Alice M. Bacon, *The Negro and the Atlanta Exposition*. Occasional Papers, no. 7 (Baltimore: Trustees of the John F. Slater Fund, 1896); and Giles B. Jackson and D. Webster Davis, *Industrial History of the Negro Race* (Richmond, Va.: Negro Educational Association, 1911.)

19. *Times-Democrat*, 24 February 1885, clipping, "Colored Department Exhibits entry," SIA, unprocessed collection; "Colored People's Day," *New York Freeman*, 7 March 1885.

20. New Orleans *Times-Democrat*, 24 February 1885, SIA, unprocessed collection.

21. Ibid.; *Times-Democrat*, clipping, 15 December 1884, in ibid.; *Times-Democrat*, clipping, 8 May 1885, in ibid.; Fairall, 38. See also David Paul Bennets, "Black and White Workers: New Orleans, 1880–1900" (Ph.D. dissertation, University of Illinois, Urbana, 1972), 198–99.

22. Burke quoted in "The World's Industrial and Cotton Centennial Exposition," *Parson's Memorial and Historical Library Magazine*, n.d., in the Archives of the Nebraska State Historical Society; and Booker T. Washington to the editor of the *Montgomery Advertiser*, 24 April 1885, in *BTW Papers*, 2:273.

23. "An Account of a Speech before the Labor Congress," Chicago *Daily Inter Ocean*, 3 September 1893, 13, in *BTW Papers*, 2:364–66; and *Atlanta Journal*, 15 November 1893, 1, in *BTW Papers*, 2:371–73.

24. Cooper, *Cotton States and International Exposition and South Illustrated*, 24–25; Booker T. Washington, *The Story of My Life and Work*, in *BTW Papers*, 1:67–68; and Winton, 35–36.

25. *Congressional Record*, 53d Congress, 2d Session, vol. 26, part 8 (10 August 1894), 8384; Cooper, *Cotton States and International Exposition and South Illustrated*, 28.

26. I. Garland Penn to Washington, 12 August 1895, quoted in Louis R. Harlan, *Booker T. Washington: The Making of a Black Leader* (New York: Oxford University Press, 1972), 209.

27. Washington, "Standard Printed Version of the Atlanta Exposition Address," 18 September 1895, in *BTW Papers*, 2:583–87; and Washington to *New York World*, 20 September 1895, cited by Harlan, *Booker T. Washington*, 222. Washington's ideas have been the subject of national debate since the day of his address. In addition to Harlan's biography and superbly annotated edition of Washington's writings, see Emma L. Thornbrough, "Booker T. Washington as Seen by His White Contemporaries," *Journal of Negro History* 53 (1968):161–82; Louis R. Harlan, "The Secret Life of Booker T. Washington," *Journal of Southern History* 37 (1971):393–416; Alfred Young, "The Educational Philosophy of Booker T. Washington: A Perspective for Black Liberation," *Phylon* 37 (1976):224–35; and Judith Stein, " 'Of Mr. Booker T. Washington and Others': The Political Economy of Racism in the United States," *Science and Society* 38 (1974–75):422–63.

28. "Illinois at the Atlanta Exposition," *New York Times*, 8 June 1895, 8; Bishop Henry M. Turner, "To Colored People," *Constitution*, 13 January 1895, 3; "The Colored Exhibit," *Constitution*, 3 April 1895, 8; Davis, 71–99; and Bacon, 19.

29. "They Do Draw It," *Cleveland Gazette*, 7 December 1895, 1; ibid., 2 November 1895, 2; and "The Negro at the Atlanta Exposition," *Literary Digest* 22 (November 1895):6, quoted in Mullis, 36.

30. "The Colored Exhibit," *Constitution*, 3 April 1895, 8; "Negro Editors Meet," *Constitution*, 22 November 1895, 11; "The Negro Exhibit," editorial, *Constitution*, 18 October 1895, 6; and "Negro Day at the Exposition," *New York Times*, 22 October 1895, 3. See also Winton, 32–38; Bacon, 5–28; and I. Garland Penn, "The Awakening of the Race," in Cooper, *Cotton States and International Exposition and South Illustrated*, 58–63.

31. "Colored Folks Meet Happily," *Nashville Sun*, 6 June 1897, 6; *Freeman*, 12 June 1897; "Negro Day at Nashville," *Afro-American Sentinel*, 12 June 1897, 1; and Anderson, quoted in Justi, 200–201.

32. "Colored Folks Meet Happily," *Nashville Sun*, 6 June 1897, 6; "Crowned with Success," *Nashville American*, 6 June 1897, 5. See also Thomas to M. F. Jordan, 4 June 1897, TCE, box 6, folder 7; The Negro Building was designed by a young Nashville architect, Frederic Thompson, future midway magnate and designer of Luna Park. See Frances A. Groff, "Exposition Moths," *Sunset* 35 (July 1915):134.

33. "The Negroes," editorial, *Nashville Banner*, 8 June 1897, 4.

34. Wright Stedman, "Vanity Fair," *Nashville American*, 1 May 1897, 7; Cooper, *Cotton States and International Exposition and South Illustrated*, 91.

35. Speer quoted in Cooper, ibid., 104, 101–08. See also Cell, 168.

36. C. A. Collier, "The Cotton States and International Exposition—Its Inception and Growth," *"Dixie"* 11 (September 1895):35.

37. "An Exhibition of Progress," *Nashville American*, 1 May 1897, 20; "Emancipation Celebration," *Nashville Sun*, 23 September 1897, 5; Justi, 202–3; and Winton, 39.

38. ["General Announcement"] in *World's Industrial and Cotton Centennial Exposition*, 4, SIA, RU 70, "Operations Records," Assistant Director, USNM, New Orleans Exposition, box 18; and, "Seen at Atlanta's Show," *New York Times*, 10 October 1895, 13.

39. [I. W. Avery to Charles A. Collier], 1 June 1895, MS 68-102129-07, Georgia State Archives, Isaac W. Avery Collection, Letters Outgoing 1895 folder (cited hereafter as Avery Collection); and "To Increase Trade South. Gen. Avery Tells of IIis Mission to South America," *New York Times*, 11 April 1895, 9. I am especially indebted to the account of Avery's activities by John C. Edwards, "Isaac Wheeler Avery and the Quest for South American Markets: A Note on the Experience of a Foreign Commissioner," *Atlanta Historical Bulletin* 17 (Spring/Summer 1973):51–59.

40. [Avery] to Collier, 1 June 1895, Avery Collection.

41. Avery to Minister of Foreign Affairs, 29 November 1894; and Avery to Porfirio Díaz, 25 April 1895, Avery Collection.

42. "The Cotton States and International Exposition to Be Held in Atlanta, Georgia, September 18–December 31, 1895," *New York Times*, 8 June 1895, 17; and "Model of the Canal," *Constitution*, 24 November 1895, 2.

43. "The Silver Exhibit from Mexico," *Times-Democrat*, 18 December 1884, clipping; "Mexico Exhibit," ibid., clipping, in SIA, unprocessed collection; "More News from Mexico," *Nashville Sun*, 17 January 1897, 7; and Justi, 335.

44. "Mexico Exhibit," *Times-Democrat*, 16 February 1885, clipping, SIA,

unprocessed collection; Edwards, 51–54; Avery to Minister of Foreign Affairs, 29 November 1894, Avery Collection; "The International Expositions to Be Held in Mexico and South America" [circular], Atlanta Historical Society, Cotton States and International Exposition Collection, box 87; "Exposition Notes," n.d., SIA, RU 70, "Incoming Correspondence," Assistant Secretary, CSIE, box 40.

45. Jacinto Lara to Avery, 14 June 1895, Avery Collection, Letters Incoming April–June 1895 folder, quoted in Edwards, 56.

46. Edwards, 56–57; *Historical Sketch Book and Guide to New Orleans and Environs* (New York: Will H. Coleman, 1885), 321; "The Exposition and the Mexican Band," *Mascot*, 13 June 1885, 9; and "Miss Bridget Magee's Society Notes," *Mascot*, 16 May 1885, 4.

47. "A Night on Vanity Fair," *Nashville American*, 3; Justi, 206; Cooper, *Cotton States and International Exposition and South Illustrated*, 89.

48. Cooper, ibid., 39–42; Justi, 433–34.

49. Justi, 207.

50. Cooper, *Cotton States and International Exposition and South Illustrated*, 89–91. Cooper's claim is easily refuted by the exhibits discussed later in this chapter, but especially by "A Dead Eskimo," *Constitution*, 25 November 1895, 8. The twenty-one-year-old man, "one of the best specimens," died of pneumonia in the Eskimo Village, "and his sudden taking off cast a gloom over his brother natives there."

51. Cooper, *Cotton States and International Exposition and South Illustrated*, 91.

52. "Maids of China," *Constitution*, 20 September 1895, 5; "Chinamen Bound for Atlanta," *New York Times*, 5 September 1895, 9.

53. "205 Chinese Arrive," *Constitution*, 15 September 1895, 14; "A Little Boy from China," *Nashville Banner*, 30 June 1897, 1; "Statement of Harry L. Mills," n.d., in TCE, box 10, folder 4; "The 'Chincks' [*sic*] Have Come to Vanity Fair," *Nashville American*, 22 April 1897, 1.

54. "Celestials Pray," *Nashville Sun*, 26 April 1897, 5; "Shot the Chutes," *Nashville Sun*, 29 May 1897, 5.

55. Cooper, 90; Edwards, 53; "Cotton Bolls," *New York Observer Exposition Supplement*, 27 June 1895, 872 (reprinted July, 1970, Atlanta Historical Society).

56. "Buffalo Bill Coming," *Constitution*, 24 October 1895, 5; *Boston Transcript* interview, [?] July 1895, quoted in Robert Toll, *Blacking Up: The Minstrel Show in Nineteenth Century America* (New York: Oxford University Press, 1974), 262–63.

57. Cooper, *Cotton States and International Exposition and South Illustrated*, 90.

58. Walter Hough, "Historical Sketch of the Division of Ethnology," 1906, National Anthropology Archives, MS 4787; Robert Earll to Mason, 29 June 1885, Letterbook, 1/23/1885–7/5/1885, 448–49, SIA, RU 70, "Outgoing Correspondence," Assistant Secretary USNM, New Orleans Exposition, box 19.

59. Otis T. Mason, "Circular Relative to the Ethnological Exhibit at the World's Industrial and Cotton Centennial Exposition. Dec. 1, 1884–May 31, 1885," SIA, RU 70, "Incoming Correspondence," Assistant Secretary USNM, New Orleans Exposition, box 17, M–Q folder.

60. Curtis M. Hinsley, *Savages and Scientists: The Smithsonian Institution and the Development of American Anthropology, 1846–1910* (Washington, D.C.: Smithsonian Institution Press, 1981), 83–143.

61. [Robert Edward Earll], *The Exhibit of the Smithsonian Institution at the Cotton

States Exposition, in SIA, RU 70, "Incoming Correspondence," Assistant Secretary, CSIE, box 40, Exposition Rules folder.

62. *Richmond Times,* 27 March 1895, quoted in J. E. Johnson to the Editor, *Richmond Times,* n.d., in SIA, RU 70, "Incoming Correspondence," Assistant Secretary USNM, CSIE, box 40, C–J folder; *Savannah Tribune,* editorial, 30 March 1895; and Goode, "Apes and Evolution," *Constitution,* 7 April 1895, 7. The starting point for the controversy can be traced to "Our Great Exposition," *Constitution,* 18 January 1895, 4, which quotes Collier as saying: "A large building is to be erected where will be presented . . . in a kind of natural panorama the life of the negro from his original state in Africa up to the most advanced types of the race in America." This display was not forthcoming, but the Dahomey Village and Old Plantation on the Midway, coupled with the Negro Building, placed adjacent to the Midway, and the display of cultural grades in the Smithsonian exhibit produced the same effect.

63. McGee and Mason quoted in [Earll], *The Exhibit of the Smithsonian Institution.* McGee always insisted that periods be omitted after his initials, and I have followed his preference.

64. Mason quoted in ibid. See also Goode to Hoke Smith, 18 May 1895, and Mrs. W. H. Felton to Smith, 14 May 1895, SIA, RU 70, "Incoming Correspondence," Assistant Secretary USNM, CSIE, box 40.

65. Quotations are from Fairall, 336–37. See too the clippings from the *Times-Democrat,* 20 December 1884, 25 December 1884, 13 January 1885, and 13 February 1885, and from the *Chicago Weekly Journal,* 21 June 1885, in SIA, unprocessed collection.

66. "National Progress Cannot Be Defeated," *Nashville Banner,* 11 June 1897, 2; "The South and the Exposition," *Constitution,* editorial, 17 November 1895, 16; "Dr. Gilman the Man," *Constitution,* 25 June 1895, 4; and "The Atlanta Exposition: Some of the Good Which It Is Accomplishing for the World," *New York Times,* 22 October 1897, 7; Higinbotham quoted in Justi, 308; Ferdinand W. Peck to Thomas, telegram, 30 October 1897, TCE, box 5, folder 1; Mention of the National Guard is made in "Exposition Notes," n.d., SIA, RU 70, "Incoming Correspondence," Assistant Secretary, CSIE, box 40; Reverend James I. Vance quoted in Justi, 259; and Grady, 37–38.

67. Attendance figures reflect the total number of visitors and are recorded in J. W. Buel, ed., *Louisiana and the Fair: An Exposition of the World, Its People, and Their Achievements,* 10 vols. (Saint Louis: World's Progress Publishing Company, 1904), 4:1264. Concerning financial records of the fairs, see Jones to Thomas, 16 March 1897, TCE, box 4, folder 10; and Thomas to Stuart R. Knott, 3 March 1897, TCE, box 6, folder 4, who says that the Atlanta fair increased the coffers of the Southern Railway by $500,000. See also Thomas to Knott, 10 May 1900, TCE, box 6, folder 14; Thomas to John H. Averill [secretary of the South Carolina Interstate and West Indies Exposition], 13 March 1900, TCE, box 6, folder 14. Killebrew claimed that Nashville's population increased by ten thousand as a direct result of the Tennessee Centennial, according to J. C. Hemphill to Thomas, 24 March 1900, TCE, box 4, folder 7. For accolades regarding the directors' accomplishments, see the untitled and undated newspaper clipping attached to W. B. Earthman to Thomas, 31 August 1897, TCE, box 3, folder 18. See also Earthman to Thomas, 2 October 1897, ibid., in which Earthman says that the "chief greatness" of the day "was the

love and admiration the people had for you." Earthman, owner of a lumber mill, was not entirely disinterested and was probably rewarded with a substantial savings on the five million feet of lumber the exposition sold back to him. See Knott to Thomas, 6 December 1897, TCE, box 4, folder 13. On Inman, see "In Grand Array," *Constitution*, 29 November 1895, 5.

68. Thomas E. Watson to the Editor, "All for the Exposition," *Constitution*, 11 January 1894, 6; "The Exposition and How to See the Sights," *People's Party Paper*, 13 December 1895, 1.

69. "People's Party Conference," *Nashville Banner*, 3 July 1897, 1; "Populists of Many States," *Nashville Banner*, 5 July 1897, 1. For a thorough discussion of Populism as an "organizing process" and cultural challenge to the economic system, see Lawrence Goodwyn, *Democratic Promise: The Populist Movement in America* (New York: Oxford University Press, 1976).

70. Louise Little Davis, "The Parthenon and the Tennessee Centennial: The Greek Temple That Sparked a Birthday Party," *Tennessee Historical Quarterly* 26 (1967):335–53. See also *Major Eugene Castner Lewis, Tribute from a Member of the Centennial Exposition Committee . . . 10 June 1937* (no imprint), 1–8, Tennessee State Library and Archives; Justi, 112–20; and Nathaniel Stephenson, "Closing Day and Scenes," in Justi, 473–74.

Chapter Four

1. Baldwin's speech is quoted in its entirety by James B. Haynes, *History of the Trans-Mississippi and International Exposition of 1898* (Omaha: [Published under direction of the Committee on History as authorized by the board of directors, 20 June 1902], 1910), 347; W. S. Harwood, "The Omaha Exposition," *Harper's Weekly* 42 (20 August 1898):822–23. Another suggestive exhibit was on display in the Agricultural Building: "A cannon, with ammunition of glass balls filled with grain, speaks 'For Cuba,' while near by a corn-blade American flag floats gracefully." This exhibit is noted in *Harper's Weekly*, clipping, n.d., Smithsonian Institution Archives (cited hereafter as SIA), Record Unit (cited hereafter as RU) 70, Exposition Records of the SI and USNM, 1875–1916, box 44. For other accounts of the Omaha fair, consult Virginia Grace Gregory, "The Trans-Mississippi and International Exposition at Omaha, 1898" (M.A. thesis, University of Nebraska, 1929); Kenneth G. Alfers, "The Trans-Mississippi Exposition" (M.A. thesis, Creighton University, 1968); Kenneth G. Alfers, "Triumph of the West: The Trans-Mississippi Exposition," *Nebraska History* 53 (1972):313–29; and Robert Bigart and Clarence Woodcock, "The Trans-Mississippi and International Exposition and the Flathead Delegation," *Montana, the Magazine of Western History* 29 (Autumn 1979):14–23.

2. "Triumphal Day of the Exposition," *Omaha World-Herald*, 13 October 1898, 1; "The Great Exposition at Omaha," *Century Magazine* 60 (1898):518–19. See also Henry Wysham Lanier, "The Great Fair at Omaha," *American Monthly Review of Reviews* 1 (18 July 1898):53–59.

3. Haynes, 29–53; "Beautifying the Grounds," *Omaha Daily Bee*, 2 June 1898, 2; "President Wattles' Address," *Omaha Bee*, 2 June 1898, 2.

4. Haynes, 50, 189; "Features of the Midway," *Omaha Daily Bee*, 21 February 1898, 8. See also Alfers, "Triumph of the West, 324.

5. Alice French [Octave Thanet], "The Trans-Mississippi Exposition,"

Cosmopolitan Magazine 25 (1898):608; W. A. Rodgers, "The Exposition at Omaha," *Harper's Weekly* 62 (8 October 1898):987; and Haynes, 53.

6. John Webster quoted in Haynes, 344.

7. "Lesson of the Exposition," *Omaha Bee*, 30 May 1898, 8. Information about the exposition's backers is provided by "Finances of the Exposition," *Omaha Bee*, 1 June 1898, 5; [John A. Wakefield], "Report of the General Secretary of the Trans-Mississippi and International Exposition, June 26, 1899" (no imprint), in Expositions and Fairs Collection, Department of Special Collections, California State University, Fresno; Gurdon Wallace Wattles, *Autobiography of Gurdon Wallace Wattles* ([New York: Scribner Press, 1927]), 65–72; and "Summary of Stock Subscriptions & etc.," October 1896, in John A. Wakefield Scrapbooks, vol. 1, original in Omaha Public Library, microfilm copy in Nebraska Historical Society (cited hereafter as Wakefield Scrapbooks, NHS).

8. "The Trans-Mississippi and International Exposition," *Omaha World-Herald*, 22 January 1898, 9; *Official Proceedings of the Eighth Convention of the Trans-Mississippi Commercial Congress Held at Omaha, Neb., November 25, 26, 27, and 28, 1895* (Omaha: Press of the Omaha Printing Company, [1895]).

9. Ed F. Morearty, *Omaha Memories* (Omaha: Swartz Printing Company, 1917), 192; Arvid E. Nelson, Jr., *The Ak-Sar-Ben Story* (Lincoln: Johnson Publishing Company, 1967), and his "The Formation and Early History of the Knights of Ak-Sar-Ben as Shown by Omaha Newspapers" (M.A. thesis, Municipal University of Omaha, 1962), esp. 136–41. See also the *Knights of Ak-Sar-Ben: Souvenir Program 1897* (no imprint), NHS.

10. The best discussion of Wooster's activities is provided by James E. Potter, "The Political Career of Charles Wooster" (M.A. thesis, University of Nebraska, 1975). Much of my information about Wooster and his activities regarding the fair is derived from this study. Quotations are from "What Shall Nebraska Do?" *Nebraska State Journal*, 20 January 1897, 5; and Wooster to Henry Stitt, 11 February 1897, Charles Wooster Papers, box 5, NHS, cited by Potter, 74.

11. A. B. Charde to W. H. Dearing, 30 August 1897, Trans-Mississippi and International Exposition Records, box 1, folder 2, NHS; (Mrs.) A. Hardy, "Women and the Exposition," *Hatchet* (March 1898), 22, NHS; and "Exposition Postage Stamps" editorial, *Omaha Bee*, 24 December 1897, 4, also mentioned by Alfers, "Trans-Mississippi Exposition," 36.

12. "History of the Indian," *Omaha Bee*, 16 August 1897, clipping, SIA, RU 70, Exposition Records of the Smithsonian Institution and United States National Museum, 1875–1916, box 44.

13. "Third Annual Parade of the Knights of Ak-Sar-Ben," *Omaha Excelsior*, 25 September 1897. See also "Opening of the Indian Congress," editorial, *Omaha Bee*, 5 August 1898, 6

14. For additional information about Mooney consult Lester George Moses, "James Mooney—Ethnologist" (Ph.D. dissertation, University of New Mexico, 1977), esp. 76–126; and William Munn Colby, "Routes to Rainy Mountain: A Biography of James Mooney, Ethnologist" (Ph.D. dissertation, University of Wisconsin, 1977), 324–26.

15. Mooney to W J McGee, 17 October 1897, National Anthropology Archives (cited hereafter as NAA), Bureau of American Ethnology (cited hereafter as BAE),

Letters Received 1886–1906, box 14, Mooney Folder, cited by Moses, 116. See also William V. Allen to Cornelius Bliss, 11 September 1897, National Archives, Record Group 75 (cited hereafter as NA, RG), Central Correspondence Files, no. 2459. Mooney's idea for a relief map is noted in "Indians at the Exposition," [*Omaha Bee*, 15 November 1897], Wakefield Scrapbooks, 3:90.

16. William V. Allen to the Secretary of the Interior, 5 December 1897, in "Congress of the Indian Tribes of the United States," (13 December 1897), Senate Report no. 397, *Senate Reports*, 1, no. 3620:2–3.

17. Ibid., 2–5. See also "Favor the Indian Exhibit," [*Omaha Bee*, 11 December 1897], 2.

18. "Bill for Indian Congress," [*Omaha Bee*, 7 January 1897], clipping, Wakefield Scrapbooks, 3:152; *Omaha Bee*, 3 July 1898, 12; Rosewater to Bliss, 20 May 1898, telegram, NA, RG 75, Central Correspondence Files, no. 23476; Rosewater to Allen, 7 February 1898, William V. Allen Papers, box 1, NHS; and Rosewater to Bliss, 20 May 1898, telegram, NA RG 75, Central Correspondence Files, no. 23476.

19. "Details for Indian Congress," *Omaha Bee*, 25 July 1898, 1. The circular is quoted in James Mooney, "The Indian Congress at Omaha," *American Anthropologist* 1 (January 1899):128.

20. Fay Fuller, "Omaha's Congress of Aborigines," *State* 2 (20 September 1898):70–71.

21. William A. Mercer to Commissioner of Indian Affairs, 19 July 1898, NA, RG 75, Central Correspondence Files, no. 33222; "Indians on Review," *Omaha Bee*, 4 August 1898, 1, 5; and "Indian Congress Is Open," *Omaha Bee*, 5 August 1898, 5.

22. "Indian Congress Is Open," *Omaha Bee*, 5 August 1898, 5.

23. "Aboriginality" is the term used in "Indians on Review," *Omaha Bee*, 4 August 1898, 1, 5.

24. "Indians Beaten in Battle," *Omaha Bee*, 11 August 1898, 5; "Sham Fight with Indians Today," *Omaha Bee*, 10 August 1898, 1; and "Red Men Avoid Battle," *Omaha World-Herald*, [11 August 1898?], clipping, Wakefield Scrapbooks, 6:38. See also Bigart and Woodcock, 14–23.

25. "Indians Beaten in Battle," *Omaha Bee*, 11 August 1898, 5.

26. Ibid.

27. Ibid.

28. Mooney to McGee, 27 September 1898, NAA, BAE Letters Received 1886–1906, box 14, Mooney folder, cited by Moses, 123. Mooney, "Indian Congress at Omaha," 129; "Foot Race and Ghost Dance," *Omaha Bee*, [8 October 1898?], clipping, Wakefield Scrapbooks, 7:39.

29. "Glimpses of Indian Life at the Omaha Exposition," *American Monthly Review of Reviews* 18 (1898):436–43; Fuller, "Omaha's Congress of Aborigines," 73; French, "Trans-Mississippi Exposition," 612.

30. Mooney, "Indian Congress at Omaha," 129; "Child Dies in Indian Village," [*Omaha Bee*, 29 August 1898], clipping, Wakefield Scrapbooks, 6:113; "Burial of a Dead Brave," [3 October 1898?], clipping, Wakefield Scrapbooks, 7:19; [John A. Wakefield], "Report of the General Secretary of the Trans-Mississippi and International Exposition," 14; and "Geronimo on Indian Wars," *Omaha Bee*, 10 October 1898, 5.

31. French, "Trans-Mississippi Exposition," 613.

32. Lanier, "Great Fair at Omaha," 58; Mary Alice Harriman, "The Congress of American Aborigines at the Omaha Exposition," *Overland Monthly*, n.s., 33 (June 1899):508; Fuller, 73; "Bill Cody's Day in Omaha," *Omaha Bee*, 28 August 1898, 5.

33. Lanier, "Great Fair at Omaha," 58–59.

34. "Features of the Midway," *Omaha Bee*, 21 February 1898, 8; "Coming to Opening," *Omaha World-Herald*, 1 June 1898, 9; "Darkey Life on the Midway," *Omaha Bee*, 23 December 1897, 5; "Glimpses of the Midway," *Omaha World-Herald*, 16 September 1898, 2; Alice French [Octave Thanet], "As Viewed by Octave Thanet," *Omaha Bee*, 31 July 1898, 19.

35. "Chinese May Come to Omaha," [*Omaha Bee*], 14 September 1897, clipping, Wakefield Scrapbooks, 8:100; "Chinese at the Exposition," [*Omaha Bee*], 9 June 1897, clipping, Wakefield Scrapbooks, vol. 2; "Many Chinese Are Coming," *Omaha Bee*, 26 October 1897, clipping, Wakefield Scrapbooks, 3:69; and "Heathen Chinee Is Smooth," *Omaha Bee*, 25 October 1898, 2.

36. "Heathen Chinee Is Smooth," *Omaha Bee*, 25 October 1898, 2; "Features of the Midway," *Omaha Bee*, 21 February 1898, 8.

37. "Great Parade of the Nations," [*Omaha Bee*], 30 August 1898, clipping, Wakefield Scrapbooks, 6:117; "Bill Cody's Day in Omaha," *Omaha Bee*, 28 August 1898, 5.

38. [Advertisement], *Omaha Bee*, 25 October 1898, 2; French, "Trans-Mississippi Exposition," 608; and "Scores Another Musical Hit," *Omaha Bee*, 24 August 1898, 1–2.

39. Haynes, 262–63; "Glimpses of the Midway," *Omaha World-Herald*, 16 October 1898, 2; "Dewey's Requisition for Soap," *Omaha World-Herald*, 22 July 1898, 4; "Character of the Filipinos," *Omaha Bee*, 23 October 1898, 18. A good discussion of the application of America's colonial policy toward Native Americans to Filipinos is offered by Walter L. Williams, "United States Indian Policy and the Debate over Philippine Annexation: Implications for the Origins of American Imperialism," *Journal of American History* 66 (1980):810–31.

40. Alfers, "Trans-Mississippi Exposition," 94–97; "President at the Fair," *Omaha Bee*, 13 October 1898, 1–2; "President McKinley's Ovation," *Omaha Bee*, 13 October 1898, 6; "President Is Here," *Omaha Bee*, 12 October 1898, 1, 5.

41. "Reception to the President," *Omaha Bee*, 13 October, 1898, 1, 5.

42. "Great Father and Indian," *Omaha Bee*, 13 October 1898, 1, 5.

43. Ibid. See also "Triumphal Day of the Exposition," *Omaha World-Herald*, 13 October 1898, 1.

44. "President McKinley Makes an Extended Call at Congress Grounds," *Omaha Bee*, 13 October 1898, 1, 5.

45. "Children at the Exposition," *Omaha Bee*, 6 March 1898, 12; (Mrs.) A. Hardy, "Women and the Exposition," 22; "Pupils Subscribe Stock," 7 November 1897, clipping, Wakefield Scrapbooks, 3:80; Haynes, 120–21; and "Holding Cleaning up Bees," *Omaha World-Herald*, 13 March 1898, 3.

46. "Kids Overrun the Exposition," *Omaha World-Herald*, 23 October 1898, 10; Thomas J. Kelly, "The Trans-Mississippi Ode for Girls and Boys," music from Joseph Barnaby's "We March to Victory," *Hatchet* (18 March 1898): 19.

47. *Omaha World-Herald,* 31 October 1898, 4; Wattles, 71; Alfers, "Triumph of the West," 326–27; and French, "Our Exposition Summed Up," *Omaha Bee,* 28 August 1898, 17.

48. *Greater America Exposition, Omaha, 1899: Prospectus* (no imprint), NHS; George W. Gaines to Secretary of Interior, 21 June 1899, NA, RG 75, Central Correspondence Files, no. 29334; and Morearty, 59.

49. William V. Cox to Frederick True, 29 June 1898, SIA, RU 70, Letterbook, 45, "Outgoing Correspondence," Official Representative, SI and USNM, Omaha Exposition, box 45.

Chapter Five

1. "Pax 1901" was the motto for the official flag of the fair. See the Buffalo *Commercial,* 20 May 1901, clipping, in Buffalo and Erie County Historical Society (cited hereafter as BHS), "Pan-American Exposition, Buffalo, New York, Newspaper Clippings," microfilm, vol. 11, n.p. (cited hereafter as Pax Newspaper Clippings); Eugene Richard Wright, "Aspects of the Pan-American Exposition," *Atlantic Monthly* 88 (1901):87; and "Architects at the Fair," Buffalo *Express,* 4 October 1901, clipping, in Pax Newspaper Clippings, vol. 11.

2. "What the Exposition Means," editorial, Buffalo *Evening News,* 13 March 1901, 2; Richard H. Barry, *The Grandeur of the Exposition* (Buffalo: Robert Allen Reid Publisher, 1901); Richard Watson Gilder, "What Shall We Name It?" in *Art Handbook: Official Handbook of Architecture and Sculpture and Art Catalogue to the Pan-American Exposition* (Buffalo: David Gray, 1901), 6, in UCLA, Department of Special Collections, Expositions and Fairs Collection, 344/1, box 1 (cited hereafter as UCLA 344/1); *Official Catalogue and Guide Book to the Pan-American Exposition* (Buffalo: Charles Ahrhart, 1901), 53, in UCLA, 344/1, box 1; and Wright, 86.

3. Hamilton Wright Mabie, "The Spirit of the New World as Interpreted by the Pan-American Exposition," *Outlook* 68 (10 July 1901):547; *Ins and Outs of Buffalo: Official Guide to the Pan-American City* (Buffalo: A. B. Floyd, 1901), 137; John Hay quoted in "The Good Done at Buffalo," *Century Magazine* 62 (1901):794.

4. "The Pan-American Exposition," *Pan-American Herald* 1 (15 July 1899):1–2; Richmond C. Hill, *Buffalo Greets the South with a Synopsis of Her History . . .* (Buffalo: Matthews-Northrup Company, [1895]); and *Report of the Board of General Managers of the Exhibit of the State of New York* (Albany: J. B. Lyon Company, 1902), 10; "President's Day," editorial, *Express,* 6 September 1901, 4. These same sentiments had been appearing in newspaper headlines throughout the country since the earliest planning stages of the exposition. See, for instance, "Buffalo's Great Pan-American Exposition: The Big Show to Be Held in 1901 Has International Significance—Its Central Idea Is Our Acquisition of South American Trade," *Cleveland Leader,* 13 November 1899, clipping, in Letterbook, Smithsonian Institution Archives (cited hereafter as SIA), Record Unit (cited hereafter as RU) 70, Exposition Records of the Smithsonian Institution and the United States National Museum, 1875–1916, box 45.

5. Nicholas Murray Butler, "The Educational Influence of the Exposition," *Cosmopolitan Magazine* 31 (1901):540; William I. Buchanan, "The Pan-American Exposition," *Colliers* 26 (December 1900): 5; Mabie, 536–37; *Nation* 72 (9 May

1901):366; "Flag Day at Buffalo Fair," *New York Times*, 15 June 1901, 8; and excerpt from *New York Tribune*, quoted in *Pan-American Herald* 1 (July 1899):8.

6. *Pan-American Exposition* (Buffalo: Pan-American Exposition Company, 1900), 1–2, BHS vertical file; "The Pan American Exposition," *Pan-American Herald* 1 (15 July 1899):2; "How the Railroads Built the Exposition," advertising supplement, *World's Work* 2 (1901):n.p., UCLA, 344/1, box 1; "Railroads Take $300,000 Stock," *Buffalo Times*, 12 March 1900, 1; "Railroads Give Big Sums to the Pan-American," Buffalo *Enquirer*, 8 May 1900, clipping, Pax Newspaper Clippings, vol. 5; "Pan-American Finances," *Buffalo Times*, 23 February 1898, 4; "$1,450,000 Now," *Commercial*, 1 August 1900, clipping, in Pax Newspaper Clippings, vol. 6; and "Success," *Buffalo Times*, 26 February 1898, 5.

7. "Builders of the Exposition," *Pan-American Herald* 1 (15 July 1899):5; "These Are the Men," *Pan-American*, n.d., clipping, in UCLA, Frederick W. Taylor Scrapbooks, vol. 1 (cited hereafter as Taylor Scrapbooks); "No Office for Mr. Goodyear," Buffalo *Evening News*, 12 March 1899, clipping, Pax Newspaper Clippings, vol. 2; *New York Times*, 12 August 1930, 21; *Who Was Who in America, 1897–1942* (Chicago: Marquis Company, 1968), 837; "Taking Definite Form," *Pan-American Herald* 1 (November 1899):4; [Isaac W. Avery] to President Charles A. Collier and the Directors of the Cotton States and International Exposition, 1 June 1895, 6–7, Georgia State Archives, Isaac W. Avery Collection, MS 68-10-2129-17, Outgoing Letter folder, 1895; Harlow N. Higinbotham to John Milburn, 22 May 1899, BHS, William I. Buchanan Papers, box 2 (cited hereafter as Buchanan Papers); and Harold F. Peterson, *Diplomat of the Americas: William I. Buchanan* (Albany: State University of New York Press, 1976).

8. "Two Will Decide," *Commercial*, 3 April 1899, and "Site Experts," *Express*, 13 April 1899, clippings, in Pax Newspaper Clippings, vol. 2; "Ethnology," *Commercial*, 2 June 1899, clipping, Taylor Scrapbooks, vol. 1; "Landscape Architect Rudolph Ulrich," *Pan-American Herald* 1 (15 August 1899):9.

9. "Indian Congress Would Be a Grand Feature," *Enquirer*, 2 June 1899, clipping, Taylor Scrapbooks, vol. 1; "Indian Congress," *Pan-American Herald* 2 (May 1900):7; "Editor Rosewater on Pan-American," *Commercial*, 11 December 1899, clipping, Pax Newspaper Clippings, vol. 4; "Indian Congress," *Evening News*, 10 June 1900, clipping, Pax Newspaper Clippings, vol. 5; "Indian Congress Awarded," Buffalo *Courier*, 2 September 1900, clipping, Pax Newspaper Clippings, vol. 6; and William I. Buchanan to Executive Committee, 31 August 1900, Copybook, box 1, Buchanan Papers.

10. Robert Grant, "Notes on the Pan-American Exposition," *Cosmopolitan Magazine* 31 (1901):458.

11. Ibid.

12. John M. Carrère, "The Architectural Scheme," in *Art Handbook*, 14–17; *Pan American Exposition: Its Purpose and Its Plan* (Buffalo: Pan-American Exposition Company, 1900); Charles Y. Turner, "The Story of the Color Scheme for the Exposition," 22 June 1901, MS in Buchanan Papers, box 6. Joann Marie Thompson, "The Art and Architecture of the Pan-American Exposition, Buffalo, New York, 1901," 2 vols. (Ph.D. dissertation, Rutgers University, 1980).

13. For biographical information concerning Turner, see "Turner Will Paint the

Exposition City," *Courier*, 10 April 1900, clipping, Taylor Scrapbooks, vol. 2; "Charles Y. Turner, *Express*, 17 June 1900, clipping, Taylor Scrapbooks, vol. 2; and assorted clippings in "Charles Yardley Turner," New York Public Library, Art and Architecture Division, Artist File. Biographical information about Bitter is from John Milburn, "Karl Bitter: Exposition Builder," *Art and Progress* 6 (1915):305–8; Edward Hale Brush, "Karl Bitter: An Appreciation," ibid., 295–301; and Oswald G. Villard, "Karl Bitter: Immigrant," ibid., 310–12. On the development of the coloring plan see C. Y. Turner, "Report of the Director of Color," 22 June 1901, MS, Buchanan Papers, box. 6.

14. John M. Carrère, "The Architectural Scheme," in *Art Handbook*, 16, UCLA, 344/1, box 1.

15. Turner, "Story of the Color Scheme for the Exposition."

16. *Pan-American Exposition: Its Purpose and Its Plan*.

17. Frank Edwin Elwell, "The Pan-American Exposition," *Arena* 25 (1901):53–58; "Its Splendors Are Not Exaggerated," *Evening News*, 14 July 1901, clipping, Pax Newspaper Clippings, vol. 14; Mabel E. Barnes, "Peeps at the Exposition," 1:4, 19, in BHS, Mabel E. Barnes Papers (cited hereafter as Barnes Papers); Christian Brinton, "Art at the Pan-American Exposition," *Critic* 38 (1901):520. Claude Bragdon, "Some Pan-American Impressions," *American Architecture and Building News* 72 (1901):43–44; Julian Hawthorne, "Some Novelties at the Buffalo Fair," *Cosmopolitan Magazine* 31 (1901):486. Maurice F. Newton, "The Pan-American Exposition: The Color Scheme," *American Architect and Building News* 71 (1901):4; Amos K. Fiske, "An Exposition as a Work of Art," *Harper's Weekly* 45 (9 March 1901):272–77.

18. Mabie, "Spirit of the New World as Interpreted by the Pan-American Exposition," 546; Herbert Croly, "Some Novel Features of the Pan-American Exposition: Impressions and Opinions," *Architectural Record* 11 (1901):592; "Pan-American Color Scheme," *New York Times*, 28 April 1901, 7.

19. "Exposition's Ethnology Building," *Enquirer*, 4 March 1901, clipping, Pax Newspaper Clippings, vol. 8. See also Richard H. Barry, *The Grandeur of the Exposition* (Buffalo: Robert Allen Reid Publisher, 1901).

20. C. Y. Turner, "Coloring and Decorating the Pan-American Exposition," *Quarterly Bulletin of the American Institute of Architects* 2 (1901):163; Minnie J. Reynolds, "Exposition as an Educator," *New York Times*, 6 October 1901, 24.

21. "For the Pan-American," *Express*, 20 May 1900, clipping, Pax Newspaper Clippings, vol. 5; A. L. Benedict to Aleš Hrdlička, 21 July 1900, BHS, A. L. Benedict Papers, box 2 (cited hereafter as Benedict Papers); "Dr. A. L. Benedict," *Pan-American Herald* 2 (May 1900): 23; [Benedict] to Buchanan, 16 April 1901, BHS, Records of the Department of Ethnology, box 63; "Ethnological Department," *World's Fair Bulletin* 2 (October 1900):5; and Richard Rathbun to Benedict, 8 August 1900, Benedict Papers, box 1.

22. [Benedict] to Buchanan, 16 April 1901, Records of the Department of Ethnology, box 63.

23. Ibid. See also [Benedict], "Report in Regard to Register [*sic*]," ibid.

24. *Pan-American Exposition: Report of William I. Buchanan, Director-General* (Buffalo, 1901), 53–54, UCLA, 344/1, box 1.

25. E. R. Rice, F. W. Taylor, and John B. Weber to the Board of Management,

United States Government Exhibit, Pan-American Exposition, 9 October 1899, SIA, RU 70, box 47; "Memorandum of Action Taken by the Board of Management, United States Government Exhibit, Pan-American Exposition, 1901, on the Proposition Submitted by the Management of the Exposition at Buffalo, for a Special Governmental Display of Exhibits from Cuba, Puerto Rico, Alaska, Hawaii and the Philippine Islands, Showing the Products, Resources, and Possibilities of these Possessions, and Particularly the Ethnological Features Available," n.d., in SIA, RU 70, box 47 (cited hereafter as "Memorandum of Action Taken").

26. William I. Buchanan to J. H. Brigham, 5 December 1899, SIA, RU 70, box 47.

27. "Memorandum of Action Taken"; W. de C. Ravenal, "Minutes of the Meeting of the Special Committee Appointed to Consider the Proposed Colonial Village Exhibit at the Buffalo Exposition," 7 December 1899, SIA, RU 70, box 47.

28. "Memorandum of Action Taken."

29. Biographical information about Hilder is derived from "Necrology—Frank Frederick Hilder," in *Twenty-second Annual Report of the Bureau of American Ethnology to the Secretary of the Smithsonian Institution: 1900–1901, Part I* (Washington, D.C.: Government Printing Office, 1901), xl–xlii; William E. Curtis to Samuel P. Langley, 11 November 1897, SIA, RU 189, "Assistant Secretary in Charge, United States National Museum, 1860–1908," box 27, folder 8; "Filipino Relics," *Commercial*, 21 September 1900, clipping, Pax Newspaper Clippings, vol. 6; "Pan-American Exposition," *Black Diamond Express* 2 (February 1900):15–16.

30. "Memorandum for Frank F. Hilder, Special Agent of the Government Board of Management for the Philippine Islands," SIA, RU 70, box 47; J. B. Guthrie to Assistant Adjutant-General and Chief Quartermaster, United States Army, Manila, 8 January 1900, SIA, RU 70, box 47.

31. William Henry Holmes, "Instructions for Collecting Ethnological Material in the Philippine Islands for the Buffalo Exposition," 22 January 1900, SIA, RU 70, box 47.

32. F. F. Hilder to F. W. True, 4 April 1900, SIA, RU 70, box 47; Hilder to True, 31 March 1900, SIA, RU 70, box 47; "Prices of Commodities and Rates of Wages in Manila," *Bulletin of the Department of Labor*, no. 32 (January 1901):29–42, clipping, in National Archives, Record Group 350, Records of the Bureau of Insular Affairs, General Classified Files, no. 1937; *San Francisco Chronicle*, 2 June 1900, clipping, in SIA, RU 70, box 47; "National Activity," *Pan-American Herald* 2 (June 1900):14–15; Hilder to True, 4 April 1900, SIA, RU 70, box 47. For general descriptions of the materials Hilder collected, see D. O. Noble Hoffman, "The Philippine Exhibit at the Pan-American Exposition," *National Geographic Magazine* 12 (March 1901):119–22. Also indispensable is Hilder's massive catalog of the display—an exhibit that eventually wound its way into the collections of the Smithsonian Institution. See the "Original Catalog of Frank Hilder for the Board of Management, United States Government Exhibit, Pan-American Exposition, 1901," in National Anthropology Archives (cited hereafter as NAA), United States National Museum, Division of Ethnology, Pamphlet and Manuscript File, box 67.

33. "Exhibits from Outlying Possessions," [summary of minutes], n.d., SIA, RU 70, box 47 (cited hereafter as "Exhibits from Outlying Possessions"); Arthur Goodrich, "Short Stories of Interesting Exhibits," *World's Work* 2 (1901):1085,

UCLA, 344/1, box 1; [Richard Rathbun?], "Expositions in Which the National Museum Has Participated," 92, SIA, RU 55, Assistant Secretary in Charge of the United States National Museum 1897–1917 (Richard Rathbun) Records, box 19, folder 9; and *New Orleans Picayune*, 8 June 1901, clipping, in NAA, Division of Ethnology, Pamphlet and Manuscript File, box 70.

34. "Exhibits from Outlying Possessions," SIA, RU 70, box 47; F. W. Clarke, "The Government Exhibit at Buffalo," *Forum* 31 (1901):654–60; and Goodrich, 1057.

35. "Report to the Concessions Committee," 12 September 1900, Letterbook of the Minutes of the Concession Committee, 66, Taylor Papers; "Great Rush for Concessions," *Pan-American Herald* 1 (July 1899):4; Buchanan to Brigham, 5 December 1899, SIA, RU 70, box 47; "National Activity," *Pan-American Herald* 2 (June 1900):14–15; "Filipino Concession Has Been Let," *Evening News*, n.d., clipping, Pax Newspaper Clippings, vol. 6; "Filipinos," *Express*, 12 November 1900, clipping, ibid., vol. 15; "Filipinos Managed by a Versatile Genius," *Courier*, 29 July 1901, clipping, ibid.; Pony Moore, "Pan-American Filipinos," *Express*, 18 November 1900, clipping, ibid., vol. 7; and Pony Moore, "Pan-American Filipinos," *Illustrated Express*, 1 January 1901, clipping, Taylor Scrapbooks, vol. 5.

36. Moore, "Pan-American Filipinos"; Minnie J. Reynolds, "Exposition as an Educator," *New York Times*, 6 October 1901, 24; Frederick Starr diary, 1901, University of Chicago, Department of Special Collections, Frederick Starr Papers, box 29; "Filipino to Be Christened," *Courier*, 3 July 1901, clipping, Pax Newspaper Clippings, vol. 13.

37. "Filipino Characteristics," *Pan-American Herald* 2 (July 1900):10–11; Richard H. Barry, *Snap Shots on the Midway of the Pan-American Exposition* (Buffalo: Robert Allen Reid Publisher, 1901), 83.

38. "Funny but Not Practical," editorial, *Evening News*, 1 April 1901, 2; "Midway to Close in Burst of Fun," *Courier*, 2 November 1901; and "Barren and Deserted Where Once Spieler's Cries Filled the Air," *Courier*, 3 November 1901, clippings, Pax Newspaper Clippings, vol. 23; "Filipino Woman Dies at Hospital of Consumption," *Courier*, 22 October 1901, clipping, Pax Newspaper Clippings, vol. 22.

39. Finley P. Dunne, "Mr. Dooley on the Midway," *Cosmopolitan Magazine* 21 (1901):476; Frederick W. Taylor, "Exhibits That Might Have Been," *Everybody's Magazine* 5 (October 1901):406; J. W. Buel, ed., *Louisiana and the Fair: An Exposition of the World, Its People, and Their Achievements*, 10 vols. (Saint Louis: World's Progress Publishing Company, 1904), 4:1270; Taylor, "Exhibits That Might Have Been," 416; Mary Bronson Hart, "The Play-Side of the Fair," *World's Work* 2 (1901):1099; and Frederick W. Taylor, "The Picturesque Midway," in *Art Handbook*, 81, UCLA, 344/1, box 1.

40. "Slavery Proposed for Pan American," *Courier*, 25 March 1900, clipping, Pax Newspaper Clippings, vol. 5; "Met in Buffalo," *Evening News*, 23 September 1900, clipping, ibid.; Buchanan to the Executive Committee, 22 March, 1901, Letterbook 3, Buchanan Papers, box 1; "Briefs of Pan-American Concession Contracts," 52–53, Taylor Papers, box 5 (cited hereafter as "Briefs of Pan-American Concession Contracts"); "Going after the Native Africans," *Courier*, 13 October 1900, clipping, Pax Newspaper Clippings, vol. 6; *Darkest Africa: Real African Life in a Real African*

Village [souvenir guide], n.d., in BHS, "Scientific Exhibits," vertical file. See also "An African Village: Ethnological Exhibit to Be of Great Interest," *Express*, 31 March 1901, clipping, Pax Newspaper Clippings, vol. 9.

41. *Darkest Africa;* Reynolds, "Exposition as an Educator," 24; Barry, *Snap Shots on the Midway*, 72–73.

42. "Briefs of Pan-American Concession Contracts," 25; Barry, *Snap Shots on the Midway*, 125–26.

43. "Plantation Most Delightful Feature," *Courier*, 11 April 1901, clipping, Pax Newspaper Clippings, vol. 9; Barry, *Snap Shots on the Midway*, 125–26; "Briefs of Pan-American Concession Contracts," 25; "Big Jim Parker Says He Saved the President from Death," *Evening News*, 9 September 1901, Pax Newspaper Clippings, vol. 19. Biographical information about Parker is from A. Wesley Johns, *The Man Who Shot McKinley* (New York: A. S. Barnes, 1970), 71.

44. "Briefs of Pan-American Concession Contracts," 39; Buchanan to Executive Committee, 26 March 1900, Letterbook 3, Buchanan Papers, box 1; "Romantic Policemen of Mexico," [*Enquirer?*], 10 April 1901, clipping, Pax Newspaper Clippings, vol. 9; Paul J. Vanderwood, "Mexico's Rurales: Reputation versus Reality," *Americas* 34 (1977):102–12; "Streets of Mexico, Pan-American," *Evening News*, 13 January 1901, clipping, Pax Newspaper Clippings, vol. 8; and "Briefs of Pan-American Concession Contracts," 39.

45. *Mexico, Old and New: A Souvenir of the "Streets of Mexico,"* n.d., BHS, "Special Events," vertical file; Barry, *Snap Shots on the Midway*, 60; "Mexican Village Too Prim," *Enquirer*, 9 May 1901, clipping, Pax Newspaper Clippings, vol. 10; "Latin Americans Unite for Harmony at Pan-American," *Buffalo Times*, 12 April 1901, clipping, ibid., vol. 9.

46. Thomas Fleming, *Around the Pan with Uncle Hank: His Trip through the Pan-American Exposition* (New York: Nut Shell Publishing Company, 1901), 196–97; Mary Bronson Hart, "How to See the Pan-American Exposition," *Everybody's Magazine* 5 (1901):491; Barry, *Snap Shots on the Midway*, 20; Fleming, 79.

47. Barry, *Snap Shots on the Midway*, 27; Frederick T. Cummins, *Historical Biography and Libretto of the Indian Congress* (no imprint), 25–26, in California State University, Fresno, Department of Special Collections, Expositions and Fairs Collection; "Old Neighbors: An Exposition Study," drawing by L. D. Johnson, *Express*, 19 May 1901, clipping, Pax Newspaper Clippings, vol. 11.

48. *Official Catalogue and Guide Book to the Pan-American Exposition*, 53; "Esau: The Man Monkey," *Evening News*, 3 June 1901, clipping, Pax Newspaper Clippings, vol. 13; and, Barnes, "Peeps at the Exposition," 2:6–7.

49. Roswell Park, "Report of the Medical Department of the Pan-American Exposition," in W. I. Buchanan, "Report of the Director General," vol. 2, Buchanan Papers; and "Hard on Eskimo," *Commercial*, 8 May 1901, clipping, Pax Newspaper Clippings, vol. 10; Fleming, 15.

50. Hart, "Play-Side of the Fair," 1097; Barnes, "Peeps at the Exposition," 2:122–27; Hart, "Play-Side of the Fair," 1097; Frances A. Groff, "Exposition Moths," *Sunset* 35 (July 1915):135.

51. Johns, 13–273; Charles Sumner Olcott, *The Life of William McKinley*, 2 vols. (Boston: Houghton Mifflin Company, 1916), 2:312–33; Howard Wayne Morgan,

William McKinley and His America (Syracuse: Syracuse University Press, 1964),
509–25; "Senator Depew Talks of Nation's Railways," *New York Times,* 29
September 1901, 24.

52. "President McKinley Favors Reciprocity," *New York Times,* 25 September
1901, 1; "Midway Was Opened," *Express,* 8 September 1901, 13.

53. "Do Not Neglect the Fair," editorial, *Express,* 25 September 1901, 4; "Hail
and Farewell," ibid., 16 September 1901, clipping, Taylor Scrapbooks, vol. 6;
"Table Showing Paid-Free and Total Admissions as per Turnstile Readings," Taylor
Scrapbooks, vol. 7. The figure of two million is an approximation and is derived from
the attendance figures given in the *Express,* 4 September and 2 November 1901;
"Midway Was Opened," *Express,* 8 September 1901, 13; "Railroad Day," ibid., 29
September 1901, 13; "Crowds Throng to See M'Kinley's Picture in Floor," *Courier,* 2
October 1901, clipping, Pax Newspaper Clippings, vol. 21; and "New York Day at
the Pan-American," *New York Times,* 10 October 1901, 7.

54. Selim H. Peabody [superintendent of the Department of Liberal Arts at the
Pan-American Exposition], quoted in Charles Edward Lloyd, "The Pan-American
Exposition as an Educational Force," *Chautauquan* 33 (1901):335.

Chapter Six

1. David R. Francis, "Response at a Reception Given at Merchant's Exchange, on
Return from European Tour, March 23rd, 1903," in *A Tour of Europe in Nineteen
Days: Report to the Board of Directors of the Louisiana Purchase Exposition on
European Tour, Made in the Interest of the St. Louis Fair, by David R. Francis,
President* (no imprint), in the Beinecke Library, Yale University; opening day speech
by David R. Francis, quoted in "Educational Value of the World's Fair," *Literary
Digest* 29 (13 August 1904):192; "Meet Me in St. Louis, Louis," words by Andrew B.
Sterling, music by Kerry Mills, in James J. Geller, *Famous Songs and Their Stories*
(New York: Macauley Company, 1931), 241–44.

2. For reference to visitors and their notebooks, see H. Phillips Fletcher, *The St.
Louis Exhibition, 1904* (London: B. T. Batsford, 1905), 79. See also "How to See the
World's Fair," *St. Louis Globe-Democrat,* 15 May 1904, 2; "Educational Value of the
World's Fair," 192; [untitled clipping], in Smithsonian Institution Archives, Record
Unit 70, Exposition Records of the Smithsonian Institution and the United States
National Museum, 1875–1916, box 63 (cited hereafter as SIA, RU 70); A. W.
Coates, "American Scholarship Comes of Age: The Louisiana Purchase Exposition of
1904," *Journal of the History of Ideas* 22 (1961):404–17; and Edo McCullough,
World's Fair Midways: An Affectionate Account . . . (New York: Exposition Press,
1966), 71.

3. "Opening of the St. Louis Fair," *Harper's Weekly* 48 (30 April 1904):665;
Slocum, quoted in "Educational Value of the World's Fair," 192. Financial
information about the fair is provided by J. W. Buel, ed., *Louisiana and the Fair: An
Exposition of the World, Its People, and Their Achievements,* 10 vols. (Saint Louis:
World's Progress Publishing Company, 1904), 4:1292–98.

4. Brief biographical accounts of exposition officials are available in *World's Fair
Immortals* (Saint Louis: Cartoonists' Club, 1905), in UCLA, Department of Special
Collections, Expositions and Fairs Collection, 344/3, box 2 (cited hereafter as UCLA,
344/3). Other relevant information about the history, organization, and financial

backing of the fair is provided by Edmund S. Hoch, "The Universal Exposition of 1904," in *Official Catalogue of Exhibits: Section II* (Saint Louis: Official Catalogue Company, 1904), 29–34, in UCLA, 344/3, box 1.

5. Buel, 4:1396–1409. See also *Official Catalogue of Exhibits: Section II*, 39, in UCLA, 344/3, box 1 (italics omitted); Charles H. Hughes, "The Louisiana Purchase Exposition: The Neurasthenic and the Brain-Tired," *Alienist and Neurologist*, reprint, n.d., 1–18, esp. 8–12, in UCLA, 344/3, box 3.

6. Fletcher, 78; "Mrs. Kate Chopin, the St. Louis Authoress, Dead," *St. Louis Globe-Democrat*, 23 August 1904, 13; Thomas Wolfe, *Look Homeward, Angel: A Story of the Buried Life* (New York: Charles Scribner's Sons, 1929), 46; Ellis Parker Butler, "The Feet of the Detwilers: A Tale of Cousin Carrie and the Louisiana Purchase Exposition," *Leslie's Monthly Magazine* 68 (1904):413–18; [?] to M. L. Richmond, n.d.; [?] to Gladys Johnson, 20 July 1904; and Roy [?] to Miss Artye Stose [?], 13 October 1904, postcards, in UCLA, box 344/3, box 2. See also Joe Mitchell Chapple, "Affairs at Washington," *National Magazine* 20 (1904):605–8.

7. "Director F. J. V. Skiff Tells of Great Work," *Atlanta Journal*, 30 April 1904, clipping, in Colorado Heritage Center, Frederick James Volney Skiff Scrapbooks, 2:17 (cited hereafter as Skiff Scrapbooks); Skiff, "Introduction," in Buel, 9:vii–viii; Fletcher, 77, provides the figure of two hundred strikes, but this may be a low estimate. F. B. Thurber, president of the United States Export Association, stated that one contractor alone "had one hundred and fifty strikes." See *Official Proceedings of the Fifteenth Session of the Trans-Mississippi Commercial Congress Held at St. Louis* (Denver: Smith-Brooks Company, 1904), 61. See also "Notable Address by Skiff," *Denver Times*, 7 June 1905, clipping, Skiff Scrapbooks, 2:583.

8. "Notable Address by Skiff"; Skiff, "The Universal Exposition" Makeesport, Pennsylvania *Journal*, 27 April 1904, clipping in Skiff Scrapbooks, 2:17.

9. Frederic W. Lehmann to D. R. Francis, 31 August 1901, in Library of Congress, Manuscripts Division, W J McGee Papers, box 3, folder F (cited hereafter as McGee Papers). See also the newspaper clippings from the *St. Louis Globe-Democrat*, 18 April 1901, 25 April 1901, and from the Saint Louis *Republic*, 28 April 1901, noting the decision made by the directors to make anthropology a significant part of the fair, in McGee Papers, box 2; and Frederick Ward Putnam to F. W. Lehmann, McGee papers, box 9, O–P folder. See also "Minutes of the Executive Committee of the Louisiana Purchase Exposition Company, May 28, 1901–November 2, 1901," 3 August 1901 entry, in Missouri Historical Society, Louisiana Purchase Exposition Collection (cited hereafter as MHS, LPX.).

10. Biographical details about McGee are derived from Curtis M. Hinsley, *Savages and Scientists: The Smithsonian Institution and the Development of American Anthropology, 1846–1910* (Washington, D.C.: Smithsonian Institution Press, 1981), 231–56; Whitney R. Cross, "W J McGee and the Idea of Conservation," *Historian* 15 (1953):148–62; and Michael James Lacey, "The Mysteries of Earth-Making Dissolve: A Study of Washington's Intellectual Community and the Origins of American Environmentalism in the Late Nineteenth Century" (Ph.D. dissertation, George Washington University, 1979), 284–342.

11. W J McGee, "The Trend of Human Progress," *American Anthropologist*, n.s., 1 (July 1899):401–47, esp. 403, 410–11, 413. I am also relying on the discussion of McGee's racial philosophy presented by John S. Haller, Jr., in *Outcasts from*

Evolution: Scientific Attitudes of Racial Inferiority, 1859–1900 (New York: McGraw-Hill, 1975), 102–8.

12. McGee, "Trend of Human Progress," 446, 414. McGee's proposals attracted the attention of Hinton Rowan Helper, apologist for antebellum slavery and ardent advocate of colonization. Helper commended McGee for his "latest contribution to a high order of science and literature" but objected to any suggestion of racial intermingling. See Helper to McGee, 28 August 1899 and 9 October 1899, McGee Papers, box 5, folder H.

13. McGee, "National Growth and National Character," address before the National Geographic Society, 28 March 1899, 19–21, copy of page proofs in McGee Papers, box 27.

14. Haller, 104.

15. McGee, "Trend of Human Progress," 42.

16. For McGee's criticism of earlier fairs, see McGee to Lehmann, 8 August 1901, McGee Papers, box 7, folder K–L; and McGee to Henry E. Dosch, 6 August 1904, McGee Papers, box 19.

17. "Prof. W J M'Gee," *World's Fair Bulletin* 4 (August 1903):29; McGee, "Anthropology," in *Louisiana Purchase Centennial: Dedication Ceremonies, St. Louis, U.S.A., April 30th and May 1st–2nd, 1903* (no imprint), 41, in California State University, Fresno, Department of Special Collections, Expositions and Fairs Collection (cited hereafter as *Louisiana Purchase Centennial Dedication Ceremonies*); McGee, "Anthropology," 43; McGee, "Anthropology and Its Larger Problems," an address at the Louisiana Purchase Exposition, n.d., 20, McGee Papers, box 27; "McGee," *Post-Dispatch*, 17 July 1904, magazine supplement. Guidebooks and popular descriptions of the exhibit kept McGee's message before fairgoers. See, for instance, McGee, "Department of Anthropology," in *Official Catalogue of Exhibits, Universal Exposition, St. Louis, 1904* (Saint Louis: Official Catalogue Company, [1904]), 9–10, 73, UCLA, 344/3, box 1; *Laird's and Lee's Standard Pocket Guide and Time Saver* (Chicago: Laird and Lee Publishers, 1904), 34; and McGee, "The Anthropology Exhibit," *Harper's Weekly* 48 (April 1904):683.

18. McGee, "Anthropology Exhibit," 683.

19. McGee, "Anthropology," 41; McGee, "Introduction," in Buel, 5:xv.

20. For Aleš Hrdlička's role in planning the anthropometry section see [Hrdlička?] to McGee, 23 February 1904; McGee to Richard Rathbun, 26 February 1904; and [Otis T. Mason] to Rathbun, 8 March 1904, in SIA, Record Unit 192, United States National Museum Permanent Administration Files, 1877, (1902–35), 1975, box 39. See also McGee to Hrdlička, 12 April 1904, National Anthropology Archives, Aleš Hrdlička Papers, box 7, McGee folder (cited hereafter as Hrdlička Papers). For a discussion of Boas's role and a discussion of the laboratories, see George W. Stocking, Jr., "Franz Boas and the Culture Concept in Historical Perspective," *American Anthropologist* 68 (1966):873–74. Boas, in a letter to C. E. Hulbert, 5 October 1901, informed the exposition management that he would help with the anthropological exhibit, in McGee Papers, box 1. Two and one half years later Boas informed McGee that he might be able to help him obtain several Eskimos for display. See Boas to McGee, 5 March 1904, McGee Papers, box 19. Additional insight concerning Boas's involvement in physical anthropology is provided by J. R.

Pole, *The Pursuit of Equality in American History* (Berkeley and Los Angeles: University of California Press, 1978), 238–41.

21. Robert S. Woodworth to McGee, 12 January 1904, and attached transcript, McGee Papers, box 19; McGee, "Monthly Report," 30 June 1904, McGee Papers, box 16; "Jury Correspondence," undated MS in McGee Papers, box 19; Frank Bruner, "The Hearing of Primitive Peoples," *Archives of Psychology*, no. 11, and Clark Wissler, "Review of Bruner," *American Anthropologist* 10 (1908), as quoted'by Stocking, 874. The jurors selected specifically to evaluate the Anthropology Department formed a distinguished cast of scientists and included Boas, Hrdlička, J. M. K. Cattell, Alice Fletcher, Joseph Jastrow, G. Stanley Hall, Putnam, George A. Dorsey, Alfred L. Kroeber, and Alice Palmer Henderson. See "Commission Confirms Long Jury List," *St. Louis Globe-Democrat*, 21 August 1904, 11.

22. Hrdlička to Livingston Farrand, 27 May 1904, Hrdlička Papers, box 5, Fa–Fo misc. folder; and Hrdlička to George S. Huntington, 25 April 1904, ibid., box 20, Huntington folder. See also *St. Louis Globe-Democrat*, 29 March 1904, in MHS vertical files. Anthropologists were not the only ones expecting the deaths of villagers. George E. Pond, the assistant quartermaster-general, informed Clarence Edwards, chief of the Bureau of Insular Affairs, that a plot large enough to contain forty graves was set aside in the National Cemetery of the Jefferson Barracks in Saint Louis. See Pond to Edwards, 18 July 1904, National Archives, Record Group 350, Records of the Bureau of Insular Affairs, General Classified Files, no. 10669-1 (cited hereafter as RBIA, RG 350). See also Mason, "Report on Department of Anthropology for the Year 1904–1905," MS, SIA, RG 158, USNM Curators Annual Reports, box 26, folder 16. Quite possibly the brains Hrdlička obtained were from the three Igorots who died of pneumonia. See A. L. Lawshe to Edwards, 28 March 1905, RBIA RG 350, General Classified Files, no. 10699-3.

23. For information concerning Starr's expedition to Japan, consult Buel, 5:1698–1701, and McGee to Hajima Ota, 12 January 1904, University of Chicago, Department of Special Collections, Frederick Starr Papers, box 2, folder 7. R. Berkeley Miller, "Anthropology and Institutionalization: Frederick Starr at the University of Chicago, 1892–1923," *Kroeber Anthropology Papers*, no. 51–52 (1978):49–60.

Starr, like many other anthropologists, was approached by the directors of the fair at an early stage in the planning of the Anthropology Department, and he offered a continuing stream of suggestions concerning the development of the department. In a letter to C. E. Hulbert, 17 August 1901, McGee Papers, box 11, folder S, Starr stated that he was "heartily in favor of such a congress of uncultured Peoples." See also Starr to McGee, 22 January 1904, McGee Papers, box 20; "Announcement to Students," n.d., McGee Papers, box 19; McGee to A. J. Smith [manager of the Cliff Dwellers exhibit], 2 September 1904, McGee Papers, box 19; and Rose Marion, "Chicago Co-eds Who Hitched Their Wagon to Prof. Starr Are Finding Anthropology a Live Study at World's Fair," *Post-Dispatch*, 11 September 1904, 1; "Starr to Guide Co-eds," *Post-Dispatch*, 31 August 1904, 1; "Co-eds Know All about Poor Lo," *Post-Dispatch*, 1 September 1904, 4; "Chicago Co-eds Will Study Pike People," *Globe-Democrat*, 28 August 1904, 9; and "Fair as Textbook for Fair Co-eds," *Post-Dispatch*, 30 August 1904, 9. A $5,000 gift by an anonymous donor to Columbia

University to help pay students' expenses to the fair underscores the educational value attributed to the exposition. See *Programme of Dedication Exercises, Montana State Building, Louisiana Purchase Exposition, World's Fair Grounds, St. Louis, Mo.* (Helena: Montana Historical Society, n.d.), 10.

24. McGee to J. E. Sullivan, 13 May 1904; McGee to Samuel M. McGowan, 13 May 1904; and, McGee to William P. Wilson, 13 May 1904, in McGee Papers, box 19; "Primitive Tribes to Meet in Interesting Athletic Contest," *St. Louis World,* 10 August 1904, 3; McGee to Sullivan, 18 August 1904, McGee Papers, box 19; "Moros Win Championship of Philippine Natives on Track," *St. Louis, Globe-Democrat,* 16 September 1904, 4; "Plan an Anthropology Meet," *St. Louis Globe-Democrat,* 3 July 1904, 9.

25. McGee, "Anthropology," 41, 43–44; Skiff to D. R. Francis, 28 September 1903, in "Minutes of the Executive Committee, 29 September 1903," MHS, LPX; William N. Swarthout, "A Descriptive Story of the Philippine Exhibit," in *Louisiana Purchase Centennial Dedication Ceremonies,* 43. A souvenir guide to the reservation makes abundant use of the term. See Alfred O. Newell, ed., *Philippine Exposition, World's Fair, St. Louis, 1904* (no imprint), in Denver Public Library, Western History Collection (cited hereafter as *Philippine Exposition*). The term "reservation" was used by the national press as well. See, for instance, Edmund Mitchell, "The Exposition as a Historical Museum," *World Today* 7 (1904):1193–1201.

26. "Philippine Exhibits Officially Dedicated," *St. Louis World,* 19 June 1904, 6. Wilson also claimed that the reservation "speaks for itself, being the largest and finest colonial exhibit ever made by any Government." See Wilson to Edwards, 21 October 1904, RBIA, RG 350, General Classified Files, no. 6683-22; Richard Drinnon, *Facing West: The Metaphysics of Indian-Hating and Empire Building* (New York: New American Library, 1980), 333–51.

27. C. H. Huttig to Elihu Root, 13 August 1901, RBIA, RG 350, General Classified Files, no. 3315. See also "Our Insular Possessions," *World's Fair Bulletin* 2 (September 1901):25; Taft, quoted in "The Philippines Display," *World's Fair Bulletin* 3 (May 1902):20. See also *Official Handbook of the Philippines and Catalogue of the Philippine Exhibit* (Manila: Bureau of Public Printing, 1903), 9–10; *Official Catalogue: Philippine Exhibits* (Saint Louis: Official Catalogue Company, 1904); *Report of the Philippine Exposition to the Louisiana Purchase Exposition and Official List of Awards . . .* (Saint Louis: Greeley Printery, 1904); and "An Act Creating a Commission to Secure, Organize, and Make an Exhibit of Philippine Products, Manufactures, Art, Ethnology, and Education at the Louisiana Purchase Exposition to Be Held at Saint Louis, in the United States, in Nineteen Hundred and Four," in SIA, RU 70, box 58. See also the Louisiana Purchase Exposition Scrapbooks, vol. 98, MHS, (cited hereafter as LPE Scrapbooks).

28. *A Resolution in Memory of William P. Wilson* (n.p., 1927), 6, in the Charles Van Pelt Library, University of Pennsylvania. This memorial provided most of the biographical data for my reconstruction of Wilson's career. See also "Dr. William Powell Wilson Dies, Founded Museum," *Philadelphia Evening Bulletin,* 12 May 1927, clipping, University of Pennsylvania Archives, Biographical File; and "Dr. W. P. Wilson," *World's Fair Bulletin* 3 (October 1902):23.

29. The history of the Commercial Museum can be gleaned from its published

annual reports. See, for instance, *Annual Report of the Philadelphia Commercial Museum for the Year 1907* (n.p., 1908), 8–15.

30. Information about Niederlein is taken from his autobiographical statement, "Niederlein's Positions and Services Rendered Aboard," MS, RBIA, RG 350, General Classified Files, no. 9330-11. See also "Dr. Niederlein's Exposition Record," *Justica*, n.d., clipping in ibid., no. 9330-11. Wilson is quoted in "Dr. Gustavo Niederlein," *World's Fair Bulletin* 3 (October 1902):30.

31. Consult Newell, *Philippine Exposition*. For information about the Philippine Commercial Museum and Preliminary Exposition, see Niederlein, "The Philippine Exposition in St. Louis," n.d., MS, RBIA, RG 350, General Classified Files, no. 3315-37; "Address of Mr. Gustavo Niederlein to the Provincial Governors at Their Official Reception at Ayuntamiento, December 15, 1903," ibid., no. 3315-213; Niederlein to Edwards, 3 April and 9 May 1901, ibid., nos. 3315-112 and 3315-113; S. B. Shirley to Edwards, 26 August 1902, ibid., no. 6211-1; Walter J. Ballard, "Museum of the Philippines," *Ohio Valley Manufacturer*, n.d., clipping, in ibid., no. 6211-10; Niederlein to [Rathbun?], SIA, RU 70, box 58; and "Address of Mr. Gustavo Niederlein to the Provincial Governors."

32. Niederlein, "Important Instructions to Bear in Mind in Making Philippine Exhibits," in *Circular Letter of Governor Taft* (Manila: Bureau of Public Printing, 1902), RBIA, RG 350, General Classified Files, no. 6111-3; "To Exhibit Man at the St. Louis Fair: Dr. McGee Gathering Types and Freaks from Every Land," *New York Times*, 1 November 1903, clipping, SIA, RU 70, box 64; and Newell, *Philippine Exposition*.

33. "Philippine Exhibits Officially Dedicated," *St. Louis World*, 19 June 1904, 6; "Teaching English to Sixty Nine Different Tribes," *Portland Oregonian*, 17 September 1905, 44. See also Francis to Taft, 15 May 1902, MHS, David R. Francis Collection.

34. Newell, *Philippine Exposition*. See also Buel, 4:1532–44.

35. Newell, *Philippine Exposition*.

36. Ibid. See also Buel, 5:1709–74; and Niederlein, "Office of the Philippine Government Board in the United States, for the Louisiana Purchase Exposition," 10 December 1904, RBIA, RG 350, General Classified Files, no. 3315-378. The arrangement of the exhibit is discussed by Buel, 4:1532–44, and is apparent in the drawing of the reservation in Newell, *Philippine Exposition*. The descriptions in the souvenir guidebook edited by Newell and in Buel's official history appear to be derived largely from Albert Ernest Jenks, "Native Races," in *Official Handbook: Description of the Philippines* (Manila: Bureau of Public Printing, 1903), 155–63, and from Jenks, "Anthropology," in *Official Catalogue: Philippine Exhibits*, 261–62.

37. Jenks, "Anthropology," 262.

38. Newell, *Philippine Exposition*; Buel, vol. 4, esp. 1540–44; "Hiram at the Fair," *St. Louis Globe-Democrat*, 24 June 1904, 8. The popularity of the reservation was apparent in many sources. See, for instance, Thomas H. Carter to Wilson, 25 June 1904, RBIA, RG 350, General Classified Files, no. 9640-8; "How the People Rush to See the Igorrotes before They Put Pants On," *Post-Dispatch*, 3 July 1904, 1; "All Roads Lead to Filipinos," *Post-Dispatch*, 1 May 1904, 6; and "The Cultural Features of the St. Louis Exposition," *Nation* 79 (22 December 1904): 499–500. The

nationwide awareness of the Igorot Village was assured by the massive publicity campaign undertaken by the exposition's publicity department and by the reservation's Department of Exploitation. A description of these publicity campaigns was provided by the Sioux Falls, South Dakota *Soo Critic*, 22 April 1904, clipping, in Skiff Scrapbooks, 2:12.

39. Alice Jenkins to Shirley and Mabel Miller, 18 October 1904, in Duke University, Perkins Library, Department of Special Collections, Joseph A. Miller Papers. The plank in the Democratic party platform of 1904 is quoted by Rubin Francis Weston, *Racism in American Imperialism* (Columbia: University of South Carolina Press, 1972), 115. For the clothing controversy, see Taft to Edwards, 23 June 1904, RBIA, RG 350, General Classified Files, no. 9640-3; Edwards to Taft, 23 June 1904, ibid., no. 9640-10; [?] Pepperman to Edwards, 24 June 1904, ibid., no. 9640-4; Charles Magoon to Edwards, 24 June 1904, ibid., no. 9640-5; and Edwards to Niederlein, 27 June 1904, ibid., no. 8640-6.

40. G. S. Johns to Herbert Stone, 29 June 1904, RBIA, RG 350, General Classified Files, no. 9640-22; [cartoon], *Post-Dispatch*, 3 July 1904, 1; Edwards to Wilson, 6 July 1904, RBIA, RG 350, General Classified Files, no. 9640-22; and "Igorrotes Not to Wear Breeches," *St. Louis Globe-Democrat*, 15 July 1904, 1. Edwards reported the following conversation with Roosevelt over the pants issue: " 'It is no pants.' The President has said so. The President took rather a more serious view of the objections than I did. With him the point was whether we were exploiting savagery to the detriment of civilization. I told him that we might as well put pants on a cow as on a Igorrote. He laughed, but his decision was made from the serious standpoint, nonetheless." Edwards, quoted in "Philippine Show May Be Fenced In," unidentified newspaper clipping, 28 July 1904, in Oregon Historical Society, Manuscripts Division, Lewis and Clark Centennial Exposition Collection, box 7, Office of President folder.

41. Newell, *Philippine Exposition;* Jenks, "Anthropology," 261–62; Buel, 5:1735; "Use Negritos to Kill Sparrows at the Fair," *St. Louis Globe-Democrat*, 12 June 1904, 8; Newell, *Philippine Exposition;* "Hints for Fair Visitors," *New York Post*, 2 July 1904, LPE Scrapbooks, vol. 196; "Filipinos Excite President's Praise," *St. Louis Globe-Democrat*, 27 November 1904, 6.

42. "Filipinos Become a Fad with Foolish Young Girls," *Post-Dispatch*, 3 July 1904; Wilson to Edwards, 9 July 1904, RBIA, RG 350, General Classified Files, no. 10032-37; "Scouts Lose First Battle with Marines," *Post-Dispatch*, 7 July 1904, 1; William Llewellyn Adams, *Exploits and Adventures of a Soldier Ashore and Afloat* (Philadelphia: J. B. Lippincott Company, 1911); "Jefferson Guard" entry, information files, MHS; and Edwards, "1st Endorsement," 12 July 1904, RBIA, RG 350, General Classified Files, no 10032-29. See also Herb Lewis, *Eb Peechcrap and Wife at the Fair* (New York: Neale Publishing Company, 1906), 206–7.

43. "The Philippines' New Era," *St. Louis Globe-Democrat*, 13 August 1904, 8; "Tribesmen for Fair," *Portland Oregonian*, 19 December 1904, 5; L. Payson Broad and H. S. Caswell-Broad to [?], 3 June 1904, in RBIA, RG 350, General Classified Files, no. 10736; and "The Talk of Washington," *New York Post*, 3 August 1904, LPE Scrapbooks, vol. 198.

44. Thomas R. MacMechen, "The True and Complete Story of the Pike and Its

Attractions," in *Louisiana Purchase Centennial Dedication Ceremonies*, 1; MacMechen, "Down 'the Pike,' the Boulevard of Gaiety at the St. Louis Exposition," *Pacific Monthly*, 12 (July 1904):30; and John A. Wakefield, Norris B. Gregg, and E. Norton White, "The Division of Concessions and Admissions," in *Louisiana Purchase Centennial Dedication Ceremonies*, 36.

45. "Concerning the Pike," *St. Louis World*, 20 January 1904, 5.

46. "Most Unique Parade in World's History Will Be Seen Here Next Week," *St. Louis World*, 21 April 1904, 2; "All Nations in the Pike Parade," *St. Louis Globe-Democrat*, 1 May 1904, 1; and "Truly Biggest Show That Ever Came over the Pike," *Post-Dispatch*, 1 May 1904, 3.

47. "Truly Biggest Show That Ever Came over the Pike," p. 3; "Terrible Battles of the Bloody Boer War," *St. Louis World*, 17 June 1904, 5; Walter Wellman, "The World's Fair as a Progress Promoter," *Success* (November 1904), clipping, in Skiff Scrapbooks, 2:40.

48. The best discussion of Japanese participation in this exposition is Neil Harris's "All the World a Melting Pot? Japan at American Fairs, 1876–1904," in *Mutual Images: Essays in American-Japanese Relations*, ed. Akira Iriye (Cambridge: Harvard University Press, 1975), 47–54. See also "Bringing Several Score of Chinese to Fair," *St. Louis Globe-Democrat*, 18 August 1904, 3; and Wellman, "World's Fair as a Progress Promoter." See also Irene E. Cortinovis, "China at the St. Louis Fair," *Missouri Historical Review* 72 (1977):59–66.

49. M. Carl Hundt, "Head of Anthropology Department of World's Fair," *Post-Dispatch*, 19 February 1904, 2; McGee, "Anthropology," in *Louisiana Purchase Centennial Dedication Ceremonies*, 42.

50. McGee's opinions are recorded in Buel, 5:1708. See also McGee, "The Beginnings of Civilization," *World Today* 7 (September 1904):1210–13; Frederick Starr, *The Ainu Group at the Saint-Louis Exposition* (Chicago: Open Court Publishing Company, 1904); "Mr. Dooley on the War in the Far East," *Post-Dispatch*, 28 August 1904, 1; Grace Griscom, "Some Quaint Little Ways of the Quaint Little Japs," *St. Louis World*, 29 May 1904, 12; Wellman, "World's Fair as a Progress Promoter"; E. P. Powell, "Some of the Reasons Why Americans Like the Japanese," *St. Louis Globe-Democrat*, 17 April 1904, supplement.

51. For descriptions of these exhibits, consult MacMechen, "True and Complete Story of the Pike and Its Attractions," 4, 18; MacMechen, "Down 'the Pike,' ", 31–32; and Stuart Seely Sprague, "Meet Me in St. Louis on the Ten-Million-Dollar Pike," *Missouri Historical Society Bulletin* 32 (1975):26–31.

52. *St. Louis Exposition 1904: Exhibit of American Federation of Labor . . . Catalogue of Exhibits* (no imprint), 14. A local labor newspaper summed up labor's discontent with the exposition: "Here we have a great World's Fair, built by the labor of the world. And in the World's Fair city thousands of people are waging a war of despair against poverty, misery, starvation. This is modern civilization!" See "The Citizen's Alliance World's Fair Opening [*sic*]" *Labor*, 23 April 1904, 1–2; Francis quoted in M. J. Lowenstein, *Official Guide to the Louisiana Purchase Exposition* (Saint Louis: Official Guide Company, 1904), 7–8.

53. Rolla and Francis, quoted in David R. Francis, *The Universal Exposition of 1904* (Saint Louis: Louisiana Purchase Exposition Company, 1913), 302, 304, vi; and "The Close of the St. Louis Exposition," *Midway* 1 (January 1905):12.

54. Questionnaires, transcripts, and tapes of oral interviews are in MHS, LPX, Oral History Collection; John Steinbeck, *The Grapes of Wrath* (New York: Viking Press, 1939), 120.

55. " 'All Aboard for Portland,' " *Post-Dispatch*, 20 November 1904, magazine supplement.

Chapter Seven

1. Paul Wessinger, A. L. Mills, and F. Dresser [subcommittee on the scope and site of the Lewis and Clark Centennial] to the Executive Committee, 5 July 1902, in ["Minutes of the Executive Committee"], MS, p. 13, Portland Public Library, John L. Wilson Room, Records of the Lewis and Clark Centennial (cited hereafter as Wilson Room). William Howard Taft, quoted in *Hearing before the Committee on Industrial Arts and Expositions of the House of Representatives: Alaska-Yukon Exposition, January 27, 1908* (Washington, D.C.: Government Printing Office, 1908), 12.

2. "Honors Brave Men," *Portland Oregonian*, 2 June 1905, 15; "James J. Hill Says Exposition Makes Unique Appeal," *Seattle Post-Intelligencer*, 2 June 1909, 1, 4.

3. E. Frances Bauer, "The Development of an Empire," *Music Trade Review, Special Edition: Lewis and Clark Exposition Number* 41 (30 September 1905):7, in Oregon Historical Society, Manuscripts Division, Records of the Lewis and Clark Centennial, box 1 (cited hereafter as OHS, LCX). The official emblem of the Seattle exposition appeared on many official documents and souvenirs. A postcard of the official seal can be found in University of California, Los Angeles, Department of Special Collections, Expositions and Fairs Collection, box 334/M (cited hereafter as UCLA, 344).

4. ["Minutes of the Executive Committee"], MS, 5 September 1902, 27, in the Wilson Room; "Portland Welcomes World to Her Great Exposition," *Oregon Daily Journal*, 1 June 1905, 1; "Hallie Ermine Rives' Impressions of Fair," *Portland Oregonian*, 3 September 1905, 48; *The World's Most Beautiful Exposition* (no imprint), in University of Washington, Pacific Northwest Collection, vertical file (cited hereafter as Northwest Collection); "The Lesson of the Fair," *Portland Oregonian*, 15 October 1905, 6; and "Portland Welcomes World to Her Great Exposition," *Oregon Daily Journal*, 1 June 1905, 1.

5. Hill quoted in *Seattle Post-Intelligencer*, 1 June 1909, 4. The importance of the depression backdrop to exposition planners was noted in Henry Reed's "Official History of the Lewis and Clark Centennial," MS, 1908, 30–34, MS 383B, microfilm in California State University, Fresno, Department of Special Collections (cited hereafter as CSUF) original in OHS. A recent history of the fair is Carl Abbott, *The Great Extravaganza: Portland and the Lewis and Clark Exposition* (Portland: Oregon Historical Society, 1981). See also John E. Chilberg, "The Organization and Management of the Business of the Alaska Yukon Pacific Exposition of 1909," MS, [1953], in University of Washington, Manuscripts Division, Miscellaneous Records of the Alaska-Yukon-Pacific Exposition, box 1 (cited hereafter as UW, MS Division).

6. Reed, "Official History of the Lewis and Clark Centennial," 30–34; and Dan McAllen to Reed, 2 May 1905, in University of Oregon, Oregon Collection, Robert

A. Miller Papers. See also Reed, "The Story of the Lewis and Clark Exposition to Date," *Pacific Monthly* 9 (January 1903):32–40.

7. Biographical information about Corbett is from Reed, "Official History of the Lewis and Clark Centennial," 57; and E. Kimbark MacColl, *The Shaping of a City: Business and Politics in Portland, Oregon, 1885–1915* (Portland: Georgian Press Company, 1976), 32, 35, 262–66, 480–82; Reed, "Official History of the Lewis and Clark Centennial," 1–89, 373–92; Reed, ibid., 386–89 also provides a brief sketch of Goode's career. The sign Goode donated to the exposition is noted in "A Generous Gift," *Lewis and Clark Journal* 1 (May 1904):7, in UCLA, 344/7.

8. "Club Endorses the Alaska Exposition," *Seattle Post-Intelligencer*, 30 July 1905, 11; William M. Sheffield, "Work of the Alaska Club," *Alaska-Yukon Magazine* 2 (October 1906):106–7; Reed quoted in *Hearing before the Committee on Industrial Arts and Expositions of the House of Representatives, January 27, 1908*, 25.

Biographical information is from Frank L. Merrick, "Alaska-Yukon-Pacific Exposition," *Alaska-Yukon Magazine* 2 (September 1906):2–7. For other details on the financing of the fair, see "How Railroads Help the Fair," editorial, *Seattle Post-Intelligencer*, 22 June 1909, 6; Will R. Parry and William Sheffield to F. G. Whitaker, 22 September 1906, in UW, MS Division, F. G. Whitaker Papers, box 1, folder 4; and Frank L. Merrick, "Financing of the Alaska-Yukon-Pacific Exposition," *Alaska-Yukon Magazine* 2 (November 1906):117–22. Henry Reed, in his statement in *Hearing before the Committee on Industrial Arts and Expositions*, 23, provided a breakdown of stock subscriptions showing that three subscribers owned $75,000 worth of stock while 2,595 subscribers held only $56,400 worth of the exposition issue. Names of the stockholders were listed in the *Secretary's Report, A.-Y.-P. Exposition* (no imprint), in the Northwest Collection. See also Barry J. McMahon, "Seattle's Commercial Aspiration as Expressed in the Alaska-Yukon-Pacific Exposition" (M.A. thesis, Washington State University, 1960), 8–49; and George A. Frickman, "Alaska-Yukon-Pacific Exposition, 1909," *Pacific Northwest Quarterly* 53 (1962):89–99.

9. "Strike Situation at the Lewis and Clark Exposition Grounds," *Portland Labor Press*, 10 March 1905, 1, 3, provided a retrospective view of labor turmoil at the fair and is the source for the quotation. See also "Fight Started against the Fair," *Oregon Daily Journal*, 2 May 1903, 8, which noted the understanding organized labor believed it had reached with the directors; and "Organized Workers May Fight the Fair," *Oregon Daily Journal*, 21 April 1903, 1.

10. "Farmers Fighting the Fair," *Oregon Daily Journal*, 17 March 1903, 1; "A Conference Is Suggested," *Oregon Daily Journal*, 5 May 1903, 3. At about the same time, rural areas in Oregon voted between 15 and 25 percent socialist. See Jeff Johnson, "The Heyday of Oregon's Socialists," *Northwest Magazine* (19 December 1976):15–18, clipping, OHS, vertical file, Socialist Labor Party folder.

11. "Organized Workers May Fight the Fair," *Oregon Daily Journal*, 21 April 1903, 1; and, "Fight Started against Fair," ibid., 2 May 1903, 8; Henry Kundert to George E. Shaver, 18 November 1904, attached to Reed to H. W. Goode, 8 March 1905, in OHS, LCX, box 7, President's Correspondence folder.

12. Kundert to Shaver, 18 November 1904; "Are in Favor of a 1905 Fair," *Oregon Daily Journal*, 6 May 1903, 5, notes the divided feelings about the fair among union members.

13. Kundert to Shaver, 18 November 1904; "Report of President Samuel Gompers to the Twenty-fourth Annual Convention of the American Federation of Labor, at San Francisco, Calif.," *American Federationist* 11 (1904):1087.

14. Reed to Goode, 8 March 1905; "Strike Situation at the Lewis and Clark Exposition Grounds," *Portland Labor Press,* 10 March 1905, 1, 3; Reed, "Official History of the Lewis and Clark Centennial," 174. Reed stated: "Labor troubles were not serious. The policy of the exposition corporation from beginning to end was the open shop, but it did not discriminate against union labor. Believing that well paid and contented workmen are as good an asset as any city can have, the corporation paid fair wages," ibid., 172–73.

15. "Strike Situation at the Lewis and Clark Grounds," *Portland Labor Press,* 10 March 1905, 1, 3; "The A. Y. P. and the Class Struggle," Seattle *Socialist,* 1 May 1909; "Progress on the Unfair A.-Y.-P. Fair," *Seattle Union Record,* 8 August 1908; M. W. O'Shea, "Opening Day at the A.-Y.-P.-E.," *Seattle Union Record,* 5 June 1909, 1. The exposition was put on the unfair list in 1908 and again in 1909 by the State Federation of Labor according to "A.Y.P.E. Boycott to Stay in Effect," *Seattle Post-Intelligencer,* 9 January 1909, 2.

16. Theodore Hardee [form letter], 27 June 1905, attached to [Hardee] to General Press Bureau, 5 July 1905, OHS, LCX, box 21, Special Events folder. Hardee observed in the letter dated 5 July that at Saint Louis "these big [industrial] concerns felt that they were being amply repaid for their generosity and expense incidental thereto from the increased value of their wage earners through a visit to the exposition."

17. "Workingmen's Day," editorial, *Oregon Daily Journal,* 3 August 1905, 4; "Toilers Throng Exposition," *Oregon Daily Journal,* 3 August 1905, 3; and "Workingmen at Fair," Portland *Evening Telegram,* 26 July 1905, 5. The idea for a Workingmen's Day seems to have originated with John A. Wakefield, who assumed charge of concessions for the Portland fair as he had at several previous expositions. See Wakefield to Reed, 17 July 1905, OHS, LCX, box 19, Reed-Wakefield folder. Average daily attendance figures were compiled by the Division of Concessions and Admissions. See [Wakefield], "Memorandum from Final Reports, Lewis and Clark Centennial Exposition, October 31, 1905," UCLA, 344/7. The total attendance on Workingmen's Day, according to the *Oregon Daily Journal,* 3 August 1905, 3, was 27,420.

18. "Free Tickets for the Fair—Nit [*sic*]" *Seattle Union Record,* 7 August 1909, 5.

19. Labor's list of grievances against the directors is compiled from "Labor Day Celebration," *Seattle Union Record,* 31 July 1909, 1, and *Seattle Union Record,* 11 September 1909, 4. A description of the Labor Day holiday as celebrated by the unions was provided by "Labor Day Grand Success," *Seattle Union Record,* 11 September 1909, 1, 5.

20. For discussions of anti-Asian sentiment and action on the Pacific Coast, see Alexander Saxton, *The Indispensable Enemy: Labor and the Anti-Chinese Movement in California* (Berkeley and Los Angeles: University of California Press, 1971); Jacobus tenBroek, Edward, N. Barnhart, and Floyd W. Matson, *Prejudice, War and the Constitution: Causes and Consequences of the Evacuation of the Japanese Americans in World War II* (Berkeley and Los Angeles: University of California Press, 1954); Richard A. Thompson, "Yellow Peril, 1890–1924" (Ph.D. dissertation, University of

Wisconsin, 1957). The quotation is from "Labor Day Celebration," *Seattle Union Record,* 31 July 1909, 1.

21. Henry Dosch to Goode, 5 October 1904, OHS, LCX, box 21, Communications from the President's Office folder; Dosch to Goode, 7 October 1904, in ibid., box 7, Office of the President folder. An anonymous letter to Erving Winslow [secretary of the Anti-Imperialist League], 21 June 1906, in the National Archives, Record Group 350, Records of the Bureau of Insular Affairs, General Classified Files, no. 9640-43 (cited hereafter as RBIA, RG 350), notes that several Igorots contracted with individuals to be exhibited in various privately operated shows after the Saint Louis fair closed. The phrase "dead exhibit" is from Dosch to Goode, 5 October 1904. See also [?] to Dosch, 2 July 1904, OHS, LCX, box 21, Correspondence from the President's Office folder; and Reed to Dosch, 12 July 1904, OHS, LCX, box 1.

22. Dosch to Goode, 11 October 1904, OHS, LCX, box 21, Correspondence from the President's Office folder.

23. Only fragmentary details exist concerning the founding of the International Anthropological Exhibit Company. The name of the firm as well as details of initial agreement made with the directors of the Portland fair are taken from the tentative contract negotiated in November 1904. See the undated and unsigned concession contract in OHS, LCX, box 9. This contract lists S. C. Simms as a partner and makes no mention of Felder. But Felder was named as a partner in the company in "Five Filipino Villages to Be on Grounds," *Lewis and Clark Journal* 3 (January 1905):6–7, in UCLA, 344/7. Biographical information about McGowan is from *Louisiana Purchase Centennial: Dedication Ceremonies, St. Louis, U.S.A., April 30th and May 1st–2nd, 1903* (no imprint), 46, in California State University, Fresno, Department of Special Collections, Expositions and Fairs Collection. See also Edmund A. Felder to Clarence B. Edwards, 22 December 1904, and attached documents, RBIA, RG 350, General Classified Files, no. 10111-8; Edwards to [Civil Governor of the Philippine Islands], [19] January 1905, RBIA, RG 350, General Classified Files, no. 10111 after 10, notes Taft's approval.

24. Details of this arrangement are sketchy but can be deduced from C. S. Moody [Hunt's business manager] and Truman K. Hunt to Goode, 22 April 1905, and Goode to Moody, 25 April 1905, in OHS, LCX, box 7, Office of the President folder. Biographical details about Richard Schneidewind are taken from J. R. McKey [memo], 3 June 1907, RBIA, RG 350, General Classified Files, no. 13431-48; H. Albert Johnson to [Secretary of State], 31 December 1913, ibid., no. 13431-71; and Schneidewind to Frank McIntyre, 25 October 1917, RBIA, RG 350, Personal Name File. For the competition concerning the concessions, see Moody and Hunt to Goode, 22 April 1905. In early October 1904, Hunt informed Dosch that the Igorot Village concession had grossed $173,000. See Dosch to Goode, 7 October 1904; Goode to Moody, 25 April 1905; See Felder to Goode, 22 April 1905, OHS, LCX, box 7, Office of the President folder.

25. [Concession contract between Felder and the directors], 9 June 1905, OHS, LCX, box 7; Goode to Taft, 23 June 1905, RBIA, RG 350, General Classified Files, no. 10111-15. H. G. Farris, along with Schneidewind, held a cigar concession on the Philippine Reservation at the Saint Louis fair. See [contract between Philippine Exposition Board and Richard Schneidewind and H. G. Farris], 2 May 1904, RBIA, RG 350, Records of the Philippine Exposition Board, Minutes of the Board.

26. "The Igorrote," *Portland Oregonian*, 30 September 1905, 8; Merle McKelvey diary, 14 September [1905] entry, MS no. 1509, OHS.

27. Goode to Felder, 23 October 1905, attached to Schneidewind, ["Report on Igorots"], 28 February 1906, RBIA, RG 350, General Classified Files, no. 13431-9. See also "The Igorrote Tribe from the Philippines," *Lewis and Clark Journal* 4 (October 1905):4, UCLA, 344/7. Testimonials and awards were noted in subsequent advertisements for the Igorot show. See, for instance, *Igorrotes: 25 Head Hunting, Dog Eating Wild People from the Philippines* [Riverview Park publicity release], in RBIA, RG 350, General Classified Files, no. 13431-21.

28. "The Call of the Wild" [broadside advertisement for Igorot Village in Chutes Park, Los Angeles], in RBIA, RG 350, General Classified Files, no. 13431-7. See also *Igorottes: 25 Head Hunting, Dog Eating Wild People from the Philippines*.

29. William H. Hammer [recruiting officer] to [military secretary], 28 February 1906, RBIA, RG 350, General Classified Files, no. 13431-10 and, Schneidewind, ["Report on Igorots"].

30. Felder to Edwards, 29 May 1906, RBIA, RG 350, General Classified Files, no. 13431-20; [?] to Mrs. Elsie Hunt, 21 February 1907, RBIA, RG 350, General Classified Files, no. 9640-45; J. R. McKey, [memo], 3 June 1907; and *Alaska-Yukon-Pacific Exposition: Official Guide* (no imprint), 44.

In 1911 Schneidewind informed Cameron Forbes, governor-general of the Philippines, that he was taking fifty Igorots on an exhibition tour of Europe (Schneidewind to Forbes, 3 February 1911, RBIA, RG 350, General Classified Files, no. 13431-54). Forbes replied that the government of the Philippines opposed the exhibition because "it creates a wrong impression of the Filipino people . . . [and] being illiterate and dependent people, they are too dependent on their employer" (Forbes to Schneidewind, 4 February 1911, ibid., no. 13431-54). Forbes subsequently told the secretary of war that the Igorot leaders vehemently opposed the planned show because of its "demoralizing" effect. The problem, Forbes noted, was the absence of any legal means to prevent the Igorots from contracting with the showmen (Forbes to [?], 23 February 1911, ibid., no. 13431-54). After the Ghent Exhibition of 1913, two Igorot translators sent an urgent appeal to Woodrow Wilson asking that the Igorots be permitted to return to the Philippines. Schneidewind, they claimed, had defrauded them of their earnings. Furthermore, they told Wilson that nine Igorots in the company had died (James Amok and Ellis Tongain [interpreters] to [Woodrow Wilson], 21 October 1913, ibid., no. 13431-56). Several weeks later the *New York Sun* reported that the Igorots were "destitute and wandering in the streets of Ghent" (*Sun*, 6 November 1913, clipping, in ibid.). In late December the government finally returned the Igorots to the Philippines, but eight had died in Ghent (H. Albert Johnson [U.S. consul] to [William Jennings Bryan], 31 December 1913, ibid., no. 13431-71). Yet even after the debacle in Ghent Schneidewind continued in the village concession business. He managed the Samoan Village at San Francisco's Panama-Pacific Exposition of 1915 before winding up in Detroit as a streetcar employee (Schneidewind to McIntyre, 25 October 1917, RBIA, RG 350, Personal Name File).

31. "Totem Poles Will Point Way," *Seattle Times*, 24 May 1908, clipping in Alaska-Yukon-Pacific Exposition Scrapbook, 4-SP-np, Northwest Collection (cited hereafter as AYPE Scrapbooks); *Alaska-Yukon-Pacific Exposition: Official Guide*, 44;

and "Alaska-Yukon-Pacific Exposition," *Hotels and Travel* (August 1908), 11–12, AYPE Scrapbooks, 16-0-TP.

32. "Fair Is Seen by 16,000 Children," *Seattle Post-Intelligencer*, 28 March 1909, 9; "How Ye College Campus Civilizes Ye Igorrote," *University of Washington Daily*, 3 November 1909, in Northwest Collection.

33. Alfred C. Haddon to Frederick Morgan Padelford, 30 June 1908, Frederick Morgan Padelford Papers, in University of Washington, University Archives, box 2, folder 15; "Fair as Laboratory for the Study of Races," *Seattle Post-Intelligencer*, 22 June 1909, clipping, AYPE Scrapbooks, 12-SP-62; "Horrors, Say Filipinos at Sight of Naked Igorrotes," *Seattle Post-Intelligencer*, 6 July 1909, 8; and "Resents Aspersions on Igorrote Village," *Seattle Post-Intelligencer*, 7 July 1909, clipping, in AYPE Scrapbooks, 12-SP-165. An advertisement for the Igorot Village in the *Seattle Post-Intelligencer*, 1 August 1908, 8, quotes Haddon as saying: "These amiable savages are fascinating." The advertisement also quotes the *Seattle Times's* praise for the village as "A Vital Issue in Living Bronze."

34. For a description of the Trail, see George L. Hutchin, "Hit the Trail Is the Favorite Diversion at the Lewis and Clark Exposition," *Lewis and Clark Journal* 3 (June 1905):48–58, in UCLA, 344/7. The description of the Old Plantation is from the contract between the Lewis and Clark Centennial Corporation and concessionaire George E. Ames, in OHS, LCX, box 9, folder A. Information about Harry L. Blitz is from " 'Haba Haba Man' to Rewed Ex-Wife," *Portland Oregonian*, 2 February 1910, 7. A description of the Vaudeville Theater was provided by Harry L. Newton, *Hiram Birdseed at the Lewis and Clark Centennial Exposition* (New York: Will Rossiter, 190[5]), 105, in the Wilson Room. Newton's protagonist describes one performance in the theater, entitled "My Coal Black Lady," in which a white man was "clean smitten on this nigger gal." The protagonist, Hiram Birdseed, expressed his views on the matter in no uncertain terms: "no nice-lookin' feller like him wuz a fallin' in love with any coal black lady." See also "Pay Streak Will Have to Be Good," *Seattle Post-Intelligencer*, 16 February 1909, clipping, AYPE Scrapbooks, 6-SP-np. Concerning the Eskimo Village, see "People of the Ice Basking under Southern Suns," *Seattle Times*, 4 October 1908, clipping in AYPE Scrapbooks, 5-SP-np; "Siberians Come from Arctic for A.Y.P. Fair," *Seattle Post-Intelligencer*, 15 November 1908, clipping, in Northwest Collection, vertical file; [*Orphanage*] *News Letter* 9 (December 1908), clipping, in National Archives, Records of the Bureau of Indian Affairs, Record Group 75, Alaska Division, General Correspondence File, "Natives (General) 1909 file"; "Building Eskimo Village Is Begun," unidentified clipping, in Northwest Collection, vertical file, miscellaneous; and undated press release in National Archives, Records of the Secretary of Interior, Record Group 48, Alaska Yukon Pacific Exposition, Office of the Alaska Exhibit, Seattle Correspondence of the Commissioner, box 6 (cited hereafter as RSI, RG 48).

35. Bauer, "The Development of an Empire," 7; "Chilberg Is Proud," *Seattle Star*, 1 June 1909, 1. According to "The A.Y.P. Exposition," *World's Work* 18 (1904):11894, "the linking of Oriental commerce, Alaskan development, and American industry is apparent all the time. No Oriental, visiting from Shanghai or Tokio, could fail to see it."

36. [Richard Rathbun?], "Expositions in Which the National Museum Has Participated," 102–20, Smithsonian Institution Archives, Record Unit 55 (cited

hereafter as SIA, RU), assistant secretary in charge of the USNM, 1897–1917
(Richard Rathbun), Records, box 19, folder 9; and *Report of the United States
Government Board of Managers, Alaska-Yukon-Pacific Exposition, Seattle,
Washington, 1909* (Washington, D.C.: Government Printing Office, 1909), 16 (cited
hereafter as *Report of the U.S. Government Board of Managers, AYPE*).

37. *Report of the U.S. Government Board of Managers, AYPE*, 10; Walter Hough
elaborated on the purpose of the Smithsonian exhibit in his "Report of the
Department of Anthropology for 1908–1909," MS, p. 106, SIA, RU 158, Curators'
Annual Reports, 1881–1964, box 27, folder 1. According to Hough: "From the
collections of the Museum was taken a large series of ethnological objects illustrative
of the aboriginal culture in the states and territories covered by the scope of the
Exposition, and afforded the primary point of view for the historical perspective
which was the dominant motive in the Government exhibit."

38. *Report of the U.S. Government Board of Managers, AYPE*, 67–70. The
newspaper account is "Exhibit Pictures Nation's History," *Seattle Post-Intelligencer*,
20 June 1909, clipping, AYPE Scrapbooks, 12-SP-53. The original typescript, "The
Exhibits of the Smithsonian Institution and United States National Museum," is in
SIA, RU 70, Exposition Records of the Smithsonian Institution and the United
States National Museum, box 80. Portions of this account also appeared in *The
Exhibits of the Smithsonian Institution and United States National Museum at the
Alaska-Yukon-Pacific Exposition* (Washington, D.C.: Judd and Detwiler, 1909), 50–
54, in ibid. Another account of the exhibit was written by T. T. Belote, one of the
exhibit installers, and appeared in "The A.-Y.-P. Exposition: What It Is," *Seattle
Post-Intelligencer*, 7 August 1909, 6.

39. Descriptions of the Filipinos are taken from "Exhibit Pictures Nation's
History," *Seattle Post-Intelligencer*, 20 June 1909, and from *Exhibits of the
Smithsonian Institution and United States National Museum at the Alaska-Yukon-
Pacific Exposition*.

40. "Philippine Exhibit," RSI, RG 48, Alaska Yukon Pacific Exposition Board of
Managers, Correspondence of Chairman, box 1.

41. A description of Dosch's activities in Japan was provided by Joseph Gaston,
Portland: Its History and Builders, 3 vols. (Portland, 1911), 1:586–88. See also
Henry E. Dosch, "Department of Exhibits," *Lewis and Clark Journal* 1 (March
1904):6–7, UCLA, 344/7; Dosch to Goode, 12 October 1904, OHS, LCX, box 21,
Correspondence from President's Office folder; and "Problems for the Congress,"
Portland Oregonian, 19 August 1905, 10. Irene E. Cortinovis, "China at the St.
Louis Fair," *Missouri Historical Review* 72 (1977):59–66.

42. For Japan's involvement in the Lewis and Clark Centennial, see Tsuneji Aiba
[Japanese vice-consul], "Japan's Relations to Fair," *Lewis and Clark Journal* 2
(October 1904):12–13, UCLA, 344/7. The Chinese boycott began in July. See
"Chinese Refuse American Goods," *Portland Oregonian*, 30 July 1905, 1. Italy's
participation was noted in "Sunny Italy's Day," ibid., 21 September 1905, 16.
Theodore Hardee, another Portland representative at the Saint Louis fair, noted that
there would be little difficulty obtaining private exhibits. See his "Foreign
Participation," *Lewis and Clark Journal* 1 (April 1904):6–7, UCLA, 344/7. When it
became apparent that the Chinese government would not send a display, the Chinese

exhibit space went "by default into the hands of a few Mongolian ornament and knick knack merchants," though merchants in the Shantung province in China evidently organized their own display and sent it to the fair. See "Shantung Makes Its Own Exhibit," *Portland Oregonian*, 8 August 1905, 8! See also "Architectural Splendors of Portland's Great Fair," *Oregon Daily Journal*, 1 June 1905, 14.

43. Benjamin Ide Wheeler, "The Relation of the Pacific Coast to Education in the Orient," in *Program, Organization, and Addresses: Lewis and Clark Educational Congress* (Portland: Anderson and Duniway Company, [1905]), 41–50.

44. Ibid., 45; quotation is from "Colors of Orient and Occident Are Mingled at Fair," *Seattle Post-Intelligencer*, 5 September 1909, clipping, in AYPE Scrapbooks, 13-AP-54.

45. Quotations are from "Seattle Opens Doors of Country to Japanese Commissioners," *Pacific Northwest Commerce* 1 (October 1909):5, 11–19. See also Hajime Ota [commissioner to the fair?], "Japan's Motive for Taking Part in A.-Y.-P. Exposition," ibid. 1 (September 1909):18–20; "America's Japanese Friends," *Seattle Post-Intelligencer*, 1 September 1909, clipping, in AYPE Scrapbooks, 13-SP-18; and McMahon, 58. Attendance figures for the turnout on Japan Day are from "Seattle Opens Doors of Country to Japanese Commissioners," 17. To start Japan Day, two thousand Japanese paraded through the downtown area. At their head was T. T. Fugosama, a labor contractor who probably had provided the Northern Pacific with workers during the previous decade. This supposition is reinforced by Yugi Ichioka's "Japanese Immigrant Labor Contractors and the Northern Pacific and the Great Northern Railroad Companies, 1898–1907" (unpublished paper, Asian American Studies Center, UCLA, 1977).

46. Baron E. Shibusawa, "Mutual Interest Grows Steadily," *Pacific Northwest Commerce* 1 (October 1909):21–22, reprints Shibusawa's speech that was given in early September. See "Welcome Japan's Masters of Trade," *Seattle Post-Intelligencer*, 2 September 1909, clipping, in AYPE Scrapbooks, 13-SP-31; and Ichioka, "Japanese Immigrant Labor Contractors."

47. *Proceedings of the First International Convention of the Asiatic Exclusion League* (n.p., 1908), 5, in UCLA, Department of Special Collections; and "Commercial Club Wants 7-Day Fair," *Seattle Post-Intelligencer*, 21 April 1909, 9.

48. J. H. McGraw, quoted in "Coast in Arms," *Chicago Chronicle*, 6 December 1906, clipping, in AYPE Scrapbooks, 1-OP; "Japs Have Big Day," *Seattle Star*, 4 June 1909, 1.

49. "The Lesson of the Fair," *Portland Oregonian*, 15 October 1905, 6. Attendance figures are from Reed, "Official History of the Lewis and Clark Centennial," 190.

50. Arthur A. Greene, "A 'Last Night' Impression," *Portland Oregonian*, 15 October 1905, 10; "The Close of the Fair as It Looks to Harry Murphy," *Portland Oregonian*, 14 October 1905, 10; and "The Lesson of the Fair," *Portland Oregonian*, 15 October 1905, 6.

51. "Portland Offers Cheer to Exposition Doubters," *San Diego Union*, 6 December 1912, 5; Jack Pement, "Few Remember Portland without a Rose Festival," *Oregon Journal*, 6 June 1977, clipping; "Lewis-Clark Fair Early Day Dream," ibid., 19 August 1977, clipping; and Michael Burton, "Rose Festival through the Years,"

Old Portland Today 3 (1 June 1905), clipping; "Guild's Lake Now City's Industrial Center," *Portland Oregonian*, 27 July 1947, clipping; all in OHS, vertical file. See also MacColl, *Shaping of a City*, 266–71, 341–42, 468–72.

52. Several of the buildings that became part of the University of Washington were noted by Roy D. Bailey in *A-P Exposition as an Educator* (no imprint), in Northwest Collection, vertical file, "National and foreign participation"; and "Non-Salaried Officers of Exposition Dined," *Pacific Northwest Commerce* 1 (December 1909):15–17.

Chapter Eight

1. [Herbert C. Hoover] to Charley Field, 29 April 1912, attached to Hoover to Frank L. Browne, 29 May 1912, in University of California, Berkeley, Bancroft Library (cited hereafter as Bancroft Library), Records of the Panama Pacific International Exposition, box 29/30A, folder 1-18-20 (cited hereafter as RPPIE). "Mission History," in "Prospectus of the 1915 Exposition in San Diego," in San Diego Historical Society, Library and Manuscripts Collection (cited hereafter as SDHS).

2. Attendance figures are from Frank Morton Todd, *The Story of the Exposition: Being the Official History of the International Celebration Held at San Francisco in 1915 to Commemorate the Discovery of the Pacific Ocean and Construction of the Panama Canal*, 5 vols. (New York: G. P. Putnam's Sons, Knickerbocker Press, 1921), 5:228, and Richard F. Pourade, *Gold in the Sun* (San Diego: Union-Tribune Publishing Company, 1965), 218. See also Elizabeth Gordon, *What We Saw at Madame World's Fair, Being a Series of Letters from the Twins at the Panama-Pacific International Exposition to Their Cousins at Home* (San Francisco: Samuel Levinson, 1915), 3–4, in University of California, Los Angeles, Department of Special Collections, Expositions and Fairs Collection, 344/5, box 2 (cited hereafter as UCLA 344/5); "General," in "Prospectus of the 1915 Exposition"; "Exposition Beautiful Welcomes World to Land of Golden Promises Fulfilled," *San Diego Union*, 1 January 1915, 1; "Exposition Is Educational," Roswell, New Mexico *Record*, 17 December 1912, clipping, in SDHS, Panama California Exposition Scrapbooks (cited hereafter as PCE Scrapbooks).

3. This phrase is taken from Katherine Delmar Burke, *Storied Walls of the Exposition* (n.p., 1915), in California State University, Fresno, Department of Special Collections, Expositions and Fairs Collection (cited hereafter as CSUF); Yorick, "On the Margin," *San Diego Union*, 10 January, 1915, 1; "Architecture," in "Prospectus of the 1915 Exposition"; [Hoover] to Field, 29 April 1912; Juliet James, *Palaces and Courts of the Exposition: A Handbook of the Architecture, Sculpture, and Mural Painting with Special Reference to the Symbolism* (San Francisco: California Book Company, 1915), 48–49, in UCLA, 344/5, box 2; Churchill quoted in "Panama Canal and Exposition Spell Prosperity for California," *San Diego Tribune*, 28 April 1913, clipping, PCE Scrapbooks.

4. Information about the continuity of exposition personnel is from Arthur H. Gaebel, comp., *Makers of the Panama-California and Southern California, San Diego, Expositions* [San Diego, 1915], in CSUF; Francis Farquar, "An Interview with Anson Herrick," February 1959, in Oral History Project, Bancroft Library; Carleton Moore Winslow, "The Architecture of the Panama-California Exposition, 1909–1915"

(M.A. thesis, University of San Diego, 1976); John D. Barry, *The City of Domes* (San Francisco: John J. Newbegin, 1915); Frances A. Groff, "Exposition Moths," *Sunset* 35 (1915):133–48; and Todd, passim.

5. Todd, 1:126–28, 109, and 2:219.

6. Ibid., 1:110–18. According to Todd, when Skiff first met Hoover he had never heard of the latter, in Todd, 1:283. The so-called labor covenant is discussed in Todd, 1:325–30. See also P. H. McCarthy to O. A. Tvietmoe, n.d., RPPIE, box 3, folder 5; P. H. McCarthy to Charles Moore, 29 July 1912, ibid. When the Associated Press carried a report that union conditions would prevail on the fairgrounds, numerous manufacturers protested. See, for instance, [?] to J. C. Ford, [22 January 1913], ibid., box 33, folder 3. Unfounded rumors also spread that Samuel Gompers had become one of the directors of the fair. See C. C. Bradley, Jr., to Moore, in ibid., folder 4. The exposition management denied all reports that the exposition was a closed shop. See Moore to Atlas Lumber and Shingle Company, 1 November 1912, ibid., folder 3; and Joseph M. Cumming to Ira E. Bennett, 22 August 1913, RPPIE, box 33, folder 7.

7. "Mission History," in "Prospectus of the 1915 Exposition"; the best source for information about the directors is Gaebel, *Makers of the . . . Expositions*, which is also the source for the quotation. For additional information on San Diego, see "Spreckles' Millions Build up San Diego," *San Diego Union*, n.d., clipping, in SDHS, San Diego Electrical Company Scrapbook (June 1912–June 1915); Dana Alan Basney, "The Role of Spreckles' Business Interests in the Development of San Diego" (M.S. thesis, San Diego State University, 1975); John Springer, "First Citizen," *San Diego Union*, 8 August 1948, clipping, SDHS, "G. Aubrey Davidson Biographical File"; "Oral Interview with Samuel Wood Hamill," by Bob Wright, 24 August 1974, SDHS, "George W. Marston Biographical File"; and "Rites Tuesday for H. O. Davis," *San Diego Tribune*, 29 August 1964, clipping, SDHS, "Harry O. Davis Biographical File"; Ben F. Dixon, "Collier Park Honors Col. D. C. Collier," MS, in SDHS, "David Charles Collier Biographical File"; "Dynamic Energy, Civic Service to San Diego Cited in Tribute to Late Col. Collier," *San Diego Sun*, 14 November 1934, clipping, in ibid.; and "Exposition's Scope, Intense Loyalty of City Amazes Visitors," *San Diego Union*, 18 May 1913, clipping, in PCE Scrapbooks.

8. The best discussion of the origins and early years of the San Francisco exposition is provided by Todd, 1:34–139. See also Joan Elaine Draper, "The San Francisco Civic Center: Architecture, Planning, and Politics" (Ph.D. dissertation, University of California, Berkeley, 1980); and Burton L. Benedict et al., *The Anthropology of World's Fairs: San Francisco's Panama-Pacific International Exposition, 1915* (Berkeley: Scolar Press, 1983).

9. See especially Basney, "Role of the Spreckles' Business Interests in the Development of San Diego," passim; "General," in "Prospectus of the 1915 Exposition"; "Some of the Objects of San Diego Show," *Arizona Gazette*, 22 July 1912, clipping, PCE Scrapbooks; and "Panama-California First Purely Constructive Exposition," *San Diego Union*, 1 January 1915, 3–4. The political situation in San Diego is noted by Florence Christman, *The Romance of Balboa Park* (San Diego: Committee of One Hundred, 1977), 28–29; and Pourade, 143–60.

10. Roger W. Lotchin, "The Darwinian City: The Politics of Urbanization in San Francisco between the World Wars," *Pacific Historical Review* 48 (1979):357–81; *The*

*Logical Point: An Illustrated Monthly for the Advancement of the World's Panama
Exposition, New Orleans*, 1915, Yale University, Sterling Library; Todd, 1:63–64.

11. Quotation is from "Definition of the Scope of the Panama California
Exposition," *San Diego Tribune*, 9 February 1912, clipping, PCE Scrapbooks. Also
consult "Exposition's Scope, Intense Loyalty of City Amazes Visitors," *San Diego
Union*, 18 May 1913, clipping, in ibid. Another account notes that the agreement to
focus the San Diego fair on ethnology and archaeology was made in 1910. See "Press
of the Southland Shows Its Loyalty to San Diego," 25 February 1912, unidentified
clipping in ibid.

12. This chronology of events is discussed by Richard Amero, "The Making of the
Panama-California Exposition, 1909–1915" (unpublished paper, 1978), SDHS. See
also "Proceedings" [minutes of a meeting between the exposition promoters and the
California delegation], in RPPIE, box 3B/4A, folder 5.

13. "Collier Raps President in Speech to Boosters," *San Diego Sun*, 29 February
1912, clipping, PCE Scrapbooks; "Rousing Welcome Is Given Collier," *San Diego
Tribune*, 29 February 1912, clipping, in ibid.; and "Million to Be Spent on the S.D.
and A. in Year," *San Diego Union*, 31 May 1912, clipping, in ibid.; "Oral interview
with Egbert Carroll (Bert) Bangs," 29 April 1959, by Edgar F. Hastings, SDHS.

14. Martin K. Gordon, comp., *Joseph Henry Pendleton, 1860–1942: Register of His
Personal Papers* (Washington, D.C.: History and Museums Division Headquarters,
United States Marine Corps, 1975), 14; Joan M. Jensen, "The Politics and History of
William Kettner," *Journal of San Diego History* 11 (June 1965):29. For discussions
of the Free Speech Movement, see Kate Haurshan Taylor, "A Crisis of Confidence:
The San Diego Free Speech Fight of 1912" (M.A. thesis, University of California,
Los Angeles, 1966); and Robert Warren Diehl, "To Speak or Not to Speak: San
Diego 1912" (M.A. thesis, University of California, San Diego, 1976).

15. "Friends Praise Collier for Triumph in Capitol," *San Diego Union*, 29 May
1915, clipping in PCE Scrapbooks; "Fair Bill's Friends Have Hard Fight to Prevent
Mutilation," *San Diego Union*, 26 May 1913, clipping, in ibid.; and "Bill for Expo.
Is Signed by Wilson," *San Diego Tribune*, 24 May 1913, clipping, in ibid.

16. G. Aubrey Davidson noted that in a meeting with Hearst in 1915 the latter
"brought up the subject of keeping the fair open another year. He told me it had to
be done; and that he was willing to aid the project in every way possible." See
"Davidson, Exposition Chief, Bubbles with Optimism after Trip to Busy East," *San
Diego Union*, 22 October 1915, 3. Another account notes that the proposal to keep
the fair originated with Chicago railroad executives. See "Move to Continue Fairs into
1916 Gains Support," *San Diego Union*, 17 July 1915, 1. Crocker, quoted in
"Spanish City Beautiful Wins Unstinted Praise from Northern Guests," *San Diego
Union*, 17 January 1915, 1.

17. "Conference between F. J. V. Skiff, Esq., and the President and Directors of
the Panama-Pacific International Exposition Company," 22 November 1911, 42–43,
in RPPIE, box 3B/4A, folder 2; Charles F. Lummis to D. C. Collier, 3 December
1911, Southwest Museum, Charles F. Lummis Papers, Collier folder (cited hereafter
as Lummis Papers).

18. "Exposition's Scope, Intense Loyalty of City Amazes Visitors," *San Diego
Union*, 18 May 1913, PCE Scrapbooks; D. C. Collier to Edgar Hewett, 4 November
1911, Lummis Papers, Hewett folder.

19. George W. Stocking, Jr., "The Sante Fe Style in American Anthropology: Regional Interest, Academic Initiative, and Philanthropic Policy in the First Two Decades of the Laboratory of Anthropology, Inc.," *Journal of the History of the Behavioral Sciences* 18 (1982):3–19.

20. Collier to Hewett, 4 November 1911, Lummis Papers, Hewett folder; Dudley Gordon, *Charles F. Lummis: Crusader in Corduroy* (Los Angeles: Cultural Assets Press, 1972), 314–15; Lummis to [Collier], n.d., Lummis Papers. Collier to Charles D. Walcott, 24 January 1912, National Anthropology Archives, Aleš Hrdlička Papers, box 9, San Diego Exposition Folder (cited hereafter as Hrdlička Papers).

21. Hrdlička to William H. Holmes, 31 January 1912, Hrdlička Papers, box 9, San Diego Exposition Folder. The most complete biography of Hrdlička is Frank Spencer, "Aleš Hrdlička, M.D., 1860–1943: A Chronicle of the Life and Work of an American Physical Anthropologist," 2 vols. (Ph.D. dissertation, University of Michigan, 1979); Spencer, 1:284.

22. Spencer, 1:381–91, 2:437–67. See also Aleš Hrdlička, "The Division of Physical Anthropology at the Panama California Exposition, San Diego," n.d., 1–13 in Hrdlička Papers, box 9; for Philip Newton's activities, see Newton to Hrdlička, 22 October 1912, ibid., box 8, Newton folder; Spencer, 2:465–67.

23. [Joseph C. Thompson], "Scientific Features at the San Diego Exposition," Hrdlička Papers, box 11, J. C. Thompson folder; Hewett to Hrdlička, 16 June 1915 (letterhead), Hrdlička Papers, box 17, Hewett folder; "Anthropological," in "Prospectus of the 1915 Exposition." Another entry in the "Prospectus," under the heading "Agricultural," notes that the ethnology display "is a vast scientific portrayal of the advance of civilization produced as only a scientific body like the institution at Washington can produce it—and it is shown for the first time at San Diego," in ibid. Notice of the "Evolution Room" is given in Hrdlička to Hewett, 12 October 1914, Hrdlička Papers, box 17, Hewett folder.

24. Hrdlička, "The Division of Physical Anthropology at the Panama California Exposition, San Diego," 17–24. The impact of the exhibits registered in "Are You a Monkey's Son? Science Says So," *San Diego Sun*, 5 June 1915, 3.

25. Hrdlička, "The Division of Physical Anthropology at the Panama California Exposition, San Diego," 23–26.

26. Ibid., 27–34.

27. Ibid., 14–16; George W. Stocking, Jr., *Race, Culture, and Evolution: Essays in the History of Anthropology* (New York: Free Press, 1968), 161–94; Hewett to Hrdlička, 25 April 1915, Hrdlička Papers, box 17, Hewett folder. Hewett wrote: "The Science of Man exhibit is a great success. I doubt you yourself realize what a service you have rendered in preparing this . . . and not only physicians and scholars, but the common people make constant and intelligent use of it."

28. Hrdlička, "Division of Physical Anthropology at the Panama California Exposition, San Diego," 4; James B. Wilkinson, "Exposition Excursions, Man's Evolution," *San Diego Union*, 16 May 1915, 2. Hrdlička's definition of eugenics is from an addresss read in 1915 at the meeting of the American Association for the Advancement of Science, "Eugenics and Its Natural Limitations in Man," *Science*, n.s., 42 (15 October 1915):546.

29. For an overview of the various congresses see Todd, 5:1–6, 100–121.

30. "Experts Warn of Race Perils," *San Francisco Examiner*, 5 August 1915, 4;

"Burbank Views Race Culture," ibid., 8 August 1915, 59; "Morality Masque Pictures the Triumph of Eugenics," ibid.

31. Henry Smith Williams, "The Greatest Migration in History," *San Franciso Chronicle*, 8 August 1915, supplement; Henry Smith Williams, "Are We Importing Lunacy?" ibid., 10 June 1915, 18.

32. Todd, 5:76–77.

33. Todd, 5:38–40.

34. Roger O'Donnell (acting representative, Department of Labor) to W. de C. Ravenel, 4 March 1915, in Smithsonian Institution Archives, Record Unit 70, Exposition Records of the Smithsonian Institution, box 83.

35. Leonard Pitt, *The Decline of the Californios: A Social History of the Spanish-Speaking Californians, 1846–1890* (Berkeley and Los Angeles: University of California Press, 1971), 309; John Higham, *Strangers in the Land: Patterns of American Nativism, 1860–1925* (New Brunswick: Rutgers University Press, 1955), 309–12, 324.

36. "Oh, Rhythmic Din, Not All Can Win," *San Francisco Chronicle*, 14 March 1915, supplement; "Little Eva Now a Zone Feature," *San Francisco Examiner*, 13 March 1915, 14. See also "News of the World from San Francisco: Latest Official Data from the Panama Pacific International Exposition" [exposition publicity release], in Library of Congress, Manuscripts Division, Booker T. Washington Papers, box 944. Groff, 132–48, is a good account of the concessionaires on the Zone.

37. Todd, 2:150, and Ralph Emmett Avery and William C. Haskins, *The Panama Canal and Golden Gate Exposition* (no imprint), 377, in CSUF; Todd, 2:149–50.

38. Todd, 2:355; "Aztec Life Is Truly Shown on the Zone," *San Francisco Bulletin*, 23 February 1915, 8; "A City of Lovely Light," *San Francisco Examiner*, 21 February 1915, supplement; Todd, 2:375.

39. Pauline Jacobson, "Seeing a Stamboul [*sic*] on the Zone," *San Francisco Bulletin*, 22 May 1915; Todd, 2:362–63; [Frank Burt?] to Moore, 16 July 1915, RPPIE, box 17B/18A, folder 3. See also Groff, 144; "Minutes of Committee on Concessions and Admissions," 5 April 1915, RPPIE, box 2B/3A, folder 6; and "Concession on Zone Ordered Closed," *San Francisco Chronicle*, 21 March 1915, 4.

40. "The Forbidden City at the Exposition," *San Francisco Chronicle*, 2 May 1915, supplement; Todd, 3:287–92.

41. Todd, 3:287–88.

42. Todd, 2:358.

43. "Indian 'Rags' Style for Tonight," *San Diego Union*, 28 August 1915, 1; "Stroll along the Isthmus" [unidentified newspaper clipping; June 1913?], in PCE Scrapbooks.

44. "Enterprise of Big Fair Astonishes Washington," *San Diego Union*, 6 August 1913, clipping, in PCE Scrapbooks; "General-Juvenile," in "Prospectus of the 1915 Exposition"; "Gleaned on Prado and Isthmus," *San Diego Union*, 28 February 1915, 6; and "Economics," in "Prospectus of the 1915 Exposition."

45. "General," in "Prospectus of the 1915 Exposition."

46. Ben Macomber, "Stories of the Exposition," *San Francisco Chronicle*, 14 March 1915, supplement.

47. "Movies to Invite the World to the Exposition," *San Francisco Bulletin*, 4 February 1915, 8; "Motion Picture Actors Arrive for Production of 'The World to

Come,' " *San Diego Union,* 15 June 1915, 1; "Grace Darling Sees World as Fairyland," *San Francisco Examiner,* 11 February 1915, 7; "Grace Darling to Get First Glimpse of Fair To-Day: Motion Picture Queen to Arrive on Great Northern," *San Francisco Examiner,* 12 February 1915, 9.

48. William F. Benedict, " 'Griffithizing' the Exposition," *San Francisco Chronicle,* 4 July 1915, supplement.

49. Todd, 5:225–30.

50. R. Duffus, *The Tower of Jewels: Memories of San Francisco* (New York: W. W. Norton, 1960), 120; Barbara Rubin, Robert Carlton, and Arnold Rubin, *L.A. in Installments* (Santa Monica, Calif.: Westside Publications, 1979), 13–18.

51. Lillian Pray-Palmer, ed., *A Book of Memories for the Ages* (San Diego, [1925]). See also Christman, 81–86.

Bibliography

Archival Materials

Major Depositories of Printed Sources

California State University, Fresno, Library, Department of Special Collections
Center for Research Libraries, Chicago
Library of Congress
National Museum of American History
New York Public Library
University of California, Berkeley, Doe Library
Yale University, Sterling and Beinecke Libraries

Manuscript Sources

Atlanta Historical Society
    Cotton States and International Exposition Collection
Buffalo and Erie County Historical Society
    Mable E. Barnes Papers
    A. L. Benedict Papers
    William I. Buchanan Papers
    Records of the Pan-American Exposition
    Vertical Files
Chicago Historical Society
    Samuel Waters Allerton Papers
    George Alfred Townsend Papers
City Archives of Philadelphia
    Annual Messages and Reports of Departments
    Bureau of Fine Arts, Official Catalogue, Department of Art
    United States Centennial Board of Finance, Election Materials
    United States Centennial Board of Finance, Minutes
    United States Centennial Commission, Correspondence and Papers, William Phipps
    Blake Copybook
    United States Centennial Commission, Scrapbooks
Claremont Colleges, Honnold Library, Special Collections Department

Joaquin Miller Papers
Colorado Heritage Center
    Frederick J. V. Skiff Scrapbooks
Duke University, Perkins Library, Manuscripts Division
    Sidney Lanier Papers
    Joseph A. Miller Papers
Georgia State Archives
    Isaac W. Avery Papers
Harvard University Archives
    Frederic Ward Putnam Papers
Historical Society of Pennsylvania
    William Bigler Papers
    Philadelphia Centennial Exhibition Collection
    John Welsh Collection
Library of Congress
    W J McGee Papers
    Booker T. Washington Papers
Missouri Historical Society
    David R. Francis Papers
    Records of the Louisiana Purchase Exposition
National Anthropology Archives, Smithsonian Institution
    Bureau of American Ethnology, Letters Received 1886–1906
    Aleš Hrdlička Papers
    Otis T. Mason Papers
    Private Papers of Charles Rau
    Mathilda Coxe Stevenson Papers
    United States National Museum, Division of Ethnology, Manuscript and Pamphlet
    Files
National Archives
    Record Group 48, Records of the Office of the Secretary of the Interior
    Record Group 75, Records of the Bureau of Indian Affairs
    Record Group 350, Records of the Bureau of Insular Affairs
Nebraska State Historical Society
    William V. Allen Papers
    Records of the Trans-Mississippi and International Exposition
    John A. Wakefield Scrapbooks (microfilm, originals in the Omaha Public Library)
    Charles Wooster Papers
New York Public Library, Art and Architecture Division
    Artist Files
Oregon Historical Society, Manuscripts Division
    Merle McKelvey Diary
    Records of the Lewis and Clark Centennial
Portland Public Library, John L. Wilson Room
    Records of the Lewis and Clark Centennial
San Diego Historical Society, Manuscripts Collection
    Biographical Files
    Panama California Exposition Scrapbooks

Smithsonian Institution Archives
  Record Unit 55, Assistant Secretary in Charge of the United States National
  Museum, 1897–1917
  Record Unit 70, Exposition Records of the Smithsonian Institution and the United
  States National Museum, 1875–1916
  Record Unit 158, United States National Museum, Curators' Annual Reports,
  1881–1964
  Record Unit 189, Assistant Secretary in Charge, United States National Museum,
  1860–1908
  Record Unit 192, United States National Museum Permanent Administration Files,
  1877, [1902–35], 1975
  Record Unit 7050, George Brown Goode Collection, 1798–1896
  Record Unit 7098, Biographical Information File
  Record Unit 7230, Department of Geology, Biographical File
Southwest Museum
  Charles F. Lummis Papers
Tennessee State Library and Archives
  Joseph Buckner Killebrew Papers
  Tennessee Centennial Exposition Collection
University of California, Berkeley, Bancroft Library
  Records of the Panama-Pacific International Exposition
University of California, Los Angeles, Department of Special Collections
  Expositions and Fairs Collection
  Frederick W. Taylor Scrapbooks
University of Chicago, Regenstein Library, Department of Special Collections
  Frederick Starr Papers
University of Colorado, Western Historical Collections
  Horace G. Benson Papers
University of Oregon, Oregon Collection
  Robert A. Miller Papers
University of Pennsylvania Archives
  Biographical Files
University of Washington, Manuscripts Division
  Miscellaneous Records of the Alaska-Yukon-Pacific Exposition
  Frederick G. Whitaker Papers
University of Washington, Pacific Northwest Collection
  Alaska-Yukon-Pacific Scrapbooks
  Vertical Files
University of Washington, University Archives
  Frederick Morgan Padelford Papers

Guidebooks, Pamphlets, Broadsides, and Similar Materials
Alaska-Yukon-Pacific Exposition: Official Guide. No imprint.
*Art Handbook: Official Handbook of Architecture and Sculpture and Art Catalogue
  to the Pan-American Exposition*. Buffalo: David Gray, 1901.
Catalogue of the Centennial Loan Exhibition. Philadelphia: J. B. Lippincott, [1875].
Centennial Exposition Guide. Philadelphia: G. Lawrence, [1876?].

Circular Letter of Governor Taft. Manila: Bureau of Public Printing, 1902.

Cooper, Peter, et al. *The Centennial Celebration and International Exhibition: Address to the People of New York by Prominent and Influential Citizens*. [New York]: New York Evening Post, n.d.

Cummins, Frederick T. *Historical Biography and Libretto of the Indian Congress*. No imprint.

Darkest Africa: Real African Life in a Real African Village. No imprint.

Historical Sketchbook and Guide to New Orleans and Environs. New York: Will H. Coleman, 1885.

Ins and Outs of Buffalo. Official Guide to the Pan-American City. Buffalo: A. B. Floyd, 1901.

The Javanese Theater, the Java Village, Midway Plaisance: World's Columbian Exposition, Chicago, 1893. Containing Also a Short Description of Java, the People, Languages, Customs, Food, Products, Etc. [Chicago]: Java Chicago Exhibition Syndicate, n.d.

Laird's and Lee's Standard Pocket Guide and Time Saver. Chicago: Laird and Lee Publishers, 1904.

The Logical Point: An Illustrated Monthly for the Advancement of the World's Panama Exposition. No imprint.

Lowenstein, M. J. *Official Guide to the Louisiana Purchase Exposition*. Saint Louis: Official Guide Company, 1904.

Magee's Centennial Guide of Philadelphia. Philadelphia: R. Magee, 1876.

Newell, Alfred O., ed. *Philippine Exposition, World's Fair, St. Louis, 1904*. No imprint.

Official Catalogue and Guidebook to the Pan-American Exposition. Buffalo: Charles Ahrhart, 1901.

Official Catalogue of Exhibits: Section II. Saint Louis: Official Catalogue Company, 1904.

Official Catalogue of Exhibits, Universal Exposition, St. Louis, 1904. Saint Louis: Official Catalogue Company, [1904].

Official Catalogue of the Japanese Section. Philadelphia: W. P. Kildare, 1876.

Official Catalogue: Philippine Exhibits. Saint Louis: Official Catalogue Company, 1904.

The Official Guide and Descriptive Book, Panama California International Exposition. San Diego: Panama-California Exposition Commission, [1915].

Official Handbook: Description of the Philippines. Manila: Bureau of Public Printing, 1903.

Official Handbook of the Philippines and Catalogue of the Philippine Exhibit. Manila: Bureau of Public Printing, 1903.

Pan-American Exposition. Buffalo: Pan-American Exposition Company, 1900.

Report of the Philippine Exposition to the Louisiana Purchase Exposition and Official Lists of Awards. . . . Saint Louis: Greeley Printery, 1904.

St. Louis Exposition 1904: Exhibit of American Federation of Labor . . . Catalogue of Exhibits. No imprint.

Sunset City and Sunset Scenes, No. 2, May 14, 1894. San Francisco: H. S. Crocker, 1894.

A Week at the Fair Illustrating Exhibits and Wonders of the World's Columbian Exposition. Chicago: Rand McNally, 1893.

World's Columbian Exposition, Plan and Classification. Chicago: Chicago World's
Columbian Exposition, Department of Publicity and Promotion, n.d.

Primary Sources

Adams, Henry. *The Education of Henry Adams*. Boston: Houghton Mifflin Company,
1961. Originally published 1907.

Adams, William Llewellyn. *Exploits and Adventures of a Soldier Ashore and Afloat*.
Philadelphia: J. B. Lippincott Company, 1911.

"An American Exposition." *Outlook* 49 (13 April 1901):97–98.

Annual Reports, Smithsonian Institution. Washington, D. C.: Government Printing
Office, 1876–1916.

"Association Welcomes Japan's Exposition Envoys to Europe and to the United
States." *Chicago Commerce* 5 (16 April 1909):5–11, 28–34.

[Avery, Isaac W.]. *City of Atlanta: A Descriptive Historical and Industrial Review
of the Gateway City of the South, Being the World's Fair Series on Great
American Cities*. Louisville, Ky.: Inter-State Publishing Company,
1892–93.

"Awakening: The Southern States and the Centennial." *Journal of the Exposition* 1
(15 November 1873):73–74.

"The A.-Y.-P. Exposition." *World's Work* 18 (1909):11889–94.

Bacon, Alice M. *The Negro and the Atlanta Exposition*. Occasional Papers, no. 7.
Baltimore: Trustees of the John F. Slater Fund, 1896.

Baird, Spencer F. "Appendix to the Report of the Secretary." *Annual Report,
Smithsonian Institution, 1875*. Washington, D.C.: Government Printing Office,
1876.

Baker, Charles H. *Life and Character of William Taylor Baker*. New York: Premier
Press, 1908.

Bancroft, Hubert Howe. *The Book of the Fair*. 2 vols. New York: Bancroft Books,
1894.

Barry, John D. *The City of Domes*. San Francisco: John J. Newbegin, 1915.

Barry, Richard H. *The Grandeur of the Exposition*. Buffalo: Robert Allen Reid
Publisher, 1901.

————. *Snap Shots on the Midway of the Pan-American Exposition*. Buffalo: Robert
Allen Reid Publisher, 1901.

Bauer, E. Frances. "The Development of an Empire." *Music Trade Review,
Special Edition: Lewis and Clark Exposition Number* 41 (30 September
1905).

Bennitt, Mark. *History of the Louisiana Purchase Exposition*. Saint Louis: St. Louis
Universal Exposition Publishing Company, 1905.

Besant, Walter. "A First Impression." *Cosmopolitan Magazine* 15 (1893):528–39.

Blake, William Phipps. "Previous International Exhibitions." In *Journal of the
Proceedings of the United States Centennial Commission at Philadelphia, 1872*.
Philadelphia: E. C. Markley, 1872.

Bloom, Sol. *The Autobiography of Sol Bloom*. New York: G. P. Putnam, 1948.

Bragdon, Claude. "Some Pan-American Impressions." *American Architecture and
Building News* 72 (1901):43–44.

Brennan, J. K., et al. "Expositions and Progress." In *The World's Work*. Vol. 10.
The Delphian Society, 93–206. New York: Doubleday, Page, n.d.

Brinton, Christian. "Art at the Pan-American Exposition." *Critic* 38 (1901):512–28.

Brush, Edward Hale. "Karl Bitter: An Appreciation." *Art and Progress* 6 (1915):295–301.

Buchanan, William I. "The Pan-American Exposition." *Collier's* 26 (December 1900):5.

Buel, J. W., ed. *Louisiana and the Fair: An Exposition of the World, Its People, and Their Achievements*. 10 vols. Saint Louis: World's Progress Publishing Company, 1904.

"Builders of the Exposition." *Pan-American Herald* 1 (July 1899):5.

Burke, E. A. "The World's Industrial and Cotton Centennial Exposition." *Parson's Memorial and Historical Library Magazine*. Nebraska Historical Society, n.d.

Burke, Katherine Delmar. *Storied Walls of the Exposition*. N.p., 1915.

Burnette, Frances Hodgson. *Two Little Pilgrims' Progress: A Story of the City Beautiful*. New York: Charles Scribner's Sons, 1895.

Burnham, Clara Louisa. *Sweet Clover*. Chicago: Laird and Lee, 1893.

Butler, Ellis Parker. "The Feet of the Detwilers: A Tale of Cousin Carrie and the Louisiana Purchase Exposition." *Leslie's Monthly Magazine* 68 (1904):413–18.

Butler, Nicholas Murray. "The Educational Influence of the Exposition." *Cosmopolitan Magazine* 31 (1901):538–40.

[Cameron, William E.; Palmer, Thomas W.; and Willard, Frances E.]. *The World's Fair: Being a Pictorial History of the Columbian Exposition*. Philadelphia: National Publishing Company, 1893.

Carrère, John M. "The Architectural Scheme." In *Art Handbook: Official Handbook of Architecture and Sculpture and Art Catalogue to the Pan-American Exposition*, 12–17. Buffalo: David Gray, 1901.

Chapple, Joe Mitchell. "Affairs at Washington." *National Magazine* 20 (1904):605–08.

———. "Affairs at Washington." *National Magazine* 21 (1904):3–21.

Clarke, F. W. "The Government Exhibit at Buffalo." *Forum* 31 (1901):654–60.

"The Close of the St. Louis Exposition." *Midway* 1 (January 1905):12.

Cockerell, T. D. A. "Spencer Fullerton Baird and the U.S. National Museum." *Bios* (1942):6–7.

Cohen, D. S. [Daisy Shortcut], and Sumner, H. B. [Array O'Pagus]. *One Hundred Years a Republic. Our Show: A Humorous Account of the International Exposition*. Philadelphia: Claxton, Remsen, and Haffelfinger, 1876.

Collier, C. A. "The Cotton States and International Exposition—Its Inception and Growth." *"Dixie"* 11 (September 1895):35.

The Columbian Gallery: A Portfolio of Photographs for the World's Fair. Chicago: Warner Company, 1894.

Congrès International d'Anthropologie et d'Archéologie Préhistoriques: Compte rendu de la dixième session à Paris, 1889. Paris: Ernest Leroux, 1891.

"Congress of the Indian Tribes of the United States (December 13, 1897). Senate Report no. 397." *Senate Reports* 1, no. 3620:2–3.

Cook, Frederick F. "An Eloquent Article on the Scene in Jackson Park." *Halligan's Weekly World's Fair* 3 (December 1893):713.

Cooper, Walter G. *The Cotton States and International Exposition and South Illustrated*. Atlanta: Illustrator Company, 1896.

_____. "The Growth of a Great Exposition." *"Dixie"* 11 (May 1895):32.

Crandall, Roy. "Friendly Cooperation." *Pan-American Herald* 2 (May 1900):23.

Croly, Herbert. "Some Novel Features of the Pan-American Exposition: Impressions and Opinions." *Architectural Record* 11 (1901):590–614.

"The Cultural Features of the St. Louis Exposition." *Nation* 79 (22 December 1904): 499–500.

Dale, James L. *What Ben Beverly Saw at the Great Exposition.* Chicago: Centennial Publishing Company, 1876.

Dall, William H. "Anthropology." *Nation* 57 (28 September 1893):226.

_____. "Science." *Nation* 57 (14 September 1893):186–87.

"Darkies Day at the Fair." *World's Fair Puck* (21 August 1893): 186–87.

"Department of Organization." *World's Columbian Exposition Illustrated* 1 (June 1891):20.

"Dr. Gustavo Niederlein." *World's Fair Bulletin* 3 (October 1902):30.

"Dr. W. P. Wilson." *World's Fair Bulletin* 3 (October 1902):23.

Douglass, Frederick. "Inauguration of the World's Columbian Exposition." *World's Columbian Exposition Illustrated* 3 (March 1893):602–4.

Douglass, Frederick, and Wells, Ida. *The Reason Why the Colored American Is Not in the World's Columbian Exposition.* No imprint. Beinecke Library, Yale University.

Duffus, R. L. *The Tower of Jewels: Memories of San Francisco.* New York: W. W. Norton, 1960.

Dunne, Finley P. "Mr. Dooley on the Midway." *Cosmopolitan Magazine* 21 (1901):476.

Duster, Alfreda M., ed. *Crusade for Justice: The Autobiography of Ida B. Wells.* Chicago: University of Chicago Press, 1970.

Eastlake, Delano W. "Moral Life of the Japanese." *Popular Science Monthly* 43 (1893):348.

Eastman, John C. "Village Life at the World's Fair." *Chautauquan* 17 (1893):602–4.

Editorial. *Harper's Weekly* 37 (7 July 1893):629.

"Educational Value of the World's Fair." *Literary Digest* 29 (13 August 1904):192.

Elwell, Frank Edwin. "The Pan-American Exposition." *Arena* 25 (1901):53–58.

"Ethnological Department." *World's Fair Bulletin* 2 (October 1900):5.

"Ethnology and Archaeology at the Exposition." *World's Columbian Exposition Illustrated* 1 (June 1891):9.

The Exhibits of the Smithsonian Institution and the United States National Museum at the Alaska-Yukon-Pacific Exposition. Washington, D.C.: Judd and Detwiler, 1909.

"Export Exposition." *Pan-American Herald* 1 (October 1899):4.

"Extract from President McKinley's Speech Delivered before the Pan-American Commercial Congress Convened at the International Opening of the Philadelphia Commercial Museum, June 1897." In *International Commercial Congress, 1899,* 420. Philadelphia: Press of the Philadelphia Commercial Congress, 1899.

Fairall, Herbert. *The World's Industrial and Cotton Centennial Exposition.* Iowa City: Republican Publishing Company, 1885.

Fifth Annual Message of William S. Stokely, Mayor of the City of Philadelphia . . . October 11, 1877. Philadelphia: E. C. Markley, 1877.

"Filipino Characteristics." *Pan-American Herald* 2 (July 1900):10–11.

Fiske, Amos K. "An Exposition as a Work of Art." *Harper's Weekly* 45 (9 March 1901):272–77.

"Five Filipino Villages to Be on Grounds." *Lewis and Clark Journal* 3 (January 1905):6–7.

Fleming, Thomas. *Around the Pan with Uncle Hank: His Trip through the Pan-American Exposition*. New York: Nut Shell Publishing Company, 1901.

Fletcher, H. Phillips. *The St. Louis Exhibition, 1904*. London: B. T. Batsford, 1905.

Ford, Frances M. "Exposition Briefs." *Hatchet* (March 1898):20.

[Francis, David R.]. *A Tour of Europe in Nineteen Days: Report to the Board of Directors of the Louisiana Purchase Exposition on European Tour, Made in the Interest of the St. Louis Fair, by David R. Francis, President*. No imprint.

————. *The Universal Exposition of 1904*. Saint Louis: Louisiana Purchase Exposition Company, 1913.

French, Alice [Octave Thanet]. "The Trans-Mississippi Exposition."*Cosmopolitan Magazine* 25 (1898):599–614.

Fuller, Fay. "Omaha's Congress of Aborigines." *State* 2 (20 September 1898):70–73.

Gaebel, Arthur H., comp. *Makers of the Panama-California and Southern California. San Diego, Expositions*. San Diego, 1915.

Gage, Lyman, *Memoirs of Lyman J. Gage*. New York: House of Field, 1937.

————. *The World's Columbian Exposition: First Annual Report of the President*. Chicago: Knight and Leonard Company, 1891.

Gardner, Dorsey, ed. *United States Centennial Commission: International Exhibition, 1876, Grounds and Buildings of the Centennial Exhibition, Philadelphia, 1876*. Philadelphia: J. B. Lippincott, 1878.

Gaston, Joseph. *Portland: Its History and Builders*. 3 vols. Portland, 1911.

"A Generous Gift." *Lewis and Clark Journal* 1 (May 1904):7.

Gilder, Richard Watson. "What Shall We Name It?" In *Art Handbook: Official Handbook of Architecture and Sculpture and Art Catalogue to the Pan-American Exposition*, 6. Buffalo: David Gray, 1901.

"Glimpses of Indian Life at the Omaha Exposition." *American Monthly Review of Reviews* 18 (1898):436–43.

"The Good Done at Buffalo." *Century Magazine* 62 (1901):793–94.

Goode, G. Brown. "America's Relation to the Advance of Science." *Science*, n.s., 1 (4 January 1895):8–9.

————. "Museums and Good Citizenship." *Public Opinion* 17 (1894):758.

————. "The Museums of the Future." In *Annual Report of the United States National Museum: Year Ending June 30, 1897*. Washington, D.C.: Government Printing Office, 1898.

Goodrich, Arthur. "Short Stories of Interesting Exhibits." *World's Work* 2 (1901):1054–96.

Gordon, Elizabeth. *What We Saw at Madame World's Fair, Being a Series of Letters from the Twins at the Panama-Pacific International Exposition to Their Cousins at Home*. San Francisco: Samuel Levinson, 1915.

Grady, Henry. "The New South." In *The New South and Other Addresses by Henry Woodfin Grady*, ed. Edna Henry Lee Turpin. New York: Charles F. Merrill Company, 1904.

"Grand Finale." *World's Fair Puck* (30 October 1893): back cover.

Grant, Robert. "Notes on the Pan-American Exposition." *Cosmopolitan Magazine* 31
(1901):451–62.

"The Great Exposition at Omaha." *Century Magazine* 60 (1898):518–19.

"Great Rush for Concessions." *Pan-American Herald* 1 (July 1899):4.

Groff, Frances A. "Exposition Moths." *Sunset* 35 (July 1915):133–48.

Hardee, Theodore. "Foreign Participation." *Lewis and Clark Journal* 1 (April
1904):6-7.

Hardy, Mrs. A. "Women and the Exposition." *Hatchet* (March 1898):24.

Harlan, Louis, ed. *The Booker T. Washington Papers*. 7 vols. Urbana: University of
Illinois Press, 1972.

Harriman, Mary Alice. "The Congress of American Aborigines at the Omaha
Exposition." *Overland Monthly*, n.s., 33 (June 1899):505–12.

Hart, Mary Bronson. "How to See the Pan-American Exposition." *Everybody's
Magazine* 5 (October 1901):488–91.

———. "The Play-Side of the Fair." *World's Work* 2 (1901):1097–1101.

Harwood, W. S. "The Omaha Exhibition." *Harper's Weekly* 42 (20 August
1898):822–23.

Hawthorne, Julian. "Foreign Folk at the Fair." *Cosmopolitan Magazine* 15
(1893):567–82.

———"Some Novelties at the Buffalo Fair." *Cosmopolitan Magazine* 31 (1901):483–
92.

Haynes, James B. *History of the Trans-Mississippi and International Exposition of
1898*. Omaha: [Published under direction of the Committee on History as
authorized by the Board of Directors, 20 June 1902], 1910.

*Hearing before the Committee on Industrial Arts and Expositions of the House of
Representatives: Alaska-Yukon Exposition, January 27, 1908*. Washington, D.C.:
General Printing Office, 1908.

Herrick, Robert. *The Memoirs of an American Citizen*. Cambridge: Harvard University
Press, 1963. Originally published 1905.

Hill, Richmond C. *Buffalo Greets the South with a Synopsis of Her History*. Buffalo:
Matthews-Northrup Company, [1895].

Hoch, Edmund S. "The Universal Exposition of 1904." In *Official Catalogue of
Exhibits: Section II*, 29–34. Saint Louis: Official Catalogue Company, 1904.

Hoffman, D. O. Noble. "The Philippine Exhibit at the Pan-American Exposition."
National Geographic Magazine 12 (March 1901):119–22.

Holley, Marietta. *Josiah Allen's Wife as a P. A. and P. I.: Samantha at the
Centennial*. Hartford, Conn.: American Publishing Company, 1877.

Howells, William Dean. *Letters of an Altrurian Traveller*, edited by Clara M. Kirk
and Rudolph King. Gainesville, Fla.: Scholar's Facsimilies and Reprints, 1961.

———. "A Sennight of the Centennial." *Atlantic Monthly* 38 (1876):92–107.

"How the Railroads Built the Exposition." *World's Work* 2 (1901), advertising
supplement.

Hrdlička, Aleš. "Eugenics and Its Natural Limitations in Man." *Science*, n.s., 42 (15
October 1915):546.

Hughes, Charles H. "The Louisiana Purchase Exposition: The Neurasthenic and the
Brain-Tired." *Alienist and Neurologist*. Reprint. N.d. UCLA, Department of
Special Collections, Expositions and Fairs Collection.

Hutchin, George L. "Hit the Trail Is the Favorite Diversion of the Lewis and Clark Exposition." *Lewis and Clark Journal* 3 (June 1905):48–58.

"The Igorrote Tribe from the Philippines." *Lewis and Clark Journal* 4 (October 1905):41.

"Indian Congress." *Pan-American Herald* 2 (May 1900):7.

Ingram, J. S. *The Centennial Exposition, Described and Illustrated: Being a Concise and Graphic Description of This Grand Enterprise Commemorative of the First Centenary of American Independence*. Philadelphia: Hubbard Brothers, 1876.

Jackson, Giles B., and Davis, Webster D. *Industrial History of the Negro Race*. Richmond, Va.: Negro Educational Association, 1911.

James, Juliet. *Palaces and Courts of the Exposition: A Handbook of the Architecture, Sculpture, and Mural Painting with Special Reference to the Symbolism*. San Francisco: California Book Company, 1915.

"Japan's Relations to Fair." *Lewis and Clark Journal* 2 (October 1904):12–13.

Jenks, Albert Ernest. "Anthropology." In *Official Handbook of the Philippines and Catalogue of the Philippine Exhibit*, 261–62. Manila: Bureau of Public Printing, 1903.

————. "Native Races." In *Official Handbook: Description of the Philippines*, 155–63. Manila: Bureau of Public Printing, 1903.

Johnson, Rossiter, ed. *A History of the World's Columbian Exposition*. 4 vols. New York: D. Appleton, 1898.

Jones, Kennard H. "Fourth Annual Report of the Chief of Police of the City of Philadelphia." In *Fifth Annual Message of William S. Stokely, Mayor of the City of Philadelphia . . . October 11, 1877*, 167. Philadelphia: E. C. Markley, 1877.

Journal of the Proceedings of the United States Centennial Commission at Philadelphia, 1872. Philadelphia: E. C. Markley, 1872.

Justi, Herman, ed. *Official History of the Tennessee Centennial Exposition*. Nashville: Brandon Publishing Company, 1898.

Kelley, Thomas J. "The Trans-Mississippi Ode for Girls and Boys." *Hatchet* (18 March 1898):19.

"Landscape Architect Rudolph Ulrich." *Pan-American Herald* 1 (15 August 1899):6.

Langley, Samuel Pierpont. "Memoir of George Brown Goode." In *Annual Report of the United States National Museum: Year Ending June 30, 1897*, 58. Washington, D.C.: Government Printing Office, 1898.

Lanier, Henry Wysham. "The Great Fair at Omaha." *American Monthly Review of Reviews* 1 (18 July 1898):53–59.

Leslie, Amy. *Amy Leslie at the Fair*. Chicago: W. B. Conkey Company, 1893.

Letters about the Exhibition, the New York Tribune Extra, no. 35. [New York, 1876].

Lewis, Herb. *Eb Peechcrap and Wife at the Fair*. New York: Neale Publishing Company, 1906.

Lewis, Sinclair. *Babbit*. New York: Harcourt, Brace, 1922.

Lloyd, Charles Edward. "The Pan-American Exposition as an Educational Force." *Chautauquan* 33 (July 1901):335.

Louisiana Purchase Centennial: Dedication Ceremonies, St. Louis. U.S.A., April 30th and May 1st–2nd, 1903. No imprint.

Mabie, Hamilton Wright. "The Spirit of the New World as Interpreted by the Pan-American Exposition." *Outlook* 68 (10 July 1901):536–37.

McCabe, James D. *The Illustrated History of the Centennial Exhibition Held in Commemoration of the One Hundredth Anniversary of American Independence.* Philadelphia: National Publishing Company, 1876.

McDowell, Edward B. "The World's Fair Cosmopolis." *Frank Leslie's Popular Monthly* 36 (October 1893):407–16.

McGee, W J. "Anthropology." In *Louisiana Purchase Centennial: Dedication Ceremonies, St. Louis, U.S.A. April 30th and May 1st–2nd, 1903,* 41–45. No imprint.

———. "The Anthropology Exhibit." *Harper's Weekly* 48 (April 1904):683.

———. "The Beginnings of Civilization." *World Today* 7 (September 1904):1210–13.

———. "Department of Anthropology." In *Official Catalogue of Exhibits, Universal Exposition, St. Louis, 1904,* 9–10. Saint Louis: Official Catalogue Company, [1904].

———. "The Trend of Human Progress." *American Anthropologist,* n.s., 1 (July 1899):401–47.

MacMechen, Thomas. "Down 'the Pike,' the Boulevard of Gaiety at the St. Louis Exposition." *Pacific Monthly* 12 (July 1904):30.

———. "The True and Complete Story of the Pike and Its Attractions." In *Louisiana Purchase Centenial: Dedication Ceremonies, St. Louis, U.S.A. April 30th and May 1st–2nd, 1903,* 1. No imprint.

Mason, Otis T. "Anthropology." In *Report of the Committee on Awards of the World's Columbian Commission: Special Reports upon Special Subjects or Groups (1901–1902).* House Report no. 4373, 154:319–22.

———. *Ethnological Directions Relative to Indian Tribes of the United States.* Washington, D.C.: Government Printing Office, 1875.

———. "Ethnological Exhibit of the Smithsonian Institution." In *Memoirs of the International Congress of Anthropology.* ed. C. Staniland Wake, 208–16. Chicago: Schute Publishing Company, 1894.

———. "Summary of Progress in Anthropology." In *Annual Reports of the Smithsonian Institution for the Year Ending July 1893,* 601–29. Washington, D.C.: Government Printing Office, 1894.

Merrick, Frank L. "Alaska-Yukon-Pacific Exposition." *Alaska-Yukon Magazine* 2 (September 1906):2–7.

———. "Financing of the Alaska-Yukon-Pacific Exposition." *Alaska-Yukon Magazine* 2 (November 1906):117–22.

Midway Types: A Book of Illustrated Lessons about the People of the Midway Plaisance. Chicago: American Engraving Company, 1894.

Milburn, John. "Karl Bitter: Exposition Builder." *Art and Progress* 6 (1915):305–8.

Miller, Joaquin. "The Great Centennial Fair and Its Future." *Independent* (13 July 1876).

———. "Song of the Centennial." In *Frank Leslie's Illustrated Historical Register of the Centennial Exposition, 1876,* 128. No imprint.

Mitchell, Edmund. "The Exposition as a Historical Museum." *World Today* 7 (1904):1193–1201.

Mooney, James. "The Indian Congress at Omaha." *American Anthropologist* 1 (1899):126–49.

Morearty, Ed F. *Omaha Memories*. Omaha: Swartz Printing Company, 1917.

"National Activity." *Pan-American Herald* 2 (June 1900):14–15.

"National School Celebration of Columbus Day: The Official Program." *Youth's Companion* 65 (8 September 1892):446–47.

"Necrology—Frank Frederick Hilder." In *Twenty-second Annual Report of the Bureau of American Ethnology to the Secretary of the Smithsonian Institution, 1900–1901, Part I*, xl–xlii. Washington, D.C.: Government Printing Office, 1901.

Newton, Harry L. *Hiram Birdseed at the Lewis and Clark Centennial Exposition*. New York: Will Rossiter, [1905].

Newton, Maurice F. "The Pan-American Exposition: The Color Scheme." *American Architect and Building News* 71 (1901):3–5.

Niederlein, Gustavo. "Important Instructions to Bear in Mind in Making Philippine Exhibits." In *Circular Letter of Governor Taft*. Manila: Bureau of Public Printing, 1902.

"Non-Salaried Officers of Exposition Dined." *Pacific Northwest Commerce* 1 (December 1909):15–17.

Northrup, Birdsley Grant. *Official Bulletin of the International Exhibition: Education Number*. Philadelphia: International Exhibition Company, 1877.

Norton, Charles B., ed. *Treasures of Art, Industry, and Manufacture Represented in the American Centennial Exhibition at Philadelphia, 1876*. Buffalo: Cossact, 1877.

"Now for Buffalo." *Century Magazine* 53 (1901):156.

Official History of the California Midwinter International Exposition. San Francisco: Press of H. S. Crocker Company, 1894.

Official Proceedings of the Eighth Convention of the Trans-Mississippi Commercial Congress Held at Omaha, Neb., November 25, 26, 27, and 28, 1895. Omaha: Press of Omaha Printing Company, [1895].

Official Proceedings of the Fifteenth Session of the Trans-Mississippi Commercial Congress held at St. Louis. Denver: Smith-Brooks Company, 1904.

"Opening of the St. Louis Fair." *Harper's Weekly* 48 (30 April 1904):665.

Oriental and Occidental: Northern and Southern Portraits. Types of the Midway Plaisance. Saint Louis: N. D. Thompson Publishing Company, 1894.

Ota, Hajime. "Japan's Motive for Taking Part in A.-Y.-P. Exposition." *Pacific Northwest Commerce* 1 (September 1909):18–20.

"Our Insular Possessions." *World's Fair Bulletin* 2 (September 1901):25.

Packer, E. E. *The White City, Being an Account of a Trip to the World's Columbian Exposition at Chicago in 1893*. San Diego, 1933.

Page, Walter Hines. "The Pan-American Exposition." *World's Work* 2 (1901):1015–48.

Palmer, Thomas W. "Presentation of the Buildings." In *Memorial Volume: Dedicatory and Opening Ceremonies of the World's Columbian Exposition*, 159. Chicago: A. L. Stone, 1893.

"Pan-American Exposition." *Black Diamond Express* 2 (February 1900):15–16.

"The Pan-American Exposition." *Pan-American Herald* 1 (July 1899):1–2.

Pan-American Exposition: Its Purpose and Its Plan. Buffalo: Pan-American Exposition Company, 1900.

Pan-American Exposition: Report of William I. Buchanan, Director-General. Buffalo, 1901.

Penn, I. Garland. "The Awakening of the Race." In *The Cotton States and International Exposition and South Illustrated*, ed. Walter C. Cooper, 58–63. Atlanta: Illustrator Company, 1896.

"The Philippines Display." *World's Fair Bulletin* 3 (May 1902):20.

Pray-Palmer, Lillian, ed. *A Book of Memories for the Ages*. San Diego, [1925].

"Prices of Commodities and Rates of Wages in Manila." *Bulletin of the Department of Labor*, no. 32 (January 1901):29–42.

Proceedings of the Dedication of the John Welsh Memorial, 23 June 1887. Philadelphia: Allen, Lane, and Scott, n.d.

"Prof. W J M'Gee." *World's Fair Bulletin* 4 (August 1903):29.

Program, Organization, and Addresses: Lewis and Clark Educational Congress. Portland: Anderson and Duniway Company, [1905].

Rapport d'Ensemble de la Délégation Ouvrière Libre à Philadelphia. Paris, 1889.

Reed, Henry. "Official History of the Lewis and Clark Centennial," 1908, MS. 383B. Oregon Historical Society, Manuscripts Division. Microfilm copy in California State University, Fresno, Department of Special Collections.

———. "The Story of the Lewis and Clark Exposition to Date." *Pacific Monthly* 9 (January 1903):32–40.

van Rensselaer, Mariana G. "At the Fair." *Century Magazine* 46 (May 1893):12–13.

Report of the Board of Commissioners Representing the State of New York at the Cotton States and International Exposition. Albany: Wynkoop Hallenbeck Crawford Company, 1896.

Report of the Board of General Managers of the Exhibit of the State of New York. Albany: J. B. Lyon Company, 1902.

Report of the Committee on Awards of the World's Columbian Commission: Special Reports upon Special Subjects or Groups (1901–1902). House Report no. 4373, vol. 154. Washington, D.C.: Government Printing Office, 1901.

Report of the Philippine Exposition to the Louisiana Purchase Exposition and Official List of Awards. . . . Saint Louis: Greeley Printery, 1904.

Report of the President to the Board of Directors of the World's Columbian Exposition. Chicago: Rand, McNally, 1893.

Report of the United States Government Board of Managers, Alaska-Yukon-Pacific Exposition, Seattle, Washington, 1909. Washington, D.C.: Government Printing Office, 1909.

The Reports of Committees of the House of Representatives for the First Session of the Fifty Second Congress, 1891–1892. House Report no. 3047. Washington, D.C.: Government Printing Office, 1892.

Rodgers, W. A. "The Exposition at Omaha." *Harper's Weekly* 62 (8 October 1898):987.

"Science at the Columbian Exposition." *Popular Science Monthly* 44 (1893):124.

"Scientific Teaching in the Colleges." *Popular Science Monthly* 16 (1880):556–59.

"Seattle Opens Doors of Country to Japanese Commissioners." *Pacific Northwest Commerce* 1 (October 1909):5, 11–19.

Sheffield, William M. "Work of the Alaska Club." *Alaska-Yukon Magazine* 2 (October 1906): 106–7.

Shibusawa, Baron E. "Mutual Interest Grows Steadily." *Pacific Northwest Commerce* 1 (October 1909):21–22.

Skiff, Frederick J. V., et al. *An Historical Account and Descriptive Account of the Field Columbian Museum*. Field Columbian Museum Publication no. 1. Chicago, 1894.

Smith, Harlan Ingersoll. "Man and His Works: The Anthropology Building at the World's Columbian Exposition." *American Antiquarian* 15 (1893):115–17.

Snider, Denton J. *World's Fair Studies*. Chicago: Sigma Publishing Company, 1895.

Starr, Frederick. *The Ainu Group at the Saint-Louis Exposition*. Chicago: Open Court Publishing Company, 1904.

———. "Anthropology at the World's Fair." *Popular Science Monthly* 43 (1893):610–21.

Stead, William. *From the Old World to the New; or, A Christmas Story of the World's Fair, 1893, Being the Christmas Number of the Review of Reviews*. N.p., 1892.

Steinbeck, John. *The Grapes of Wrath*. New York: Viking Press, 1939.

Stevens, Charles M. [Quondam]. *The Adventures of Uncle Jeremiah and Family at the Great Fair*. Chicago: Laird and Lee, 1893.

Sullivan, Louis H. *The Autobiography of an Idea*. New York: W. W. Norton, 1926.

"Taking Definite Form." *Pan-American Herald* 1 (November 1899):4.

Tateno, Gozo. "Japan." *North American Review* 156 (1893):34–43.

Taylor, Frederick W. "Exhibits That Might Have Been." *Everybody's Magazine* 5 (October 1901):406–19.

Telang, Rao. *A World's Fair Souvenir: Impressions of the World's Fair and America in General*. San Francisco: Pacific Press Publishing Company, 1893.

Todd, Frank Morton. *The Story of the Exposition: Being the Official History of the International Celebration Held at San Francisco in 1915 to Commemorate the Discovery of the Pacific Ocean and Construction of the Panama Canal*. 5 vols. New York: G. P. Putnam's Sons, Knickerbocker Press, 1921.

Trout, S. Edgar. *The Story of the Centennial of 1876: Golden Anniversary*. N.p., 1929.

Truman, Ben C. *History of the World's Fair*. Philadelphia: Mammoth Publishing Company, 1893.

Turner, C. Y. "Coloring and Decorating the Pan-American Exposition." *Quarterly Bulletin of the American Institute of Architects* 2 (1901):159–63.

Turner, Frederick Jackson. "The Significance of the Frontier in American History." In *The Significance of the Frontier in American History*, ed. Harold P. Simonson. New York: Frederick Ungar Publishing Company, 1963.

Twenty-second Annual Report of the Bureau of American Ethnology to the Secretary of the Smithsonian Institution: 1900–1901, Part I. Washington, D.C.: Government Printing Office, 1901.

United States Centennial Commission. *International Exhibition, 1876: Reports of the President, Secretary, and Executive Committee together with the Journal of the Final Session of the Commission*. Philadelphia: J. B. Lippincott, 1879.

Villard, Oswald G. "Karl Bitter: Immigrant." *Art and Progress* 6 (1915):310–12.

Wake, C. Staniland, ed. *Memoirs of the International Congress of Anthropology*. Chicago: Schute Publishing Company, 1894.

[Wakefield, John A.]. *Report of the General Secretary of the Trans-Mississippi and International Exposition, June 26, 1899*. No imprint.

Wakefield, John A.; Gregg, Norris B.; and White, Norton E. "The Division of Concessions and Admissions." In *Louisiana Purchase Centennial: Dedication Ceremonies, St. Louis. U.S.A., April 30th and May 1st–2nd, 1903*. No imprint.

Walker, Charles Howard. "The Great Exposition at Omaha." *Century Magazine* 60 (1898):518–19.

Walker, Francis A. *The World's Fair*. New York: A. S. Barnes, 1878.

Wattles, Gurdon Wallace. *Autobiography of Gurdon Wallace Wattles*. [New York: Scribner Press, 1927].

Wellman, Walter. "The World's Fair as a Progress Promoter." *Success* (November 1904):40.

Wheeler, Benjamin Ide. "The Relation of the Pacific Coast to Education in the Orient." *Program, Organization, and Addresses: Lewis and Clark Educational Congress*. Portland: Anderson and Duniway Company, [1905].

White, Annie Randall. *The Story of Columbus and the World's Columbian Exposition . . . Designed for Young Folks*. Chicago: Monarch Books Company, [1892].

Wilcox, Ella Wheeler. "The Americas to the World." *Cosmopolitan Magazine* 31 (1901): 529–30.

"Within the Midway Plaisance." *World's Fair Special Number: Illustrated American* (n.d.):59.

Wolfe, Thomas. *Look Homeward, Angel: A Story of the Buried Life*. New York: Charles Scribner's Sons, 1929.

World's Columbian Exposition: Plan and Classification. Chicago: Chicago World's Columbian Exposition, Department of Publicity and Promotion, n.d.

World's Fair Immortals. Saint Louis: Cartoonists' Club, 1905.

Wright, Eugene Richard. "Aspects of the Pan-American Exposition." *Atlantic Monthly* 88 (1901):85–92.

Secondary Sources

Abbot, Carl. *The Great Extravaganza: Portland and the Lewis and Clark Exposition*. Portland: Oregon Historical Society, 1981.

————. "Norfolk in the New Century: The Jamestown Exposition and Urban Boosterism." *Virginia Magazine of History and Biography* 85 (1977):86–96.

Alfers, Kenneth G. "The Trans-Mississippi Exposition." M.A. thesis, Creighton University, 1968.

————. "Triumph of the West: The Trans-Mississippi Exposition." *Nebraska History* 53 (1972):313–29.

Allwood, John. *The Great Exhibitions*. London: Studio Vista, 1977.

Altick, Richard D. *The Shows of London*. Cambridge: Harvard University Press, 1978.

Amero, Richard. "The Making of the Panama-California Exposition, 1909–1915." Unpublished paper, 1978, San Diego Historical Society.

Andrews, William D. "Women and the Fairs of 1876 and 1893." *Hayes Historical Journal* 1 (1977):173–83.

Asad, Talal. *Anthropology and the Colonial Encounter*. London: Ithaca Press, 1973.

August, Thomas G. "Colonial Policy and Propaganda: The Popularization of the Idée Coloniale in France, 1919–1939." Ph.D. dissertation, University of Wisconsin, 1978.

Badger, Rodney Reid. *The Great American Fair: The World's Columbian Exposition and American Culture*. Chicago: Nelson-Hall, 1979.

———. "The World's Columbian Exposition: Patterns of Change and Social Control in the 1890s." Ph.D. dissertation, Syracuse University, 1975.

Bannister, Robert. *Social Darwinism: Science and Myth in Anglo-American Social Thought*. Philadelphia: Temple University Press, 1972.

Basney, Dana Alan. "The Role of the Spreckles' Business Interests in the Development of San Diego." M.S. thesis, San Diego State University, 1975.

Benedict, Burton, et al. *The Anthropology of World's Fairs: San Francisco Panama-Pacific International Exposition, 1915*. Berkeley: Scolar Press, 1983.

Bennets, David Paul. "Black and White Workers: New Orleans, 1880–1900." Ph.D. dissertation, University of Illinois, Urbana, 1972.

Berger, Peter L., and Luckmann, Thomas. *The Social Construction of Reality: A Treatise in the Sociology of Knowledge*. New York: Anchor Books, 1967.

Bigart, Robert, and Woodcock, Clarence. "The Trans-Mississippi and International Exposition and the Flathead Delegation." *Montana, the Magazine of Western History* 29 (Autumn 1979):14–23.

Blicksilver, Jack. "International Cotton Exposition of 1881 and Its Impact upon Economic Development of Georgia." *Cotton History Review* 1 (1960):175–94.

Braun, Judy. "The North American Indian Exhibits at the 1876 and 1893 World Expositions: The Influence of Scientific Thought on Popular Attitudes." M.A. thesis, George Washington University, 1975.

tenBroek, Jacobus; Barnhart, Edward N.; and Matson, Floyd W. *Prejudice, War, and the Constitution: Causes and Consequences of the Evacuation of the Japanese Americans in World War II*. Berkeley and Los Angeles: University of California Press, 1954.

Brown, Dee. *The Year of the Century: 1876*. New York: Charles Scribner's Sons, 1976.

Burg, David F. *Chicago's White City of 1893*. Lexington: University of Kentucky Press, 1976.

Burt, Jesse C. "History of the Nashville, Chattanooga and St. Louis Railroad, 1873–1916." Ph.D. dissertation, Vanderbilt University, 1950.

Cary, Francine Curro. "Shaping the Future in the Gilded Age: A Study of Utopian Thought, 1888–1900." Ph.D. dissertation, University of Wisconsin, 1975.

Cawelti, John. "America on Display, 1876, 1893, 1933." In *America in the Age of Industrialism*, ed. Frederic C. Jaher, 317–63. New York: Free Press, 1968.

Cell, John. *The Highest Stage of White Supremacy: The Origins of Segregation in South Africa and the American South*. London: Cambridge University Press, 1982.

Chang, Su Cheng. "Contextual Framework for Reading Counterpoint." *Amerasia* 5, no. 1 (1978):115–29.

Christman, Florence. *The Romance of Balboa Park*. San Diego: Committee of One Hundred, 1977.

Coates, A. W. "American Scholarship Comes of Age: The Louisiana Purchase Exposition of 1904." *Journal of the History of Ideas* 22 (1964):404–17.

Colby, William Munn. "Routes to Rainy Mountain: A Biography of James Mooney, Ethnologist." Ph.D. dissertation, University of Wisconsin, 1977.

Cortinovis, Irene. "China at the St. Louis Fair." *Missouri Historical Review* 72 (1977):59–66.

Crook, David H. "Louis Sullivan, the World's Columbian Exposition, and American Life." Ph.D. dissertation, Harvard University, 1963.

Cross, Whitney R. "W J McGee and the Idea of Conservation." *Historian* 15 (1953):148–62.

Cunningham, Hugh. *Leisure in the Industrial Revolution*. London: Croom Helm, 1980.

Curti, Merle. "America at the World's Fairs, 1851–1893." *American Historical Review* 55 (1950):833–56.

Darnell, Margaretta Jean. "From the Chicago Fair to Walter Gropius: Changing Ideals in American Architecture." Ph.D. dissertation, Cornell University, 1975.

Darnell, Regna Diebold. "The Development of American Anthropology, 1879–1920: From the Bureau of American Ethnology to Franz Boas." Ph.D. dissertation, University of Pennsylvania, 1969.

Darney, Virginia Grant. "Women and World's Fairs: American International Expositions, 1876–1904." Ph.D. dissertation, Emory University, 1982.

Davis, David Brion. *The Problem of Slavery in the Age of Revolution, 1770–1823*. Ithaca: Cornell University Press, 1975.

Davis, Julia F., et al. "American Expositions and Architecture." *Journal of the Society of Architectural Historians* 35 (1976):272–79.

Davis, Louise Little. "The Parthenon and the Tennessee Centennial: The Greek Temple That Sparked a Birthday Party." *Tennessee Historical Quarterly* 26 (1976):335–53.

Davis, Mary Roberts. "The Atlanta Industrial Expositions of 1881 and 1895: Expressions of the Philosophy of the New South." M.A. thesis, Emory University, 1952.

Deahl, William E., Jr. "A History of Buffalo Bill's Wild West Show, 1883–1913." Ph.D. dissertation, Southern Illinois University, 1974.

Dexter, Ralph W. "The Impact of Evolutionary Theories on the Salem Group of Agassiz Zoologists." *Essex Institute Historical Collections* 115 (1979):144–71.

———. "Putnam's Problems Popularizing Anthropology." *American Scientist* 54 (1966):315–32.

———. "The Role of F. W. Putnam in Founding the Field Museum." *Curator* 13 (1970):21–26.

Diehl, Robert Warren. "To Speak or Not to Speak: San Diego 1912." M.A. thesis, University of California, San Diego, 1976.

Ditter, Dorothy E. C. "The Cultural Climate of the Centennial City: Philadelphia, 1875–1876." Ph.D. dissertation, University of Pennsylvania, 1947.

Doenecke, Justus D. "Myths, Machines, and Markets: The Columbian Exposition of 1893." *Journal of Popular Culture* 6 (1973):535–49.

Donaldson, Christine Hunter. "The Centennial of 1876: The Exposition and Culture for America." Ph.D. dissertation, Yale University, 1948.

Draper, Joan Elaine. "The San Francisco Civic Center: Architecture, Planning, and Politics." Ph.D. dissertation, University of California, Berkeley, 1980.

Drinnon, Richard. *Facing West: The Metaphysics of Indian-Hating and Empire Building*. New York: New American Library, 1980.

Druyvesteyn, Kenten. "The World's Parliament of Religions." Ph.D. dissertation, University of Chicago, 1976.

Edwards, John C. "Isaac Wheeler Avery and the Quest for South American Markets: A Note on the Experience of a Foreign Commissioner." *Atlanta Historical Bulletin* 17 (Spring/Summer 1973):51–59.

Falke, Wayne. "Samantha at the Centennial." *Hayes Historical Journal* 1 (1977):165–71.

Fishel, Leslie H. "The Utility of 1876." *Hayes Historical Journal* 1 (1977):211–15.

Foner, Philip S. "Black Participation in the Centennial of 1876." *Negro History Bulletin* 39 (1976):533–38.

Ford, Guy Stanton. "Expositions, International." In *Encyclopedia of the Social Sciences*, 6:23–27. London: Macmillan, 1932.

Fredrickson, George. *The Black Image in the White Mind: The Debate on Afro-American Character and Destiny, 1817–1914*. New York: Harper Torchbooks, 1971.

————. *White Supremacy: A Comparative Study on American and South African History*. New York: Oxford University Press, 1981.

Frickman, George A. "Alaska-Yukon-Pacific Exposition, 1909." *Pacific Northwest Quarterly* 53 (1962):89–99.

Gaston, Paul M. *The New South Creed: A Study in Southern Mythmaking*. New York: Alfred A. Knopf, 1970.

Genovese, Eugene D. *In Red and Black: Marxian Explorations in Southern Afro-American History*. New York: Pantheon Books, 1968.

Godley, Michael R. "China's World Fair of 1910: Lessons from a Forgotten Event." *Modern Asian Studies* 12 (1978):503–22.

Goldstein, Jonathan. *Philadelphia and the China Trade, 1682–1846: Commercial, Cultural, and Attitudinal Effects*. University Park: Pennsylvania State University Press, 1978.

Goodwyn, Lawrence. *Democratic Promise: The Populist Movement in America*. New York: Oxford University Press, 1976.

Gordon, Dudley. *Charles F. Lummis: Crusader in Corduroy*. Los Angeles: Cultural Assets Press, 1972.

Gordon, Martin K., comp. *Joseph Henry Pendleton, 1860–1942: Register of His Personal Papers*. Washington, D.C.: History and Museums Division Headquarters, United States Marine Corps, 1975.

Gossett, Thomas F. *Race: The History of an Idea in America*. New York: Schocken Books, 1965.

Gregory, Virginia Grace. "The Trans-Mississippi and International Exposition at Omaha, 1898." M.A. thesis, University of Nebraska, 1929.

Haller, John S., Jr. *Outcasts from Evolution: Scientific Attitudes of Racial Inferiority, 1859–1900*. New York: McGraw-Hill, 1975.

Haller, Mark. *Eugenics: Hereditarian Attitudes in American Thought*. New Brunswick: Rutgers University Press, 1963.

Hardy, Donald Clive. "The World's Industrial and Cotton Centennial Exposition." M.A. thesis, Tulane University, 1964.

Harlan, Louis R. *Booker T. Washington: The Making of a Black Leader*. New York: Oxford University Press, 1972.

———. "The Secret Life of Booker T. Washington." *Journal of Southern History* 37 (1971):393–416

Harris, Marvin. *The Rise of Anthropological Theory*. New York: Thomas Y. Crowell, 1968.

Harris, Neil. "All the World a Melting Pot? Japan at American Fairs, 1876–1904." In *Mutual Images: Essays in American Japanese Relations*, ed. Akira Iriye, 24–54. Cambridge: Harvard University Press, 1975.

———. "Cultural Institutions and American Modernization." *Journal of Library History* 16 (Winter 1981):28–47.

———. *Humbug: The Art of P. T. Barnum*. Boston: Little, Brown, 1973.

———. "Museums, Merchandising, and Popular Taste: The Struggle for Influence." In *Material Culture and the Study of American Life*, ed. Ian M. G. Quimby, 141–74. New York: W. W. Norton, 1978.

Hicks, John Henry. "The United States Centennial Exhibition of 1876." Ph.D. dissertation, University of Georgia, 1972.

Higham, John. *Strangers in the Land: Patterns of American Nativism, 1860–1925*. New Brunswick: Rutgers University Press, 1955.

Hilton, Suzanne. *The Way It Was: 1876*. Philadelphia: Westminster Press, 1975.

Hines, Thomas S. *Burnham of Chicago: Architect and Planner*. New York: Oxford University Press, 1974.

Hinsley, Curtis. "The Development of a Profession: Anthropology in Washington, D.C., 1846–1903." Ph.D. dissertation, University of Wisconsin, Madison, 1976.

———. *Savages and Scientists: The Smithsonian Institution and the Development of American Anthropology, 1846–1910*. Washington, D.C.: Smithsonian Institution Press, 1981.

Hirschfeld, Charles. "America on Exhibition: The New York Crystal Palace." *American Quarterly* 9 (1957):101–16.

Hoare, Quinton, and Smith, Geoffrey Nowell, eds. *Selections from the Prison Notebooks of Antonio Gramsci*. New York: International Publishers, 1971.

Hofstadter, Richard. *Social Darwinism in American Thought*. Boston: Beacon Press, 1955.

Holland, Norman. *Poems in Persons: An Introduction to the Psychoanalysis of Literature*. New York: W. W. Norton, 1973.

Horowitz, Helen L. "Animal and Man in the New York Zoological Park." *New York History* 57 (1975):426–55.

———. *Culture and the City: Cultural Philanthropy in Chicago from the 1880s to 1917*. Lexington: University of Kentucky Press, 1976.

———. "Seeing Ourselves through Bars." *Landscape* 25, no. 2 (1981):12–19.

Horowitz, Helen L., and Bridges, William. *Gathering of Animals: An Unconventional History of the New York Zoological Society*. New York: Harper and Row, 1974.

Jackson, Joy J. *New Orleans in the Gilded Age: Politics and Urban Progress, 1880–1896*. Baton Rouge: Louisiana State University Press, 1969.

Jensen, Joan M. "The Politics and History of William Kettner." *Journal of San Diego History* 11 (June 1965):26–39.

Johns, A. Wesley. *The Man Who Shot McKinley*. New York: A. S. Barnes, 1970.

Johnson, Jeff. "The Heyday of Oregon's Socialists." *Northwest Magazine* (19 December 1976):15–18.

Jordan, Winthrop D. *White over Black: American Attitudes towards the Negro, 1550–1812*. Baltimore: Penguin Books, 1968.

Karabel, John. "Revolutionary Contradictions: Antonio Gramsci and the Problem of Intellectuals." *Politics and Society* 6 (1976):123–72.

Kasson, John F. *Amusing the Millions*. New York: Hill and Wang, 1978.

Knutson, Robert. "The White City—The World's Columbian Exposition of 1893." Ph.D. dissertation, Columbia University, 1956.

Kohlstadt, Folke. "Formal and Structural Innovations in American Exposition Architecture, 1901–1939." Ph.D. dissertation, Northwestern University, 1973.

Kouwenhoven, John A. "The Eiffel Tower and the Ferris Wheel." *Arts Magazine* 54 (February 1980):170–73.

Kovel, Joel. *White Racism: A Psychohistory*. New York: Vintage Books, 1971.

Kraditor, Aileen S. "American Radical Historians on Their Heritage." *Past and Present*, no. 56 (August 1972):136–53.

Lacey, Michael James. "The Mysteries of Earth-Making Dissolve: A Study of Washington's Intellectual Community and the Origins of American Environmentalism in the Late Nineteenth Century." Ph.D. dissertation, George Washington University, 1979.

Lathrop, John Clarke. "The Philadelphia Exhibition of 1876: A Study of Social and Cultural Implications." M.A. thesis, Rutgers University, 1936.

Lears, T. J. Jackson. *No Place of Grace: Anti-Modernism and the Transformation of American Culture, 1880–1920*. New York: Pantheon Books, 1981.

Lederer, Francis L., II. "Competition for the World's Columbian Exposition: The Chicago Campaign." *Journal of the Illinois State Historical Society* 45 (1972):365–81.

Lester, Joan. "A Museum's Eye View." *Indian Historian* 5 (Summer 1972):25–31.

Loewenberg, Peter. "The Psychology of Racism." In *The Great Fear: Race in the Mind of America*, ed. Gary B. Nash and Richard Weiss. New York: Holt, Rinehart and Winston, 1970.

Lotchin, Roger. "The Darwinian City: The Politics of Urbanization in San Francisco between the World Wars." *Pacific Historical Review* 48 (1979):357–81.

Luckhurst, Kenneth W. *The Story of Exhibitions*. London: Studio, 1951.

Maass, John. "The Centennial Success Story." In *1876: A Centennial Exhibition*, ed. Robert Post, 11–23. Washington, D.C.: National Museum of History and Technology, Smithsonian Institution, 1976.

———. *The Glorious Enterprise*. Watkins Glen, N.Y.: American Life Foundation, 1973.

———. "Who Invented Dewey's Classification?" *Wilson Library Bulletin* 47 (December 1972):335–41.

MacColl, E. Kimbark. *The Shaping of a City: Business and Politics in Portland, Oregon, 1885–1915*. Portland: Georgian Press Company, 1976.

McCullough, Edo. *World's Fair Midways: An Affectionate Account of American Amusement Areas from the Crystal Palace to the Crystal Ball*. New York: Exposition Press, 1966.

McMahon, Barry J. "Seattle's Commercial Aspiration as Expressed in the Alaska-Yukon-Pacific Exposition." M.A. thesis, Washington State University, 1960.

Mandell, Richard D. *Paris 1900*. Toronto: University of Toronto Press, 1967.

Massa, Ann. "Black Women in the White City." *Journal of American Studies* 8 (1974):319–37.

May, Henry. *The End of American Innocence*. Chicago: Quadrangle Books, 1964.

Mayer, Harold M., and Wade, Richard C. *Chicago: Growth of a Metropolis*. Chicago: University of Chicago Press, 1969.

Miller, R. Berkeley. "Anthropology and Institutionalization: Frederick Starr at the University of Chicago, 1892–93." *Kroeber Anthropology Papers*, no. 51–52 (1978):49–60.

Montague, M. F. Ashley. "Aleš Hrdlička, 1869–1943." *American Anthropologist* 46 (1944):113–17.

Morgan, Howard Wayne. *William McKinley and His America*. Syracuse: Syracuse University Press, 1964.

Moses, Lester George. "James Mooney—Ethnologist." Ph.D. dissertation, University of New Mexico, 1977.

Mullis, Sharon M. "Extravaganza of the New South: The Cotton States and International Exposition, 1895." *Atlanta Historical Bulletin* 20 (Fall 1976):17–36.

Nelson, Arvid E., Jr. *The Ak-Sar-Ben Story*. Lincoln: Johnson Publishing Company, 1967.

————. "The Formation and Early History of the Knights of Ak-Sar-Ben as shown by Omaha Newspapers." M.A. thesis, Municipal University of Omaha, 1962.

Neufeld, Maurice F. "The Contribution of the World's Columbian Exposition of 1893 to the Idea of a Planned Society in the United States." Ph.D. dissertation, University of Wisconsin, 1935.

Oehser, Paul H. *Smithsonian Institution*. New York: Praeger Books, 1970.

Olcott, Charles Sumner. *The Life of William McKinley*. 2 vols. Boston: Houghton Mifflin Company, 1961.

Parmet, Robert D. "Competition for the World's Columbian Exposition: The New York Campaign." *Journal of the Illinois State Historical Society* 45 (1972):382–94.

Peterson, Harold F. *Diplomat of the Americas: William I. Buchanan*. Albany: State University of New York Press, 1976.

Pierce, Bessie L. *A History of Chicago, 1871–1893*. 3 vols. New York: Alfred A. Knopf, 1957.

Pitt, Leonard. *The Decline of the Californios: A Social History of the Spanish-Speaking Californians, 1846–1890*. Berkeley and Los Angeles: University of California Press, 1971.

Pole, J. R. *The Pursuit of Equality in American History*. Berkeley and Los Angeles: University of California Press, 1978.

Post, Robert, ed. *1876: A Centennial Exhibition*. Washington, D.C.: National Museum of History and Technology, Smithsonian Institution, 1976.

Potter, James E. "The Political Career of Charles Wooster." M.A. thesis, University of Nebraska, 1975.

Pourade, Richard. *Gold in the Sun*. San Diego: Union-Tribune Publishing Company, 1965.

Rabineau, Phyllis, "North American Anthropology at the Field Museum of Natural History." *American Indian Arts Magazine* 6 (1981):30–37.

Rodgers, Phyllis A. "The American Circus Clown." Ph.D. dissertation, Princeton University, 1979.

Roemer, Kenneth M. *The Obsolete Necessity: America in Utopian Writings, 1888–1900*. Kent, Ohio: Kent State University Press, 1976.

Rogin, Michael P. *Fathers and Children: Andrew Jackson and the Subjugation of the American Indian*. New York: Alfred A. Knopf, 1975.

Rowe, Kenneth E. "Bishop Simpson's Centennial Prayer." *Methodist History* 15 (1976):68–72.

Rubin, Barbara. "Aesthetic Ideology and Urban Design." *Annals of the Association of American Geographers* 69 (1979):339–61.

Rubin, Barbara; Carlton, Robert; and Rubin, Arnold. *L.A. in Installments*. Santa Monica, Calif.: Westside Publications, 1979.

Rudwick, Elliot, and Meier, August. "Black Man in the 'White City,' Negroes and the Columbian Exposition, 1893." *Phylon* 26 (1965):354–61.

Rydell, Robert W. "The Trans-Mississippi and International Exposition: 'To Work out the Problem of Universal Civilization.' " *American Quarterly* 33 (1981):587–607.

———. "Visions of Empire: International Expositions in Portland and Seattle, 1905–1909." *Pacific Historical Review* 52 (1983):37–65.

———. "The World's Columbian Exposition of 1893: Racist Underpinnings of a Utopian Artifact." *Journal of American Culture* 1 (1978):253–75.

Saxton, Alexander P. "Blackface Minstrelsy and Jacksonian Ideology." *American Quarterly* 27 (1975):3–28

———. "Historical Explanations of Racial Inequality: A Review Essay." *Marxist Perspectives* 2 (Summer 1979):146–68.

———. *The Indispensable Enemy: Labor and the Anti-Chinese Movement in California*. Berkeley and Los Angeles: University of California Press, 1971.

———. "Review Essay." *Amerasia* 4, no. 2 (1977):141–50.

Schenck, William Ziegler. "Negro Participation in Three Southern Expositions." M.A. thesis, University of North Carolina, 1970.

Schlereth, Thomas J. "The Philadelphia Centennial as a Teaching Model." *Hayes Historical Journal* 1 (1977):201–10.

Schneider, William. "Colonies at the 1900 World's Fair." *History Today* 31 (1981):31–34.

Shannon, Fred A. *The Centennial Years*. Garden City, N.Y.: Doubleday, 1967.

Shavin, Norman. "The Great Cotton Exposition of 1895." *Atlanta Magazine* 5 (October 1965):32–37.

Silverman, Debora L. "The 1889 Exhibition: The Crisis of Bourgeois Individualism." *Oppositions* 8 (1978):71–91.

Smith, Carl S. "Fearsome Fiction and the Windy City; or, Chicago in the Dime Novel." *Chicago History* 7 (1978):2–11.

Smith, Samuel Boyd. "Joseph Buckner Killebrew: Tennessee Spokesman for the New South." M.A. thesis, Vanderbilt University, 1960.

Spencer, Frank. "Aleš Hrdlička, M.D., 1869–1943: A Chronicle of the Life and Work of an American Physical Anthropologist." 2 vols. Ph.D. dissertation, University of Michigan, 1979.

Spiess, Philip D., II. "Exhibitions and Expositions in Nineteenth Century Cincinnati." *Cincinnati Historical Society Bulletin* 28 (1970):171–92.

Sprague, Stuart Seely. "Meet Me in St. Louis on the Ten-Million-Dollar Pike." *Missouri Historical Society Bulletin* 32 (1975):26–31.

Stein, Judith. " 'Of Mr. Booker T. Washington and Others': The Political Economy of Racism in the United States." *Science and Society* 38 (1974–75):422–63.

Stocking, George W., Jr. "Franz Boas and the Culture Concept in Historical Perspective." *American Anthropologist* 68 (1966):867–82.

————. *Race, Culture, and Evolution: Essays in the History of Anthropology*. New York: Free Press, 1968.

————. "The Santa Fe Style in American Anthropology: Regional Interest, Academic Initiative, and Philanthropic Policy in the First Two Decades of the Laboratory of Anthropology, Inc." *Journal of the History of the Behavioral Sciences* 18 (1982):3–19.

Stott, Jeffrey R. "The American Idea of a Zoological Park: An Intellectual History." Ph.D. dissertation, University of California, Santa Barbara, 1981.

Takaki, Ronald T. *Iron Cages: Race and Culture in Nineteenth Century America*. New York: Alfred A. Knopf, 1979.

Taylor, Kate Haurshan. "A Crisis of Confidence: The San Diego Free Speech Fight of 1912." M.A. thesis, University of California, Los Angeles, 1966.

Thompson, Joan Marie. "The Art and Architecture of the Pan-American Exposition, Buffalo, New York, 1901." 2 vols. Ph.D. dissertation, Rutgers University, 1980.

Thompson, Richard A. "Yellow Peril, 1890–1924." Ph.D. dissertation, University of Wisconsin, 1957.

Thornbrough, Emma L. "Booker T. Washington as Seen by His White Contemporaries." *Journal of Negro History* 53 (1968):161–82.

Toll, Robert. *Blacking Up: The Minstrel Show in Nineteenth Century America*. New York: Oxford University Press, 1974.

Trachtenberg, Alan. *The Incorporation of America*. New York: Hill and Wang, 1982.

Trennert, Robert A. "A Grand Failure: The Centennial Indian Exhibition of 1876." *Prologue* 6 (1974):118–29.

Turner, Frank M. "The Victorian Conflict between Science and Religion: A Professional Dimension." *Isis* 69 (1978):356–76.

Vanderwood, Paul J. "Mexico's Rurales: Reputation versus Reality." *Americas* 34 (1977):102–12.

Wagenknecht, Edward. *Chicago*. Norman: University of Oklahoma Press, 1964.

Walthew, Kenneth. "The British Empire Exhibition of 1924." *History Today* 31 (1981):34–39.

Waters, H. W. *A History of Fairs and Expositions*. London: Reid Brothers, 1939.

Weimann, J. M. *The Fair Women*. Chicago: Academy Press, 1981.

Weston, Rubin Francis. *Racism in American Imperialism*. Columbia: University of South Carolina Press, 1972.

Wiebe, Robert H. *The Search for Order, 1877–1920*. New York: Hill and Wang, 1967.

Williams, Raymond. *Marxism and Literature*. New York: Oxford University Press, 1978.

Williams, Walter L. "United States Indian Policy and the Debate over Philippine Annexation: Implications for the Origins of American Imperialism." *Journal of American History* 66 (1980):810–31.

Winslow, Carleton Moore. "The Architecture of the Panama-California Exposition, 1909–1915." M.A. thesis, University of San Diego, 1976.

Winton, Ruth M. "Negro Participation in Southern Expositions, 1881–1915." *Journal of Negro Education* 16 (Winter 1947):34–43.

Woodward, C. Vann. *Origins of the New South, 1877–1913.* 1951; reprinted. Baton Rouge: Louisiana State University Press, 1974.

Young, Alfred. "The Educational Philosophy of Booker T. Washington: A Perspective for Black Liberation." *Phylon* 17 (1976):224–35.

Ziff, Larzer. *The American 1890s: The Life and Times of a Lost Generation.* New York: Viking Press, 1966.

Index

References to illustrations are printed in boldface type.

Adams, Henry, 3, 46, 68
Africa: exhibits at Buffalo fair, 145–46; exhibits at Philadelphia fair, 32; expeditions to, 146, 221
Afro-Americans: caricatured, 53, 54, 87–88; exhibits, 27–29, 52–55, 80–89, **82,** 97, 119, 146–47, 230, 259n.62; Negro Day at Chicago fair, 53, **54;** Negro Day at Nashville fair, 86–87. *See also* Villages; *and specific fairs*
Aguinaldo, Emilio, 144
Ainus, 181
Ak-Sar-Ben, Knights of, 109, 111
Alaska: exhibit at Buffalo fair, 139; exhibit at Seattle fair, 189, 199, 201
Alaska-Yukon-Pacific Exposition (Seattle, 1909), **187:** Alaska exhibit, 201; anthropology and, 197–200; and Asian markets, 201–5; attendance at, 205; China and, 200; Chinese Village, 199; financing of, 279n.8; Hawaiian exhibit, 201; Igorot Village, 193, 197–99, **198;** Japan and, 203–5, 285n.45; Japanese Village, 199; and labor resistance, 192–93; legacy of, 206–7; midway (Pay Streak), 197–200; Native American exhibits, 199–201; official seal, **187;** origins of, 185, 189; Philippine Islands exhibit, 201–2; purpose of, 185, 189; Smithsonian Institution and, 201–2

Algerian Village, 62
Allen, Frederick, 211
Allen, William V., 112–13
American Institute of Archaeology, 219
Anderson, Charles W., 86
Anderson, G. M., 228
Anderson, George, 27
Anthropologists, 273n.21; Boas, Franz, 55, 57, 64, 69, 223, 272n.20; Brinton, Daniel G., 58; Cushing, Frank Hamilton, 24–25; Farrand, Livingston, 165; Fletcher, Alice, 55; Goode, G. Brown, 7, 43–46, 56, 58, 97–99, 100; Haddon, Alfred C., 199; Hewett, Edgar L., 220–24; Holmes, William Henry, 57, 58, 137, 141, 220; Hough, Walter, 6, 97; Hrdlička, Aleš, 164–65, **165,** 220–23, 235; Jastrow, Joseph, 57; Jenks, Albert W., 167; Klemm, Gustav, 23–24; Lummis, Charles F., 220; McGee, W J, 160–67, **163,** 170, 181; Mason, Otis T., 23–24, 55–60, **58,** 97, 100, 137, 235; Matiegka, Jindrich, 221; Mička, Frank, 221; Mooney, James, 55, 111–12, **112,** 116–18; Moore, Riley, 221; Powell, John Wesley, 23, 55, 57, 99, 111, 113; Powers, Stephen, 23; Pratt, R. H., 252n.51; Putnam, Frederic Ward, 55, 57, 62–65, **65,** 69, 130, 137; Rau, Charles, 24–25; Rutot, A., 221; Schuck, Voltjetch, 221; Sickles, Emma, 63; Smith, Harlan Ingersoll, 57; Starr, Frederick, 92, 143, 174,

317

273n.23; Stevenson, Elizabeth Coxe,
55; Stolyhwo, Kazimierz, 221; Swan,
James G., 23, 25; Wilson, Thomas,
55–56, 57; Wissler, Clark, 164. *See
also* Bureau of American Ethnology
Anthropology: American Institute of
Archaeologists, 220; buildings, 57,
132, 136–44, 164, 220, 233,
272n.20; exhibits, 22–27, 55–71,
97–101, 111–18, 160–78, 181, 193–
202, 219–23; exhibit techniques, 57–
60; expeditions, 145–46, 221; focus
of expositions, 7–8, 117, 145, 160–
78, 217–23; hegemonic function of,
235–36; international congress of, 58;
jury of awards, 273n.21. *See also*
Expeditions; Midways; Villages
Apache, Antonio, 63, 130
Argentina, exhibit at Atlanta fair, 91
Armour, Philip, 42
Arthur, Chester A., 73
Asia, United States economic expansion
and, 29–32, 48–52, 73–74, 119,
142–44, 167–78, 180–82, 185–86,
200–205, 228–29
Asians. *See* Chinese; Filipinos; Japanese
Astor, John Jacob, 79
Astor, William Waldorf, 42
"Atlanta Compromise," 83–84
Atlanta *Constitution*, 78
Atlanta Cotton States and International
Exposition. *See* Cotton States and
International Exposition
Atwater, Wilbur O., 7
Aunt Jemimah, 119
Avenue of Progress, **216**
Avery, Isaac W., 77–78, 90, 92, 130

BAE. *See* Bureau of American Ethnology
Baird, Spencer F., 235; role at
Philadelphia fair, 22–27
Balboa Park, 209, 233
Baldwin, John, 105
Bancroft, Hubert Howe, 51, 60
Bannister, Edward M., 27
Bartholdi, Frederic, 13
Bellamy, Francis J., 46
Belmont, August, 42
Benedict, A. C., 137–38
Benson, Horace G., 40
Berger, Peter L., on "symbolic
universe," 2

Bigler, William, 19
Biograph, 142
Bissel, Herbert P., 129
Bitter, Karl, 132–34, 211–12
Blake, William Phipps, 18, 20–21; on
legacy of Philadelphia fair, 9
Bliss, Cornelius, 113
Bloom, Sol, 62–63
Boas, Franz, 55, 57, 64, 69, 223,
272n.20
Boer War, 179–80, **180**
Bostock, Frank, 150
Bowen, J. W. E., 85
Brazil: at Atlanta fair, 90–91; at
Philadelphia fair, 15, 22
Brigham, J. H., 139
Brinker, John M., 128–29
Brinton, Daniel G., 58
Bryan, Mrs. William Jennings, 149
Bryan, William Jennings, 109, **150,**
216
Buchanan, William I., 130, 138
Buckner, John C., 84
Buffalo Bill's Wild West show, 63, 96–
97, 119–20, 194
Buffalo Pan-American Exposition. *See*
Pan-American Exposition
Buffalo Society of Natural Sciences, 146
Bumpus, Hermon, 165
Burbank, Luther, 224
Bureau of American Ethnology (BAE), 7;
at Buffalo fair, 140–42; at Chicago
fair, 55–60, 111; at Omaha fair, 111–
12, 116–17; at Philadelphia fair, 22–
27; at Saint Louis fair, 160; at Seattle
fair, 201; at southern fairs, 97–101,
111
Burke, E. A., 77–78, 82
Burnett, Frances Hodgson, 39
Burnham, Daniel, 48, 94, 130

Campbell, John L., 17, 21
Conkling, Roscoe, 28
Carrère, John M., 132, 136
Cary, George, 132
Centennial Board of Finance, 17–18
Centennial City, 33–35
Centennial Commission, 10, 19
Centennial Exhibition (Philadelphia,
1876): attendance at, 10; and
Bicentennial, 36; blacks and, 27–29;
and Chicago fair, 39; Chinese

participation, 14, 29–32;
classification of exhibits, 20–22, 29;
contrasting perceptions of Africans
and South Africans, 31–32; Corliss
engine, 15–16, **16**, 35; as
"counterculture," 33–35; early
opposition to, 2, 10; and expanding
overseas markets, 29–32; financing
of, 17–18; fine arts at, 13–14; foreign
exhibits, 21–22; impact on libraries,
21; industrial depression and, 10–11;
Japanese participation in, 29–32;
Latin American exhibits, 21–22;
Machinery Hall, **15;** Main Building,
14; midway (*see* Centennial City);
moral influence of, 35–37; Native
Americans and, 23–27; opening
ceremonies, 15; origins of, 17–19;
popular entertainment, 12, 33–35;
racial violence at, 14; railroads and,
18; sanitary fairs and, 10; and
sectional reconciliation, 18–19;
Smithsonian Institution and, 19–27;
Smithsonian Institution exhibit, 25,
25; United States government exhibit,
22–27; United States government
support, 17–18; Walt Whitman at, 16;
women and, 11–13, 28; working class
and, 32–35
Chicago Association of Commerce, 69
Chicago Railway Exhibition (1883), 43
Chief Joseph, 163
Children's literature, 39–40, 46, 48,
209
Chile, exhibit at Atlanta fair, 91
China, and United States economic
expansion, 31, 49, 51–52, 95–96,
119, 180–82, 185–86, 200–205,
228–29. *See also* Chinese
Chinese: American perception of, 14,
30–31, 49–52, 95–96; exhibits, 29–
32, 49–52, 89, 95–97, **98**, 202–3,
228–29; protest against treatment, 95,
202–3. *See also* Villages; *and specific
fairs*
Churchill, Winston, 211
Cincinnati, industrial exhibitions at, 10,
17, 43
City Beautiful, 39, 106, 123, 186–88
Clarke, F. W., 142
Clarkson, George, 18
Classification of exhibits: at Chicago fair,

43–46; at Philadelphia fair, 20–22;
and racial hierarchy, 29, 64–67,
160–63
Cleveland, Grover, 42, 46, **47**, 73, 75,
87, 130
Cody, William. *See* Buffalo Bill's Wild
West show
Collier, Charles A., 77, 78, 84, 88–90
Collier, David C., 214–20
Colonial Villages. *See* Villages
Columbian Historical Exposition
(Madrid, 1892), 43, 44
Congrès Internationale d'Anthropologie et
d'Archéologie Prehistoriques, 55–56
Cook, Frederick F., 71
Cook, Walter, 132
Cooper, Walter G., 95
Corliss engine, 15–16, **16**, 35
Costa Rica, exhibit at Atlanta fair, 91
Cotton States and International
Exposition (Atlanta, 1895), **75,** 108;
Afro-Americans exhibited at, 74, 87–
88, **88,** 97, 259n.62; anthropology
exhibits, 97–101; attendance at, 102;
black protests at, 84–85; Chinese
exhibit, 95–96, 98; construction by
chain gangs, 76, 80; endorsed by
National Association of Manufacturers,
93; financing of, 78; hegemonic
function of, 101–4; and immigration
to South, 75; and labor unrest, 75,
80, 87; Latin American people and
resources on display, 89–94; Liberty
Bell, 74; midway (Midway Heights),
94–97; Negro Building, 83–85, **86;**
Negro department at, 80, 84–85;
"Negro Question" linked to Western
imperialism, 88–89; New South
ideology and, 73–104; Old Plantation,
88; Populists and, 102–3;
Smithsonian exhibit at, 97–101;
treatment of midway villagers, 95–97
Coxey, Jacob, 103
Crocker, William H., 213, 219
Croly, Herbert, 136
Crystal Palace Exhibition of 1851
(London), 8, 20, 127
Crystal Palace Exhibition of 1853 (New
York), 20
Cuba: exhibit at Buffalo fair, 139, 148;
village at Atlanta fair, 95
Cummins, Frederick, 130, **150,** 227

Cushing, Frank Hamilton, 24–25
Custer, George Armstrong, 27
Czolgosz, Leon, 152

Dabney, Charles W., 100
Dahomey Village, 61, 66, **66**
Dall, William H., 55
"Darkest Africa." *See* Villages
Darwin, Charles, 27, 127, 150
Davidson, G. Aubrey, 214
Davis, Harry O., 214
Debs, Eugene, 216
Department M. *See* Midway Plaisance
Depew, Chauncey, 42, 153
Dewey, Melvil, 21
Díaz, Porfirio, 91, 148
Dime novels, 6
Donnelly, Ignatius, 103
Dorsey, George A., 55, 69
Douglass, Frederick, 28, 52–53
Dundy, Elmer S., 146, **147**
Dunne, Finley Peter, 144

Earll, Robert Edward, 97
Eaton, Hubert, 232
Education Congress, 225
Eiffel Tower, 43, 56
Esau, 150, **151**
Esenwein, August, 132
Eskimos, 199, 221; contract diseases at
   Buffalo fair, 148–50
Ethnology. *See* Anthropology
Eugenics: exhibits at San Diego and San
   Francisco fairs, 223–27; pageant,
   224; popularized at expositions, 5
Evolution, 150; in classifications, 25,
   159; controversy at Atlanta fair,
   259n.62; emphasis at Chicago fair,
   41–42, 57; Evolution of Man show at
   Buffalo fair, 149–50; "Evolution
   Room" at San Diego fair, 221–22; and
   international expositions, 57, 98–100,
   150, 209, 221–23, 235; popularized
   at expositions, 5, 209–13, 219–26;
   popularized through art and
   architecture, 132, 209–13
Exclusion Act of 1882, 49
Exhibitions, international. *See*
   Expositions, international
Expeditions, 23, 145–46, 166, 221
Expositions, international: amusement
   and, 6; and anthropology, passim;

class conflict and, 32–35, 39, 87, 94,
   102–3, 110, 152, 159, 189–93, 218,
   236, 271n.7; cumulative legacy of,
   233; and economic expansion, 29–32,
   48–52, 70, 73–74, 76, 79, 89, 119,
   142–44, 167–78, 180–86, 200–205,
   228–29; as educators, 5, 7, 33, 46,
   155, 162, 166, 199; financing of, 17–
   19, 42–43, 78–80, 83, 129, 144,
   155–57, 188–89, 215, 235, 279n.8;
   hegemonic function of, 2–3 passim;
   and immigration, 5, 51–52, 75–76,
   119, 152, 161, 180, 203–5, 225–26;
   as "organizing processes," 103; as
   popularizers of evolution, 5, 209–13,
   219–26 passim; popular response to
   2–6, 183, passim; progress defined
   at, 4–8; racism at, 4–8 passim;
   religious significance of, 15, 36–37;
   science and, 5–7, 20, 22, 45–46,
   164, 220, 223–24, 226, 230, passim;
   United States government and, 3–8
   passim; as worldwide imperial
   phenomena, 8. *See also* Anthropology;
   Midways; Villages; *and specific fairs*

Fairs: etymology of, 3. *See also* Expo-
   sitions, international; *and specific fairs*
Farrand, Livingston, 165
Fatima, 62
Felder, Edmund A., 94
Ferris, George, 68
Ferris wheel, 60, **61,** 62
Fiction, and fairs, 6, 26, 39–40, 46,
   48, 50, 53, 67–69, 148, 158, 209
Field, Marshall, 39, 42, 69
Field Columbian Museum, 69, 99
Filipinos: anticipated deaths of, 165,
   273n.22; competition for village
   concession, 194–95, 281n.24; deaths,
   144, 165; exhibited at Buffalo fair,
   142–44; exhibited at Omaha fair,
   120; reservation at Saint Louis fair,
   160–78, **171, 173–77, 176;**
   traveling exhibit, 196–97, **198;**
   282n.30; tuberculosis contracted at
   Buffalo fair, 150. *See also* Villages
Fish, Stuyvesant, 79
Fiske, John, 68
Fletcher, Alice, 55
Foreign Exhibition (Boston, 1883), 43
Forest Lawn Cemetery, 232

Francis, David R., 154, 157, 170, 203
Franklin Institute, 17
Free Speech Movement, 210
French, Alice, 118

Gage, Lyman, 42, 43, 211, 213
Gaines, Wesley H., 83
Gardner, Dorsey, 21
Geronimo, 117, 163
Gilder, Richard Watson, 127
Gilman, Daniel Coit, 101
Goode, G. Brown, 43–46, **44,** 56, 58,
    235; controversy over Afro-American
    exhibit, 100; introduces "museum
    idea" to South, 97–99; observations
    on Smithsonian and expositions, 7
Goodyear, Charles W., 129
Gorman, Anthony, 96
Goshorn, Alfred T., 10, 17, 18
Gould, Jay, 42
Grady, Henry, 77, 78
Gramsci, Antonio, 239n.4
Grant, Abram L., 83
Grant, Ulysses S., 15, 22
Grant, Ulysses S., Jr., 213
Grauman, Sid, 228
Greater American Exposition (Omaha,
    1899), 124–25, 130
Green, Edward B., 132
Gresham, Walter Q., 90
Griffith, David W., 231–32

Haddon, Alfred C., 199
Hamlin, Harry, 129
Harrison, Benjamin, 42, 46
Harvey, Fred, 228, 230
Hawaii, 148, 201
Hawaiians, contract disease at Buffalo
    fair, 150
Hawley, Joseph R., 15, 17, 32
Hawthorne, Julian, 64
Hay, John, 127
Hearst, William Randolph, 213, 231
Helper, Hinton R., 272n.12
Hemphill, William A., 77, 78
Henry, Joseph, 22
Herrick, Robert, 38
Hewett, Edgar L., 220, 224
Higinbotham, Harlow N., 39–40, 69–
    70, 101–2
Hilder, Frank F., 140–41

Hill, Richard C., 86
Hobson, Richard Pearson, 128
Holland, Norman, "reader-response"
    theory, 3–4
Holmes, Charles, 42
Holmes, William Henry, 57, **59,** 137,
    141, 220
Ho-o-den Palace, 48
Hoover, Herbert, 208, 211, 213
Hough, Walter, 6, 97
Howard, John G., 132
Howe, Julia Ward, 73
Howells, William Dean: on blacks and
    Native Americans at Philadelphia fair,
    26, 29; on utopian significance of
    Chicago fair, 40
Hrdlička, Aleš, 164–65, 165, 235;
    exhibits for San Diego fair, 220–23
Huxley, Thomas H., 27, 68

Igorot Village, 172–76, **173, 174,**
    194–99, **198**
Iller, P. E., 124
Immigration restriction, 5, 51–52, 75–
    76, 119, 152, 161, 180, 203–5,
    225–26
Imperialism, United States, 4–8, 108,
    120, 170, 236–37; in Asia, 29–32,
    48–52, 73–74, 119, 142–44, 167–
    78, 180–82, 185–86, 200, 205,
    228–29; in context of Western
    imperialism, 8; illustrations of, **12,
    70, 129, 210;** in Latin America,
    21, 73–74, 89–94, 127–29, 218; in
    Philippines (see Filipinos; Philippine
    Islands). See also Midways; Racism;
    Villages
Improved Order of Red Men, 114
Indian Congress, 111–18, 130; visited
    by McKinley, 121–23
Indians. See Native Americans
Industrial exhibitions, 10, 17, 43
Industrial Workers of the World, 218
Inman, Samuel, 77, 102
Intelligence Quotient test, 225
International Congresses, 41, 59, 68,
    83, 223–26
International Congress of Anthropology,
    59
International Congress on Evolution, 68
International Electrical Exhibition
    (Philadelphia, 1884), 43

International Fisheries Exhibitions, 43,
44
International Harvester, 230

Jamestown Tercentenary Exposition
(1907), 73, 197
Japan, and United States economic
expansion, 29–32, 49–52, 180–82,
185–86, 200–205, 228–29. *See also*
Japanese
Japanese: American perceptions of, 14,
48–52, 180–82, 185–86, 200–205,
228–29; exhibits, 29–30, 48–49,
49, 204, 228, 230
Jastrow, Joseph, 57
Javanese Village, 61, 66
Jenks, Albert, 167
Jordan, C. P., 95
Joy Zone, **227**
Justi, Herman, 80

Kellogg, D. Otis, 14
Kellogg, John H., 224
Kettner, William, 218
Killebrew, Joseph B., 77, 79
Kiowas, exhibited at Omaha fair, 116–
17
Klemm, Gustav, 23–24
Kushibiki, Yumeto, 228

Labor Congress, 83
Laemmle, Carl, 231
Lam, Leong, 95
Langley, Samuel Pierpont, 43, 56
Latin America, 21–22, 89–94, 147–48.
See also specific countries
Letters of an Altrurian Traveller, 40
Lewis, Arthur W., 227, 228
Lewis, Edmonia, 27
Lewis, Eugene C., 77, 79
Lewis, Sinclair, 69
Lewis and Clark Centennial Exposition
(Portland, 1905), **186;** anthropology
and, 193, 200; and Asian markets,
185–86, 200–203; attendance at,
205; China and, 202–3; Chinese
Village, 199; financing of, 188–89;
Igorot Village, 193–97; Japan and,
202–3; Japanese Village, 200; labor
turmoil, 188–91, 280n.14; legacy of,

205–7; midway (Trail), 193–200,
200; origins of, 188–89; Philippine
Islands exhibit, 193–200; purpose of,
185–88; Smithsonian Institution and,
201
Liberty Bell, 73, **74,** 215
Living ethnological exhibits. *See*
Anthropology; Midways; Villages
Los Angeles Chamber of Commerce,
216–17
Louisiana Purchase Exposition (Saint
Louis, 1904), 124, 144, 153, **158,**
214; anthropology and, 160–67,
272n.20; and Asian markets, 167–78,
180–82; attendance at, 155; Boer
War, 179–80, **180;** China and, 181–
82; Chinese Village, 180; educational
value of, 273n.23; financing of, 155–
57; Igorot Village, 171–76, **173,**
174; Japan and, 180–81; Japanese
Village, 180–81; and labor turmoil,
277n.52; legacy of, 182–83; midway
(Pike), 178–82; Native American
exhibits, 163–66; Negrito Village,
171–75, **171;** opening day, **156;**
origins of, 155–57; Philippine
Reservation, 157, 163, 167–78,
176, 273n.22; purpose of, 155–57;
Smithsonian Institution and, 160, 164;
Visayan theater, **177**
Luckmann, Thomas, on "symbolic
universe," 2
Lummis, Charles F., 220

McCarthy, Patrick Henry, 213
McClellan, Fred, 147, 227
McConnell, Emmett, 119, 143, 227
McCormick, Cyrus, 42, 78
McGarvie, H. F., 148
McGee, W J, 100, 160–67, **163,** 170,
181; "Overlord of the Savage World,"
163
McKinley, William, 4, 108, 120, 121–
22, **122, 152;** assassination, 128,
147, 152–53; expositions as
"timekeepers of progress," 4, 152;
speech at Nashville fair, 101
MacMechen, Thomas R., 178
Maloney, Charles, 94
Mardi Gras, 109
Marietta, Ohio, Exposition (1889), 43

Marston, George W., 214
Martin, T. H., 92–93
Mason, Otis T., 57–60, **58**, 97, 137,
    235; exhibit of "modern savagery,"
    100; exhibits at Chicago fair, 55–60;
    involvement in Philadelphia fair, 23–
    24; popularizes evolution, 98–99
Matiegka, Jindrich, 221
Mattox, Frank, 115
"Meet Me in St. Louis, Louis," 154
Mercer, Edward, 28
Mercer, William A., 113–18
Mexico: exhibit at Atlanta fair, 91;
    exhibit at Buffalo fair, 147–48;
    exhibit of natural resources at
    Nashville fair, 92; exhibit at New
    Orleans fair, **92**, 97; exhibit at
    Philadelphia fair, 22; Mexican band at
    New Orleans fair, 93; mineral exhibit
    at New Orleans fair, 92; Revolution
    and San Diego fair, 218
Mička, Frank, 221
Middle East, United States economic
    expansion and, 181–82
Midway Plaisance, 235–36;
    anthropological significance of, 40;
    Chinese on, 51–52; description of,
    60–61; hierarchical organization of,
    64–66; impact on subsequent fairs,
    94; as "living museum of humanity,"
    60–68; origins of, 56–62; relation to
    White City, 64–68
Midways: and anthropology, 40, 137–38;
    at Atlanta fair (Midway Heights), 95–
    97; at Buffalo fair (Pan), 144–51,
    145; at Chicago fair (see Midway
    Plaisance); deaths of villagers, 150;
    financing of shows, 144; imperialistic
    function of, 88, 235–36; as living
    ethnological villages (see Villages); at
    Nashville fair (Vanity Fair), 94–97; at
    Omaha fair (Midway), 118–20; at
    Philadelphia fair (see Centennial City);
    at Portland fair (Trail), 193–200,
    200; profile of showmen, 144–45; at
    Saint Louis fair (Pike), 178–82; at
    San Diego fair (Isthmus) and San
    Francisco fair (Zone), 214, 227–32,
    227; at Seattle fair (Pay Streak),
    197–200; spieler caricatured, 229;
    treatment of villagers, 93–97. See also
Anthropology; Villages; *and specific
    fairs*
Midwinter Exposition (San Francisco,
    1893–94), 51, 109, 148, 188
Milburn, John, 126, 129–30, 152
Miller, Joaquin, 15–16, 29, 76
Millet, Frank, 132
Minstrel shows, 6
"Missing Link," 175, **175**
Mooney, James, 55, 111–12, **112,**
    116–18
Moore, Charles C., 213, 232
Moore, "Pony," 143
Moore, Riley, 221
Morgan, J. P., 42
Morrell, Daniel J., 17, 35–36
Motion pictures, 142
Mucklé, M. Richards, 17
Museums, popular, 6, 43–46, 69, 97–
    99, 168–72, 233. See also
    Smithsonian Institution

Nashville, Tennessee, Centennial
    Exposition. See Tennessee Centennial
    Exposition
National Association of Manufacturers,
    93
Native Americans, 221; deaths at Omaha
    fair, 117; delegations, 26; exhibited at
    Atlanta fair, 95; exhibited at Buffalo
    fair, 149–50, **149;** exhibited at
    Chicago fair, 63–64; exhibited at
    Omaha fair, 111–12; exhibited at San
    Diego fair, 230; exhibited at San
    Francisco fair, 228; exhibited at
    southern fairs, 100; exhibits at
    Chicago fair, 57; exhibits at
    Philadelphia fair, 23–27; William
    Dean Howells and, 26; Indian
    Congress at Omaha fair, 108, 113,
    118; sham battle at Omaha fair, 114–
    16, **115;** United States government
    policy and, 99
New Orleans, competition for 1915 fair,
    216–17
New Orleans World's Industrial and
    Cotton Exposition. See World's
    Industrial and Cotton Exposition
New South, ideology expressed at
    southern fairs, 73–104
Newton, Philip, 221

New York, competition for 1983 fair,
    41–42
Nicaragua, Revolution, and San Diego
    fair, 218
Northrup, Birdsley Grant, 31
Norton, Charles B., 17, 32

Odell, Benjamin, 153
Olmsted, Frederick Law, Jr., 130
Olmsted, John C., 211
Olympic Games (1904), 155, 166
Omaha Trans-Mississippi and
    International Exposition. *See* Trans-
    Mississippi and International
    Exposition
Owyang, Kee, 95, 229

Palmer, Potter, 46, 47–48
Palmer, Thomas, 56, 62
Panama-California Exposition (San
    Diego, 1915–16), **215**, 218;
    anthropology and, 217, 219–23;
    architecture, 209–14; Asians and,
    230; attendance at, 209; central court,
    218; Chinese Village, 230; eugenics
    and, 223; financing of, 216; Industrial
    Workers of the World and, 218;
    legacy of, 232–33; local and national
    politics and, 216–19; midway
    (Isthmus), 227–32; motion pictures
    and, 231–32; Native Americans and,
    230; origins of, 214–19; reopening of,
    288n.16; rivalry with San Francisco
    fair, 216–19; Smithsonian Institution
    and, 213, 219
Panama-California International
    Exposition. *See* Panama-California
    Exposition
Panama Canal, 91, 209, 214, 216;
    concession at San Francisco fair, 227
Panama-Pacific International Exposition
    (San Francisco, 1915), **212**;
    anthropology and, 219; architecture,
    209–14; Asians and, 228–30;
    attendance at, 209; Avenue of
    Progress, **216**; Chinese Village, 229;
    congresses, 223–25; eugenics and,
    223–27; financing of, 215; labor and,
    215; legacy of, 232; midway (Zone),
    227–32, **227**; motion pictures and,
    231–32; origins of, 214–16; rivalry

with San Diego fair, 215–19;
    Smithsonian Institution and, 213, 219
Pan-American Exposition (Buffalo,
    1901), **127, 131, 133;**
    anthropology and, 132, 136–37;
    architectural style, 128; artistic
    allegory of progress, 131;
    assassination of McKinley at, 128,
    147, 152–53; attendance at, 153;
    Carrère's plan for, 132–37; Electric
    Tower, 135–36, **135**; Ethnology
    Building, 132, 136–37; evolution in
    coloring and artistic scheme, 132–37;
    expanding Latin American markets,
    128; financing of, 128–30; Fountain
    of Man, 136, **137**; hegemonic
    function of, 128; importance of
    colonial exhibits, 139–40; Indian
    Congress, **149**, 149; Latin American
    exhibits, 147–49; McKinley's
    entrance, **152**; midway (Pan), 137,
    144–51, **145**; Native Americans at,
    138, 149, 150; origins of, 128;
    Philippine Islands exhibit, 138–44,
    142; problem of novelty, 130–31;
    sculpture at, 132–34; Smithsonian
    Institution and, 137–38, 139–42;
    United States Government Board and,
    139–42
Paris Exhibition of 1867, 18, 20
Paris Exhibition of 1889, 55, 62;
    colonial villages at, 7, 56
Park, Roswell, 150
Parker, Hale G., 52
Parker, Jim, 147
Parthenon, 79, 103–4, **103**
Patent Centennial (1891), 43
Peabody, R. S., 132
Peace Jubilee, at Omaha fair, 108, 120–
    21
Pedro, Dom, 15
Pene, Xavier, 145–46
Penn, I. Garland, 84
Philadelphia Centennial Exhibition. *See*
    Centennial Exhibition
Philadelphia Commercial Museum, 168–
    69
Philippine Islands: at Buffalo fair, 136,
    138–44, **142**; at Omaha fair, 120,
    124–25; Philippine Reservation at
    Saint Louis fair, 167–78, **171,
    173–77**, 176, 235, 274n.26; at

Portland fair, 193–200; at Saint Louis fair, 155–78, 273n.22; at Seattle fair, 193–200, **198**, 202. *See also* Filipinos

Plessy v. Ferguson, 76

Popular amusements. *See* Midways

Populists: opposition to Omaha fair, 110; southern fairs and, 102–3

Powell, John Wesley, 23, 55, 57, 99, 111, 113

Powers, Stephen, 23

Pratt, R. H., 252n.51

Progress: definition of, 4; in exposition organization, 134–37; and expositions, 17, 19–22, 24, 46, 60, 73, 96–97, 104, 127, 149–50, 162, 193, 219; ideology of at fairs, 4–8; "racial progress," 178, 213

Puerto Rico, 139

Pullman, George, 42, 78

Putnam, Frederic Ward: 55, 57, **65,** 69, 130, 137; and Midway Plaisance, 62–65

Pygmies, 221

Quannah Parker, 163

Race Betterment, National Conference on, 224

Race Betterment Foundation, 224

Racism: in classification of exhibits, 21, 31, 64–67, 101, 160–63; defined, 5; racial violence, 14, 177

Rainbow City. *See* Pan-American Exposition

Rathbun, Richard, 6

Rau, Charles, 24–25

Ravenel, W. de C., 201

Rensselaer, Mariana G. van, 47

Richardson, Edmund, 78

Rockefeller, William, 42

Roltair, Henry, 120

Roosevelt, Franklin D., 213

Roosevelt, Theodore, 214–16, 276n.40

Root, Elihu, 42

Rosewater, Edward, 110–13, 130

Rutot, A., 221

Samoan Village, 61, 66–67, 228, 282n.30

San Diego Museum Association, 233

San Diego Panama-California Exposition. *See* Panama-California Exposition

San Francisco Midwinter Exposition. *See* Midwinter Exposition

San Francisco Panama-Pacific International Exposition. *See* Panama-Pacific International Exposition

Sanitary fairs, 10

Scarborough, William S., 84

Schneidewind, Richard, 228, 281n.25, 282n.30

Schuck, Voltjetch, 221

Science, and international expositions, 5–7, 20, 22, 45–46, 164, 220, 223–24, 226, 230 passim. *See also* Anthropology

Science of Man exhibit, 289n.27

Selznick, Lewis J., 231

Sheply, George B., 132

Shimm, Sarah H., 81

Sickles, Emma, 63

Sioux City Corn Palace, 130

Skiff, Frederick J. V., 69, 211, 219

Skilton, James A., 68

Smith, Dudley, 109

Smith, Harlan Ingersoll, 57

Smith, Hoke, 79

Smith, John Q., 27

Smithsonian Institution: ambivalence of officials regarding fairs, 6–7; award received in 1876, 27; Bicentennial exhibit, 36; and Buffalo fair, 137–42; and Chicago fair, 56; controversy over Afro-American exhibit, 99–100; controversy over evolution, 259n.62; exhibit techniques, 25–26, 57–59, 100; importance to expositions, 6–7, 235; and Omaha fair, 111–12, 116–17; and Philadelphia fair, 22–27, **25;** and Portland fair, 201; and Saint Louis fair, 160, 164–65; and San Diego fair, 219–22, 230; and San Francisco fair, 219; and Seattle fair, 201–2; and southern expositions, 97–101

Snider, Denton J., 64–65

Socialists, 189–93, 216

South Africa, exhibit at Philadelphia fair, 31–32

South Carolina Interstate and West Indian Exposition (Charleston, 1901–2), 73

Southern Exposition (Louisville, 1884), 43
Southern Exposition (Raleigh, North Carolina, 1891), 52
Southwest Museum, 220
Spanish-American War, 108, 113, 120–21, 128, 141
Spaulding, Albert G., 215
Speer, Emory, 88
Spellman, J. J., 81
Spencer, Herbert, 68
Spreckles, John D., 213, 214
Spreckles, Rudolph, 213
Starr, Frederick, 92, 143, 174, 273n.23
Stephenson, Nathaniel, 103–4
Stevens, William Bacon, 19
Stevenson, Elizabeth Coxe, 55
Stieringer, Luther, 130
Stolyhwo, Kazimierz, 221
Straker, David A., 81
Suffragists, caricatured at San Francisco fair, 227
Sullivan, John E., 166
Sullivan, Louis, 68
Swan, James G., 23, 25
Swift, Gustavus, 42

Taft, William Howard, 168, 172, 184, 217
Talmadge, T. Dewitt, 76
Tateno, Gozo, 48
Taylor, Frederick W., 130, 144
Taylor, James Knox, 132
Telang, Rao, 60–61
Temple of Music, 152–53
Tennessee Centennial Exposition (Nashville, 1897), 108; Afro-Americans and, 74, 80, 85–87, 89–90; anthropology and, 97–101; attendance at, 102; Chinese Village, 96; financing of, 78–79; hegemonic function of, 101–4; Latin American people and resources on display, 89–94; midway (Vanity Fair), 94–97; Negro Building, 85–86, 89, 90; Negro Day, 86–87; Negro department, 80, 85–87, 89; New South ideology and, 73–104; northern businessmen and, 79–80; as "organizing process," 103; Parthenon, 79, 103, 103–4; Populists and, 102–3; promotion of

immigration to South, 75; railroads and, 78–79; Smithsonian Institution and, 97–101
Terman, Lewis, 225
Thomas, John W., 77, 78, 86–87, 102
Thomas, Theodore, 14
Thompson, Frederic, 147, 151, 227
Thompson, Joseph, 221
Tillman, Ben, 75
Todd, Frank Morton, 225
Tokyo Exposition of 1917, 70
Tonner, A. C., 113
Trans-Mississippi and International Exposition (Omaha, 1898): anthropology and, 111–18; architecture, 106–7; attendance at, 106, 124; Children's Day, 121–24; Chinese Village, 119; financing of, 108; Grand Court, 107; Indian Congress, 108, 111–18, 135; industrial depression and, 108; lack of popular support, 110; Maine, 109; Midway, 118–20; pageantry, 109–10; Peace Jubilee Week, 108, 120–21; Populist opposition to, 110; response of visitors, 107; sham battle, 114–16, 115, 122–23; Smithsonian Institution, 111–12, 116–18; Spanish-American War and, 108, 113, 120–21; United States Government Building 108, 121; White City, 106; women and, 110, 123
Trans-Mississippi Commercial Congress, 108
Trip to the Moon, 151
True, Frederick W., 139
Turner, Charles Y., 132
Turner, Frederick Jackson, 47
Turner, Henry A., 80–81

Ulrich, Rudolph, 106, 130
United States Bureau of Education, 142
United States Bureau of Indian Affairs, 113, 116, 235
United States Bureau of Insular Affairs, 235
United States Centennial Board of Finance. See Centennial Board of Finance
United States Department of Agriculture, 7

United States Department of Interior, 22–27, 142

United States Department of Labor, 141

United States Department of State, exhibit at New Orleans fair, 101

United States International Exhibition. *See* Centennial Exhibition

United States National Museum (USNM), 6, 201, 220–21; exhibits at southern expositions, 97–101; involvement at Buffalo fair, 141. *See also* Smithsonian Institution

United States Treasury Department, 139, 141

United States War Department, 141

Universal expositions. *See* Expositions, international

University of California, 203, 215

University of Michigan, 97

Urban, George, Jr., 129

Vanderbilt, Cornelius, 42

Venezuela, exhibit at Atlanta fair, 91, 93

Vienna International Exhibition of 1873, 17

Villages: African Villages, 61, 66, **66**, 95, 118, 145–46, 179–80, 228; Algerian Village, 62; Chinese Villages, 49–52, 95–96, 119, 180, 199, 229, 230; Cuban Village, 95; Dahomey Village, 61, 66, **66**; "Darkest Africa," 145–46; Eskimo Village, 148–50, 199, 221; as ghettos, 227; Igorot Village, 172–76, **173, 174**, 194–99, **198;** Japanese Villages, 51, 119, 180–81, 199, 228, 230; Javanese Village, 61, 66; as living ethnological exhibits, 64–65, 138, 144 passim; Mexican Villages, 96, 147–48, 228; Native American Villages, 27, 63, 95–97, 111–18, 121–23, 130, 149, **149**, 163, 166, 227–28, 230; Negrito Village, 171–75, **171;** Old Plantation, 87–88, **88**, 119, 146–47, 199; at Paris Exhibition (1889), 7, 56; Philippine Villages, 120, 142–44, 167–78, **171, 173–77**, 193–99, **198**, 235, 274n.26; Samoan Villages, 61, 66–67, 228, 282n.30; Streets of

Cairo, 60, 118, 179, 199. *See also* Midways

Visayan theater, **177**

Wagner, Richard, music for Philadelphia fair, 14

Walcott, Charles D., 220, 221

Walker, Francis A., 36–37

Wanamaker, John, 36

Washington, Booker T., 72; "Atlanta Compromise" speech, 74–75, 84; on discrimination, 82–83; Emancipation Day speech, 89; support for Atlanta fair, 83–84

Wattles, Gurdon, 107, 121

Webster, John L., 108

Wells, Ida, 52–53

Welsh, Herbert, 113

Welsh, John, 17, 35–36

White supremacy. *See* Racism

Whitman, Walt, 15–16

Wild animal show, 96, 150

Wild West show, 6, 63, 96–97, 115. *See also* Indian Congress

Wilkinson, James, 223

Williams, Henry Smith, 224–25

Wilson, Thomas, 55–56, 57

Wilson, William Powell, 168–69, 194, 274n.26

Wilson, Woodrow, 213, 218

Wissler, Clark, 164

Woman's Building, at Chicago fair, 59; at Philadelphia fair, 12–13, 28

Women: and Chicago fair, 52, 59–60; and New Orleans fair, 73; and Omaha fair, 110, 123; and Philadelphia fair, 11, 13, 28; and Saint Louis fair, 173–74; suffragists caricatured at San Francisco fair, 227

Wooster, Charles, 110

Working class: efforts to educate, 18, 32–33, 102–3, 182–83, 188–93; labor unrest, 75, 80, 87, 188–93, 218, 271n.7, 277n.52

World's Columbian Exposition (Chicago, 1893), **41**, 100, 130, 132; Henry Adams on, 3, 46, 68; Afro-Americans and, 52–55; anthropology and, 55–71; architecture, 40, 48; attendance at, 40; chidren and, 46; Chinese at, 49–52; "Colored People's Day," 53,

54; competition for site, 41–42;
congressional support, 42–43; Court
of Honor, **39;** Dahomey Village, 61,
66, **66;** dedication ceremonies, 46;
Department of Ethnology, 40, 57;
education and, 46; financing of, 42–
43; importance of evolutionary ideas
at, 40–41; influence on museums, 69;
influence on Omaha fair, 106;
international congresses, 41, 68;
Japanese Building, **49;** Japanese
participation, 48–52; Labor Congress,
83, 84; midway (*see* Midway
Plaisance); museum development and,
43–46; Native Americans and, 57,
63–64; as "New Jerusalem," 48;
opening day ceremonies, **47;** Paris
Exhibition of 1889 and, 55–56;
Pledge of Allegiance introduced at,
46; racist underpinnings of a utopian
artifact, 48; results of, 68–70;
Smithsonian Institution and, 43–46,
55–60; the South on display at, 76;
speech by Booker T. Washington, 83–
84; utopian dimension of, 46–47;
Woman's Building, 59
World's Congress Auxiliary, 68
World's Industrial and Cotton Exposition
(New Orleans, 1885), 43, **77;** Afro-
Americans and, 74, 80, 82;
anthropology and, 97–101; attendance
at, 102; Chinese and, 97, **98;**
"Colored Department," 80–82, **82;**
financing of, 77–78; Latin American
markets and, 89–94; legacy of, 101;
Mexican "pagoda," **92;** mining
exhibits, 79; Native Americans and,
99; New South ideology and, 73–104;
origins of, 73–74, 77; Smithsonian
Institution and, 43, 97–101; Woman's
Department, 73
World's Parliament of Religion, 68
Wounded Knee, 95

Yerkes, Charles T., 42

Zoological gardens, 6
Zulus, 221

15022333R00203

Made in the USA
San Bernardino, CA
11 September 2014